MEDIEVAL MAIDENS

MANCHESTER
UNIVERSITY PRESS

MANCHESTER MEDIEVAL STUDIES

SERIES EDITOR Dr S. H. Rigby

SERIES ADVISORS Professor J. H. Denton
Professor R. B. Dobson   Professor L. K. Little

The study of medieval Europe is being transformed as old orthodoxies
are challenged, new methods embraced and fresh fields of inquiry
opened up. The adoption of inter-disciplinary perspectives and the
challenge of economic, social and cultural theory are forcing medievalists
to ask new questions and to see familiar topics in a fresh light.

   The aim of this series is to combine the scholarship traditionally
associated with medieval studies with an awareness of more recent
issues and approaches in a form accessible to the non-specialist reader.

ALREADY PUBLISHED IN THE SERIES

The commercialisation of English society, 1000–1500
Richard H. Britnell

Picturing women in late medieval and Renaissance art
Christa Grössinger

The politics of carnival
Christopher Humphrey

Law in context
Anthony Musson

Chaucer in context
S. H. Rigby

MANCHESTER MEDIEVAL STUDIES

MEDIEVAL MAIDENS

YOUNG WOMEN AND GENDER IN ENGLAND, 1270–1540

Kim M. Phillips

Manchester University Press
Manchester and New York
distributed exclusively in the USA by Palgrave

Published by Manchester University Press
Oxford Road, Manchester M13 9NR, UK
and Room 400, 175 Fifth Avenue, New York, NY 10010, USA
http://www.manchesteruniversitypress.co.uk

Distributed exclusively in the USA
by Palgrave, 175 Fifth Avenue, New York, NY 10010, USA

Distributed exclusively in Canada
by UBC Press, University of British Columbia, 2029 West Mall,
Vancouver, BC, Canada V6T 1Z2

British Library Cataloguing-in-Publication Data
A catalogue record for this book is available from the British Library

Library of Congress Cataloging-in-Publication Data applied for

ISBN 0 7190 5963 1 *hardback*
ISBN 0 7190 5964 X *paperback*

First published 2003

11 10 09 08 07 06 05 04 03   10 9 8 7 6 5 4 3 2 1

Typeset in Monotype Bulmer
by Koinonia, Manchester
Printed in Great Britain
by Bell & Bain Limited, Glasgow

For Martin

and for
Rebecca, Madeline and Willow Rose

The future accumulates like a weight upon the past. The weight upon the earliest years is easier to remove to let that time spring up like grass that has been crushed. The years following childhood become welded to their future, massed like stone, and often the time beneath cannot spring back into growth like new grass: it lies bled of its green in a new shape with those frail bloodless sprouts of another, unfamiliar time, entangled one with another beneath the stone.

(Janet Frame, *An Angel at My Table*)

CONTENTS

LIST OF ILLUSTRATIONS   *page*   ix
PREFACE   xi
LIST OF ABBREVIATIONS   xiii
NOTE ON TEXTS   xv

INTRODUCTION   1

Medieval youth   4
Constructing femininity   9
Approach and sources   15

1   Attributes   23

Bodies   24
Minds   30
Exit points   36
Perfect age   43
Conclusion   51

2   Upbringing   61

Modes of learning   62
Teachers   73
Messages   77
Varieties of conduct   83
Conclusion   97

3   Work   108

Noble service   109
Town and country   120
Conclusion   135

4   **Sexualities**   143

Sexual boundaries   146
Flirtation and fantasy   162
Conclusion   167

5   **Voices**   177

'Send more clothes'   179
'Marry me'   182
'Ave Maria'   185
Restive voices   194
Conclusion   196

CONCLUSION   202

BIBLIOGRAPHY   207
INDEX   239

ILLUSTRATIONS

1 Woman in her perfect age. St Dorothy, from Bancroft Library
MS UCB 150 (*The Heller Hours*, *c*. 1470–80), fol. 245v. Reproduced
by kind permission of The Bancroft Library, University of California,
Berkeley.   *page* 48

2 The Virgin Mary in her perfect age, at her death, assumption and
coronation. Pierpont Morgan Library MS M. 302 (*The Ramsey Psalter*,
c. 1300–10), fol. 4r. Reproduced by kind permission of The Morgan
Library, New York.   50

3 St Anne teaching the Virgin, with Saints Katherine, Margaret and Barbara.
British Library MS Add. 24686 (*The Alphonso Psalter*, *c*. 1284–1316),
fol. 2v. Reproduced by kind permission of The British Library, London.   69

4 Margaret of York, an English princess resident in the Low Countries,
at prayer with her ladies. Bodleian Library MS Douce 365 (1465), fol. 115r.
Reproduced by kind permission of The Bodleian Library, Oxford.   72

5 The Knight of the Tower instructs his daughters. British Library
MS Royal 19C VII (*Le Livre de la Tour Landry*), fol. 1r. Reproduced
by kind permission of The British Library, London.   84

6–8 The damsel refuses the old knight and takes off with the young one;
the two knights fight and the old knight kills the young; the old knight
goes away with his greyhound and leaves the damsel alone for her
'unnaturalness'. British Library Yates Thompson MS 13 (*The Taymouth
Hours*, *c*. 1325), fols 65r, 67r, 67v. Reproduced by kind permission of
The British Library, London.   91

9 The perils of dancing. Bodleian Library MS Bodley 264 (*The Romance of
Alexander*, *c*. 1400–10), fol. 58r. The work was produced in the Low
Countries but had English owners. Reproduced by kind permission of
The Bodleian Library, Oxford.   189

PREFACE

This book began as a doctoral thesis on 'The Medieval Maiden', but for publication has been completely rewritten, with much extra material added. The thesis was produced under the incomparable supervision of Jeremy Goldberg and Felicity Riddy, and I am tremendously grateful for their years of inspiration, generosity, encouragement and criticism. For their suggestions on turning the thesis into a book I thank Chris Given-Wilson, Alastair Minnis, Ruth Parr, Barry Reay, Jane Thorniley-Walker, and the anonymous readers of my proposal.

Staff and fellow students at the Centre for Medieval Studies at York created a dream research community. Particular thanks go to Cordelia Beattie and Katherine Lewis for sharing so many ideas and research leads, and to John Arnold, Peter Biller, Jim Binns, Chris Humphrey, Joanna Laynesmith (Chamberlayne), Christian Liddy, Lisa Liddy (Howarth), Noël James Menuge, Mark Ormrod and Sarah Williams, as well as all the friends who created a memorable social atmosphere. Christian Turner, Julian King, Katherine Lewis, Lara McClure and Adrian Clayton provided hospitality on recent trips to London and York, while Gordon and Pamela Jones welcomed me into their family. In Auckland I have learned a great deal from my colleagues and students, and thank Barry Reay in particular and my postgraduate students for their lively ideas, while Tracy Adams kindly translated some passages from Old French at short notice. Beyond York and Auckland, I owe particular debts to Caroline Barron and Steve Rigby for their very wise, considered and constructive comments on the draft manuscript, also to Caroline Barron for generosity with sources, to Judith Bennett and Stephanie Trigg for their warm encouragement and advice, to the patient and cheerful staff at Manchester University Press, and to my teachers and undergraduate lecturers in Melbourne who inspired my interest in history, feminism and all things medieval.

The research was mostly funded by the Commonwealth Scholarships Commission through the Association for Commonwealth Universities and the British Council, whose generosity made my studies at York possible, and through University of Auckland research grants. Thanks also go to the staff of the many libraries and record offices used, for their help both in person and over long distance. The section in Chapter 1 subtitled 'Perfect age' is a revised and much shortened version of my article, 'Maidenhood as the perfect age of woman's life', in Katherine J. Lewis, Noël James Menuge and Kim M. Phillips (eds), *Young Medieval Women* (Stroud, 1999), and appears here with the permission of Sutton Publishing Ltd.

On a personal note I am grateful to my parents Brian and Marie Phillips for their love, and for encouraging me to follow my passions rather than a more sensible path. The book is dedicated with much love and gratitude to Martin, who bravely came with me to the other side of the world and has helped and encouraged me in so many ways, and to three little girls – my nieces Rebecca and Madeline and my god-daughter Willow Rose – with hope for the future.

ABBREVIATIONS

BIHR   Borthwick Institute for Historical Research, York

BL   The British Library, London

Book of the Knight   William Caxton (trans.), *The Book of the Knight of the Tower*, ed. M. Y. Offord, EETS ss 2 (London, 1971)

Bracton   G. E. Woodbine (ed.) and Samuel E. Thorne (trans.), *Bracton on the Laws and Customs of England*, 4 vols (Cambridge, MA, 1968)

Byerly and Byerly 1   Benjamin F. Byerly and Catherine Ridder Byerly (eds), *Records of the Wardrobe and Household, 1285–1286* (London, 1977)

Byerly and Byerly 2   Benjamin F. Byerly and Catherine Ridder Byerly (eds), *Records of the Wardrobe and Household, 1286–1289* (London, 1986)

CL   Alison Hanham (ed.), *The Cely Letters, 1472–1488*, EETS os 273 (London, 1975)

CLRO   Corporation of London Record Office

Collection of Ordinances   Society of Antiquaries of London (ed.), *A Collection of Ordinances and Regulations for the Government of the Royal Household* (London, 1790)

CP   Cause paper

CPM   A. H. Thomas and Philip E. Jones (eds), *Calendar of Plea and Memoranda Rolls of the City of London, 1323–1482*, 6 vols (Cambridge, 1926–61)

CPR   *Calendar of Patent Rolls* (London, 1891–1986)

Documenta   'Documenta matris ad filiam', in R. Girvan (ed.), *Ratis Raving and Other Early Scots Poems on Morals*, Scottish Text Society, ser. 3, 2 (Edinburgh, 1937)

EETS   Early English Text Society

es   extra series

Glanvill   G. D. G. Hall (ed. and trans.) with guide to further reading by M. T. Clanchy, *The Treatise on the Laws and Customs of the Realm of England Commonly Called Glanvill* (Oxford, 1993)

Good Wife   'The Good Wife Taught Her Daughter', in Tauno F. Mustanoja (ed.), *The Good Wife Taught Her Daughter, The Good Wyfe Wold a Pylgremage, The Thewis of Gud Women* (Helsinki, 1948)

Letter Books   Reginald R. Sharpe (ed.), *Calendar of Letter Books of the City of London*, 11 vols (London, 1899–1912)

LL   Muriel St Clare Byrne (ed.), *The Lisle Letters*, 6 vols (Chicago, 1981).

Manual   Alfred E. Hartung and Jonathan Burke Severs (eds), *Manual of the Writings in Middle English*, 9 vols (New Haven, 1967–)

MED   Hans Kurath and Sherman M. Kuhn (eds), *Middle English Dictionary* (Ann Arbor, 1952–)

NHB   Thomas Percy (ed.), *The Regulations and Establishment of the Household of Henry Algernon Percy at His Castles of Wreshill and Likinfield in Yorkshire* (a.k.a. *Northumberland Household Book*) (London, 1827)

NRO   Norfolk Record Office

os   original series

PC   Thomas Stapleton (ed.), *The Plumpton Correspondence*, Camden Society os 4 (London, 1839)

Pilgrimage   'The Good Wyfe Wold a Pylgremage', in Tauno F. Mustanoja (ed.), *The Good Wife Taught Her Daughter, The Good Wyfe Wold a Pylgremage, The Thewis of Gud Women* (Helsinki, 1948)

PL and P   Norman Davis (ed.), *The Paston Letters and Papers of the Fifteenth Century*, 2 vols (Oxford, 1971–6)

Pollock and Maitland   F. Pollock and F. W. Maitland (eds), *The History of English Law Before the Time of Edward I*, 2 vols (Cambridge, [1895] 1968)

PR   Probate register

PRO   Public Record Office, Kew

Sandler, *Gothic Manuscripts*   Lucy Freeman Sandler, *Gothic Manuscripts 1285–1385*, 2 vols, in J. J. G. Alexander (general ed.), *A Survey of Manuscripts Illuminated in the British Isles* (London, 1986)

Scott, *Later Gothic Manuscripts*   Kathleen L. Scott, *Later Gothic Manuscripts 1390–1490*, 2 vols, in J. J. G. Alexander (general ed.), *A Survey of Manuscripts Illuminated in the British Isles* (London, 1996)

SL and P   Christine Carpenter (ed.), *Kingsford's Stonor Letters and Papers, 1290–1483* (Cambridge, 1996)

ss   supplementary series

TE   J. Raine *et al.* (eds), *Testamenta eboracensia: A Selection of Wills from the Registry at York*, 6 vols, Surtees Society 4, 30, 45, 53, 79, 106 (Durham, 1836–1902)

Thewis   'The thewis off gudwomen', in R. Girvan (ed.), *Ratis Raving and Other Early Scots Poems on Morals*, Scottish Text Society ser. 3, 2 (Edinburgh, 1937)

WAM   Westminster Abbey Muniments

NOTE ON TEXTS

All references to canon-legal texts are to E. Friedberg (ed.), *Corpus iuris canonici*, 2 vols (Leipzig, 1879), and citations of canon law follow the conventions outlined in James A. Brundage, *Medieval Canon Law* (London, 1995), Appendix 1. All references to Chaucer are to Larry D. Benson (ed.), *The Riverside Chaucer*, 3rd edn (Oxford, 1987).

Quotations in Middle English have in most instances been rendered in modern spelling (though the syntax has not been altered), to make the work more accessible to a wider readership, though where no current equivalent of a word exists I have retained the original term (sometimes modifying the spelling) and offered a translation in square brackets. Exceptions to this rule occur with quotations from well-known works of Middle English literature, such as those by Chaucer and the Pearl Poet, where modernisations are less necessary and more likely to grate. Translations from Latin are my own unless otherwise stated.

INTRODUCTION

Early on a January morning in 1464, before matins, a maiden in service accompanied her mistress Elizabeth Sharp to St Ewen's Church in Bristol. She carried a cake with candles and a lavishly embroidered sacrament cloth. 'Full womanly', Mistress Sharp offered up the items to the parson and parish worthies gathered there, and prayed, 'Father parson and my ghostly Father and all being here present, I am right fain and glad of this good end that is had and concluded between my husband and you and this church. And in token whereof, after my decease, I give you this same towel.'[1] As all present would have been aware, the point of this small ceremony was to accomplish the reconciliation of Elizabeth Sharp's husband, John, with the officials of the church.

Such a small, rather homely scene will be overlooked by readers looking for the epic or dramatic moments of history. But in its very ordinariness is expressed as revealing an account of idealised medieval femininity as Froissart's tale of the pregnant Philippa of Hainault's intercession for the lives of the Calais burgers.[2] What did Elizabeth Sharp do which was so 'womanly'? Bake a cake, offer it up, make a certain gesture or movement, provide the embroidered cloth? Perhaps femininity was encoded in all of these actions but most important was the intercessory or peace-making purpose they served, signalled by Mistress Sharp's prayer for reconciliation between her husband and the Church. John Sharp, a Bristol merchant, was notable for his absence that morning – unsurprisingly, as until the previous week he had owed forty-one years' rent to the parish for his shop in the city. It was no accident that after so many years of dispute it fell to Sharp's wife to heal the rift, help seal the agreement and kiss the parson and procurators, and with subtle drama draw her family back into the parish fold.[3]

If Elizabeth Sharp's actions are easy to overlook, how much more likely is it that the reader will miss the presence of her 'mayden', probably a young woman in her teens or early twenties? Her role that morning was both passive and active. As an observer of her mistress she learned the forms of respectable adult womanhood expected of a merchant's wife, while as agent her presence added to the impact of Elizabeth Sharp's actions as a visual reminder of another form of idealised femininity. The youthful maiden, unmarried yet sexually mature, no longer a child but not yet an adult, served as a profound symbol of ideal womanhood throughout English culture of the later Middle Ages. The twin themes of maidenhood as a time of learning feminine roles, and as itself a powerful image of perfect womanhood, will be the subject of this book.

Of course, not all young women were ideal figures, either in life or in representation. Elizabeth Sharp's maid may not have been receptive to the spectacle her mistress presented, and not all young medieval women learned approved womanly ways. On the manor of Halesowen in the late thirteenth century, young villein women joined in the widespread resistance of servile tenants against their monastic landlords. In late 1293 Christina, daughter of Roger de Honeford, went with her sister Julian and Amice Green to the site where the abbot's bailiffs had erected gallows ready to punish some mutinous tenant, and she managed to knock the structure to the ground. The three women fled, and were never found or punished, though the court rolls recorded their deeds.[4] Their actions make sense against the backdrop of tenant resistance to the oppressions of their lord, the abbot of the Premonstratensian Abbey of Halesowen, throughout the late thirteenth century.[5] Though male householders of the manor took the leading roles in the rising, women and girls took part too, tearing up and burning the lord's hedges, running away from the manor and being fined in the manor court (as Matilda de Hiddeley was in 1280) for verbally abusing the abbot.[6] Their actions cannot be understood by a focus on their gender or youth alone, but rather through their membership of villein society and local communities.

The aristocratic daughters of Lady Honor Lisle two and a half centuries later were also deeply influenced by the values and concerns of their family and social rank, and round out the social and chronological range covered in this book. In the 1530s, living in an aristocratic household in north-eastern France, thirteen-year-old Anne Basset wrote letters to her mother which display a narrowness of mental horizons and an expectation of privilege. Her letters contain little more than frequent requests for more, or more fashionable, clothing and trinkets, for items which she might give as gifts to her new-found friends in high society, and for small sums of money which she claimed to need for her devotions (but which her mother was anxious she would misspend, probably in gambling), all expressed with a formal *hauteur* which her upbringing had inculcated as an essential mark of breeding.[7] For a girl of her status, care for appearance, fashion, gift exchange and exaggeratedly proper forms of address were suitable virtues, and fit her well for the life as a royal maiden-in-waiting which was eventually procured for her.

These young women had profoundly different experiences of growing up in later medieval England, but what they shared in common was their identity as 'maidens', that is, young unmarried women past childhood but not yet fully adult. In modern terms these were adolescent girls, but the medieval word 'maiden' better captures the contemporary meanings associated with their life phase. It is a term with common application in Middle English texts, defined by the *Middle English Dictionary* as primarily 'an unmarried woman, usually young', while in their translation of thirteenth-century texts on virginity Bella Millett and Jocelyn Wogan-Browne comment that although they generally sought modern equivalents of medieval terms they made an exception for maiden, 'since there is no current English word which can mean both "girl" and "virgin"'.[8]

Secular, life-cycle maidenhood (as opposed to the state of perpetual virginity), as an experience and in cultural representation, has not been granted extended scholarly consideration before, although scholarship on topics concerning medieval English women and femininity is expanding rapidly and in ever more sophisticated forms. While works by P. J. P. Goldberg, Judith M. Bennett, Mavis E. Mate and Barbara A. Hanawalt have made invaluable contributions to our knowledge of young women's lives within broader studies of women across the life cycle or of childhood and adolescence, youthful maidens, like Elizabeth Sharp's maid, have proved easy to overlook.[9] The actions of the adult male leaders of the late thirteenth-century resistance at Halesowen or the political fortunes of Arthur Plantagenet, Lord Lisle, overshadow the experiences of their daughters or step-daughters. Yet young women's marginalisation within the historical record is at odds with their prominence in contemporary idealised representations. The maiden as a feminine type would have been firmly before the view of medieval English contemporaries, both male and female. When they walked into a parish church, or (if they had access to books) opened an illuminated prayer book, contemporaries would have been confronted with images not only of the enormously popular virgin martyrs including St Katherine and St Margaret but also of the most holy saint herself, the Virgin Mary, which celebrated the appearance and qualities of the idealised maiden. Those images of teenaged girls with long blonde hair, garlands or crowns, and conventional beauty celebrated the unique combination of sexuality and virginity which most strongly defined maidenhood as a phase in the life cycle. Though the ideology and the lived reality by no means perfectly matched one another any more than the modern ideology of childhood innocence lines up precisely with the experience of actual children, the realms of ideas and experience did overlap in some ways. The lives of girls were partly defined and influenced by wider cultural ideas of what it meant to be a maiden.

What age of woman's life corresponded with maidenhood? Throughout the present study 'maiden' refers to a young unmarried woman in her teens and early twenties. As will be discussed in the first chapter, the boundaries of the phase were set at the lower end by the onset of puberty and the advent of legal responsibilities and abilities in the early to midteens, and at the upper end by consummated marriage or its expectation in the later teens to mid-twenties (though it is not possible to set firm boundaries by age in years). There will be no particular discussion of the small minority of girls destined for the convent rather than marriage. Maidenhood was a phase experienced by most women across the social strata, though with certain differences according to status. With such a wide social spectrum to cover and as the first extended discussion of the subject, this book will necessarily leave much work to be done, but aims to provide a broad view with certain scenes sketched in detail, while opening up the subject for a range of closer studies.

Medieval youth

If female youth is to be studied as a distinct period in the lives of medieval Englishwomen, one must accept that medieval culture could conceive of a separate age intervening between childhood and adulthood.[10] Few scholars who have turned their attention to 'youth' or 'adolescence' in premodern Europe would now dispute that a distinct stage of this kind existed, both as a concept and experience, in that era.[11] The challenge has become not so much to demonstrate the existence of the phase as to understand the meanings and forms it took in specific cultures. Another challenge, not yet fully explored, is to understand the gendered forms of youth, alongside its class forms. Female youth is rarely given the attention paid to the male variety, and some sociologists have noted that in contemporary society adolescence itself is often characterised by masculine themes. 'Femininity and adolescence as discourses [are] subversive of each other. All of our images of the adolescent – the restless, searching teen; the Hamlet figure; the sower of wild oats and tester of growing powers – these are masculine figures.'[12] Scholarly awareness of premodern youth risks becoming similarly constrained, focused on the rowdy apprentice, the courtly lover or the young scholar. To redress the balance, and because it held qualities which make it quite distinct from medieval male youth, young womanhood is here treated in its own right.

In an anthropological study of 186 non-Western societies, Alice Schlegel and Herbert Barry III found male adolescence in all the cultures studied and female adolescence in almost all. Their argument depends on the broadest possible definition of adolescence, as a recognised stage between childhood and adulthood.[13] The special attributes of the phase, however, differ from one culture to another. To this extent, adolescence (like other life stages) is a cultural construct. Within the wide range of possible constructions, two broad conceptions recur: adolescence primarily as a transitional stage between childhood and adulthood, and adolescence as a stage *sui generis*, that is with its own important distinctive features.[14] English medieval conceptions of adolescence comprised both of these perceptions.

Male youth had a strongly transitional identity as an age of preparation for masculine adulthood, though the formal structures designed as preparation for manhood also gave the age its own characteristics. Thus, among the nobility, it was common for boys to be taken from the care of women after around the age of seven and put under the training of a private tutor.[15] In their teens they might be sent to a royal or noble household to begin a career in service, with specific duties and behaviour outlined for them. Others, particularly of gentry status, entered university in their early or mid-teens to prepare for a career in the law, Church or royal service, while some entered the Inns of Court for specialised legal training.[16] In urban areas – especially London – apprenticeship provided the clearest distinctive structure for male youths of artisan and merchant status, with its formal contracts and enrolment procedures and its ceremonies of admission and graduation.[17] Towns also increasingly provided grammar schools, serving mostly boys in their early or mid-teens, and Barbara Hanawalt has noted that with a rising age of entry to apprenticeship in London from the late fourteenth century more boys attended grammar schools before entering a trade, in response to masters' wishes that they hold a better educational standard.[18] Fewer distinctive institutions of male adolescence were apparent in peasant society, apart from the 'yonglings' guilds which some rural as well as urban parishes maintained, and at twelve boys were expected to enrol in a tithing, thus beginning their involvement with the public life of the village.[19] The shift to adulthood in peasant society seems more abrupt, at least in terms of institutional structures, than in artisan, mercantile or noble society.

Male adolescence did have some features *sui generis*. Some expressions of the 'ages of man' theme described it as a distinct phase characterised by the predominance of blood among the youth's humours. This inclined the young man towards lustiness, hot-headedness, and sometimes (as with Chaucer's Squire) romantic temperament.[20] Hanawalt's study of youth in late medieval London demonstrates the existence of both an adult concern with the rowdy behaviour of youths, and its frequent actual occurrence.[21] Male adolescence did possess some features which made it a life phase with its own defining characteristics, but predominantly it marked a period of passage, immaturity and incomplete masculinity.

Women's youth shared many of these transitional characteristics.[22] Female apprenticeships did exist in a few trades, some girls received a little formal schooling, some aristocratic girls had governesses, and many at all social levels left home to serve in the households of others. Their generally informal upbringing and training also stressed the learning of proper adult womanhood. But far fewer girls than boys went to school or entered apprenticeships, and those that were apprenticed experienced no ceremonies of entry and exit. Of course, none attended university. Women's general exclusion from public life meant that structures such as tithing groups were closed to them. One partial exception to this rule was the existence in some parishes of 'maidens' guilds', devotional associations usually run by young women themselves. Those who entered service in a great household rarely had their duties outlined as clearly as did boys.

Lacking the structures that channelled boys into manhood in a regulated fashion, maidenhood had a less formalised identity as a period of passage (though that is certainly not to deny that it had a transitional nature). But it had a clearer identity than male youth as a distinct phase of its own sort. The literary and artistic figure of the maiden, especially in representations of the virgin martyrs and the Virgin Mary in her apotheosis, had profound cultural importance as a depiction of ideal femininity. Indeed, as will be argued in Chapter 1, maidenhood, more than any other age, represented the perfect age of woman's life.

A model of maidenhood was outlined in John Trevisa's late fourteenth-century translation of Bartholomaeus Anglicus' *De proprietatibus rerum*:

> A maiden child and a wench is called *puella*, as it were clean and pure as the black of the eye, as sayeth Isidore.[23] For among all that is loved in a wench chastity and cleanness is loved most. Men shall take heed of wenches for they be hot and moist of complexion; and tender, small, pliant and fair of disposition of body; shamefast [modest], fearful, and merry, touching the affection; delicate in clothing. For as Seneca says, seemly clothing beseems them well that be chaste wenches. *Puella* is a

name of soundness without wem [flaw], and also of honesty [honour]. So says Isidore. For commonly we used to call maidens wenches. And a maid is called *virgo* and has that name of green age, as *virga*, 'a yard' [twig] is said as it were *viridis* 'green'. Otherwise a maid has that name *virgo* of cleanness and incorruption as it were *virago*, for she knows not the very passion of women.[24]

Though both the author (a thirteenth-century Franciscan friar) and medieval translator (a late fourteenth-century vicar and Oxford scholar) should have had limited personal experience of the *puellae*, maidens or wenches of their interest, the image does provide a neat summary of contemporary characterisations of girlhood or young womanhood. From the list of attributes – chastity, purity, delicacy and beauty of body, modesty, humility and openness of manner, freshness, incorruption, and lack of 'feminine passions' – the dominant impression is that a maiden possessed all the attractive qualities of femininity but was free of the faults. Lacking the particular passions of women, the flaws and corruptions that come with adult womanhood, the maiden is an unusually appealing feminine type to these writers. Though they represent a narrow, masculine and clerical point of view, their image fits a wider English ideology of feminine youth.

Maidenhood in late medieval England was a stage characterised primarily by a tension between sexuality and virginity. The medieval maiden was a woman caught between the asexuality and innocence of childhood, and the sexual and psychological maturity of adult womanhood. This tension brought in its train concerns about the maintenance of chastity – and those concerns had an impact on the lives of young women from most backgrounds, though not all equally – but it was not merely an age which was looked upon with alarm or anxiety. It was also the stage of women's life cycle most easily celebrated, in secular literature, in hagiography and in the visual arts. The very tension between the achievement of sexual maturity and the requirement of chastity became the focus of a kind of desire. Thus medieval maidens, both as abstract figures and as real girls, were subject both to protection and display, anxiety and appreciation. This is, of course, to generalise, and maidenhood cannot always be pinned down to a neat definition. Both the social status of the maidens under consideration and their diversity of representation in text and image have a destabilising influence on the meaning of the phase.

As far as an orthodoxy on the nature and meanings of young medieval womanhood exists among scholars, it asserts that youth was a time of unusual autonomy for women. Judith Bennett and Amy Froide make this

7

claim in their recent collection on medieval singlewomen, and Bennett has elsewhere written of unmarried women's relative legal and economic independence in pre-Plague Brigstock and fifteenth-century Ramsey.[25] Roberta Krueger also employs 'autonomy' as a key word throughout her discussion of maidens in French literature, even though her account offers much greater subtlety and complexity than the term would suggest. She finds maidenhood in courtly narratives an often troubled time of not only 'courage, fortitude, patience, generosity, forbearance and trust' but also of 'vulnerability, displacement, and the fragmentation of … identity', of 'discomfort, separation, loss, and crisis', and of dependence on other women.[26] Goldberg seems more chary of the term, but his work on unmarried women in service is underpinned by a perception of 'the high degree of emotional and economic independence' which employment away from the natal home allowed young women. Richard Smith and Felicity Riddy have also offered optimistic perspectives on young women in service, Riddy speaking of 'spirited and daring girls' who left their family homes as teenagers and plunged into unconventional and exciting lives of their own choosing in towns.[27]

While some maidens probably did find their youthful years a happy time, to view independence as a desirable state may be to impose too modern a perspective on the past. We shall see that the evidence concerning young women's economic position is not so rosy as sometimes painted. Moreover, what to modern eyes may resemble autonomy would more likely have felt like insecurity to medieval contemporaries: that is, something more like the discomfort, separation, loss and crisis which Krueger's study reveals. The whole notion of autonomy (however phrased) is a fundamentally modern value, which tends to be a focus of feminist scholars' analysis because of our own social conditioning to emphasise the freedom of the individual, deriving from nineteenth-century liberalism, and in particular a broadly liberal-feminist conviction (in a lineage from Wollstonecraft and Taylor to the present) that women's best chance of liberation is to move away from constraints of family, husbands and children and pursue independent work and public roles. Yet full individual autonomy seems an unrealistic goal even in the present, and as a concept is both too simple and too anachronistic to help in interpreting the lives of young medieval women.

Constructing femininity

Though this book is partly a study of youth, it is equally a study of the construction of femininity. In the introduction to their valuable reader of key articles in the field of gender and history, Robert Shoemaker and Mary Vincent lament the paucity of historical studies of female adolescence, and the broad potential of such studies: 'These topics require much more attention if we are to understand fully the processes by which gender roles have been historically constructed and perpetuated, not only in discourse but also in social practice.'[28]

Adolescence was the time at which the differences between the sexes began to be delineated with greater sharpness, when the construction of fully gendered selves for medieval boys and girls began in earnest. Although gender differentiation had some place in childhood roles and identities, the distinction of sexes was far less important than later in life. This can be glimpsed through educational practice for elite groups, where boys were separated from girls at around seven. The literary example of Floris and Blancheflour – a boy and girl who are intimate friends in infancy and become distraught at age seven when Floris' father decides his son should go to school without Blancheflour – seems grounded in the noble practice of the day.[29] Eileen Power, writing about the education of male and female children in nunneries, notes that in general boys were not supposed to remain in the nunnery past the age of nine or ten. A Cistercian statute of 1256–7 and ordinances of specific houses forbade the presence of boys in nunneries altogether, but the lax application of the rule implies that boys under ten were not perceived to pose a sufficiently masculine threat to the enclosed world of the nunnery to exclude them in practice.[30] In a noble domestic setting, boy and girl children could share bedrooms during childhood but be separated at puberty, as indicated by the example of John of Gaunt's household where his daughters and son shared a bedchamber until the eldest daughter reached puberty.[31] Such separation was of course enabled only by wealth, and is irrelevant in considering the small houses of artisan or peasant families.

The pronouns used in romance and other literature to refer to characters before and after puberty are also revealing, with pre-pubescent children often referred to as 'it' rather than 'he' or 'she'.[32] For example, in the Middle English translation of Marie de France's *Lay le Freine*, the heroine is referred to by the neuter pronoun up to the age of twelve, but thereafter by feminine pronouns exclusively.[33] Barbara Hanawalt has found that in peasant society although some degree of sexual division of

9

labour began to become apparent as early as the ages of two or three, it was most marked from age thirteen onwards.[34] To study medieval youth, then, is partly to study the processes by which young people were socialised into the gender roles and identities appropriate to their social group, and to study medieval maidens is in part to examine how girls became women. This, however, raises some important questions. What do we mean by a 'medieval woman'? How did this process of socialisation in gender occur, who controlled it and to what ends, and what role was played by the maidens themselves? None of these may be easily answered, but some attempt at providing partial answers at least is essential if the late medieval English process of socialisation in femininity is to be understood even imperfectly.

First, then, what is a 'medieval woman'? Page duBois makes a point about writing the history of women in classical society which is just as relevant to studies of medieval society: 'And when we do historical work on women, we may just be producing women as a category *for ourselves*, for ourselves to inhabit as we continually produce it in discourse.'[35] When modern scholars approach the history of female persons in past societies, as when they approach the history of young people, we need to be alert to the possibility that historical conceptions of such groups differ markedly from current ones. This is particularly important within those branches of history, such as women's history, the history of race, or the history of sexualities, which have arisen out of a modern political impetus to produce the histories of oppressed groups as a way of enhancing their visibility and significance in the present. In producing medieval women as a category 'for ourselves to inhabit', are we (especially when guided by feminist principles) simply producing women in our own likeness?

A further objection to the project of writing women's history arises out of the insights generated by socialist, black and post-structuralist feminist scholars who have disputed the unity of the category 'women' even in the present.[36] Categories of identity such as race, class, religious affiliation, occupation and age can be so powerful as to break down any purported unity within the category of sex. More recently, though, scholars such as Toril Moi have argued that it is important to avoid recent academic feminism's 'critical anorexia', its 'tendency to make the word women slim down to nothing'.[37] She agrees that it is essential to take into account the other facets of identity that contribute to the individual female person's make-up, because every human being is always in a 'specific situation' (racial, regional, class, religious, occupational, etc.), and therefore 'woman is not one'. But neither is she *infinitely* plural.

This kind of approach can help us to see medieval women and men in a way which encourages the recognition of multiplicity and conflictedness in gender identities, while also being alert to common patterns within a culture which serve to mark out dominant femininity or masculinity. We should look beyond plurality and seek patterns within complexity, to do justice to specific historical constructions of gender. A number of recent admirable collections dealing with medieval masculinity assert the necessity to accept the diversity of medieval masculinities, but also acknowledge that certain versions of masculinity were dominant and others subordinate or resistant.[38] 'Although gender studies has urged on us the need to think in terms of pluralities of masculinities and femininities, we must be aware of the fact that many authors in the Middle Ages sought to impose very rigid modes of behaviour.'[39] One recurring theme or pattern in medieval masculinity was the link with forms of power or authority.[40] To speak of power more generally, too pluralistic an approach ignores the processes by which dominant ideologies of gender are formed and maintained. Also, without a quest for historically contextualised patterns it is easier to fall into the trap of anachronism and premature empathy. As Page duBois warns, let us not be too hasty about producing historical women who resemble ourselves.

A fundamental feature of medieval attitudes towards women was the view of them as *secondary* or *subordinate* creatures in relation to men. This no doubt seems obvious, but the point is that this is a different dominant view of women from that which prevails in contemporary Western society. In the latter, women have come in recent decades to be defined less as inferior than as essentially *different* from men, especially in their bodies. Though the extent of the difference is contested by many feminists, wider cultural understandings of the sexes are fundamentally predicated on the opposition of male and female. The modern organisation of sexuality around the poles of heterosexual and homosexual is one of the strongest illustrations of the importance of difference. Although modern society is not free of the notion of women as lesser beings, nor medieval culture without the notion of women as different from men, what has changed is the degree of emphasis, and thus medieval education in gender did not consist of the same messages as it does today.

Medieval theology emphasised that woman was created second, to be a helper 'meet' for man, while natural philosophy turned to Greek authorities, for the claim that a woman was 'as it were, a deformed male', because of her lesser quantity of vital 'heat'. The male, says Bartholomaeus, 'passes the female in perfect complexion ... for in comparison to the female the male is hot and dry, and the female againward [the opposite]'.[41] It was her lack of heat, rather than her reproductive aspect, which was the cause of her menstruation, and made her contribution to reproduction less than a man's.[42] It also gave her a smaller, frailer body, in contrast to a man's heat and dryness which endowed him with sinews and brawn, great and strong bones and joints, and his larger heart making him more 'bold and hardy' than a woman. His physical superiority brought him closer than a woman to the 'dignity and worthiness of the image and likeness of God', and for this reason 'a man passes a woman in authority and might of sovereignty'.[43] Thus biological theories lent validity to scripture, and reinforced the physical, emotional, intellectual and moral superiority of masculinity. Legal codes show that the theory of female inferiority had force in daily reality. Though women were not without legal rights and abilities, these were almost always subordinated to the rights of men. Unmarried women and widows enjoyed greater legal abilities than wives, but even they were largely excluded from 'public' offices of any kind.[44]

The cultural construction of women as the secondary sex needs to be understood alongside other aspects of identity. Aristocratic and gentry women were subordinate to their male peers in their daily dealings, but not to men of lower social status. A widow could control a household that included male apprentices, servants and journeymen. A female mystic might command greater spiritual respect than a secular man. An independent silkwoman enjoyed better status and income in her profession than a male labourer in his. Questions of class, occupation, marital status and age add great complexity to constructions of women, but never completely override the theme of social, economic, political and cultural subordination.

On the other hand, women were generally not despised nor utterly reviled in daily life. 'No man should have woman in despite, for it is no wisdom to despise that [which] God loves', a preacher in the late fourteenth or early fifteenth century told his listeners.[45] One can overstate the extent to which misogyny – which it is useful to distinguish from anti-feminism – pervaded medieval culture.[46] Most misogynistic texts were Latin works or vernacular translations composed probably as 'amusing' texts of dubious taste for a learned male elite who smugly enjoyed their own erudition in recognising classical and biblical allusions. Vernacular misogynistic works such as the Scottish fifteenth-century *The Spectacle of Luf* can be found, but what is more notable about the great majority of vernacular literature is its avoidance of such explicitly hate-filled diatribes.[47]

Because of the centrality of the family and household to the economic organisation of later medieval English society, laymen of all classes could not afford to shun women. Ever since historians in the early twentieth century began to examine the lives of medieval laywomen they have consistently commented on the importance of peasant, urban and noble-women's contributions to the household economy, through work, child-bearing and raising, and in bringing property and money with them into marriage. Women's contributions also took less directly economic forms, such as mediation or peace-making, as seen in the example of Elizabeth Sharp. To coin a phrase, the prescribed roles and identities for medieval English women could be called 'active docility'. During their youth, maidens were taught not to be completely passive, nor to be dominant, but to acquiesce in being subordinate while still playing important roles, in the family, religious life, and in economic contributions. When Elizabeth Sharp's maidservant watched her mistress take over the staging of her husband's reconciliation with his parish, she was watching a virtuoso performance of active docility.

This example offers a vivid answer to the second question posed above, of how the socialisation in femininity occurred. Because the active but subordinate woman was central to the smooth running of society and the success of family units, it was in the interests of many groups to produce adult women with these characteristics. Mothers as well as fathers, sisters as well as brothers, female teachers, mistresses and employers as well as male ones, all participated in the production of approved femininity in young women. Ultimately, men, at all social levels, were those best served by this socialisation within patriarchy, but they needed the participation, compliance and assistance of women to make such socialisation work. They received it. Though a number of male and female authors, including Christine de Pisan (whose *Cité des dames* had some English women readers),[48] produced polemics against misogyny, the place of women as second-class citizens was not generally challenged.

Why would women not desire to better their social position, even if the structures surrounding them would crush their aspirations? It is an important task of women's history to understand how and why women accept, even defend, social circumstances apparently disadvantageous to themselves. There are two possible reasons within the medieval context – one economic, the other ideological. The medieval economy, while it waxed and waned, was never wealthy or flexible enough to give the majority of women the option of autonomy from family life. Moreover, the persistence of the household as the chief economic unit, regardless of other economic conditions, entrenched the secondary nature of woman's position in her role as wife and helpmeet. Only in widowhood, as several studies have shown, could women escape something of this secondary status, and only well set-up women had this opportunity.[49] Alternatives to marriage existed in the cloister (especially for women of well-off urban and gentry status), and in lifelong singleness, but the former was open only to a few and, because of the poverty of most contemporary English nunneries, probably attractive only to those with a genuine vocation or outright aversion to marriage, while lay singleness was likely to entail poverty, marginalisation and sometimes outright hostility.[50] Perhaps some women chose single status over marriage because they could not abide the latter's institutionalised subordination. But in a society where resistance to social norms was both less tolerated than today (though even the modern West tolerates only a degree of resistance) and more difficult in a pragmatic and economic sense, it is unreasonable to expect wide-scale defiance, or even many individual examples.

The ideological sweeteners that made the blunt pragmatism of compliance more bearable included notions of status, which ensured that a noblewoman need never feel inferior to a social subordinate and made upward mobility an achievable aspiration for women. This lack of fit between class and gender, in a culture obsessed with status, would have meant that many women would never have thought themselves disadvantaged by their sex. Other important sweeteners included the idealisation of certain feminine types, notably sainted women – especially the Virgin Mary, the virgin martyrs, mystics such as Bridget of Sweden and laywomen of exceptional piety such as Elizabeth of Hungary – and romance heroines. The highly visible presence of such female figures in the textual and visual cultures of late medieval England provided a distraction from the realities of women's subordination.

What about maidens themselves? Did they play a part in this socialisation to subordination? Questions about the formation of gendered selves are necessarily one part of wider questions about the formation of the self, and the role of the subject in that formation. Morwenna Griffiths argues that the self is a creation both of the individual and the circumstances in which the formation takes place, taking a spider's spinning of its web as a useful metaphor. As the shape of a web depends both on the spider weaving it and the physical circumstances in which the web is placed, so the constituents of the self are made both by the context of time and space and by the subject spinning the web of herself within those limits.[51] The self 'is made of nearly invisible, very strong threads attached to the circumstances of its making and under the control of its maker. It ... is made to suit the purposes of its maker, but the circumstances of the making are not under her control.'[52] As Griffiths acknowledges, the web metaphor imparts an artificial simplicity to the process – the 'individual' is hardly a being whose existence is not already shaped by circumstances – but her formulation has the advantage of acknowledging some personal agency in the process, unlike a strongly post-structuralist stance which would view the self as entirely a product of circumstances, and especially of language. The problem for the historian interested in the shaping of past identities is that while the surroundings of the web are relatively visible (as social structures, class and locational groupings, occupational categories, life cycle patterns, and so on) the individuals undertaking the weaving are often invisible, or at best very dim and shadowy. This is especially the case for women, and even more for young unmarried women (even of elite groups), whose near-silence in the written record means that voices of individual maidens, heavily mediated by concerns of discourse and audience, are few and far between. One could say this does not matter, and be content to study the teachings on gender that the culture imposed on individuals, but in order to understand the extent to which those teachings had any real influence, or were even partly shaped or adapted by indivi-duals, it is necessary to pay at least some attention to the latter. For this reason, while much of this book will discuss the teachings on femininity that directed young women's socialisation and daily experiences, the webmakers will be remembered throughout and come to the fore in the final chapter, which will endeavour to listen to some of the voices and watch some of the actions of maidens themselves, to attempt some analysis of young women's role in shaping their gendered selves. Though some will be seen to rebel against aspects of their own circumstances, such as unappealing arranged marriages, or subordination within the constraints of villein society, these instances of resistance did not add up to defiance of a gender system. The limitations which the economic structures surrounding them imposed upon their lives did not allow the privilege of resistance without uncomfortable consequences.

Approach and sources

This is an interdisciplinary study of young womanhood, both in the types of sources used and the approach taken to them. Given the broad nature of the topic, and because no single set of sources provides a really substantial body of information, it has been necessary to cast a very wide net. This necessity, however, has a potentially desirable outcome, as it produces a wide-ranging study which encourages comparisons between groups of maidens. Evidence from across England, both in rural and urban areas, across the social status groups, from the late thirteenth to early sixteenth centuries, is employed.[53] The chronological framework spans around 1270 to around 1540 (the 'circas' are taken as read in the book's title). The later thirteenth century is a useful starting point, as increasing numbers of documents and other materials survive from that time onwards, while 1540 or thereabouts is chosen over the conventional '*c.* 1500' because the English Reformation, well underway by 1540, better marks the end of the medieval era and (particularly relevant here) the decline of the veneration of the Virgin Mary and the cult of saints. Neither the primary nor secondary sources are limited to those traditionally belonging to a particular discipline. Sources traditionally associated with 'history', including legal treatises and court cases, manorial records, civic ordinances, household accounts, travel narratives, churchwardens' accounts, family letters and apprenticeship records will be employed, among many others. Sources from theological literature, dealing with notions of the age of consent and ages at first reception of the sacraments, have a place. Medical or scientific literature, especially discussing the age at puberty, is also considered. Instructive or didactic literature has an important role, especially in the form of conduct books addressed to young women and some sermon, homiletic and vices-and-virtues material. Devotional literature, such as hagiography dealing with virgin martyrs, is analysed, as are genres more often associated with the purely 'literary' – especially romances, but also drama and lyrics.

Although the range of sources used is made deliberately broad, attention is given to the nature and function of the sources in question. For example, literary representations of young womanhood are understood within the framework of genre, authorship, audience and purpose, not as reflections of reality. Literary works could sometimes serve a mild didactic function, but could also offer a conceptual space for exploring possible behaviours beyond the boundaries of acceptable daily life. At the same time, approaches to 'historical' sources such as legal records are informed by literary approaches which alert one to the kinds of discourse operating within and around a given text. Although constraints of space will not allow full discussion of the choice and analysis of sources in each instance, the guiding principles throughout have been firstly to establish a range of evidence, and secondly to ascertain each source's relevance for young laywomen. Texts which would have had little influence upon the lives of young women of any social group, such as theoretical works on theology, medicine or natural philosophy circulating amongst an educated elite, or any works not known to have circulated in England, are mostly ignored or given brief attention. While primary sources are employed as much as possible, some sets of sources dealing especially with lower-status women (such as manor court rolls) are best examined in the kind of close detail which a more narrowly focused monograph offers. Studies by other scholars are relied upon to a greater extent in such instances.

The first chapter explores the key attributes associated with maidenhood, sketching the phase's boundaries (the legally, socially and culturally defined entry and exit points of the age), examining perceptions of the particularity of maidens' bodies and minds, and ending with the contention that maidenhood was understood by many as the 'perfect age' of woman's life and was therefore an important ideal of femininity. The second chapter moves away from conceptions of maidenhood to examining the practice of bringing up young women, especially their 'education' in femininity, considering the modes of learning, teachers and messages, and the differences found according to social status. Chapter 3 is concerned with maidens' experiences of work and service, especially outside the natal home, again considering the variations found between status groups and ultimately challenging the scholarly orthodoxy concerning young women's autonomy. Chapter 4 picks up the theme of sexuality, which is a thread running throughout the book, and considers in greater depth the nature of the sexuality prescribed for young women, the boundaries of licit and illicit behaviour and opportunities for pushing those boundaries through flirtation and literary fantasy. Chapter 5 takes up the challenge of considering the perspective of young women themselves and their role in shaping or challenging prescribed femininity, through brief case studies of young women from a range of backgrounds. Throughout the book two themes remain constant. Maidenhood was an age of intense socialisation in preferred forms of femininity, and was also itself, with its characteristic combination of sexuality and virginity, considered an ideal of womanhood.

Notes

1 Betty R. Masters and Elizabeth Ralph (eds), *The Church Book of St Ewen's, Bristol, 1454–1584*, Bristol and Gloucestershire Archaeological Society 6 (Gloucester, 1967), pp. 60–1.

2 Jean Froissart, *Chronicles of England, France and the Adjoining Countries*, trans. Thomas Johnes, 5 vols (n.p., 1803), vol. 1, p. 367; Paul Strohm, 'Queens as intercessors', in *Hochon's Arrow: The Social Imagination of Fourteenth-Century Texts* (Princeton, 1992).

3 Masters and Ralph (eds), *St Ewen's*, pp. xxix–xxxii, 58–60.

4   John Amphlett, Sydney Graves Hamilton and R. A. Wilson (eds), *Court Rolls of the Manor of Hales 1272–1307*, 3 vols, Worcestershire Historical Society (Oxford, 1910–33), vol. 1, p. 245 (hereafter *Hales Court Rolls*).

5   Zvi Razi, 'The struggles between the abbots of Halesowen and their tenants in the thirteenth and fourteenth centuries', in T. H. Aston *et al.* (eds), *Social Relations and Ideas: Essays in Honour of R. H. Hilton* (Cambridge, 1983), though he does not discuss women's participation.

6   Amphlett (ed.), *Hales Court Rolls I*, pp. 116–17, 121, 122, 232, 247, 257, 261, 270–1, 325, 348.

7   *LL* 3, pp. 142–3, 150, 158, 169–71.

8   *MED* s.v. 'maiden', 'maid', 'mai'; Bella Millett and Jocelyn Wogan-Browne (eds), *Medieval English Prose for Women: Selections from the Katherine Group and Ancrene Wisse* (Oxford, 1990), p. xliii. 'Adolescence' will be used sparingly as it carries the baggage of twentieth-century concepts of the phase, such as struggle against parents and authority, which are not necessarily cross-cultural: see for example Margaret Mead, *Coming of Age in Samoa: A Study of Adolescence and Sex in Primitive Societies* (Harmondsworth, 1943), p. 12 (Mead's point here stands up despite several criticisms of her work in Samoa more generally).

9   For a survey of recent work on medieval women see Miri Rubin, 'A decade of studying medieval women, 1987–1997', *History Workshop Journal*, 46 (Autumn, 1998), 213–39. P. J. P. Goldberg, *Women, Work, and Life Cycle in a Medieval Economy: Women in York and Yorkshire, c. 1300–1520* (Oxford, 1992) and Judith M. Bennett, *Women in the Medieval English Countryside: Gender and Household in Brigstock before the Plague* (Oxford, 1987) included groundbreaking examinations of young single womanhood within their broader studies of women of lower orders, added to recently by Mavis E. Mate, *Daughters, Wives and Widows after the Black Death: Women in Sussex, 1350–1535* (Woodbridge, 1998). Barbara A. Hanawalt includes some discussion of adolescent girls alongside boys in *Growing Up in Medieval London: The Experience of Childhood in History* (Oxford, 1993). Judith M. Bennett and Amy M. Froide's collection *Singlewomen in the European Past, 1250–1800* (Philadelphia, 1999) deals with young unmarried women under the broader heading of 'singlewomen', which includes life-long 'spinsters', and none of the essays deals specifically with English maidens of the period *c.* 1270–1540. For a collection dealing solely with young women see Katherine J. Lewis, Noël James Menuge and Kim M. Phillips (eds), *Young Medieval Women* (Stroud, 1999). See now also Fiona Harris Stoertz, 'Young women in France and England, 1050–1300', in *Journal of Women's History*, 12 (2001), 22–46, and Konrad Eisenbichler (ed.), *The Premodern Teenager: Youth in Society, 1150–1650* (Toronto, 2002), both of which appeared after the manuscript of the present book was completed.

10 Few readers will be unaware that the debate over whether premodern Europeans had concepts of childhood or adolescence was sparked by Philippe Ariès's 1960 classic, *L'Enfant et la familiale sous l'ancien régime*, translated in 1962 as *Centuries of Childhood* by Robert Baldick (New York, 1962). His claims that 'in medieval society the idea (*sentiment*) of childhood did not exist' (p. 128) and that before the eighteenth century 'people had no idea of what we call adolescence'

(p. 29) were seized upon with enthusiasm in the mid-1970s by Lawrence Stone and Edward Shorter among others although Ariès himself had acknowledged the failings of his argument by 1973: see Danièle Alexandre-Bidon and Didier Lett, *Children in the Middle Ages: Fifth–Fifteenth Centuries*, trans. Jody Gladding (Notre Dame, 1999), p. 1. The claims were then as vigorously rebutted in the 1980s and early 1990s by Adrian Wilson, Linda Pollock, Lorraine Attreed, Barbara Hanawalt, Shulamith Shahar and others. Several recent studies provide useful summaries of the debate, especially James A. Schultz, *The Knowledge of Childhood in the German Middle Ages, 1100–1350* (Philadelphia, 1995), pp. 2–9; Paul Griffiths, *Youth and Authority: Formative Experiences in England 1560–1640* (Oxford, 1996), pp. 1–16; and Sally Crawford, *Childhood in Anglo-Saxon England* (Stroud, 1999), pp. 1–8. Hugh Cunningham's summary in *Children and Childhood in Western Society Since 1500* (London, 1995), pp. 2–9, 30–40, is especially useful in pointing out ways in which Ariès has been mistranslated, misread or over-simplified by some. Rather than reiterate their points I direct readers to these works, and hope discussion on youth can move on.

11 See the essays by Barbara A. Hanawalt, Kathryn L. Reyerson and Stanley Chojnacki in *Journal of Family History*, 17 (1992), 341–95; Hanawalt, *Growing Up*; Ilana Krausman Ben-Amos, *Adolescence and Youth in Early Modern England* (New Haven, 1994); Griffiths, *Youth and Authority*; Giovanni Levi and Jean-Claude Schmitt (eds), *A History of Young People*, vol. 1, *Ancient and Medieval Rites of Passage*, trans. Camille Naish (Cambridge, MA, 1997). James A. Schultz in his article 'Medieval adolescence: the claims of history and the silences of German narrative', *Speculum*, 66 (1991), 519–37, argued that Middle High German romances contain no evidence of the concept of adolescence, but his more recent *Knowledge of Childhood* makes clear that what he did not find was a *twentieth-century* notion of adolescence, as a time of physiological development and psychological struggle: see pp. 131–2 and p. 132, n. 149.

12 Barbara Hudson, 'Femininity and aolescence', in Angela McRobbie and Mica Nava (eds), *Gender and Generation* (Houndmills, 1984), p. 35.

13 Alice Schlegel and Herbert Barry III, *Adolescence: An Anthropological Inquiry* (New York, 1991). The authors found that even where marriage occurs before puberty a kind of adolescence follows. In some societies where girls marry upon or shortly after puberty they are not deemed adult until becoming mothers, usually a few years later. In general, they find that the beginning of adolescence is usually marked by biological changes and is therefore relatively easy to locate, but the demarcation of the end of adolescence is harder to identify, and that in most cases girls' adolescence is shorter than boys'.

14 Schlegel and Herbert note that sociologists tend to emphasise the former, while anthropologists also consider the latter, p. 6.

15 Nicholas Orme, *From Childhood to Chivalry: The Education of the English Kings and Aristocracy, 1066–1530* (London, 1984), pp. 17–18.

16 Orme, *Childhood to Chivalry*, pp. 66–79.

17 Hanawalt, *Growing Up*, esp. ch. 8.

18 Hanawalt, *Growing Up*, pp. 21, 113, 144. On grammar schools in northern England

see Jo Ann Hoeppner Moran, *The Growth of English Schooling, 1340–1548: Learning, Literacy, and Laicization in Pre-Reformation York Diocese* (Princeton, 1985), ch. 2.

19 On yonglings see Katherine L. French, *The People of the Parish: Community Life in a Late Medieval English Diocese* (Philadelphia, 2001), pp. 127–9, 172, 173. To become a member of a tithing or frankpledge meant that a boy had reached an age at which he could be subject to criminal law, and was a member of a group whose duty it was to report crimes committed within their communities to the sheriff at annual views of frankpledge; Pollock and Maitland 1, pp. 531–2, 580–2.

20 J. A. Burrow, 'Chaucer's *Knight's Tale* and the three ages of man', in *Essays in Medieval Literature* (Oxford, 1984), p. 30, and *The Ages of Man: A Study in Medieval Writing and Thought* (Oxford, 1986), pp. 12–54. See also Mary Dove, *The Perfect Age of Man's Life* (Cambridge, 1986), p. 8; Elizabeth Sears, *The Ages of Man: Medieval Interpretations of the Life Cycle* (Princeton, 1986), esp. ch. 1; Michael E. Goodich, *From Birth to Old Age: The Human Life Cycle in Medieval Thought 1250–1350* (Lanham, MD, 1989), pp. 105–26.

21 Hanawalt, *Growing Up*, pp. 120–8.

22 All the following topics will be discussed in subsequent chapters.

23 That is, *puella* is derived from *pupilla*, according to Isidore.

24 M. C. Seymour *et al.* (eds), *De puella* in *On the Properties of Things: John Trevisa's Translation of Bartholomaeus Anglicus De proprietatibus rerum. A Critical Text*, 2 vols (Oxford, 1975), vol. 1, lib. 6, cap. 6.

25 Judith M. Bennett and Amy M. Froide, 'A singular past', in Bennett and Froide (eds), *Singlewomen*, p. 8; Bennett, *Women in the Medieval English Countryside*, pp. 76–82; and 'Medieval peasant marriage: an examination of marriage license fines in *Liber gersumarum*', in J. A. Raftis (ed.), *Pathways to Medieval Peasants* (Toronto, 1981).

26 Roberta L. Krueger, 'Transforming maidens: singlewomen's stories in Marie de France's *Lais* and later French courtly narratives', in Bennett and Froide (eds), *Singlewomen*, quotations at pp. 156, 160 and 179.

27 Goldberg, *Women, Work, and Life Cycle*, quotation at p. 327; Richard M. Smith, 'Geographical diversity in the resort to marriage in late medieval Europe: work, reputation, and unmarried females in the household formation systems of northern and southern Europe', in P. J. P. Goldberg (ed.), *Women in Medieval English Society* (Stroud, 1997), esp. pp. 41–6; Felicity Riddy, 'Mother knows best: reading social change in a courtesy text', *Speculum*, 71 (1996), 66–86, esp. p. 86.

28 Robert Shoemaker and Mary Vincent (eds), *Gender and History in Western Europe* (London, 1998), p. 16.

29 'Floris and Blancheflour', in Donald Sands (ed.), *Middle English Verse Romances* (Exeter, 1986), lines 1–24.

30 Eileen Power, *Medieval English Nunneries, c. 1275–1535* (Cambridge, 1922), p. 263.

31 Anthony Goodman, *John of Gaunt: The Exercise of Princely Power in Fourteenth Century Europe* (Harlow, 1992), p. 321.

32 *MED*, s.v. 'hit'. The *MED* gives only one example of reference to an adult by the neuter pronoun, in *Havelock the Dane*, line 2264.

33 'Lai le Freine', in Sands (ed.), *Middle English Verse Romances*, pp. 238–41. The poet calls Freine 'it' twenty-three times and uses feminine pronouns only three times between lines 134 and 236, that is, from soon after her birth to her twelfth birthday.

34 Barbara A. Hanawalt, *The Ties that Bound: Peasant Families in Medieval England* (Oxford, 1986), pp. 157–61.

35 Page duBois, 'The subject in antiquity after Foucault', in David H. Larmour, Paul Allen Miller and Charles Platter (eds), *Rethinking Sexuality: Foucault and Classical Antiquity* (Princeton, 1998), p. 96.

36 Denise Riley, 'Does sex have a history?', in *Am I That Name? Feminism and the Category of 'Women' in History* (London, 1988), pp. 1–2; Joan Wallach Scott, 'Introduction', to Joan Wallach Scott (ed.), *Feminism and History* (Oxford, 1996).

37 Toril Moi, 'What is a woman? Sex, gender, and the body in feminist theory', in *What is a Woman? And Other Essays* (Oxford, 1999), p. 7. The term 'critical anorexia' is Susan Gubar's. Other feminist scholars whose recent work has called for a move away from the further reaches of Judith Butler-inspired scholarship include Lynne Segal, *Why Feminism?: Gender, Psychology, Politics* (Cambridge, 1999), esp. pp. 70–7.

38 Jacqueline Murray, 'Introduction', in Jacqueline Murray (ed.), *Conflicted Identities and Multiple Masculinities: Men in the Medieval West* (New York, 1999), p. xvii.

39 D. M. Hadley, 'Introduction: medieval masculinities', in D. M. Hadley (ed.), *Masculinity in Medieval Europe* (London, 1999), pp. 6–7.

40 Clare A. Lees, 'Introduction', in Clare A. Lees, with the assistance of Thelma Fenster and Jo Ann McNamara (eds), *Medieval Masculinities: Regarding Men in the Middle Ages* (Minneapolis, 1994), p. xxi.

41 *De prop. rerum*, lib. 6, cap. 12.

42 Joan Cadden, *Meanings of Sex Difference in the Middle Ages: Medicine, Science and Culture* (Cambridge, 1993), pp. 170–7.

43 *De prop. rerum*, lib. 6, cap. 12.

44 For summaries of medieval Englishwomen's legal rights see Ruth Kittel, 'Women under the law in medieval England 1066–1485', in Barbara Kanner (ed.), *The Women of England from Anglo-Saxon Times to the Present: Interpretive Bibliographical Essays* (London, 1979); Janet Senderowitz Loengard, '"Legal history and the medieval Englishwoman" revisited', in Joel T. Rosenthal (ed.), *Medieval Women and the Sources of Medieval History* (Athens, GA, 1990); Caroline M. Barron, 'The "Golden Age" of women in medieval London', *Reading Medieval Studies*, 15 (1989), 35–58.

45 Woodburn O. Ross, *Middle English Sermons*, EETS OS 209 (London, 1940), p. 137. Though of course texts of this sort cannot be proven to have been ever preached in entirely the form in which they have been preserved, it seems likely that they at least served as guides to preachers.

46 Misogyny is the hatred of women, anti-feminism is the belief that women should be subordinate to men. A discussion of the distinction with numerous examples from late medieval England is in S. H. Rigby, *English Society in the Later Middle Ages: Class, Status and Gender* (Houndmills, 1995), pp. 246–52.

47 John Asloan, 'The spectacle of luf', in W. A. Craigie (ed.), *The Asloan Manuscript: A Miscellany in Verse and Prose*, 2 vols, Scottish Text Society, ser. 2, 14–16 (Edinburgh, 1923–5), vol. 1.

48 Carol M. Meale, '"… alle the bokes that I haue of latyn, englisch, and frensch": laywomen and their books in late medieval England', in Carol M. Meale (ed.), *Women and Literature in Britain, 1150–1500*, 2nd edn (Cambridge, 1996), pp. 134–5, 143.

49 Louise Mirrer (ed.), *Upon My Husband's Death: Widows in the Literature and Histories of Medieval Europe* (Ann Arbor, 1992); Sue Sheridan Walker (ed.), *Wife and Widow in Medieval England* (Ann Arbor, 1993); Caroline M. Barron and Anne F. Sutton (eds), *Medieval London Widows, 1300–1500* (London, 1994).

50 On the social groups usually found in East Anglian nunneries see Marilyn Oliva, 'Aristocracy or meritocracy? Office-holding patterns in late medieval English nunneries', in W. J. Sheils and Diana Wood (eds), *Women in the Church*, Studies in Church History 27 (Oxford, 1990). On singlewomen see Bennett and Froide (eds), *Singlewomen*, and Cordelia Beattie, 'Meanings of singleness: the single woman in late medieval England' (D.Phil. thesis, University of York, 2001).

51 Morwenna Griffiths, *Feminisms and the Self: The Web of Identity* (London, 1995), esp. pp. 1–3.

52 Griffiths, *Feminisms and the Self*, p. 2. Though she does not cite him, this idea strongly echoes Anthony Giddens's 'structuration' theory, which he developed in response to Foucault's (and others') removal of the individual agent from the formation of subjectivity: see for example Anthony Giddens, *The Constitution of Society: Outline of the Theory of Structuration* (Cambridge, 1984).

53 The present study follows Chris Given-Wilson in using the term 'noble' to cover both lower and higher levels of elite landed society, and 'gentry' and 'aristocracy' when more specific terms are needed: *The English Nobility in the Late Middle Ages: The Fourteenth-Century Political Community* (London, 1987), p. vii.

1

Attributes

A fourteenth-century English translation of Marie de France's *Lai le Freine* tells of the moment when the young heroine, brought up in a nunnery, begins to grow from a child into a woman.

> Freine thrived from year to year
> Men thought she was the abbess's niece.
> The abbess began to teach and train her.
> By the time she was twelve winters old
> In all England there was no
> Fairer maiden than she.
> And when she knew something of human nature,
> She bade the abbess teach and advise her
> Which were her kin.[1]

It was at twelve, too, that the orphan Goldboro of *Havelok the Dane* developed boldness of speech, knowledge of courtesy, and began to speak of love, and when Osbern Bokenham's St Christina not only 'had great bodily beauty / But also she was wise, prudent and sage / Past all the women of that city'.[2] Twelve stood, conceptually and in some ways actually, as a watershed age in the lives of women. Though other texts specified ages in the early to mid-teens as the turning point, few identified an earlier age. At twelve girls were perceived to begin the gradual transition through maidenhood to adult womanhood. There was no clear-cut switch from one phase to another, no *rite de passage*, but at ages ranging mostly from twelve to fifteen, girls were seen in medicine, law and literature to move towards new forms of maturity and responsibility, as in such practices as putting girls out into service and apprenticeship. Becoming mature sexually and in psychological, intellectual and moral capacity, girls entered a potentially hazardous age but one also subject to a peculiar idealisation.

The bodily and mental qualities of maidenhood, the boundaries of the phase and the notion of maidenhood as woman's 'perfect' age together demonstrate the distinctive attributes of this phase of women's life.

Bodies

At puberty the similarities of male and female childish bodies began to slip away, replaced by the distinctions of physical sex intimately linked with what we now call gender. In premodern scientific thought it was not anatomy that was woman's destiny so much as her 'complexion', her essential coldness and wetness.[3] This humoural composition, compared with a man's heat and dryness, began to become apparent in a girl's early teens. A commentator on the thirteenth-century *De secretis mulierum* explained that girls began to menstruate at twelve, thirteen or fourteen, because this was when the vital heat of childhood began to fail.[4] Because children were perceived by some scholars to be born with a supply of vital 'heat' which dissipated with the years, ending finally in the coldness of decrepitude and death, the explanation for girls' menarche fits with the view that females had less vital heat to begin with.[5] A version of the *Prose Salernitan Questions* which was in Peterhouse, Cambridge, by 1418, posited that girls did not menstruate before the age of twelve or fourteen because before that age either her membranes were undeveloped, the vagina was constricted, or because of change in heat.[6] Losing the heat that in childhood enabled her to burn off her superfluous humours, by puberty those collected in the body and had to be purged in the form of monthly menses. A male's superiority of heat enabled him to deal with such humours by other means – turning them into beards and body hair to be pushed through his wider, warmer pores, or in the commotion of intercourse concocting them into foamy sperm, supplying the formative substance for a new embryo nurtured in the female's more passive womb.[7] At puberty a girl took up her particular biological burden, of the coldness and wetness that would define her physiological and psychological destiny as a lesser, more feeble creature than a man.

Such were the messages young men undertaking studies in natural philosophy or theology at English universities would have received, in any case. Certainly, the tiny handful studying medicine at Oxford and Cambridge or more venturesome scholars who crossed the channel to study at the great medical schools at Paris, Montpellier, Padua or Bologna would certainly have explored questions of sex difference in depth.[8] But how relevant were these beliefs about female physiology beyond academe?

Girls, even of the literate elite, at home or in service, are unlikely to have encountered many of the twisting and turning debates of the scholars. Yet theories of women's cold and wet nature, and its link with menstruation, were beginning to turn up in fourteenth- and fifteenth-century vernacular manuscripts. Versions of *The Sekenesse of Wymmen* make the link clear: 'we shall understand that women have less heat in their bodies than men and more moistness for default of heat that should dry their humours and their moistness. But nevertheless nature has ordained [for] women a purgation at certain time, of bleeding, to make their bodies clean and whole from sickness. And they have such purgations from the time of twelve winters age unto the age of fifty winters.'[9] Contemporary English versions of the 'Trotula' text (the most popular of which, 'Trotula A' or *The Knowing of Woman's Kind in Childing*, survives in five copies) state that 'the coldest man is hotter than the hottest woman', and that therefore women must menstruate to purge themselves of humours.[10] In many instances such works may have had lay male readerships, but their circulation in the vernacular among lay society suggests that the link between women, cold and wet humours and the onset of menstruation had potential currency among literate laywomen. The scribe of the 'Trotula A' text in BL MS Sloane 421A claims that he translated the text from Latin 'at the pleasure of my lady', hinting at the interest a gentle or noble woman might take in matters of biology and gynaecology.[11] What the illiterate majority made of the changes of puberty is impossible to know.

Medical texts conveyed a variety of opinions regarding the age at first menstruation. *The Sekenesse of Wymmen* states that women menstruate from the ages of twelve to fifty, while many vernacular translations of 'Trotula' place the age range at fifteen to fifty.[12] The *De secretis mulierum* of Pseudo-Albertus Magnus gives twelve, thirteen or fourteen as common ages of menarche, while Latin copies of Trotula's *De mulierum passionibus* of English provenance cite ages from thirteen to fifteen.[13] It is almost certain that this kind of variation existed in life as well as in theory. Poorly nourished girls, in particular, may not have reached menarche until their mid-teens or even later, while instances of women bearing children at twelve or thirteen did occasionally occur among royalty and aristocracy where nutrition levels could be high enough to allow early puberty. Mary de Bohun bore Henry Bolingbroke's first child when she was twelve, though the boy died shortly afterwards, and Lady Margaret Beaufort bore the future Henry VII at thirteen.[14] Yet even in this social group, as we shall see, such experiences were exceptional.

The standard medical opinion viewed first menstruation as marking the onset of reproductive capacity. This was described poetically in both vernacular and Latin versions of 'Trotula A': 'For right as the Creator of all things ordained trees to blossom and flower and thereafter to bear fruit, in the same manner he has ordained to all women they have the purgation which is called flowers, without which may no child be engendered or conceived.'[15] An alternative tradition, however, envisaged the lapse of a few years between the first menstruation and readiness for childbearing. Authors including Hildegard of Bingen and (more influentially) Albertus Magnus stated that while the physical changes associated with puberty enabled boys and girls to feel desire and enter sexual relations, the 'seed' in both parties was either too weak or not yet emitted, so that weak offspring or none at all were the result. Such authorities saw puberty as a 'process and a period, rather than just a moment', to quote Joan Cadden, but they were in the minority.[16] The notion that intercourse and childbearing at too early an age had deleterious effects had a greater authority, however, in some views of Aristotle, transmitted by Giles of Rome in his *De regimine principum* and translated in England by John Trevisa. In what Peter Biller has called a eugenicist ethics, it was argued that early childbearing resulted in feeble and imperfect children: 'for when a thing engenders and brings forth another, if the thing that engenders is imperfect, the thing that is engendered must be imperfect'. In addition to enfeebling the child, the practice is undesirable because it prompts lechery and intemperance in young women, and harms the bodies of both women and young men. The 'deed of wedlock' should therefore be delayed until the age of eighteen for women, and twenty-one for men, with the ending of the 'waxing' or growing time.[17] Though the English translation of Giles's text survives in only one copy, numerous Latin copies circulated in English hands, suggesting the transmission of the eugenicist theory among members of the Latin literate.[18] Moreover, a similar idea may be found in the vernacular in copies of 'Trotula A', or *The Knowing of Woman's Kind in Childing*, which condemn female sexual activity before the age of fifteen because it may result in barrenness, a tendency to lascivious or loose sexual behaviour later in life, and even bad breath.[19] In summary, although the view of puberty as a process, with a delay between menarche and childbearing age, seems to have held only slight credence as an argument that girls aged twelve to fifteen *could not* produce children, it does seem to have influenced the view that they *should not* conceive for a few years after menarche. The latter view is well documented in social practice.

Even if some understanding of the humoural explanation for female puberty had entered lay literate households, its significance was rather abstract and lacking in practical implications compared with teachings reaching budding canon lawyers in university law faculties. Their readings of Gratian's *Decretum* and the more influential *Liber extra* (*The Decretals of Gregory IX*) provided them with an understanding of the physiological changes during female and male puberty which had enormous ramifications for the application of the canon law and its prohibition of marriage below the age of consent. Any student of medieval marriage knows that twelve was the minimum age at which a woman could be married, and for males the minimum age was fourteen. This age was variously called the age of consent, *aetas nubilis*, canonical age, *pubertas* and *perfecta aetas*. On valid marriage in general, note that in the later medieval period the Lombard, or Parisian, theory of marriage formation prevailed. Marriage could be legally contracted in two ways – through the exchange of words of present consent, with no requirement for subsequent sexual intercourse, or through the exchange of words of future consent, ratified through subsequent sexual intercourse.[20] In both cases certain capacities, intellectual or physiological, were required, and these were held to be absent in children. A betrothal could be validly contracted at the age of seven (in practice sometimes earlier), but had a suspended quality, and upon reaching canonical age one party or the other could apply to have the match annulled. Around 1466 Thomas Stonor and Thomas Rokes drafted a contract of marriage between their underage children, with the requirement that if Rokes's son at fourteen and Stonor's daughter at thirteen wished to terminate the match the contract would be void, and occasionally dissatisfied suitors did manage to bring actions to the Church courts for annulment of marriage upon reaching puberty.[21] A valid marriage could therefore only be made where the parties were of an age deemed sufficiently mature, though canon law did provide for marriages made in the cradle *pro bono pacis* – a convenient loophole for royalty in particular but hardly relevant for the great majority.[22]

Gratian's *Decretum* of *c.* 1140 states that marriage could not be properly contracted before the parties had reached the age of consent, or discretion. 'Where there is not consent on both sides, there is no marriage. Therefore those who give girls to boys in the cradle, and vice versa, do nothing.'[23] It is evident from other chapters that Gratian assumes that the 'age of consent' is twelve for girls and fourteen for boys. In his discussion on entry to religious life he argues that as up to the age of twelve a girl is subject to her father's will her decision to take the veil could be immediately revoked by her parents or guardians, and elsewhere that 'boys before the age of fourteen' and girls 'if of girlish age living in [their] father's house' may not be compelled to testify in court.[24] Thomas Aquinas appealed to Gratian's authority in citing the ages at which girls and boys could enter religious life.[25]

Gratian was primarily interested in intellectual development as a guide to the minimum age of marriage and made no mention of physical development or capacity for reproduction. This is odd, given his requirement that a valid marriage be made by both mutual consent and sexual intercourse. Rather, it is in some post-Lombardian texts that physical development is seen as a defining characteristic of marriageable age. The most significant statements came in the *Liber extra* of *c.* 1234, which devotes fourteen decretals to *desponsatio impuberum*, and which acquired greater authority in the universities and Church courts of Europe than Gratian's work.[26] Its discussion of consent quotes Isidore of Seville's etymological definition of puberty based on physical condition:

> *Adults are, in respect to marriage, those who are able to conceive and procreate from the condition of the body.* Adults [*puberes*] are named after the pubes, that is after the shameful parts of the body: because these places first become fleecy. Certain people think that puberty is determined by years, that is, he who has completed fourteen years is an adult, even though he is late in showing physical signs of puberty. What is certain is that someone who demonstrates his puberty from the condition of his body, and is able to generate seed, is an adult. And there are women in childbed who are able to give birth in childish years.[27]

Questions of relative heat and coldness, dryness and wetness, are insignificant here. Rather, for males and females alike the fundamental bodily change experienced at puberty is the onset of reproductive ability. With the changes signalled by the appearance of pubic hair, boys at or around fourteen are able to generate seed while girls display their sexual maturity by the ability to bear a child. The author is wary of stating too precisely the years at which these capacities are reached, as some individuals achieve them earlier or later than others. Other decretals further blur the boundaries by introducing loopholes which could allow for the marriage of underage parties if it could be shown that they were capable of sexual intercourse, of conception, or were *proxima pubertati* – that is, within about six months of canonical age.[28] Twelve and fourteen, however, are the ages which recur in the discussions on consent, and upon which the practice of marriage law was based. The difference between the ages of consent for boys and girls was accounted for by biological ideas in a discussion by the thirteenth-century canonist Hostiensis, who argued that as females were colder and more adaptable than males they therefore matured more quickly and died at an earlier age.[29]

Two weeks before Christmas, 1364, a clandestine wedding which illustrates many of these themes took place in a room within the walls of St Mary's Abbey, in York, between John Marrays and a young heiress, Alice de Rouclif.[30] Alice was either ten or eleven years old. If the latter, she was *proxima pubertati*, as her birthday fell in Lent. According to her half-brother who was present, she made her vows 'with a cheerful countenance, compelled neither by force nor fear'. The following week, according to John's sister Anabilla Wastelayne, the couple lay together alone and naked all night in a room in her house, while several other witnesses affirmed that the match was consummated by the following summer (that is, after Alice's birthday). The abbot of St Mary's reported that Joan de Rolleston, Alice's bedpartner at Anabilla's house, told him how she lay beside them one night in July when John and Alice slept together, and she 'heard a noise from them like they were making love together, and how two or three times Alice silently complained at the force on account of John's labour as if she had been hurt then as a result of this labour'. Despite her grimaces, a number of witnesses claimed that Alice was unhappy only about the marriage's secrecy, which in her eyes rendered it less than complete. She told one, 'I am old enough and mature enough to be his wife, but not his mistress' – 'leman' in English. Sadly we do not hear directly from Alice herself, as she was deemed too young to testify before the consistory court. In a case before the Norwich consistory court a fifteen-year-old girl was judged too young to give sound evidence, and Goldberg has found fourteen to be the youngest age of any female deponent in York.[31] Shortly afterwards Alice was abducted by a relative, Sir Brian de Rouclif, against whom John Marrays brought his case for restitution of conjugal rights that November.

John's case was to prove that Alice had been eleven at the time of the marriage, but had since turned twelve, and had ratified the match by her consent and intercourse. Sir Brian had to demonstrate that she had been only ten at the time of the wedding, and thus by the time of the case of no age to be capable of consent. The question of whether Alice was physically ready for marriage was central. Two witnesses for Marrays, his sister Anabilla and the abbot, William Marrays (presumably a relative), spoke of her physical development. Anabilla claimed that Alice looked to be fourteen years old from her appearance, and the abbot said that she was obviously of age 'by reason of her physical appearance, as anyone examining her can clearly see'. However William Potell, John Marrays's servant, told the court that he had joked lewdly with Alice, 'May you grow up sufficiently that he is able to do with you as is fitting', to which Alice reportedly made the rather adult reply that she was 'quite adequate to be his wife but not his whore'. Marrays won his case, and we hear no more of Alice de Rouclif. Such cases of underage marriage are far from common-place in English records, however, and it is a mistake to assume that girls were frequently married at extremely young ages.[32] Where they did occur, the youthful parties were rarely in a position to defend the rights which canon law theoretically gave them.

For practical purposes, canon law was required to be fairly clear cut on the age at which puberty occurred. Medical literature did not require such regularity, and as a result probably provides a better (though by no means watertight) guide to common ages of puberty among late medieval English girls, with twelve at the lower end of the scale of a girl's age at first menstruation. What both sets of evidence indicate is that a woman's maidenhood formed a distinct stage in the history of her body. She was beginning to lose her childish heat, and take on the cold, wet complexion which would shape her gendered body and character. She was entering a reproductive capacity, but only of a weak and incomplete sort. She was partially sexualised, in her appetites, in her abilities, and in her desir-ability, but not fully so. She knew not 'the very passion of women'. Such liminality made her unusually precious within the peculiarities of medieval sexual culture.

Minds

As the bodies of maidens began to mature, so did their minds. The clearest voices on this were the theorists and practitioners of law representing the Church, Crown, borough or manor, discussing the ages at which boys and girls passed from the legal incapacities of childhood into the abilities and duties of adulthood. Church authorities were also concerned to define ages at which children should first receive sacraments. The ages of perceived maturity varied widely, but here too, in most instances, girls were thought to achieve mental maturity before boys.

We have seen that canon law on consent contained a psychological as well as a physiological justification. Gratian's notion of an age of discretion was based on ideas about rational development, while the *Liber extra* was influenced by the work of the twelfth-century scholar Huguccio, who argued that in some cases marriage and the taking of religious vows could be valid where the boy or girl was below canonical age so long as they were *doli capax* (capable of trickery, fraud or cunning), because then *malitia supplet aetatem* (wickedness supplements age). Possession of *prudentia* could have the same effect.[33] These ideas introduced flexibility into the canon law on age at marriage, but also supported the idea that changes in judgement usually occurred in the early teens.

Clerics also debated the ages for first reception of the sacraments, but aimed to set guidelines rather than rules and so presented a variety of views. The Fourth Lateran Council's statement in 1215 on first reception of penance and communion set the benchmark, requiring 'all the faithful of both sexes' to make their confession once a year as soon as they attained the 'years of discretion'.[34] Unlike *aetas nubilis* this age was not precisely defined, with different authors setting it at seven, others around ten, and others at the age of puberty.[35]

Opinions on minimum age at confirmation also varied.[36] The early medieval principle that it should be performed by a bishop at the same time as baptism was gradually replaced by the rise of infant baptism, and a gradual increase in the number of years elapsing between baptism and confirmation. By the fourteenth century the Church, perhaps making a virtue of necessity, began to recommend seven as a *minimum* age for confirmation, and by the sixteenth century confirmation below seven was prohibited by the Council of Trent. The 1549 English Prayer Book required that children be able to demonstrate a certain level of doctrinal instruction before being confirmed.

The trend with each of the three sacraments was towards an emphasis on the psychological maturity necessary for the sacrament's reception. Late medieval English commentators often felt that all three sacraments went together. William of Pagula stated that no one should be admitted to communion before confirmation, and that confirmation should take place at 'perfect age, that is twelve or fourteen years old', and should be preceded by confession, but his late fourteenth-century successor John de Burgh pushed the age at first communion and confirmation down to around ten or eleven, while maintaining that first confession should take place at twelve or fourteen (dependent on sex). He argued, on the first point, that it is at around ten or eleven that 'signs of discretion and reverence towards the sacrament appear in them'.[37] There seems to have been a growing sense of a need to delay the conferring of the sacraments until the recipient had reached an appropriate level of understanding, and possessed moral and intellectual readiness to enter the Church as a full participant. The opinion of John Myrc, who in the mid-fifteenth century advised that children be confirmed 'within the fifth year', is unrepresentative of the trend.[38]

The spiritual development required for reception of sacraments was often perceived to arrive earlier than the physical and psychological maturity necessary for marital consent, but secular codes of common, borough and customary law regulating the ages of inheritance, exit from wardship, trial for felonies, responsibility for debts or other civil business, usually placed the turning point above canonical age. Again, the ages for girls were regularly lower than for boys, but the secular codes lacked canon law's consistency and instead took social status as an important consideration.

Common law's clearest statements on age of majority were in the treatises *Glanvill* and *Bracton*, texts which influenced legal practice until the rise of Parliament as a legislative body in the fourteenth century.[39] They explained the customary age of majority for males in terms of social position, sons of the nobility reaching majority at twenty-one, of sokemen at fifteen, and of burgesses when they could count money properly, measure cloth, and perform other tasks related to their fathers' business (free and servile peasants are not mentioned).[40] *Bracton* explained that the differing ages of majority for sons of sokemen and knights was because the latter required greater capacity both in judgement and strength.[41] Such fine class-distinctions in male majority did not necessarily hold in practice. In a case from the Court of Common Pleas in 1310 dispute arose over whether fourteen or twenty-one was the correct age of majority for a boy in socage.[42] Holdsworth argues that the age of majority in the knightly class came to apply to all classes, and so the law for the elite came to be the law for all.[43]

Majority for females was conceived from similar principles. According to *Bracton* a woman in socage reaches full age 'whenever she can and knows how to order her house and do the things that belong to the arrangement and management of a house', provided she understands what pertains to 'coffer and key', which cannot be before her fourteenth or fifteenth year, since such things require discretion and understanding (that is, the same age as her brothers). The age of majority for the daughters of burgesses was also generally held to be the same as that for boys; that is, not a fixed age, but when she became capable of carrying out the tasks required of a woman of her station. *Bracton* was less sure about majority for daughters of holders of military fees. Fifteen was the generally preferred age, for then 'she can order her house and marry a husband, who, by himself or by another, can perform the military obligations', and she achieved full age earlier than men of her station 'because she is held legally responsible for her actions earlier than a man, and because she is ready for marriage earlier than a man'. Yet the author was uneasy about the contrast, as it implied that 'below the lawful age of twenty-one years she could plead and be impleaded by writ of right', and concluded that women in military fees should reach majority at twenty-one.[44] The idiosyncratic *Mirror of Justices*, *c.* 1289, also found the laws confusing and unsatisfactory.[45] A number of examples from the common-law courts demonstrate the lack of hard and fast rules on female majority. In Frowyk v. Leuekemore, before the Court of Common Pleas in 1310, it was stated that 'the same age is fixed for the tenant in socage that is fixed for the female tenant in chivalry to have her land – namely, the age of fourteen years'.[46] Yet in the proof of age of an heiress from 1329, it was proved that Alice, daughter and co-heiress of the late Peter de Southcherche, 'is twenty-one' (the proof shows that she was indeed twenty-five; the point is to show that she was over twenty-one).[47] The will of Margaret Paston (dated 1482) bequeathes to Custaunce, bastard daughter of John Paston, 'when she is twenty years of age ten marks'.[48]

The confusion probably arose from the conflict of gender and status concerns. According to the latter and the standard set by majority for males, women must come of age at twenty-one. But, considering their sex, it was often more desirable to lower that age to fourteen or fifteen for reasons little to do with notions of psychological maturity and more to do with the institution of wardship. Wardship was an investment, and could be very profitable. The guardian of a royal ward held rights in the person, marriage and lands of the young heir.[49] Rents and profits from the land were due to the guardian, who could also make a significant sum through selling the ward's marriage, and to whom damages were payable in cases of his or her abduction.[50] It was desirable that female wards come into their inheritance earlier than males, as female heirs would usually share the property with any sisters in the system of parcenage.[51] Thus the marrying-off of female wards was perhaps more profitable than the rents and services of their land. Moreover, female wards were highly desirable property to young men seeking a fief and a fortune, and guardians stood to make useful allies through making swift matches. To secure these ends, elite girls of fourteen or fifteen could be deemed of sufficient emotional maturity to enter marriage without long delay.

Customary and borough law were more variable than common law in their statements on age of majority. Manorial custom on inheriting age varied from manor to manor, and separate ages for girls are not usually apparent. In Halesowen males could take up tenancies from the age of twenty, in Kibworth Harcourt at twenty-one, while on Sussex manors both boys and girls could inherit at fifteen.[52] Bennett notes that few manor courts specified the ages of girls' and boys' legal maturity, and bases her own interpretation partly on entry to tithing, which occurred for boys at the age of twelve and to which girls were not admitted (see below).[53] The age at which one might legally inherit land, however, was not necessarily the same as that at which one could be held criminally responsible. Borough customs on full age are more explicit. In towns boys came of age variously at twenty or twenty-one, fourteen or fifteen, even as young as twelve, but the pattern of generally more youthful majority for girls emerges. Thus girls were considered of full age at twelve when their brothers had to wait for fourteen, and at sixteen when the boys had to wait until twenty-one.[54]

What rights and liabilities were achieved with the age of majority? Infants (the usual legal term for anyone underage) had limited property rights. They could inherit and own property, but the common-law principle was that they should not control it until of full age. Single underage women had similar property rights to men, though a son would always be preferred to a daughter, and heiresses often had to share inherited lands.[55] A 1362 case from the Court of King's Bench shows that an underage female could own but not control property. Thomas Darell claimed he had been unlawfully deprived of tenements formerly granted him by a woman named Joan, and her defence was that she was underage at the time of making the grant and that the action was therefore invalidated.[56] Similarly, in the Court of Common Pleas in 1310 a woman attempted to retrieve tenements she had previously quitclaimed, on the grounds that she had been underage at the time.[57] And in 1317 a married woman was excused until she reached full age from answering a writ against her claim over her tenements.[58] Limitations on the powers of the infant were perceived to be due to immature intellectual capacity. In 1311 Maud Hesbath brought a writ against Robert Hesbath, claiming to be heir to certain tenements through her grandfather and Robert answered that the grandfather had previously surrendered the property to him. Maud's counsel answered that she was 'within age and knoweth not how, nor is competent, to establish her title against the fine'.[59] Though legally competent to hold property, she was not intellectually capable of defending her tenancy in court.

Similar principles guided the ages of criminal and civil responsibility, and were no more straightforward. Pollock and Maitland claim that infants might sue or be sued, and appear in court either to make a complaint or defend themselves, and Holdsworth states they were liable if guilty of dispossessing another, or of committing waste or trespass, of not paying rent or performing the services due of their land. He also claims that in civil actions infants were apparently as liable as anyone else and were required to pay damages. [60] Yet the practice of law was not this clear-cut. In 1313 at the Eyre of Kent a woman was excused from paying a debt at least while she remained under age, as it was claimed that in the custom of Gavelkind there was no liability for debt until twenty-one.[61] In the Court of Common Pleas in 1319 the defendant pleaded that he was underage when his debt was incurred.[62] In these examples, infant incapacity was invoked by lawyers to protect their underage clients.

The age of criminal responsibility was also contested. Though it was generally agreed that an infant under seven convicted of a felony could not be judged or punished 'because he knoweth not of good and evil',[63] once he or she was over the age of seven the court's judgement hinged on whether the infant could be said to be *doli capax*, capable of trickery.[64] So at the 1313–14 Eyre of Kent a boy of eleven was found guilty of stealing certain chattels and killing a child. The fact that he had hidden the body of the murdered child was taken as evidence of his 'heinous malice'.[65] In 1319 a child underage was accused and found guilty of breaking into a house, and it was 'awarded that he be hanged despite his nonage'.[66] In general, while twelve and fourteen were the ages at which girls and boys became *doli capaces*, the ages between seven and twelve or fourteen represent a period in which the judge might use his own discretion in assessing the criminal capacity of the accused.

In village society the tithing or frankpledge system meant that at twelve a boy became subject to criminal law, as it was at that age that he had to join the tithing, taking an oath that he would not be a thief or a party to thieving.[67] His fellow tithingmen would then be responsible for bringing him to justice for any felony. Girls did not enter tithings, but manorial courts punished unmarried daughters for a range of criminal and civil activities.[68] The age at which they became responsible for their actions is not recorded, but given the patterns established elsewhere it was unlikely to have been below twelve.

As with theories on the development of the female body, legal notions of young women's development towards psychological maturity were multiple, and to an extent were a matter for debate. No single age marked a rite of transition to adulthood. Rather, from twelve to around fifteen girls experienced a process of change which could vary from one individual to another, from one social group to another. By her mid-teens a girl had left childhood well behind. But the age she found herself in the midst of was not full adulthood, though she had achieved certain rights and responsibilities, but rather an intervening phase which might continue for as little as a year or as many as ten years. In cases where her youthful singleness endured for some years she could enter institutions such as service or apprenticeship which were characteristic of this time of life, and some individual girls were able to enjoy economic and legal rights before marriage placed most of the control of those matters in the hands of her husband.[69] Some young women never married, but they were in the decided minority. The age at marriage, expected age at marriage, or – where marriage was very early – age at first motherhood, provided an upper boundary to the phase of maidenhood, though it is as rash to posit a swift or smooth movement from one life-cycle phase to another at the end as at the beginning of maidenhood.

Exit points

In 1447 Sir Thomas Clifford betrothed his six-year-old daughter Elizabeth to Robert, heir of Sir William Plumpton. The girl was so young that John Garthe 'bore her in his arms' to the chapel. Within three years Robert died, the match unconsummated, and so in 1453 Elizabeth, aged twelve, was married to the second son, William. On this occasion 'the said Sir William promised the said Lord Clifford that they should not lie together until she came to the age of sixteen years. And when she came to eighteen years she had Margaret, now Lady Roucliffe.'[70]

There was nothing in canon law to prevent the marriage of Elizabeth and William from being immediately consummated. At twelve Elizabeth was in theory a grown woman, both physically and psychologically, and in exceptional circumstances some such matches were consummated. But the concerns of her father that her first experience of sex and possible conception be delayed until sixteen mirror a wider social concern to protect girls from being forced too young into adult roles. Late medieval English evidence of ages at marriage and motherhood indicates that canon-legal theory on women's marriageable age offers a very limited perspective, and that social beliefs and practice provide a more reliable view of girls' transition to adulthood. While marriages at very young ages could and sometimes did take place, particularly for girls of high social status, it would be a mistake to see marriage below or around the age of puberty as the norm even for young noblewomen. A space opens up between the legal (twelve) or the real (probably between twelve and fifteen) ages of puberty, and the ages at marriage, consummation or motherhood.

Emerging evidence is eroding the stereotype of medieval child marriage. Goldberg and Smith's work on low- and lower-middle-status women has refuted Hajnal's argument for generally early marriage for medieval women.[71] Even Razi's 'early' age at marriage for girls in Halesowen hardly indicates child marriage, as a large proportion of his sample married between the ages of eighteen and twenty-two.[72] Smith has argued that Herlihy and Klapisch-Zuber's 'medieval' marriage regime in Tuscany, where girls in their late teens married men around ten years older than themselves, should be seen as Mediterranean rather than medieval. Goldberg has offered evidence from fourteenth- and fifteenth-century Yorkshire showing that urban girls tended to marry in their early to mid-twenties and rural girls married in their late teens to early twenties, and both groups married men who were close to them in age.[73] Perhaps even more useful than data on marriage age is Goldberg's argument that service was, in England, primarily an occupation of young unmarried men and women who left home to enter service during their teens and twenties. Although recent work by Mavis Mate and Mark Bailey suggests a slightly earlier age at marriage than Goldberg does, the existence of institutions such as teenage service and apprenticeship demonstrate the existence of a distinct youthful phase in the lives of many rural and urban girls as well as boys.[74]

Whether the stage existed for women of the gentry and aristocracy is more open to question. Jennifer Ward comments that children of the nobility were usually married in their teens, and sometimes well below canonical age,[75] yet individual instances of early marriage age may offer a misleading view of the preferred marriage age for girls. We are more likely to know about the marriages of heiresses than other girls, and heiresses are more likely to have been betrothed or married young. Thus we know that Margaret Plumpton, daughter of Elizabeth Clifford, whose youthful marriages have already been mentioned, was betrothed in 1463 at four by her grandfather, Sir William Plumpton, who (falsely) asserted that Margaret and her sister Elizabeth were his heirs.[76] Moreover, we are more likely to know about marriages that come into dispute, and underage marriage was one cause of such disputes: thus we know that Alice de Rouclif was married at ten or eleven.[77] We also hear of girls' age at marriage if they were children when their parents died, partly because the daughters would then pass into wardship – with subsequent legal documentation, and often early marriage for the financial benefit of the guardian – and because the age at which their parents would like them to marry or enter a convent was sometimes specified in the will. When Beatrix Lady Greystoke made her will in 1505, she outlined her vision of her children's careers. Her thirteen-year-old son was to go to Cambridge and on to the Inns of Court at eighteen, and her six-year-old son to go to grammar school once he reached the age of twelve. For her two daughters she provided that

> when my daughter Elizabeth shall come to the age of twelve years, and she be then disposed to be a nun, that then my executors shall pay or cause to be paid unto the said Master of Watton £20.... If any convenient marriage for my daughter Jane shall happen to be purveyed before she be of the age of fourteen or after, then my executors shall cast and evenly rate and divide all such goods as then shall be in their possession ... amongst my said children.

If Elizabeth would not agree to taking the veil money should go to Thomas or Anne Rokby 'for her exhibition' for two years, then at fourteen a marriage sought for her. If Jane were not married by thirteen the Rokbys should have money for supporting her for a further seven years.[78] In such cases parents were most concerned to ensure that the futures of children of both sexes be settled in advance. It does not necessarily follow that daughters who were not heiresses, and whose parents were alive and well, would have been married in childhood or soon after puberty.

Thomas Hollingsworth's demographic study of the English peerage suggests that even within this exalted social group, child or pubescent brides were not the norm.[79] The mean age at marriage of duke's daughters from 1330 to 1479 was 17.1 years, but while a significant proportion of daughters had married by the age of fifteen the rate then slowed considerably, with a number still unmarried by the age of thirty, and thereafter a handful who never married. Moreover, he finds that more duke's daughters married between twenty and twenty-five than between fifteen and twenty, so the average of 17.1 is slightly misleading.

Within examples of very young marriage by girls of the social elite, it is evident that early marriage took place for pure expedience rather than any sense that wedlock was suitable for pubescent girls. The celebrated example of Lady Margaret Beaufort, mother of Henry VII, provides an excellent illustration.[80] As heiress of John Beaufort, her wardship was highly valuable and was first granted to William de la Pole, who betrothed her to his son when she was six. Within three years the contract was dissolved and the wardship transferred to Jasper Tudor. She was married at twelve to Edmund Tudor in 1455, and was pregnant within a few months. Made a widow when six months pregnant, she gave birth to the future Henry VII while only thirteen years old. Both the marriage and the pregnancy were politically convenient for Edmund Tudor, and do not provide evidence of what was considered desirable for pubescent girls. Marriage and the begetting of heirs had an importance for the social elite which sometimes overrode other beliefs, including the preference to allow girls a period of growing up before marriage and sexual activity. Unease about Margaret's youth during her experiences of marriage and childbirth shows in the words of her sixteenth-century eulogist, who commented on the difficulty of the birth due to her lack of physical development – 'not a woman of great stature … she was so much smaller at that stage'.[81] Her modern biographers suggest that permanent physical damage resulted from the birth, and she had no more children. Her own experiences led to an antipathy to early marriage, attested later in her life when she opposed the marriage of one of her granddaughters to James IV of Scotland, fearing James would not wait to consummate it.[82]

Still on the highest rung of the social ladder, John Carmi Parsons' survey of eighty-seven marriages among the Plantagenets, Mortimers and Hollands from 1150 to 1500 finds a tendency to delay consummation of marriage where the female party was below fifteen at the wedding.[83] Over half the daughters were not married until fifteen or older (forty-nine out of eighty-seven), and of those married under fifteen there was apparently a decision to delay consummation. Fifteen of the thirty-eight girls married under fifteen remained childless, and of the remaining twenty-three most waited three or more years for consummation. Of the seven who bore children while under fifteen, five were kings' wives or daughters. He feels that female relatives had a good deal to do with this caution.

A close look at the ages at first marriage of English princesses illustrates these points further. Examining the marriages of the daughters of kings from Edward I to Henry VII, it is clear that though marriage negotiations and sometimes formal betrothals occurred when the girls were very young they were not married until much later, and usually had their first children later still.[84] Of the twenty princesses for whom marriages were sought (others died in infancy and a small number entered nunneries), the mean age at which marriage negotiations were begun or betrothals sought was about five and a half, but of those who went on to marry (three died early), the mean age at first marriage was 16.65. Of these seventeen girls, five were married between the ages of ten and fourteen, eleven between fifteen and twenty, and one – Isabella, eldest daughter of Edward III, despite marital negotiations beginning in her infancy and a failed betrothal at around fourteen – not until thirty-three. Only three of the princesses bore their first child before the age of twenty. A still clearer impression is gained from individual circumstances. Of all the English princesses of the era only Blanche, eldest daughter of Henry IV, was married below canonical age. Henry had sought marriages for his infant daughters as soon as possible after becoming king, and after a proposed match between Blanche and a member of the French royal house was declined he secured Louis, son of the emperor Rupert, and the wedding took place in 1402 when Blanche was about ten. His second daughter, Philippa, was also one of the youngest English princesses to marry, wedding the king of Sweden at thirteen. The very high status of these matches and Henry's precipitous haste in securing them are indicative of his tentative hold on the throne and eagerness to bolster it with powerful alliances, rather than of any strong approval of early marriage. Blanche was also the youngest of the princesses to have a child, a stillborn son, at fifteen. She died at sixteen, giving birth to her second child.[85]

Despite the low age of consent, medieval English culture was not insensitive to the dangers of early marriage and childbearing. The development of a 'eugenicist' ethics, already mentioned, may have been reinforced by events such as the early death of Princess Blanche and her infants. In some cases, considerations other than reaching puberty determined the age at which a maiden was considered physically ready to begin sexual relations. The marriage of Edward I's eldest daughter Eleanor, though she had been betrothed at eleven to Alphonso, prince of Aragon, was delayed because of her perceived youth. Even when she had reached seventeen, and pressure to hasten the marriage was being imposed from Aragon, Edward wrote requesting a delay of another year and a half or two years, because the girl's mother and grandmother (themselves both married when young) had protested, 'on account of her tender age'.[86] Here, as with the example of Lady Margaret Beaufort's concern about her granddaughter and the women's interventions in younger women's marriages examined by Parsons, it was older women's concerns for the welfare of young women which held in check the political and dynastic fixations of powerful men.

Moving down the social ladder to the gentry we find, within letters of the Paston and Stonor collections, anxieties about the youth of prospective brides. Though the adjective 'young' is sometimes used favourably of eligible women in the Paston letters and letters of the mercantile Celys, one could have too much of a good thing.[87] John Paston II (Sir John) wrote to his younger brother, John Paston III, about a young Mistress Barley, who had received inspection as a prospective bride for the younger John before the latter's betrothal to Margery Brews: 'as for this matter of Mistress Barley, I hold it but a bare thing. I feel well that it passes not … marks. I saw her for your sake. She is a little one; she may be a woman hereafter, if she be not old now: her person seems thirteen years of age, her years men say be full eighteen.'[88] The Paston brothers were little interested in taking such pubescent-looking women as this 'little one' as brides, but found women in their late teens more promising. William Paston III wrote to John Paston III of a 'young gentlewoman' Margaret Alborow, whose wealth and beauty appealed, and who was 'by all likelihood eighteen or nineteen years at the furthest'.[89] Young women's ages were assessed chiefly on the basis of their appearance rather than by their reported age, supporting the impression that physical development could be a deciding factor in a gentleman's choice of bride.

The letters from Thomas Betson concerning his young betrothed, Katherine Ryche, stepdaughter of his business partner William Stonor, are most revealing of the unease of an adult man facing the prospect of marriage to a young girl. Katherine was twelve or thirteen at the time of their betrothal, and fifteen at their marriage. Betson never seemed comfortable with the youth of his betrothed:

> And if you would be a good eater of your meat always, that you might wax and grow fast to be a woman, you should make me the gladdest man of the world, by my troth: for when I remember your favour and your sad [solemn] loving dealing towards me, forsooth you make me even very glad and joyous in my heart: and on the other side again when I remember your young youth. And see well that you be no eteter [picky eater] of your meat, the which should help you greatly in waxing.[90]

Though his letter has been called 'charming' by Eileen Power and 'delightful' by Christine Carpenter,[91] it is more revealing of the confusion aroused by such a mismatch of ages. At times it reads as a conventional love letter – 'whereas you, full womanly and like a lover, remember me with manifold recommendations in divers manners' – and at others as an address to a child – 'I pray you greet well my horse, and pray him to give you four years to help you withall: and I will at my coming home give him four of my years.'[92]

Katherine's level of spiritual and moral maturity presented further cause for concern. Shortly before their wedding Betson wrote to Sir William Stonor, expressing gratitude for the latter's efforts in seeing to the good upbringing of his stepdaughter, as without that 'she could not be of that disposition virtuous and goodly, her youth remembered and considered.'[93] Yet doubts lingered: 'I shall when I speak with her tell her every word, and if I find the contrary our vicar here, so God help me, shall cry out upon her within these ten weeks and less, and by that time I shall be ready in every point with God's grace, and so I would she were.'[94] Betson's unease even crept into his dreams, as he relates to Katherine's mother: 'I dreamt once she was thirty winters of age; and when I woke I wished she had been but twenty: and so by likelihood I am sooner like to have my wish than my dream.'[95]

That marriage sometimes occurred at, soon after, or even before canonical age for girls of the late medieval English gentry and aristocracy is not in doubt. That it occurred at all does indicate a greater tolerance for girls' swift passage from childhood to adult womanhood than prevails in the modern West. But what I have hoped to show in this discussion is that such marriages were not as ubiquitous as has sometimes been suggested, that they were not necessarily considered normal and certainly were often regarded as undesirable. Where early marriages did occur they tell us less about late-medieval ideas of female youth than about political or social aspirations. Marriage turns out to be an unreliable exit point of 'maidenhood', as consummation was often delayed when the girls were in their early teens (and not all women married). Stanley Chojnacki has argued that in Renaissance Venice daughters of the patriciate often married in their early teens but did not immediately achieve adulthood. Rather, they entered an 'uxorial cycle', comprising 'bridehood', mature wifehood and motherhood, and widowhood, and during bridehood were viewed as not yet ready for the full responsibilities expected of an adult woman. 'Marriage for women was not the diploma of adulthood but rather the tuition beginning the passage to it', and the same could be said of those English maidens coaxed or coerced into early marriage.[96]

Still, a rough outline of maidenhood may be drawn, beginning with puberty and intellectual development around twelve to fifteen, and ending with 'full' marriage or the age at which it might be expected. That age could vary from around sixteen as a usual minimum for women of high status to the early and mid-twenties for working women. In many cases, then, maidenhood was a shorter life-cycle phase for elite women. The evidence resists neatness in definitions, yet it becomes clear that maidenhood was a commonly perceived and experienced phase in women's life cycle. It was the age at which a woman was developing sexually, but was supposed to be sexually inactive. She could be considered desirable, but was expected to be chaste. She had entered a phase of moral and intellectual development which marked her as an adult, though she would lose some of its legal benefits and responsibilities on marrying. The concept of maidenhood as a life-cycle phase was not only widespread in late medieval English culture, it shaped some of the most powerful contemporary images of ideal femininity.

Perfect age[97]

The theme of the 'ages of man', which had roots in ancient writings and appeared in medieval medical theory and natural philosophy, literature and art, regularly portrayed one age as the peak, prime or 'perfect' age of man.[98] This peak was middle age, usually called *iuventus* in Latin works. The phase had a variable span in years, but roughly covered about the mid-twenties to the mid-forties. According to medieval writers this was the perfect age of man's life as he was then in the prime of his physical and mental powers. Where youth was characterised by physical health but undeveloped mental capacity, and old age by wisdom but ailing health, middle age represented a perfect balance of strong body and mind.[99]

This philosophical, literary and artistic model overlapped with theological views on the resurrection of the body. Theologians from St Augustine to Peter Lombard took inspiration from Ephesians 4.13, 'until we all meet into the unity of faith and of the knowledge of the Son of God, unto a perfect man, unto the measure of the age of the fullness of Christ'. Taking this literally, commentators argued that the resurrected body reflected the perfect age of Christ. Augustine said Christ's prime was at thirty, the age at which he began his ministry, while Ælfric, Peter Lombard and others preferred thirty-three, Christ's age when crucified.[100] Either way, Christ's prime and the age of the Christian body at resurrection fell neatly within *iuventus*, the perfect age of man.

When Paul imagined Corinthian confusion over the bodies of the resurrected, 'With what manner of body shall they come?' (1 Cor. 15.35), he probably did not have sexual distinctions in mind. But we may rephrase the question: 'With what manner of body shall the women come?' Neither the ages-of-man scheme nor the theology of the resurrection provides an adequate account of the perfect age of woman. As Mary Dove says, 'We need to remind ourselves that "man" in the Ages of Man is not normally an inclusive term, and that when I talk about "man's life" I am not being inclusive either'.[101] Woman's perfect age was not middle age. Instead, representations of the perfected woman's body in death depict the woman as a maiden. The bodies of the 'Pearl Maiden', of the virgin martyr saints and of the Virgin Mary at her death, assumption and coronation, offer

43

examples of feminine figures who have achieved the perfection of bodies in the afterlife and all are depicted in death as maidens of youthful years.

In the Middle English poem *Pearl*, written in the late fourteenth century by an unknown author and surviving in a single manuscript, the male speaker experiences a dream vision in which he is confronted by his daughter, his 'Pearl', who had died at the age of two but appears to him as a beautiful and courtly young woman.[102] The Pearl Maiden therefore has two ages. Though a 'faunt' or infant (line 161), in death she has taken on the body of a 'mayden of menske' (line 162), a 'damyselle' (line 361) – that is, of a courtly young woman. Her physical appearance is described at length (lines 197–228). Her dress is in the style of a fashionable young woman of the late fourteenth century, and her dress is all white and covered in pearls (lines 197–204).[103] Her skin is the purest white – whiter than whale bone, or passing the 'flour de lys' (lines 212, 753) – and she wears a crown of pearls and flowers (lines 205–8). Her hair is golden and hangs unbound around her face and on her shoulders (lines 213–14), she has grey eyes, and likens herself to a rose (lines 254, 269). The dreamer marvels at her 'fayre fygure' and dazzling beauty (lines 747–53). These physical characteristics are all aspects of the courtly ideal of feminine beauty, which can be found in almost any youthful heroine of late medieval English romance or courtly lyric. The Pearl Maiden's appearance is meant to represent her physical state on entering heaven, and at the close of the poem she joins a procession of a hundred thousand virgins, all crowned, dressed in white and covered with pearls (lines 1095–152). At that moment her childish age and her maidenly body seem combined, as the dreamer is moved to see his 'lyttel quene', making merry with her friends (lines 1147–50). Her childish years represent her soul's innocence, made clear during her debate with the dreamer over the parable of the vineyard (lines 481–660), but she appears in the form of a young maiden.

Many have linked the Pearl Maiden's physical state to the theology of the resurrection. The poet could not, strictly speaking, represent her in resurrected form, as that would imply that the raising from the dead had already occurred, but still 'it is appropriate that this body should have the appearance of the one which, according to the highest patristic authority, she will assume after the General Resurrection'.[104] She is not represented in the body of a woman in her mid-thirties, reflecting the perfect age of man; rather, her age may be suggested by comparison with Boccaccio's *Olympia*, a poem which bears a striking similarity to *Pearl* as a dream vision in which a father sees and speaks to his daughter, who had died at five and a half but appears to her father as a girl of marriageable age.[105]

Thirty or thirty-three was by no means the most desirable marriageable age for women, particularly in Tuscany. We would expect her to appear, rather, in the body of a young woman in her mid- to late teens.

Three elements of her representation indicate that she was imagined as a maiden rather than an older woman: her courtly beauty, her loose golden hair and her crown. Conventions concerning feminine beauty were remarkably consistent in later medieval England. The beautiful woman almost always, in both literary and visual media, has long blonde hair, very fair skin, fine features, sparkling eyes, curved dark eyebrows, red lips and a long and slender body with small breasts but a protruding belly. She often has grey eyes, though at other times they are blue, a cleft chin and delicately rosy cheeks.[106] Matthew of Vendôme and Geoffrey of Vinsauf supply sample descriptions of the beautiful woman in their guides to poetical writing, and the convention is also prominent within romances and lyrics, from *Guy of Warwick's* description of Felice to the Harley Lyrics' 'Fair Maid of Ribbesdale'.[107] A prominent aspect of the ideal is youthfulness, implied in physical slenderness and delicacy, and literary heroines are usually young, though their age is only occasionally stated. In addition to twelve-year-old Freine and Goldboro, Chaucer's Alison is eighteen, and his Virginia – a 'mayde in excellent beautee' – is fourteen.[108] When January of *The Merchant's Tale* states that his ideal wife 'shal nat passe twenty yeer, certayn' and likens thirty-year-old women to dried beanstalks and coarse fodder he was being satirised as an old man with unsuitable desires, yet his ideal was a common one.[109] An ugly woman, in contrast, is usually old, with loose skin, a forest of wrinkles and breasts like deflated bladders.[110] Some of those who have discussed the subject of beauty in history have argued that feminine beauty is ahistorical, eternal and unchanging, but tastes alter with time and representations of women must be read within their cultural contexts.[111] The representation of the idealised beautiful woman as a slender teenage girl is not a constant across history or cultures and should be read within the historical context of its production. In later medieval England it was an aspect of the wider ideal of maidenhood as an age of consummate femininity.

The Pearl Maiden's long loose blonde hair is a powerful signal of her maidenly status. Long, uncovered and loose hair had a variety of meanings in late medieval English culture. It could be a sign of uncivilised or anti-social nature, as in images of the hairy wild men and women, or penitence, as in representations of Mary Magdalene and Mary of Egypt.[112] Hair long enough to cover the body could provide modesty, as in the life of St Agnes, whose hair grows to cover her nakedness when she is stripped and thrown into a brothel, and in the legend of Lady Godiva.[113] Yet long loose hair was also a sign of sexual availability. The London *Liber albus* required the cutting of a prostitute's hair at her third conviction, and professed virgins were required to cut their tresses and 'take the veil' during the ritual of consecration.[114] During wedding ceremonies brides might wear their hair loose and uncovered, as Chaucer's Griselda and Guinevere of the *Prose Merlin* do, and so did queens during coronation, a ritual which bears many similarities to the rituals of consecration and marriage.[115]

Loose unbound hair signified an apparently contradictory state – at once sexually attractive and available, and virginal. It is therefore the sign *par excellence* of maidenhood, an age in which sexual desirability and virginity are intermingled. This is better seen as a tension than a contradiction. The unbound golden hair of the Pearl Maiden is meant as a sign that she is not meant to be imagined as a sober, respectable woman in her mid-thirties, but rather as a perfectly chaste and gloriously desirable maiden, probably somewhere in her teens.

The Maiden's crown of pearls and flowers offers another key to her maidenly state. The author of the thirteenth-century exhortation to chastity, *Hali Meiðhad*, was conventional in her or his image of virgins in heaven, each wearing 'a circlet shining brighter than the sun, called *aureola* in Latin'.[116] The crown could be a symbol of singleness, and thus of permanent virginity in the secular life, as in *The Good Wyfe Wold a Pylgremage*: 'If thou wilt no husband have, but wear thy maiden's crown', or of the permanent virginity of the woman professed to the religious life: 'Your virginity … will be radiant in a golden diadem.'[117] May Games involved gathering flowers and crowning of a May King and Queen, and brides often wore garlands or circlets on their wedding day.[118] The crown of virgins symbolised both victory over death through the promise of eternal life, and virginity through its association with marriage and fertility, and the image of the virgin as the bride of Christ.[119] The Pearl Maiden's crown consisted both of flowers and pearls. The latter symbolised purity and virginity, an analogy played upon by Jacobus de Voragine in his introduction to the life of St Margaret (from *margarita* – Latin for 'pearl').[120] The Maiden's white garments also contribute to her representation as pure, innocent and virginal.[121] The pearls, the crown, the loose hair and the white garments combine with the Pearl Maiden's conventional beauty to present a complex yet harmonious image of a woman who combines the most admired feminine traits – chastity, and sexual desirability. In her case and others, this is the image of woman in death.

Her appearance is in many ways mirrored in the virgin martyrs and the

Virgin Mary at death, assumption and coronation. The virgin martyrs were the most popular type of female saint of the era and included Katherine, Margaret, Lucy, Christina, Cecilia, Dorothy, Agnes, Barbara and Agatha.[122] The virginity, steadfastness of will and popularity among women readers of virgin martyrs' lives have received most attention from commentators. Their age has been little mentioned, but it is central to their idealisation. Of those whose actual ages are given all are in their teens: Agnes is thirteen, Margaret is fifteen, Katherine is eighteen, and Christina is twelve when her torments begin.[123] The others also occupy this post-pubescent phase. They must all be of *aetas nubilis* because the plot of each virgin martyr's life hinges on her sexual attractiveness and the efforts of her suitor/tormentor to make her marry him, while the upper limit of their age may also be suggested by their eligibility and also by the language used to describe them. In Osbern Bokenham's collection they are called 'maidens', and the corresponding Latin of the *Legenda aurea* is *puella*.[124] Moreover, the lives frequently describe the martyrs as 'young' or of 'tender age', or as *tenerae puellae*, tender girls. Lucy is 'a maiden young and delicate', Agatha is a 'damsel young', Faith is 'in her tender age'.[125] There can be little doubt that all the virgin martyrs would have been perceived as young women in their teens.

According to medieval authors on the resurrection, Christ died at thirty-three because he had reached the peak of his life and it would not have been appropriate for him to experience physical decline.[126] By corollary, perhaps the virgin martyrs died in their teens because that was the peak of the lives of their feminine bodies. The late medieval rewriting of the life of St Apollonia is revealing. In earlier lives, including the thirteenth-century *Legenda aurea*, she was an ageing deaconess, whom Jacobus de Voragine called 'an admirable virgin, well along in years'.[127] But by the fifteenth century in England she was represented visually as a young maiden, alongside youthful martyrs such as Agnes.[128] Increasingly, youth was becoming a necessary element of ideal femininity.

The virgin martyrs do not wear the white clothes of the Pearl Maiden but they share her conventional beauty, long blonde hair and, in many cases, her crown or garland (see Figure 1). Bokenham's description of the beauty of Margaret when first seen by the prefect Olibrius – her lily-white forehead, curved dark eyebrows and grey eyes, cherry cheeks and fine nose, red lips and cleft chin – engages explicitly with courtly ideals of feminine beauty.[129] From Bokenham's allusions to both Geoffrey of Vinsauf and Matthew of Vendôme elsewhere within the life it is clear that he made his appeal to secular courtly ideals quite consciously.[130] The conventional beauty of the virgin martyrs is significant as it demonstrates that these saints were not meant to be conceived of in sexually neutral terms, nor that through their virginity they had 'become men'. Not only are they represented in uncompromisingly female form, they fit the image of the

1 Woman in her perfect age. St Dorothy

desirable ideal, and although their physical perfection was probably intended to mirror their spiritual eminence it is significant that they were made to resemble young courtly beauties, rather than stately older women.

The unbound hair of the martyrs takes on the meanings it does for the Pearl Maiden, of the woman who is both desired and untouched. The symbolism of their crowns or garlands is more complex. As with the Pearl Maiden, they symbolise virginity and dedication to Christ, as shown by the example of Cecilia and her chaste husband Valerian, to whom angels offer crowns of roses as signs of their chastity.[131] But they are also crowns of martyrdom. Peter Abelard in the twelfth century had written of the double crown of the virgin martyrs: of lilies for virginity, and of roses for martyrdom.[132] In the case of St Katherine, a royal princess, the crown also points to regal status. Yet the significance of the crown or wreath as a symbol of youthful and potentially fertile virginity remains, and is appropriate to their age.

Representations of the Virgin Mary at her death, assumption and coronation offer perhaps the most powerful expression of the idea that a woman's perfect age was her maidenhood. Tradition had it that she, unlike her son, lived on well into old age, and thus well past the perfect age of the body.[133] Voragine's account of the assumption says that she was fourteen when she conceived Christ and fifteen when she gave birth to him – at woman's perfect age – then after his death at thirty-three survived another twenty-four years, dying at seventy-two (another account gives her age at death as sixty).[134]

Turning to visual representation of the Virgin's death, assumption and coronation, one might expect to find her represented as an old woman, if the artists concerned took a naturalistic course. But a wimpled matronly figure is not favoured. Rather, as queen of heaven she has the unbound hair and crown of a maiden on her wedding day. Composite depictions of her death, assumption and coronation in the Sherborne Missal and the Ramsey Psalter offer vivid illustrations of this (see Figure 2).[135] Contemporary English depictions of the coronation of the virgin, such as those found in the De Lisle Psalter, the Peterborough Psalter, the Hours of Alice de Reydon and the Carmelite Missal among many others, are especially revealing, regularly depicting a mother who looks considerably younger than her son.[136] The bearded, stately and sombre figure of Christ contrasts with the demure, pretty, youthful and maidenly figure of Mary. The popularity of this image in works owned by the wealthy laity as well as religious houses testifies to its wide appeal.

Mary's representation is more complex than the Pearl Maiden or virgin

2   The Virgin Mary in her perfect age, at death, assumption and coronation

martyrs. While she too is a conventional beauty with flowing golden hair,[137] her crown holds slightly different meanings from those of the others. While the iconography of 'Maria Regina', or the Virgin as queen, dates to the sixth century, the theme of the act of the coronation of the virgin dates from the twelfth and thirteenth centuries.[138] Its appearance is linked to the theological development of the Virgin as royal intercessor, who in her heavenly role shared with queens on earth the privilege of direct mediation and intercession with Christ on behalf of the faithful.[139] Although virgin martyrs, like other saints, could also intercede for those who prayed to them, only the Virgin sat at Christ's right hand as his queen, and she held the strongest powers of intercession.[140] Yet the multi-layered meanings of the representations of the Virgin do not detract from the observation that she is, in English art of the later Middle Ages, regularly depicted in the body of a conventionally desirable young maiden at the moment of her bodily ascension and of her crowning. The contrast with the peak of masculinity represented by her son suggests a clear distinction in notions of the perfect age of man and of woman.

Conclusion

Maidenhood was in many respects an age of transition in women's lives. As a period of developing bodily, moral and intellectual attributes, it had much in common with the youth of men, though it tended to arrive earlier and, especially for noble girls, finish sooner. But unlike male youth, in which that half-way status represented incompletion or immaturity, maidenhood attained the status of perfected womanhood. The images of the Virgin Mary in death and apotheosis, the virgin martyrs at the time of their passion and the Pearl Maiden grown from infant to damsel in a dream vision indicate that the female soul took on the perfected female body of the maiden. Still, although maidenhood was a symbol of female bodily perfection, like the youth of men it was socially an age of incompletion. In the course of a woman's life it was not hoped that her maidenhood would represent the end or culmination but should instead be a stepping-stone between the shores of childhood and wifehood. In life, if not in imagery, it formed a transitional stage, providing an essential period of 'education' for maidens learning adult femininity, which is the subject of the next chapter.

Notes

1 Sands (ed.), *Middle English Verse Romances*, lines 235–43, my adaptation. The translation differs from the Anglo-Norman original which does not specify her age in years: 'Quant ele vint en tel ée / que Nature furme beuté, / En Bretaine ne fu si bele / Ne tant curteise dameisele', Jean Rychner (ed.), *Les Lais de Marie de France* (Paris, 1966), p. 51. The choice of words in the translation must have been to stress Freine's changes upon reaching twelve.

2 Sands (ed.), *Middle English Verse Romances*, lines 192–5; Osbern Bokenham, *Legendys of Hooly Wummen*, ed. Mary S. Serjeantson, EETS os 206 (London, 1938), pp. 58–9.

3 The best account of medieval notions of sex differences is Cadden's *Meanings of Sex Difference*, esp. pp. 169–88. For *loci classici* on women's greater coldness see Aristotle, *Generation of Animals*, trans. A. L. Peck (London, 1943), pp. 93–5, 103, 387, and Galen, *On the Usefulness of the Parts of the Body*, trans. Margaret Tallmadge May, 2 vols (Ithaca, NY, 1968), vol. 2, pp. 628–31.

4 Pseudo-Albertus Magnus, *Women's Secrets: A Translation of Pseudo-Albertus Magnus' De secretis mulierum*, ed. and trans. Helen Rodnite Lemay (Albany, 1992), pp. 60–70.

5 Avicenna said children derived a stock of heat from the semen from which they were generated and that ageing is caused by its dissipation: Mazhar H. Shah, *The General Principles of Avicenna's Canon of Medicine* (Karachi, 1966), p. 33. Albertus Magnus mentioned women's greater coldness when puzzling over whether men or women had greater longevity. *By nature*, a man lives longer because of his heat, but *by accident*, women actually live longer because their work is less taxing, they are regularly cleansed by menstruation, and are less debilitated by sexual intercourse: Albertus Magnus, *Quaestiones super De animalibus*, ed. Ephrem Filthaut, vol. 12 of *Opera omnia*, ed. Bernhard Geyer (Münster, 1955), pp. 263–4.

6 Brian Lawn (ed.), *The Prose Salernitan Questions*, Auctores Britannici Medii Aevi 5 (London, 1979), pp. 233–4.

7 Cadden, *Meanings of Sex Difference*, pp. 117–30, 173–7, 181–3; Danielle Jacquart and Claude Thomasset, *Sexuality and Medicine in the Middle Ages*, trans. Matthew Adamson (Princeton, 1988), pp. 52–60, 71–3.

8 On medical education see Nancy G. Siraisi, *Medieval and Early Renaissance Medicine: An Introduction to Knowledge and Practice* (Chicago, 1990). On the transmission of texts see Cadden, *Meanings of Sex Difference*, pp. 110–17.

9 BL MS Royal 18 A.vi, fol. 35r. See also BL MS Sloane 5, fol. 158r, and M. R. Hallaert (ed.), *The 'Sekenesse of Wymmen'*, Scripta: Mediaeval and Renaissance Texts and Studies 8 (Brussels, 1982), p. 27, and for a slightly different version of the text see Sloane 249, fol. 180v, and Sloane 2463, fol. 194v (this last was edited by Beryl Rowland in *Medieval Woman's Guide to Health: The First English Gynecological Handbook* (London, 1981), see p. 58.). A full list of the manuscripts of versions 1 and 2 of *The Sekenesse of Wymmen* and a critique of their earlier identification by editors is in Monica H. Green, 'Obstetrical and gynecological texts in Middle English', in *Women's Healthcare in the Medieval West: Texts and*

Contexts (Aldershot, 2000), pp. 72–82. See also her 'Women's medical practice and health care in medieval Europe', *Signs*, 14 (1989), 434–74, especially pp. 463–8.

10 BL MS Sloane 421A, fol. 5v; see also BL MS Additional 12195, fols 161v–162r. For a list and discussion of English versions of 'Trotula' see Green, 'Obstetrical and gynecological texts', pp. 63–72, and for editions of the Douce and Cambridge versions of the text and full discussion see Alexandra Barratt (ed.), *The Knowing of Woman's Kind in Childing: A Middle English Version of Material Derived from the Trotula and Other Sources* (Turnhout, 2001).

11 BL MS Sloane 421A, fol. 2r. Barratt argues that the texts did have a female audience, *Knowing of Woman's Kind*, pp. 1–5.

12 For *The Sekenesse of Wymmen* see note 9 above, and for 'Trotula A' on menarche see BL MS Sloane 421A, fol. 4r and 6v–7r, and BL MS Additional 12195, fol. 159v and 160r.

13 Pseudo-Albertus Magnus, *Women's Secrets*, pp. 69–70; J. B. Post, 'Ages at menarche and menopause: some mediaeval authorities', *Population Studies*, 25 (1971), 83–7, esp. p. 85.

14 James Hamilton Wylie (ed.), *History of England under Henry the Fourth*, 4 vols (London, 1884–98), vol. 4, pp. 132–3; John Fisher, 'Mornynge remembraunce had at the moneth mynde of the noble Prynces Margarete Countesse of Rychmonde and Darbye', in John E. B. Mayor (ed.), *The English Works of John Fisher*, part 1, EETS ES 27 (London, 1876), pp. 292–3; Michael K. Jones and Malcolm G. Underwood, *The King's Mother: Lady Margaret Beaufort, Countess of Richmond and Derby* (Cambridge, 1992), pp. 35–40.

15 BL MS Additional 12195, fol. 157v. See also BL MS Sloane 421A, fol. 2v, and Monica H. Green (ed. and trans.), *The* Trotula: *A Medieval Compendium of Women's Medicine* (Philadelphia, 2001), p. 72.

16 Cadden, *Meanings of Sex Difference*, pp. 86–7, 146–7.

17 David C. Fowler, Charles F. Briggs, and Paul G. Remley (eds), *The Governance of Kings and Princes: John Trevisa's Middle English Translation of the* De regimine principum *of Aegidius Romanus* (New York, 1997), pp. 194–6. Cf. Aristotle, *Politics*, ed. and trans. H. Rackham (Cambridge, MA, 1932), pp. 617–21, which argues along very similar lines, but where the ideal age for men to marry is the much later age of thirty-six. On Giles of Rome and the idea of a eugenicist ethics in the later Middle Ages see Peter Biller, '"Demographic thought" around 1300 and Dante's Florence', in John C. Barnes and Cormac Ó Cuilleanáin (eds), *Dante and the Middle Ages: Literary and Historical Essays* (Dublin, 1995), esp. p. 67.

18 The work was outstandingly popular across Europe, with nearly two hundred and fifty manuscripts extant, and fifty-three of these are of medieval English origin or provenance. See C. F. Briggs, 'Manuscripts of Giles of Rome's *De regimine principum* in England, 1300–1500: a handlist', *Scriptorium*, 47 (1993), 60–73.

19 BL MS Sloane 421A, fols 6v–7r, and BL MS Additional 12195, fol. 163v.

20 Cf. the earlier theory espoused by Gratian and the school of Bologna, that the marriage would not be completed until consummation had taken place (rejected because it implied that the marriage of Joseph and the Virgin Mary had not been

fully legitimate): James A. Brundage, *Law, Sex, and Christian Society in Medieval Europe* (Chicago, 1987), pp. 236–7, 264–9; R. H. Helmholz, *Marriage Litigation in Medieval England* (Cambridge, 1974), pp. 26–7.

21　*SL and P* 1, no. 87; Helmholz, *Marriage Litigation*, p. 98, and for transcriptions of BIHR CP E 23 and E 76, both actions for annulment brought by boys upon reaching the age of consent, see pp. 200–4.

22　X 4. 2. 2. For examples of papal dispensations to marry outside canon-legal restrictions including the impediment of age see Joel T. Rosenthal, 'Aristocratic marriage and the English peerage, 1350–1500: social institutional and personal bond', *Journal of Medieval History*, 10 (1984), 181–94.

23　C. 30 q. 2. c. un.

24　C. 20 q. 2 c. 2, and C. 22 q. 5 c. 15.

25　Thomas Aquinas, *Summa theologiae* (London, 1973), 2a 2ae, q. 189, art. 5.

26　X 4.2.1–14; Brundage, *Law, Sex, and Christian Society*, p. 237.

27　X 4.2.3. Italics in original.

28　On intercourse as ratification of underage marriage see X 4.2.8–9; William Lyndwood, *Provinciale (seu constitutiones Angliae)* (Oxford, 1679), p. 272, s.v. 'non pervenerit'; A. Esmein, *Le Mariage en droit canonique*, 2 vols (New York, [1891] 1968), vol. 1, pp. 212–13; W. Onclin, 'L'Âge requis pour le mariage dans la doctrine canonique médiévale', in Stephan Kuttner and J. Joseph Ryan (eds), *Proceedings of the Second International Congress of Medieval Canon* Law (Vatican City, 1965), pp. 240–1. On *proximus pubertati* see X 4.2.6 and 9; Esmein, *Le Mariage* 1, pp. 213–14; Onclin, 'L'Âge requis', p. 242.

29　Brundage, *Law, Sex, and Christian Society*, p. 434.

30　BIHR CP E 89. For a translation of many of the depositions contained in the roll see P. J. P. Goldberg (ed. and trans.), *Women in England, c. 1275–1525* (Manchester, 1995), pp. 58–80. I am very grateful to Dr Goldberg for his generous help with this and other cause papers.

31　E. D. Stone (ed.), *Norwich Consistory Court Depositions, 1499–1512 and 1518–30*, Norfolk Record Society 10 (Norwich, 1938), no. 126; Goldberg, *Women, Work, and Life Cycle*, p. 219.

32　Helmholz, *Marriage Litigation*, pp. 98–9, says few cases of reclamation against marriages made in childhood appear in the Act Books, either because few were made or many which were did not come before the court. It is also possible that few were made because of the relatively low proportions of individuals marrying in childhood.

33　See for example X 4.2.9 and 14; Onlin, 'L'Âge requis', p. 241.

34　'Concilium lateranense IV', in *Sacrosancta concilia*, 15 vols (Paris, 1671), vol. 11, part 1, cols 172–3, cap. 21.

35　H. C. Lea, *A History of Auricular Confession and Indulgences in the Latin Church*, 3 vols (New York, 1896), vol. 1, pp. 400–2, and Thomas N. Tentler, *Sin and Confession on the Eve of the Reformation* (Princeton, 1977), p. 70, n. 1, provide summaries of the opinions of canon-legal commentators on minimum age at confession. See also J. D. C. Fisher, *Christian Initiation: Baptism in the Medieval West*, Alcuin Club Collections 47 (London, 1965), pp. 105–6.

36 The following is based on Fisher, *Christian Initiation*, pp. 101–37, and Nicholas Orme, 'Children and the Church in medieval England', *Journal of Ecclesiastical History*, 45 (1994), 563–87.

37 Orme, 'Children and the Church', pp. 573–6.

38 John Myrc, *Instructions for Parish Priests*, ed. Edward Peacock, EETS os 31 (London, 1868), p. 7.

39 J. H. Baker, *Introduction to English Legal History*, 3rd edn (London, 1990), pp. 200–2; T. F. T. Plucknett, *A Concise History of the Common Law*, 5th edn (London, 1956), pp. 258–64.

40 *Glanvill*, p. 82; *Bracton* 2, p. 250, Pollock and Maitland 2, p. 438; William Holdsworth, *A History of English Law*, 16 vols (London, 1942), vol. 3, p. 510.

41 *Bracton* 2, p. 251.

42 F. W. Maitland (ed.), *Year Books of Edward II*, vol. 2, *2 and 3 Edward II, A.D. 1308–9 and 1309–10*, Selden Society 19 (London, 1904), pp. 157–62.

43 Holdsworth, *History of English Law*, vol. 3, p. 510.

44 *Bracton* 2, p. 251.

45 W. J. Whittaker (ed.), *The Mirror of Justices*, Selden Society 7 (London, 1893), p. 160.

46 *Year Books* 2, p. 162.

47 Jennifer Ward (ed. and trans.), *Women of the English Nobility and Gentry 1066–1500* (Manchester, 1995), p. 71.

48 *PL and P* 1, no. 230.

49 On wardship see Scott Waugh, *The Lordship of England: Royal Wardships and Marriages in English Society and Politics, 1217–1327* (Princeton, 1988); Noël James Menuge, *Medieval English Wardship in Romance and Law* (Woodbridge, 2001); Sue Sheridan Walker, 'Widow and ward: the feudal law of child custody in medieval England', in Susan Mosher Stuard (ed.), *Women in Medieval Society* (Philadelphia, 1976); Pollock and Maitland 1, pp. 318–22.

50 *Glanvill*, pp. 82–5; *Bracton* 2, pp. 252–4.

51 *Glanvill*, pp. 95–7; Pollock and Maitland 2, pp. 306–7.

52 Zvi Razi, *Life, Marriage and Death in a Medieval Parish: Economy, Society and Demography in Halesowen 1270–1400* (Cambridge, 1980), p. 61; Cicely Howell, *Land, Family and Inheritance in Transition: Kibworth Harcourt 1280–1700* (Cambridge, 1983), p. 256; Mate, *Daughters, Wives and Widows*, p. 25.

53 Bennett, *Women in the Medieval English Countryside*, pp. 67–8.

54 Mary Bateson (ed.), *Borough Customs*, 2 vols, Selden Society 18 and 21 (London, 1904–6), vol. 2, pp. 158–60.

55 See *Year Books* 14, pp. 9–20 for a case under common law involving a dispute over property between two sisters. One of them is under age and, though her position in relation to points of court procedure is debated because of her age, her entitlement to freehold tenancy is not questioned.

56 G. O. Sayles (ed.), *Select Cases in the Court of King's Bench under Edward III*, vol. 6, Selden Society 82 (London, 1965), pp. 130–1.

57 *Year Books* 2, pp. 189–92.

58 *Year Books* 22, pp. 45–7.

59 *Year Books* 11, pp. 14–17.

60 Pollock and Maitland 2, pp. 440–3; Holdsworth, *History of English Law*, vol. 3, pp. 516, 375.

61 *Year Books* 7, p. 29.

62 *Year Books* 24, p. 23.

63 *Year Books* 5, p. 109.

64 Holdsworth, *History of English Law*, vol. 3, pp. 372, 511.

65 *Year Books* 5, pp. 148–9.

66 *Year Books* 25, p. 123.

67 *Bracton* 2, p. 351; Pollock and Maitland 1, pp. 531–2, 580–2.

68 Bennett, *Women in the Medieval English Countryside*, pp. 76–87.

69 Useful summaries of married women's rights are in Pollock and Maitland 2, pp. 399–436; Charles Donahue, Jr, 'What causes fundamental legal ideas? Marital property in England and France in the thirteenth century', *Michigan Law Review*, 78 (1979), 59–88; Barron, '"Golden Age"'; Kittel, 'Women under the law'; Loengard, '"Legal history and the medieval Englishwoman"'.

70 *PC*, p. lxiv.

71 John Hajnal, 'European marriage patterns in perspective', in D. V. Glass and D. E. C. Eversley (eds), *Population in History: Essays in Historical Demography* (London, 1965); Razi, *Life Marriage and Death*, pp. 60–3.

72 Razi, *Life, Marriage and Death*, p. 63.

73 David Herlihy and Christiane Klapisch-Zuber, *Tuscans and their Families: A Study of the Florentine Catasto of 1427* (New Haven, 1985), pp. 87, 210–11, 215; David Herlihy, *Medieval Households* (Cambridge, MA, 1985), pp. 103–11; R. M. Smith, 'The people of Tuscany and their families in the fifteenth century: medieval or Mediterranean?', *Journal of Family History*, 6 (1981), 107–28, and 'Geographical diversity'; Goldberg, *Women, Work, and Life Cycle*, esp. pp. 225–32.

74 Mark Bailey, 'Demographic decline in late medieval England: some thoughts on recent research', *Economic History Review*, 49 (1996), 1–19; Mate, *Daughters, Wives and Widows*, pp. 21–31.

75 Jennifer C. Ward, *English Noblewomen in the Later Middle Ages*, (Harlow, 1992), p. 13.

76 *PC*, p. 8.

77 BIHR CP E 89.

78 *TE* 4, pp. 237–8. See also Ward (ed. and trans.), *Women of the English Nobility and Gentry*, p. 34, for the 1383 will of Sir William Berland, who states that his daughters 'should be married before the age of fifteen if they want to be married' or else take the veil.

79 T. H. Hollingsworth, 'A demographic study of the British ducal families', in Glass and Eversley, *Population in History*, pp. 364–5, tables 17 and 18.

80 Fisher, 'Mornynge remembraunce', pp. 292–3; Jones and Underwood, *The King's Mother*, pp. 35–40.

81 Oration quoted in J. Lewis, *Life of John Fisher*, 2 vols (London, 1855), vol. 2, p. 265.

82 Jones and Underwood, *King's Mother*, p. 40.

83 John Carmi Parsons, 'Mothers, daughters, marriage, power: some Plantagenet evidence, 1150–1500', in John Carmi Parsons (ed.), *Medieval Queenship* (Stroud, 1994), pp. 66–7.

84 The following is collated from information in Mary Ann Everett Green, *Lives of the Princesses of England from the Norman Conquest*, 6 vols (London, 1849–55).

85 Green, *Lives of the Princesses*, vol. 3, pp. 303–36.

86 Green, *Lives of the Princesses*, vol. 2, pp. 286–7.

87 See for example *PL and P* 1, nos. 174, 304, 380, 407; *CL* nos. 117, 165.

88 *PL and P* 1, no. 303.

89 *PL and P* 1, no. 407.

90 *SL and P* 2, no. 166.

91 Eileen Power, *Medieval People* (London, 1924), p. 119; Christine Carpenter, 'Introduction', *SL and P*, p. 24.

92 *SL and P* 2, no. 166.

93 *SL and P* 2, no. 218.

94 *SL and P* 2, no. 166.

95 *SL and P* 2, no. 211.

96 Stanley Chojnacki, 'Measuring adulthood: adolescence and gender in Renaissance Venice', *Journal of Family History*, 17 (1992), 371–95 (quotation at p. 385).

97 This is an abbreviated version of my article 'Maidenhood as the perfect age of woman's life', in Lewis, Menuge and Phillips (eds), *Young Medieval Women*.

98 Mary Dove, *Perfect Age, passim*; Burrow, *Ages of Man*, esp. pp. 5–11; Sears, *Ages of Man*, pp. 45, 56, 119.

99 Dove, *Perfect Age*, p. 21; Burrow, *Ages of Man*, pp. 6–11.

100 Burrow, *Ages of Man*, pp. 135–44; Caroline Walker Bynum, *The Resurrection of the Body in Western Christianity, 200–1336* (New York, 1995), esp. pp. 98, 122; J. A. Tasioulas, 'Seeds of perfection: the childlike soul and the resurrection of the body', in P. J. P. Goldberg and Felicity Riddy (eds), *Youth in the Middle Ages* (York, forthcoming).

101 Dove, *Perfect Age*, p. 25.

102 E. V. Gordon (ed.), *Pearl* (Oxford, 1953), and Malcolm Andrew and Ronald Waldron (eds), *The Poems of the Pearl Manuscript* (Exeter, 1987). References are to the Andrew and Waldron edition unless otherwise stated.

103 Gordon notes that the Maiden's dress is 'a very simple form of the aristocratic dress of the second half of the fourteenth century', with the very long sleeves characteristic of aristocratic dress, *Pearl*, p. 56, n. 228.

104 Ian Bishop, *'Pearl' in Its Setting* (Oxford, 1968), p. 101.

105 Giovanni Boccaccio, *Eclogues*, trans. Janet Levarie Smarr (New York, 1987), pp. 156–69. It has not proved possible to confirm whether the Pearl Poet was influenced by *Olympia*: Richard Newhauser, 'Sources II: scriptural and devotional sources', in Derek Brewer and Jonathan Gibson (eds), *A Companion to the Gawain-Poet* (Cambridge, 1997), p. 268. I am indebted to Felicity Riddy and Nick Havely for their help on this subject.

106 D. S. Brewer, 'The ideal of feminine beauty in medieval literature, especially

"Harley Lyrics", Chaucer, and some Elizabethans', *Modern Language Review*, 50 (1955), 257–69; Walter Clyde Curry, *The Middle English Ideal of Personal Beauty; As Found in the Metrical Romances, Chronicles, and Legends of the XIII, XIV, and XV Centuries* (Baltimore, 1916).

107 Matthew of Vendôme, *The Art of Versification*, trans. Aubrey E. Galyon (Ames, 1980), p. 43; Geoffrey of Vinsauf, *The Poetria nova*, translated in Ernest Gallo, *The Poetria nova and Its Sources in Early Rhetorical Doctrine* (The Hague, 1971), pp. 45–7; Julius Zupitza (ed.), *The Romance of Guy of Warwick*, EETS ES 42, 49 and 59 (London, 1883–91), lines 65–74; Rossell Hope Robbins (ed.), *Secular Lyrics of the XIVth and XVth Centuries* (Oxford, 1955), pp. 120–8, 144–5, 183, 223; G. L. Brook (ed.), *The Harley Lyrics: The Middle English Lyrics of Ms. Harley 2253* (Manchester, 1968), pp. 33–4, 37–41.

108 Geoffrey of Vinsauf, *Poetria nova*, p. 45; *The Miller's Tale*, lines. 3221–70, *The Physician's Tale*, lines. 7–8, 30–8.

109 *The Merchant's Tale*, lines 1417–22.

110 Matthew of Vendôme *Versification*, p. 44. The female grotesque found literary expression in the Loathly Lady – see for example 'The Wedding of Sir Gawain and Dame Ragnell', in Sands (ed.), *Middle English Verse Romances*, lines 231–43.

111 Kenneth Clark, *The Nude: A Study of Ideal Art* (London, 1956) and *Feminine Beauty* (London, 1980); Arthur Marwick, *Beauty in History: Society, Politics and Personal Appearance c. 1500 to the Present* (London, 1988). Cf. Angela Carter, 'I could have fancied her', *London Review of Books*, 16 (February, 1989), p. 8; Anne Hollander, *Seeing through Clothes* (New York, 1975); Margaret Miles, 'The Virgin's one bare breast: female nudity and religious meaning in Tuscan early Renaissance culture', in Susan Rubin Suleiman (ed.), *The Female Body in Western Culture: Contemporary Perspectives* (Cambridge, MA, 1986).

112 Timothy Husband with Gloria Gilmore, *The Wild Man: Medieval Myth and Symbolism* (New York, 1988); Jacobus de Voragine, *The Golden Legend: Readings on the Saints*, trans. William Granger Ryan, 2 vols (Princeton, 1993), vol. 1, pp. 227–9, 374–83; Margaret R. Miles, *Carnal Knowing: Female Nakedness and Religious Meaning in the Christian West* (Boston, 1989), pp. 48–51; Katherine L. French, 'The legend of Lady Godiva and the image of the female body', *Journal of Medieval History*, 18 (1992), 3–19, esp. pp. 15–16.

113 Ryan (ed.) *Golden Legend* 1, pp. 101–4; French, 'Lady Godiva'.

114 Henry Thomas Riley (ed.), *Liber albus in munimenta Gildhallae Londoniensis*, Rolls Series 12, 3 vols (London, 1859–62), vol. 1, p. 459; J. B. L. Tolhurst (ed.), *The Ordinale and Customary of the Benedictine Nuns of Barking Abbey*, Henry Bradshaw Society 65 and 66 (London, 1927–8), vol. 2, pp. 353–5; William Maskell (ed.), *Monumenta ritualia ecclesiae Anglicanae*, 3 vols (London, 1846–7), vol. 2, pp. 308–31.

115 *The Clerk's Tale*, lines. 379–80; Henry B. Wheatley (ed.), *Merlin, or The Early History of King Arthur*, EETS OS 10, 21, 36, 112 (London, 1865–99), p. 453; Phillis Cunnington and Catherine Lucas, *Costumes for Births, Marriages and Deaths* (London, 1972), pp. 92–3; Elizabeth Danbury, 'Images of English queens in the later Middle Ages', *The Historian*, 46 (1995), 3–9; John Carmi Parsons, 'Ritual

and symbol in English medieval queenship to 1500', in Louise Olga Fradenburg (ed.), *Women and Sovereignty* (Edinburgh, 1992), p. 62; Joanna L. Chamberlayne, 'Crowns and virgins: queenmaking during the Wars of the Roses', in Lewis, Menuge and Phillips (eds), *Young Medieval Women*, p. 56.

116 Millet and Wogan-Browne (eds and trans), 'Hali Meiðhad', in *Medieval English Prose for Women*, p. 21.

117 *Pilgrimage*, line 67; Osbert of Clare, writing to his niece Cecilia, quoted in Barbara Newman, 'Flaws in the golden bowl: gender and spiritual formation in the twelfth century', *Traditio*, 45 (1989–90), 111–46, esp. p. 127.

118 Ronald Hutton, *The Rise and Fall of Merry England: The Ritual Year 1400–1700* (Oxford, 1994), pp. 29–30, 117; Cunnington and Lucas, *Costumes*, p. 92.

119 René Metz, 'La Couronne et l'anneau dans la consécration des vierges', *Revue des sciences religieuses*, 28 (1954), 113–32.

120 C. A. Lutrell, 'The medieval tradition of the Pearl virginity', *Medium Ævum*, 31 (1962), 194–200; James W. Earl, 'Saint Margaret and the Pearl Maiden', *Modern Philology*, 70 (1972), 1–8; Ryan (ed.), *Golden Legend* 1, p. 368.

121 Cunnington and Lucas, *Costumes*, p. 41; Bishop, *Pearl*, pp. 114–21; Tolhurst (ed.), *Ordinale*, p. 353; S. B. Meech and H. E. Allen (eds), *The Book of Margery Kempe*, EETS OS 212 (London, 1940), pp. 32, 124; Mary C. Erler, 'Margery Kempe's white clothes', *Medium Ævum*, 62 (1993), 78–83; Dyan Elliott, 'Dress as mediator between inner and outer self: the pious matron of the high and later Middle Ages', *Mediaeval Studies*, 53 (1991), 279–308, esp. pp. 294–5.

122 On the popularity of virgin martyrs' lives see Katherine J. Lewis, *The Cult of St Katherine of Alexandria in Late Medieval England* (Woodbridge, 2000); Jocelyn Wogan-Browne, 'Saints' lives and the female reader', *Forum for Modern Language Studies*, 27 (1991), 314–32 and 'The virgin's tale', in Ruth Evans and Lesley Johnson (eds), *Feminist Readings in Middle English Literature: The Wife of Bath and All Her Sect* (London, 1994); Eamon Duffy, 'Holy maydens, holy wyfes: the cult of women saints in fifteenth- and sixteenth-century England', in Sheils and Wood (eds), *Women in the Church*.

123 Ryan (ed.), *Golden Legend* 1, pp. 102, 368; 2, p. 334; Bokenham, *Legendys*, pp. 12, 58, 85, 113, 175.

124 Jacobus de Voragine, *Legenda aurea vulgo historia Lombardica*, ed. Thomas Graesse (Osnabrück, 1969), e.g. pp. 31, 178, 402, 621, 633, 635, 776, 791.

125 Bokenham, *Legendys*, pp. 99, 232, 254.

126 Burrow, *Ages of Man*, p. 143.

127 Ryan (ed.), *Golden Legend* 1, p. 268.

128 David Hugh Farmer (ed.), *The Oxford Dictionary of Saints* (Oxford, 1992), p. 28. For a visual example of St Apollonia represented alongside and resembling the other virgin martyrs see the reproduction of the south rood screen at Westhall Church, East Anglia, in Duffy, 'Holy maydens', p. 183, plate 2. I owe the example of Apollonia to Katherine Lewis. Similarly, the *Alphonso Psalter* (*c.* 1284–1316) depicts St Barbara as an older woman alongside more youthful saints (Figure 3), in contrast to later panel paintings.

129 Bokenham, *Legendys*, p. 13.

130 Bokenham, *Legendys*, pp. 12, 32.
131 Ryan (ed.), *Golden Legend* 2, p. 319.
132 André Grabar, *Christian Iconography: A Study in Its Origins* (London, 1969), p. 41; Newman, 'Golden Bowl', p. 123.
133 Ryan (ed.), *The Golden Legend* 2, p. 78; Peter Meredith (ed.), *The Mary Play from the N Town Manuscript* (London, 1987).
134 Ryan (ed.), *Golden Legend* 2, p. 78.
135 For the *Sherborne Missal*, see Scott, *Later Gothic Manuscripts I*, plate 51.
136 Sandler, *Gothic Manuscripts I*, plates 39, 85, 111, 167, 169, 194, 281; Scott, *Later Gothic Manuscripts I*, plates 6 and 408.
137 On the Virgin's late medieval resemblance to courtly beauties see Michael Camille, *The Gothic Idol: Ideology and Image-Making in Medieval Art* (Cambridge, 1989), pp. 220–41.
138 Rosemary Muir Wright, 'The virgin in the sun and in the tree', in Louise Olga Fradenburg (ed.), *Women and Sovereignty* (Edinburgh, 1992); Marina Warner, *Alone of All Her Sex: The Myth and Cult of the Virgin Mary* (London, 1976), pp. 81–117.
139 Elizabeth A. Johnson, 'Marian devotion in the Western Church', in Jill Raitt (ed.), *Christian Spirituality: High Middle Ages and Reformation* (New York, 1987), pp. 405–10.
140 See Sandler, *Gothic Manuscripts I*, plates 39 and 40.

2

Upbringing

To paraphrase Simone de Beauvoir, in medieval England a girl was not born but rather became a woman. While the process of socialisation in gender began in childhood, it developed in earnest during maidenhood. 'With puberty the future not only approaches: it takes residence in her body: it assumes the most concrete reality.'[1] Although medieval maidens were not imbued with the extreme passivity de Beauvoir ascribes to the experience of French adolescent girls in the mid-twentieth century ('While the adolescent boy makes his way actively towards adulthood, the young girl awaits the opening of this new, unforeseeable period, the plot of which henceforth is woven and towards which time is bearing her. … Her youth is consumed in waiting. … She is awaiting Man'), they shared with them a period of intense socialisation in femininity and in roles appropriate to their status. For most maidens this meant preparation for wifehood and education in the active and useful but docile qualities valued in adult women. For girls of the nobility, wifehood was often only a few years away, while lower-status maidens experienced a longer period of learning and labour before marriage. The 'education' of medieval English maidens, which bore very little resemblance to modern education, had one ultimate aim: to produce women as the useful secondary sex. Medieval maidens were not taught to be downtrodden or despised but to fit uncomplainingly within larger structures of family, household, community and status group in eternally supporting roles. But the messages on femininity were not all about dreary obedience. There was room for imagining, and even for a little practice in, wilfulness, playfulness, making demands of would-be lovers, and even experiencing sexual passion.

The danger with the term 'education' is that it is too easily confused with modern schooling, and especially the training in literacy and numeracy which now forms its basis. Medieval women's education was rarely formal-ised, and the types of 'literacy' it encompassed (where at all) were far more varied than now. 'Education's' root in *educare*, 'to lead out', is helpful; we should consider not schooling so much as the processes by which girls were led out of childhood. Variations in literacy and the existence of textual communities will be discussed here, but merely as 'modes of learning' or aids in the more fundamental education in womanhood rather than as the ends in themselves they have become. Work training was of course a vital part of maidens' education at all social levels, and indeed it is artificial to maintain a strict distinction between 'learning' and 'work' for young women in this context, but for convenience activities which usually attracted some financial or material reward will be dealt with in the following chapter.

Modes of learning

The education of girls varied markedly from one social group to another, but a universal characteristic was the predominantly oral nature of instruction. Where reading literacy existed it supplemented oral culture. Written works such as *The Good Wife Taught Her Daughter* and *The Good Wyfe Wold a Pylgremage* acknowledged the primacy of the spoken word by feigning the voice of a mother speaking to her child.[2] Texts were frequently employed in an oral or auditory context, such as the group readings of devotional or romance literature, priests' readings of sermons and instructional matter, and the intonations of prayers. Purely oral forms of instruction were surely more important still: repetition of proverbs, verbal chastisement and instructions from parents, guardians, priests or chaplains, masters or mistresses, siblings, relatives, community members, or other young women themselves. Purely oral evidence cannot be pre-served, though representation is sometimes available in records such as ecclesiastical court defamation proceedings, which reveal the community's role in policing the conduct of young women.[3] On the whole we are limited to texts considered important or interesting enough to be written down and transmitted, leaving questions of what, why and by whom. The media of maidens' instruction varied according to social position, but could include conduct texts, romance literature, saints' lives, liturgical and devotional texts, apprenticeship indentures, sermons and prayers, cycle and parish plays and visual media (which will be only briefly mentioned in this chapter) in books, glass, panel painting and sculpture. Teachers included mothers, priests, employers or mistresses, communities of the household, parish or village, and, just for a handful, governesses, schools and nunneries.

Questions of female literacy levels still perplex scholars, as seemingly contradictory evidence comes to light and contrasting views are expressed.[4] Puzzlement over whether significant numbers of women could read and/or write is partly the product of a stubborn application of modern notions of literacy to a medieval context and partly the persistence of a 'common sense' approach. If women of the merchant class and higher are known to have been keen purchasers of books of hours in the later Middle Ages and visual depictions of holy women show them evidently reading such books, then higher-status women at least must have known some Latin, runs one argument.[5] If wives and widows of artisan and merchant society were active in running household businesses then some basic literacy skills must have been necessary, runs another.[6] Michael Clanchy's careful distinctions between varieties of medieval 'reading strategies' and Paul Saenger's delineation of separate 'phonetic' and 'comprehension' literacy among readers of books of hours seem overlooked by the first argument, while the second fails to take into account that much business in the present developing world is carried out by illiterate persons.[7] Women's literacy in later medieval England needs to be understood not by comparison with modern literacy, nor even with medieval male literacy. For example, Clanchy's often-invoked *litteratus/illiteratus* distinction is not as useful for late medieval women as for high-medieval men.[8] Literacy encompassed varying knowledges of Latin, French and English, and spanned abilities from phonetic reading (the ability to distinguish and pronounce words on the page without necessarily understanding them), to pragmatic literacy in the forms and content of legal documents, to the ability to read with comprehension in one or more of the languages, to skills in both reading and writing. Every variation counts, and it is unhelpful to set a single definition of what made an individual 'literate', such as the ability to sign one's name.[9] We need to develop a model of specifically female medieval literacy. In its fundamental elements, medieval female literacy was supplementary to orality, widely varying in forms and standards, rarely included Latin comprehension, and was not necessarily the marker of high or respectable status which it has attained in more recent centuries.[10]

John Paston III, penning a hurried and flirtatious note to a woman addressed only as 'Mistress Annes' (Agnes) at midnight on a journey homeward to Norwich in July 1474, added in a postscript, 'Mistress Agnes, I am proud that you can read English', as that would enable her to keep his love letters secret. Little more is known about this young woman's identity, though she may have been 'Stockton's daughter', mentioned in one of John II's letters of that year, and probably lived at Blackfriars.[11] Paston's enthusiasm for pursuing her, in any case, would suggest that she was of wealthy family – a merchant's daughter or a young gentlewoman. Despite her likely background, which one might expect to have entailed some training in reading, he appears to have been paying her a compliment for her skills. Perhaps some other young women of Paston's acquaintance had less ability.

In comparison, Eleanor Haute, who had been a damsel in Margaret of Anjou's household in the 1450s when in her early or mid-teens and continued in service with Elizabeth Woodville, had a relatively high literate capacity.[12] Evidently a favourite niece of poet Sir Richard Roos, he saw her as a fit recipient of his splendid volume of three French Arthurian romances.[13] As French retained something of its status as a language of the court well into the fifteenth century, and, more importantly, Eleanor's royal mistress was French, it is likely that she was able to read the romances.[14] English, at any rate, seems not to have been a problem for her, as on the back flyleaf she scrawled 'thys boke ys myne dame alyanor haute' in a hand far more confident than the uncertain autographs of E[lizabeth] Woodville, the princesses Elizabeth (later queen) and Cecily, and Jane Grey in the same volume.[15] These fragments of evidence suggest a level of tolerance for or expectation of variation in women's literate capacities, and point the way to modern scholars to be less demanding of consistency.

What kinds of reading skills in Latin, French and English were possessed by women of different status, and how did these change across the period? Little girls (and boys) of the aristocracy and gentry and increasingly the merchant classes were first taught to 'read' prayers and psalms in Latin liturgical books, though this reading was probably phonetic. Eleanor de Montfort, daughter of Simon de Montfort and Eleanor, countess of Leicester, was six or seven in 1265 when money was sent to a friar in Oxford to buy twenty dozen leaves of fine parchment in London and produce a breviary for her.[16] In October 1290 Eleanor of Castile paid for a psalter and seven primers. Of her daughters, Elizabeth at eight and Mary at twelve were likely recipients of some of the books.[17] Henry Bolingbroke's daughters Blanche and Philippa were about seven and five respectively in 1398 when they were given their ABCs, a new kind of compilation of religious books, 'A' containing the elementary prayers and teachings (Pater, Ave, Ten Commandments, Credo, graces), 'B' holding slightly more advanced material in the psalter, and 'C' the primer, or book of hours.[18] Margaret Roucliffe was only four in 1463 when she was said to have 'near hand learned her psalter', which raises the question of what this 'learning' comprised.[19] A four-year-old could not learn all one hundred and fifty psalms, nor would be expected to. Her little book would have contained the heavy-going 'Penitential Psalms' (6, 32, 38, 51, 102, 130, 143) and perhaps the generally more uplifting 'Gradual Psalms' (120–34), both sets being common components of books of hours.[20] Margaret had probably learned simply to pronounce the Latin aloud. The purchase of basic devotional, liturgical or paraliturgical books (that is, service books, psalters, books of hours and so on) for little girls of the nobility continued into the early sixteenth century. Bridget Plantagenet, boarding at St Mary's Abbey, Winchester, was nine when the abbess incurred costs for the mending of her two matins books in 1535.[21] Her older stepsister Mary Bassett, boarding in France from 1534 to 1538 aged eleven to fifteen, was given a paternoster, but by this age she probably wanted a smarter book or an older one had worn out.[22]

In the late thirteenth and fourteenth centuries, daughters of the gentry and aristocracy often possessed their own Latin devotional books, with the example of the earliest known book of hours, the De Brailes Hours (made around 1240 for Susanna, probably an unmarried woman of the minor nobility), setting the tone for later patterns of association between those books and women of gentle status.[23] By the fifteenth century, middle-status households, enabled by the production of cheaper books following the development of the book trade and introduction of paper, and inspired by an increasing emphasis on lay education in piety in the aftermath of Archbishop Thoresby's reforms, were also purchasing such books. A grocers' inventory of the 1390s lists among their remaining stock a primer worth 16*d*, among other inexpensive books.[24] Such volumes would have been affordable even in better-off artisan and peasant households.[25] Thus by the fifteenth century, urban girls' first textual encounters were often with Latin primers and prayer books.[26]

We will return to the question of how far girls had any comprehension of those prayers, even though they may not have been able to construe Latin. Girls or women with the best reading comprehension of Latin may, indeed, not have been those of high status, with the brilliant exception of individuals such as Dame Eleanor Hull, but rather the small handful trained as scriveners.[27] Girls apprenticed in that trade were probably taught to understand as well as write documents in Latin, French and English, for although legal documents were formulaic they were different enough from one another to require the scribe to have some comprehension and skills of composition. Only three such women have yet been discovered in England, however.[28] And despite their best efforts, Sylvia Thrupp, Jo Ann Hoeppner Moran and Caroline Barron have not found any firm evidence for English girls attending grammar schools.[29] The great majority of girls who had contact with Latin texts had very limited understanding of the words on the page.

The ability to read French was steadily replaced in the fourteenth century and after by a preference for English, and girls' training in French declined accordingly. Studying women's bequests of religious books from 1350 to 1500, Anne Dutton found that bequests of French books, while always less common than of English books, ceased altogether after 1450.[30] On the other hand Carol Meale has argued for the enduring popularity of French romances among aristocratic readers up to the end of the fifteenth century, though gentlewomen were becoming proud owners of English romances at the end of the period.[31] It seems that gentry and merchant women readers, increasingly numerous, skipped the French interlude in the history of literature in England and went directly to English texts (which many could understand) for entertainment and devotion, and Latin texts (which most could not) for religious services. Some may have had an ability to 'read' Latin, but not English. Aristocratic women's retention of French was probably meant as a way to delineate social distinctions between themselves and the gentry. By the early sixteenth century, though, French was on the wane among this group too. When Anne and Mary Basset went to board with French families in the 1530s they knew no French but quickly picked some up, and in 1536 Mary wrote to her elder sister Philippa, 'If I might have my wish I would be every day an hour with you, that I might teach you to speak French'. As the letter was written in French maybe Mary was indicating a distinction between reading and speaking ability (the latter of course is much more difficult), or perhaps Philippa had a secretary translate it aloud for her.[32] By the 1520s Latin began to undergo a revival in aristocratic girls' education, advocated especially by Juan Luis Vives and his English translator Richard Hyrd who was tutor to Thomas More's learned daughter Margaret and associated with Frances Brandon, future mother of the educated Lady Jane Grey.[33]

The general exclusion of girls from Latin learning, in the sense of full comprehension and the ability to compose, had political implications. As long as it was the most important language of scholarship, Church and law it was deemed unsuitable for women. Aristocratic women were permitted to learn French, as was appropriate to their status, but even they were usually kept away from the more powerful, and more masculine, language.

It was only in the early to mid-sixteenth century, when Latin had lost much of its force as a language of power and was in a sense neutered, that girls could safely be encouraged to learn Latin again.

At urban artisan level some girls were attending informal schools where they would have gained an elementary reading education in English, though many or most may well not have even received that much.[34] In upper and lower village society, both the opportunities and the need for literacy would have been much less. The example of Robert Reynes, a rural artisan, reeve's son and churchwarden who compiled his own commonplace book in the later fifteenth century, shows that by the later fifteenth century it was not impossible that girls might encounter books in better-off, respectable village households such as this one, but whether they learned to read them is anyone's guess.[35] Steven Justice has convincingly reassessed our understanding of the type and extent of literacy among men of the lower orders in light of the events of 1381, arguing for extensive pragmatic literacy ('a savvy about the forms and functions and powers of documentary usage'), especially knowledge of the contents of documents which concerned land tenure and servile status.[36] This suggests a kind of literacy gained not in youth or childhood but as an adult active in local courts. Male villagers would have had greater opportunity than female ones to achieve pragmatic literacy, because it was possible for them to hold public offices (as Reynes did) and they were more likely to be landholders and household heads, but as some women were tenants in their own right they may have developed levels of pragmatic literacy. This would have had little impact on their ability to read texts which conveyed messages on femininity, however, making oral sources far more important for this group.

An emphasis on variation within female literacy can help us answer the question that has troubled many scholars: could women write? While 'women' had no such collective ability, some individual women were indeed taught to write. Royal wardrobe accounts sometimes reveal that princesses were bought wax tablets, such as the tablets bought for Edward I's eldest daughter Eleanor for her writing in 1285 when she was about twenty-one.[37] The scarcity of such references, though, alerts us to the possible rarity of writing, even among women of highest status. By the fifteenth century limited orthographic abilities may have been on the increase among aristocratic and gentlewomen, witnessed by the vogue for leaving one's signature on books. The autographs of five high status women are preserved in Eleanor Haute's collection of romances, while Eleanor Guildford signed her copy of the *Prose Merlin*, and Elizabeth Frances and Elizabeth Cotton signed *Sir Degrevant* in the Findern Manuscript and indeed probably also collaborated as scribes of the romance.[38] Still, ability to sign one's name did not necessarily indicate much. In the 1530s, Anne Basset, though of high aristocratic birth and with a successful career at court, said she could write nothing in English except her name, and had only picked up a little ability to write French during her years abroad, which shows that she was given no training in writing at home as a child.[39]

The gentry and merchant letter collections indicate women of those groups often had basic orthographic skills, with Margery Paston (née Brews) and Anne Stonor among those sometimes signing their own names or appending brief messages. Elisabeth Clere possibly wrote her own letters, while Jane Stonor, according to Kingsford, did so, and her daughter-in-law Elizabeth, a London alderman's daughter and merchant's widow, wrote at least one letter entirely herself, and appended final sentences or postscripts and signed her own name to several letters scribed by secretaries.[40] Thomas Betson, by late 1477 a disgruntled suitor to fourteen-year-old Katherine Ryche (daughter of Elizabeth Stonor by her first marriage), made a revealing complaint to her mother:

> I am wrath with Katherine, because she sends me no writing: I have to her divers times, and for lack of answer I wax weary: she might get a secretary, if she would, and if she will not it shall put me to less labour to answer her letters again.[41]

This could be read two ways: Katherine could herself have penned a reply, and in any case could easily have found a secretary to do it; or, though unable to write herself, she could in any case have found a scribe to do the job for her. The former is perhaps more likely, given her mother's abilities. In either case Betson's remarks reveal that he did not scorn a letter penned by an amanuensis as being anything but a letter 'by' Katherine. In summary, many women of merchant and gentry status could write a little, but not so well that it was preferable to write a whole letter themselves rather than seek a secretary's aid (indeed, it was a show of status to use a secretary). Leaving the middle and upper groups it seems unlikely that many girls of artisan or peasant families had either the opportunity or the need to learn to write, with the exception of the few girls apprenticed to scriveners.

Iconographic portrayals of women writing were becoming more widely available by the early sixteenth century with early printed primers depicting Bridget of Sweden writing the book of her revelations.[42] Though this does not provide evidence for women's actual writing practice in England it does offer an ideological counterpoint to the didactic statements circulating in the fifteenth-century English copies of *The Book of the Knight of*

3   St Anne teaching the Virgin; St Katherine; St Margaret; and St Barbara

the Tower, that writing is a skill less desirable in women than reading: 'as for writing it is no force if a woman can [knows] nought of it but as for reading I say that good and profitable it is to all women. For a woman that can read may better know the perils of the soul and her salvation.'[43] The social implications of images of St Anne teaching the Virgin to read, common in English visual media from the twelfth century (see Figure 3), have often been explored, but the fact that some such images depict the Virgin with an implement resembling a stylus or pen in her hand has attracted less attention.[44] In some such images, such as the famous example of the East Window in All Saints, North Street, York, from *c*. 1430, the Virgin is clearly following the letters on an already written page, but perhaps she is using her stylus-like implement to follow the shapes of the letters and thus to replicate them elsewhere. Other examples such as the Cassey brass of *c*.1400 in Deerhurst church, Gloucestershire, are too small to enable one to determine whether the Virgin is following letters or actually writing them, but do show her holding an object resembling a stylus to the book in her hand.[45]

Girls' and young women's training in literacy was, in sum, patchy, varied, focused (where it existed) on phonetic reading in Latin and comprehension reading in English, with a little French for daughters of the elite and sometimes orthographic training. The fragmentary nature of the evidence will frustrate some who might hope for an El Dorado of hidden riches, but the broken and contradictory nature of the evidence is in fact the point. One should neither have high expectations of reading and/or writing abilities, nor (as far as the better-off artisan groups and above are concerned) be too surprised when they appear. While most well-off women would have had some reading ability at least, degrees of literacy and illiteracy coexisted for women even of high status, and to attempt to apply a single definition of 'literate' simply invites confusion and needless debate. From highly skilled trilinguists such as Dame Eleanor Hull, to women who could only pronounce aloud the prayers and services of their primers without proper understanding, and every form of French, English and Latin literacy in between, female literacy was marked by its fundamental variety. Female status and respectability were not intrinsically bound to literacy, and a modern parallel might be with computer literacy. Even girls of high status had variable levels of literacy while widely different standards in dress, airs and manners would never have been tolerated, just as a modern middle-class Englishwoman is expected to speak within a fairly narrow range of accents but would not (yet) be socially condemned for computer illiteracy. And in a culture where books supplemented rather than replaced oral culture, it was not necessary to own books or be able to read them in order to have access to worthy or useful teachings. For the great majority of the female population, listening was the only way to have such access.

More important than personal literacy in maidens' education, because it reached a much wider social cross-section, was their participation in 'textual communities', where readers could convey the message of a text to non-readers.[46] Others have written of the circles of aristocratic, gentle and urban women who read devotional works or romances aloud together and discussed them as part of what Riddy calls a 'predominantly oral and memorialising culture', even for such elite women as Lady Margaret Beaufort and Cecily, duchess of York.[47] In Cecily's household young maidens in service were included in the textual community at suppertime, when the duchess repeated the lessons of the readings heard at dinner, and after supper when she chatted and enjoyed 'honest mirth' with her gentle-women.[48] Andrew Taylor has written of the social role of romance and chronicle accounts of battle in forming ideals of courage and 'chivalry' amongst young men in conversation, and depictions of romance heroines may equally have played a role in the construction of urban and gentle feminine identities.[49] The spoken and sung nature of most prayer and liturgy, and thus its essentially oral nature, needs to be emphasised too. Representations of female figures at prayer following the service in a book, such as the illumination depicting Margaret of York (an English princess resident in the Low Countries) and her damsels in a domestic chapel in Margaret's French collection of moral and religious treatises, fail to depict the priest or chaplain conducting the service (see Figure 4). Cecily, duchess of York, said matins every morning with her chaplain before receiving mass in her chamber, and after breakfast heard divine service and two low masses in her chapel, also conducted by her chaplain.[50] The 'Harleian Regulations', which outline in extraordinary detail the daily routine of a late-fifteenth-century aristocrat's household, describe how the lord and lady together with a number of male and female attendants heard matins and low mass in a 'closet' adjoining the great chamber, the household chaplain officiating, before taking breakfast.[51] Though private prayer was becoming more common, fostered by the production of books of hours, worship was normally a communal experience, and an oral and aural one.

For the majority of the population the parish church was the chief point of contact with textual culture, in the singing of the daily services and the recitation of sermons and saints' lives in the vernacular on Sundays and

4   Margaret of York, at prayer with her ladies

feast days. Sundays and the Lenten season were commonly devoted to vernacular instruction in the tenets of the faith, especially after the late thirteenth- and mid-fourteenth-century reforms of Peckham and Thoresby.[52] From the second half of the fourteenth century craft guilds in York, Beverley, Chester, Coventry, Newcastle and Wakefield were staging mystery or cycle plays, while miracle plays are extant from the early fourteenth century. The allegorical and didactic 'morality' plays, common from the mid-fourteenth century, also enlivened lay spiritual education, while groups and guilds connected to parish churches mounted 'folk' drama at particular festivals which sometimes took religious themes, such as the 'St George' pieces, and sometimes secular, such as the Robin Hood plays.[53] Parish drama was one means by which guilds devoted to particular saints (among whom John the Baptist, George, and the Virgin Mary were popular choices) educated themselves about their patron. The literacy of some parish men, at least, is attested by their recording of accounts and activities in the churchwarden account books, and their abilities would have helped the formation of parochial textual communities.[54] Some songs or lyrics, though preserved in student and court manuscripts, may have supplemented more orthodox forms of Christian teaching on the perils of sexual temptation for young women.[55] In the strongly oral and communal cultures of later medieval England young unmarried women formed part of wider communities and participated as listeners, and to some extent as tellers, of exemplary tales and moral doctrine, but in a culture which also allowed room for more expansive or even subversive fantasies of femininity.

Teachers

Mothers and other women were the primary teachers of girls and young women, though the roles of male clerics, family members and employers and of wider communities were also important. The oral and often feminine nature of the teaching of girls is acknowledged in the conduct texts for maidens which begin to appear in the mid-fourteenth century, and Richard Hyrd's 1529 translation of Vives advocated maternal pedagogy: 'if the mother can [knows] skill of learning, let her teach her little children her self, that they may have all one, both for their mother, their nurse, and their teacher.'[56] Caxton recognised the marketing value of the combination of aristocracy, femininity and maternity in his prefaces (read sales-pitches) for such edifying works as *The Book of the Knight of the Tower* and the rather virtuous romance of *Blanchardyn and Eglantine*. Women were the teachers of boys up to the second phase of childhood too, that is up to about seven. The femininity of early education was acknowledged in language and in metaphor, such as the common use of the term 'nurture' to refer to upbringing.[57] A version from *c.* 1415 of Walter de Bibbesworth's *Tretiz* was entitled *Femina*, because, as its author states, it teaches youths to speak French 'just as a woman teaches an infant to speak his maternal tongue'.[58] A closer link between maternal education and French literacy among the elite is present in the original and other versions of the *Tretiz*, where Walter claims to have made his text for the use of one Dionysia de Munchensy to aid her in teaching French to her children.[59]

These literary and rhetorical examples show a clear symbolic link between women and early literacy, but an entry in Queen Isabella's account book concerning expenses incurred while travelling north in 1312 demonstrates practice. Her alms and oblations accounts record her gifts to an orphan boy 'Little Thomelinus, the Scot', including bed clothes and cloth for a robe, and 'to the same, sent to London to stay with Agnes, the wife of John, the French organist, to learn his letters from her ... 40s'. She paid for his textbook too: 'For one alphabet for little Thomelinus for learning, 4*d.*'[60] Agnes may have used the alphabet to teach Thomas reading, writing, or both. It was not only little boys who received education from women.

When Sir Anthony Windsor removed Bridget Plantagenet from the care of St Mary's Abbey, Winchester, more than two centuries later, he promised her father that 'she shall lack for nothing in learning, nor otherwise that my wife can do for her'.[61] In these cases the women were appointed as surrogate mothers to the children in the important task of elementary literacy teaching, and it is one of the paradoxes of history that we are more likely to find records of such surrogacy than the surely much more frequent occurrence of mothers themselves teaching their children, as the latter normally requires no recording.

In the highest social groups a mother's duties in elementary schooling were taken by a *magistrissa*, a female servant of high birth resident in noble or royal households, who might when younger have entered the household as a *domicella*.[62] The choice of term *magistrissa* when others such as *dame* or *domicella*, *nourrice*, or 'rocker' (for cradle tenders) were available suggests that they had a teaching rather than simply supervisory role. Boys were usually placed under male tutelage at around seven, but girls remained in female hands. The careers of some royal 'mistresses' can be traced from household accounts. Around 1281 Eleanor of Castile took Edeline Popiot and her husband Philippe, both from her county of Ponthieu, into her household as damsel and valet respectively.[63] In 1285/6 Edeline was mentioned among the *domicellae*, and in the same year embroidery thread for fourteen-year-old Princess Joan was paid for by Edeline.[64] A year or two later Edeline was explicitly Joan's *magistrissa*.[65] The career path of damsel to governess could be reversed, however, as Edward II's former governess Alice de la Legrave was among Queen Isabella's *domicellae* in 1311–12.[66] Other children and young women brought up at court sometimes brought their own governesses with them, as Edward I's niece Mary of Brittany did when she joined the royal court in 1286/7, accompanied by her *magistrissa* Lady Marquesia.[67] It is likely that in aristocratic rather than royal households, where the tasks of female servants were less specialised and demarcated, women described simply as ladies, damsels or gentlewomen took on the duties of mistress or governess to the young daughters of the household. When Elizabeth Berkeley, countess of Warwick, travelled with her household from Berkeley in March 1421 to meet her husband in Essex, two of her daughters rode on horseback with their mother, while the youngest, Elizabeth, travelled in the carriage behind with the damsels, one or more of whom could have been her governess.[68]

The intellectual achievements of *magistrissae* have gone unrecorded but were unlikely to have been particularly elevated. A chronicler reveals the moral emphasis of their duties in recounting the dismissal in 1399 of Lady Mary de Coucy, governess to little Queen Isabella. King Richard asks the queen's chamberlain and his physician whether Lady de Coucy is 'good, gentle and wise enough to be guardian and mistress' of such a great lady, and they reply that she is not sufficiently prudent or *honourable* for the post. The physician elaborates with disapproval her high way of living – outstripping the queen herself in her extravagance in the numbers of horses kept, employment of goldsmiths, embroiderers, tailors and furriers, and in building a private chapel.[69] Though there were other likely reasons for Lady de Coucy's banishment (Froissart tells a very different story and locates her dismissal and the break-up of the queen's household within the wider political attempt to overthrow Richard),[70] the first narrator's account of suitable or unsuitable qualities in a governess remains revealing. Virtue, high birth, prudence, combined with suitable modesty of living relative to her mistress's, were important traits, and point to the governess's role as exemplar of conduct and character as much as or more than 'teacher' in a more restricted educational sense. Chaucer's *The Physician's Tale* is the best-known account of a governess's duty to teach girls and maidens virtue by example.[71] They would certainly be expected to perform a range of tasks with their young charges. *Magistrissa* Katherine Waterton, for example, sewed furring and lining with seven-year-old Princess Philippa in 1401, and was one of Philippa's female attendants when she travelled to Denmark to marry King Eric in 1406.[72]

Nunneries occasionally provided a feminine educational environment for girls of gentry and noble status, but doubts have been cast on the extent of such practice since Power's work of the 1920s.[73] While some daughters were placed in nunneries for booklearning, as Elizabeth and Jane Knight in the 1450s were taken in by the prioress of Cornworthy Priory in Devon 'to teche them to scole' when they were seven and ten respectively, the correspondence between Abbess Elizabeth Shelley and Lady Lisle during Bridget Plantagenet's stay at St Mary's said nothing about any studies.[74] Power makes a crucial point: most children who were sent to nunneries stayed only for short periods. She cites stays of between six and forty weeks for nine different children at Swaffham Bulbeck in 1483. Her conclusion is that 'it is much more likely that girls were sent to the nuns for elementary schooling than for the acquirement of worldly accomplish-ments',[75] but it is just as possible that the primary purpose of sending children to nunneries was to find a safe and respectable location in which aristocratic parents could stow their young children when need arose. Such was the case for Bridget Plantagenet, whose sister Elizabeth stayed in

England with her half-brother and whose stepsisters Anne and Mary were sent out to board in France when Lord and Lady Lisle relocated to Calais on royal business in 1533. When Margaret, duchess of Clarence, travelled to Normandy in November 1419 with her household to join her husband there, she kept her sons with her but left her daughters Joan and Margaret in the charge of the prioress at Dartford.[76] As the children sent to convents were usually young (under fourteen for girls and under nine or ten for boys), they were not yet of an appropriate age for boarding in other or greater noble households. Nunneries supplied a service for busy gentry and aristocracy which better bears the label 'child care', in which some education in prayers, reading and needlework might take place, than the distracting term 'school'. Despite such limitations, within the broad definition of 'education' as upbringing, nunneries could certainly function as highly appropriate venues for imbuing young girls of elite groups with the valued feminine qualities of piety, modesty and chastity, even during short stays.

In urban households, mistresses and female employers played a central part in the upbringing of young women working within the household. Female apprentices were usually indentured to train under a female artisan, usually in textile industries (though the male householder might also be named in the contract), and Riddy has argued conduct texts such as *The Good Wife Taught Her Daughter* were probably used in the fifteenth century by women with young female servants in their employ.[77] Older sisters could take part in this culture too, and endorse it, as York singlewoman Katherine Stevenson did in her will of 1459, promising the residue of her estate to her mother for the use of her sister Elena, on the condition that Elena 'submit and conduct herself to the good rule and direction of her said mother in future'.[78] It is much more difficult to establish whether mothers or other women held exceptional importance in the upbringing of girls in village society, because of the lack of appropriate sources. The role of community through groups such as members of the parish is noticeable, but it is difficult to see whether women had a particularly significant role for girls.

Indeed, though women were often the primary educators of girls and maidens, wider communities at all social levels – such as the household, the kin group, the status group, the neighbourhood, the parish and the village – were involved in their upbringing and therefore men too played a role. Fathers, brothers, priests and chaplains, employers, masters, and male members of parish and village society all had profound influences on the upbringing of girls. Even when mothers and women had a more direct role, girls were trained in cultures and models of femininity which were undeniably patriarchal. Men held influence both through individual positions of authority in their dealings with girls, and, very importantly, as producers of most of the texts young women read or had read to them. Both maidens and older women were complicit and active in producing and reinforcing patriarchal society. However, the literatures of entertainment such as romances, and even some religious literatures, offered some space for playing with gender. The boundaries of femininity in fantasy were wider than the model of active docility which conservative discourses and practices so strongly emphasised, and are illustrated through the wide-ranging messages on femininity which circulated through later medieval English culture.

Messages

Although messages on femininity varied from village to castle, hovel to townhouse, and the media and means of teaching differed also, the teachings of the Church had at least the potential to reach all women and possessed many compelling exempla of womanhood among its holiest saints. St Anne offered a model of diligent and loving motherhood for maidens to aspire to in their married futures, while the virgin martyrs displayed the strong-minded chastity which young women were exhorted to emulate while still maidens. But the Virgin Mary offered the most universally available model of femininity to women. Though she was revered by all Christians, male and female, because she was often visually depicted in maidenly form (at the annunciation, obviously, but also in motherhood and even at death, assumption and coronation) she provided an image with which maidens could identify. That many maidens' guilds had a particular devotion to the Virgin will be seen in Chapter 5.

The cult of the Virgin was important enough to shape the structures of time in the daily and yearly cycles of Christian devotion. A devout laywoman following the Hours of the Virgin in her own primer might begin her day with matins and an account of the Virgin's miraculous conception and birth, her dedication to the temple, and annunciation. Through the services of the day, which follow the life and passion of Christ, the narrative returns frequently to the Virgin until at compline the day closes with the great finale of the Virgin's death, assumption and coronation.[79] The Virgin's life also helped shape the Church year, with the celebration of Mary's immaculate conception during Advent on 8 December, and her assumption marking the year's winding-down on 15 August, the cycle beginning its renewal with the feast of Mary's nativity on 8 September (and other Marian feasts were distributed through the calendar).[80] The very timetable and calendar of worship emphasised the centrality of the Virgin in Christian life. And although as the chosen mother of God and most exalted of saints she possessed a level of virtue and grace which no mortal could aspire to, and as both virgin *and* mother she was literally inimitable, still she was held up as a model for lay imitation. While some preachers used her as an example for all the faithful to follow, both male and female, she held particular exemplary qualities for young women. One sermon that emphasises her model role for all Christians provides a descriptive passage that reads like contemporary conduct literature on the properly demure, chaste, pleasant and humble manner desirable in young women:

> This going of this maid was measured, without dissolution, her eyes declaring all chastity, her face full of delights and amiable to angels. The words that she spoke were full sweet and full easy, ever sounding to the thanking of God. We read in her life that when she was praised of anybody for any privilege other [or] virtue that God had given unto her, she with a lowly heart and a meek countenance answered, 'Deo gracias – loving [praise] be to God thereof'.[81]

In his book for his daughters the Knight of the Tower describes some of Mary's imitable qualities: her engagement in prayers and devotions at the time of her annunciation; her fear and caution when approached by a strange man (the archangel Gabriel); her humility when told of her selection as the mother of God; her kindness and courtesy towards her cousin Elizabeth during the latter's confinement; her pity and sympathy at the plight of the wineless Galileans at their wedding; her patience in the face of the suffering brought on by the tribulations of her son; and her charity, which inspired saints Elizabeth, Lucy, Cecily and others to acts of charity.[82] His discussion shows how readily contemporaries could find mundane and worldly parallels to the conduct of this most eminent saint.

In some villages and towns, in addition to hearing of Mary's meekness and mildness and her intercessory role through sermons and vernacular prayers, young female parishioners watched dramatic presentations of her life in parish and cycle plays. The mid-fifteenth-century 'Mary Play' of the 'N-Town' manuscript (which was probably not part of a cycle but written and performed by an East Anglian religious guild) depicted the life of the Virgin from her immaculate conception to the visitation.[83] The players spoke of Mary as the 'mother of mercy' (lines 9, 261), emphasised her humility and incredulity that as a 'simple' girl she could be 'God's wife' (lines 287–94), her busyness in 'holy occupacion' rather than 'things vein' during her youth (lines 579–80), her character as a child 'so gracious' and 'so mild' that she was a model of children's behaviour towards their parents everywhere (lines 341–2), and at her betrothal her mother's advice to her to in marriage 'Be low and buxom, meek and mild,/ Sad and sober and nothing wild' (lines 966–7). Once married she occupies herself in Joseph's absence with reading her psalter, a 'holy labour' she highly recommends (lines 1002–29). Parish maidens may have been not only spectators at this feast, but players too, given their active roles in many religious guilds (see Chapter 5). Goldberg has recently challenged the assumption that male actors monopolised the parts in mystery plays before the late fifteenth century, given women's occupational participation in relevant craft guilds, and young women's common involvement in religious guilds may have meant that the young Virgin was played by a local maiden rather than some beardless youth.[84]

Mary's meekness, mildness and intercessory qualities are so ubiquitous in vernacular as well as Latin texts that enumeration of examples seems pointless.[85] A firmer aspect to her character is, however, evident in some of the York cycle plays. While in youth and before maternity she fits the usual meek mould, after the birth of Jesus she begins to display a more forthright character, disputing with Joseph over the wisdom of their flight into Egypt and again when their twelve-year-old son is missing. In the latter instance Mary takes the lead upon finding Jesus in the temple, approaching the scholars with whom her son has been conversing, while Joseph hangs back, unsure. In her role as mother Mary is permitted greater authority than as a maiden or childless wife, suggesting that different forms of womanhood were modelled for the varieties of women in the audience. Throughout the plays, though, the worthiness of her character is contrasted with the unbuxomness of such women as Eve and Noah's wife, and the proud and lascivious wife of Pilate (the latter two apparently played for laughs, but disapprovingly nonetheless).[86]

As a final point on the Virgin, although up to the mid-fifteenth century at least the prayers which made up the Hours of the Virgin or were used in devotions more generally may have been in Latin, that does not mean that the Latin illiterate would have no comprehension of them at all. For one thing, these teachings from sermons, works on conduct and drama gave audiences a general understanding of the character and chief roles of the Virgin, and they would therefore have had a reasonable sense of what their Latin recitations of exaltation or petition of the Virgin meant. For another, priests and chaplains may well have offered a verbal gloss on the prayers, in the way that fifteenth-century works aimed at lay audiences began to do in written form.[87] And finally, English speakers would almost certainly have been able to comprehend something of the Latin words as they heard them or read them aloud, though they could not have provided anything approaching a full translation. Reading or hearing one of the most important prayers to the Virgin – 'Obsecro te, Domina Sancta Maria, mater Dei, pietate plenissima, summi Regis filia, mater gloriosissima, mater orphanorum, consolatio desolatorum, via errantium, salus et spes in te sperantium. Virgo ante partum, virgo in partu et virgo post partum, fons misericordie, fons salutis et gratie' – a young layperson may have only been able to guess at one word in three or four, but would have been left with a sense that the figure she was praying to was above all else representative of kindness, maternity, consolation, virginity and grace.

Offering maidens an altogether fiercer model of femininity were the tremendously popular virgin martyrs. These saints provided a more immediate role model to young women as their peers in age who, unlike the Virgin Mary, died during maidenhood and so did not exemplify adult womanhood. This did not keep them from high popularity among adult women, as is apparent especially in the commissioning of virgin-martyr *vitae* by high-status wives in the fifteenth century,[88] but their suitability as tales for maidens in particular was expressed by both the Knight of the Tower and Christine de Pisan in her *Cité des dames*.[89] It is possible that young female readers and listeners were attracted to the defiance and determination of these figures, and this may help to explain their prominence in the devotion of contemporary laywomen especially, but they were tolerated and promoted by such conservative or semi-conservative figures as the Knight of the Tower and Christine de Pisan because their defiance was entirely directed at those who would challenge their adherence to the Christian faith and their carefully guarded virginity. In a culture where young womanhood was perceived as a time of sexual tension and potential danger, when maidens would need to do battle against the lures of men who would spoil their incorruption and against temptation within themselves, the resistance modelled by virgin martyrs could hardly have been more appropriate for young women.[90] It is notable that forms of resistance beyond protection of their faith or their virginity are not a feature of the *vitae*. The virgins defy their parents and other figures of authority only when those groups threaten their religion or sexual purity. Chaucer noticed and exaggerated this uneasy combination of defiant will to preserve virginity and proper acquiescence to parental authority when he turned Livy's tale of Virginia into a virgin martyr legend in *The Physician's Tale*, in which the virgin's father takes it upon himself to smite off the head of his daughter to preserve her from lechery, 'for love, and nat for hate' (line 225). The girl sadly yields to her father's will with tears but no protest.[91] Chaucer altered the genre of the tale from a parable of bad government to a virgin martyr's tale probably in response to the latter's popularity in his own day, and taking the opportunity to draw attention to the genre's extreme violence. The response of the Host (lines 287–302) seems designed to enhance the audience's sense of disgust.

Through tinkering with the virgin-martyr theme Chaucer produces a tale that is technically unfaithful to the genre in erasing the virgin's defiance, yet at the same time draws attention to a deeper message of the *vitae* – that resistance in young women is appropriate only where their most precious virtues are besieged. Virgin martyr's lives, in the end, are complex entities, conservative enough to win the approval of moralising writers and to ensure a place among the sermons preached over the Church year, yet containing a theme of resistance which may have conveyed more to some readers than just protection of conventionally approved virtues of chastity and steadfast faith.[92] The latter is an attractive conclusion to modern readers, though not ultimately provable.

Apart from the virgins' *vitae*, the messages most obviously relevant to maidens conveyed in sermons and religious works were homiletic narratives such as the rape of Dinah, and lessons on the dangers of pride and lechery, singing and dancing. Though scepticism exists about the extent to which surviving texts represent exactly what laypeople read or heard, some themes concerning women recur so frequently that they must have had wide currency within lay spiritual edification.[93] The precariousness of maidens' and women's grasp on their own chastity is a constant refrain. Usually, unlike in more openly misogynist literature where women's lecherous desires overwhelm themselves and their male victims, the threats are external:

as Dinah, Jacob's daughter, that walked out of her inn to see women of the country that she woned [lived] in, and was ravished and enforced and lost her maidenhood. Nice [foolish] maidenhood is likened to Jephthah's daughter, that walked about in the mountains two months for to weep her maidenhood. So do nice maidens that walk about in meads and in fair places leading dances and singing, as it were showing themselves to lose their maidenhood, and making sorrow that they have been so long maidens. For it befalls to maidens to be in stillness and enclosed, as our Lady Saint Mary was when the angel came to her and found her in a privy chamber and not standing nor walking by streets.[94]

If girls go about the streets and fields, dancing and singing, and are ravished by the men they meet, they have only themselves to blame. Songs and dances are hazardous because they open up the heart to lechery, making external dangers internal.[95] The most often-voiced fear, though, relates to maidens' and ladies' interest in fashionable dress. This features heavily in pastoral manuals under discussions of pride and lechery, such as *Jacob's Well*'s account of a fine countess who found herself in hell despite a lifetime of good works and prayer, for her pride in the array of her head and body, her trains and the broad horns of her headdresses, and Robert Mannyng's tale of a lord's wife who in life was so proud of the arrangement of her hair and headgear that she was condemned to be endlessly burnt to ash on a wheel.[96] Discussions of lechery in particular denounce women's care for clothing, as fine attire tempts men to sin and thus damns two souls in one act:

> To behold these ladies and these maidens and damsels arrayed and apparelled, that often sithe [time] apparel them more quaintly and gaily for to make nice [foolish] lookers to look on them, and wene [think] not to do great sin ... But certainly they sin well grievously, for they make and be the cause of loss of many souls, and where-through many men are dead and fall into great sin; for men say in old proverbs, 'Ladies of rich and gay apparel are arrow-blast of [against] the tower'. For she has no member on her body that is not a grin [snare] of the devil, as Solomon says, wherefore they must yield accounts at the day of doom of all the souls that by reason of them are damned.[97]

The modern judge's attitude that if an attractively dressed woman is raped it is her own fault turns out to have an ancient lineage. The Knight of the Tower manages to combine condemnation of feminine interest in clothing with the theme of the wandering woman who deserves her own rape in his version of the tale of Dinah, saying she left her father's house out of a desire to see 'the attire or array of the women of another land'.[98] Young women received decidedly mixed messages on the matters of beauty, appearance and dress, however, as those of high status were expected to dress finely in accordance with their social position, and visual representations of the Virgin Mary and virgin martyrs emphasised their conventional beauty and, in the case of the martyrs especially, their rich and fashionable garments.[99]

Maidens of non-elite status would have had at least some access to these messages on desirable femininity through sermons and confession, if in probably attenuated form, but girls who entered apprenticeships were confronted with aspects of the ideal more directly in the agreements drawn up between themselves and their new mistress and master. Extant male and female indentures are almost identical in their listings of the duties of both apprentice and master or mistress for the term of apprenticeship, but differ on the regulation of the apprentice's sexual conduct. William of Lincoln was bound in York in 1364 to commit neither adultery nor fornication within the house of his master, nor in any way with the daughter, wife or maidservant, and Nicholas of Kyghlay was enjoined in 1371 to refrain from adultery or fornication with his master's wife and daughter, and both were forbidden to visit brothels.[100] But in London Margaret Bishop (1378), Katherine Nougle (1392) and Elizabeth Eland (1454) were ordered not to commit fornication either within the house of their masters *or outside*, and Eleanor Fincham (1447) was bound not to commit fornication 'in any way at all'.[101] The difference between male and female directions seems all the more significant when two prototype indentures included in a fifteenth-century formulary book are taken into account, where both the boy's and girl's model indentures contain the same clause, ordering that they should not engage in fornication either in the house of their master *or* outside.[102] Control over boys' behaviour was looser in practice than theory.

The question of class or status differences in the messages on young womanhood offered to maidens deserves our closer attention. This can be achieved through comparing conduct literature aimed at higher-status girls with those aimed at slightly lower orders, and literary genres depicting girls of different groups.[103] It will become clear that girls were not all expected to aspire to the same forms of femininity.

Varieties of conduct

Conduct literature on the whole seems to have been aimed at audiences ranging from gentry and merchant groups to respectable artisan households, thus excluding the very high- and very low-status groups.[104] The term 'courtesy literature' is sometimes used for the books which will be discussed here, but that term is better reserved for the numerous books aimed at teaching boys etiquette and manners while in service in great households. Aspirant members of middling and moderately elite social groups formed the genre's target audience, while members of the higher nobility had less need for such books. They learned 'good' behaviour at home or in other great houses, as John of Gaunt's daughter Elizabeth Lancaster did in 1387 when she entered the royal court 'to study the behaviour and customs of courtly society', and Anne and Mary Bassett did when sent to aristocratic households in France to be finished in the ways of high society.[105] Better-off artisan households similarly aspired to improve the conduct of their inhabitants, especially by the fifteenth century.

William Caxton astutely recognised the new market for direction on conduct among the mercantile and gentry groups when in 1484 he selected for translation a late fourteenth-century French nobleman's book written purportedly for his daughters (see Figure 5).[106] *The Book of the Knight of the Tower*, mentioned several times already in this chapter, was written by Geoffrey de la Tour Landry in 1371–2, and though first translated into English in a unique manuscript from the time of Henry VI seems to have had its greatest impact outside France in the late fifteenth and early sixteenth centuries.[107] The work has much in common with the kinds of homiletic and moralising literature already discussed, and the Knight plundered the pre-1300 Franciscan work *Miroir des bonnes femmes* for his stories. To this clerical tone he added courtly elements appropriate to his own background, such as the lengthy debate over the relative virtues and dangers of young women taking paramours.[108] Clerical and courtly discourses thus converge in the work to make an attractive package for an aspiring but morally conservative mercantile and gentry audience. The Knight uses clerical models of behaviour, but for secular ends. Many of his moral tales deal with women going to court, singing, dancing, feasting and playing at dice with men, or living with their husbands. Many deal with reputation and honour, and only some are concerned with one's eternal

5   The Knight of the Tower instructs his daughters

soul. The book represents an intersection of clerical and noble ideals of feminine character and conduct, but its relative obscurity until the late fifteenth century and subsequent appearance in print indicates that its greatest appeal was for a socially aspiring lay book-buying public. It is not known whether or not maidens actually read or heard the book, though daughters of Caxton's customers would mostly have had the ability, and John Fitzherbert, in his *Book of Husbandry* of 1534, certainly thought that women were included in its audience, when he condemned the author who by the book 'made both the man and woman to know more wickedness, subtlety, and craft, than ever they should have known, had the book been obscured'.[109] Conservative though the book is, it was too explicit in parts for a sixteenth-century audience which was warming to the stricter messages of Vives and others.[110]

Despite this, the book's messages on femininity are on the whole as conservative and unsurprising as its origins. Say your prayers. Be courteous and speak graciously to everyone you meet. Pay little attention to fashion, and care little for clothes (but dress as befits your position, and dress appropriately on holy days). Beware of the dangers of gluttony and drunkenness. Do not be alone in the company of men, nor go wandering about the countryside. Be obedient to your husband. Keep a still and calm posture, and be modest of speech. Do not be argumentative. Be charitable and merciful. And although (as is clear from Fitzherbert's concerns) there is a great deal of material which focuses on sexual matters, explicitness does not imply approval.

Some of the narratives are indeed sexually frank, such as the tale of the man and the woman who made love in a church 'joined together as a dog is to a bitch', and were stuck fast and on view to all who came through the church for a day.[111] This bluntness and crude humour suggests that noble and mercantile parents of the fifteenth century did not expect their well-bred daughters to be ignorant of sex, even though the book's models of feminine conduct are sexually conservative. The Knight condemns young women's use of flirtation or feminine wiles in order to charm men and win a husband, offering a tale he claims is drawn from his own life. He went to visit a lady whom he thought to marry, and engaged her in a courtly game of conversation and lewd *double entendre*. 'I said to her, damsel I would well and had liefer [rather] be your prisoner than any others, and I think that your prison should not be so hard nor cruel as is the prison of English men.' She replied in kind, and the conversation went on in this way for some time, but when they parted he resolved he would not marry her because of 'the over great malpertness and the light manner that me seemed to see in her'. And he thanked God for his decision, for within a year and a half she fell prey to scandal 'and soon after she died'.[112] The Knight's hypocrisy results from the collision of two discourses: the clerical, which emphasises seriousness and moral virtue, steadiness and humility, and the courtly, which approves of lightheartedness, wit, flirtatiousness, and playfulness.[113] It is significant that courtly discourse is associated with moral blame. Its real danger, though that is not stated outright here, is that it opens up a space for the female subject: it gives her a voice, it offers her (through 'feminine wiles') a method by which she can claim some control over her interaction with men.

Women's use of speech is central to the Knight's rejection of the maiden, and indeed to any conservative account of femininity. Several of his exemplary tales deal with the trouble befalling women who are not 'of little speech', such as the daughter of the king of Denmark, rejected by the English king because she spoke very much, often without understanding what was said to her, while her younger sister was approved because though not beautiful she 'spoke but little, and that was well demurely'. A daughter of the king of Aragon succeeded in winning the heart of the king of Spain where her sister lost, because she was meek and humble and non-argumentative in speech. Another quarrelsome maiden lost her reputation, when she argued with a cheating knight over dice and in revenge he spread rumours that she was in the habit of entering men's chambers at night, and kissing and embracing them 'without candle'.[114]

An eligible young woman, in the Knight's book, is seen and little heard. She is one who will not question the authority of her husband, particularly before others. 'It is but honour to a good woman to suffer and hold her in peace and leave the haultain [high] language to her husband and lord. And also it is in the contrary to a woman great shame and villainy to strive against her husband be it wrong or right, and in especial before the people.'[115] Public forms of speech were barred to women because they were not culturally characterized as feminine, while others were barred because as feminine registers they were a source of danger – gossip, jangling, chatter and boasting. The denial of women's access to public forms of speech is a major feminist issue for Cora Kaplan:

> In western societies (and in other cultures as well) public speech is a
> male privilege and women's speech [is] restricted by custom in mixed
> sex gatherings, or if permitted, still characterized by its private nature,
> an extension of the trivial domestic discourse of women ... the refusal of
> access to public language is one of the major forms of the oppression of
> women within a social class as well as in trans-class situations.[116]

To Deborah Cameron the exclusion of women from public discourse is a form of imposed 'silence', which keeps women from prestigious linguistic modes and restricts them to 'silent' or 'unimportant' forms such as gossip, storytelling, private correspondence and diaries.[117] Repression of language use goes beyond speech and is relevant to wider questions concerning women's education. The Knight of the Tower sees himself as a relative liberal in advocating that daughters learn to read so they can learn about worthy women yet he sees no value in their learning to write, while a few decades later Vives (through Hyrd's English translation) assumes young noblewomen will be taught to write but recommends their textual models be scriptures or the sayings of philosophers rather than 'void verses' and 'wanton or trifling songs'.[118] The Knight's conduct book, in both its aristocratic and its clerical aspects, attempts to shape noble maidens' identities within strictly defined boundaries, and encourages maidens to adopt ready-made femininities. But other types of reading material popular among daughters of the wealthy allowed for imagining of rather different femininities.

Romance literature, widely popular among late medieval Englishwomen of well-off social background, presents a model of femininity which differs in significant ways from that offered in clerical and conduct literature. The genre's fashionable status is apparent, with tales of *Guy of Warwick*, *Sir Degrevant*, *Merlin*, *Generydes* and Arthurian romances prominent among the books mentioned in women's wills or containing women's signatures, and versions of *Tristan* and *Lancelot* were especially favoured.[119] While parents and other figures of authority may have hoped their daughters would listen to the homilies of *Book of the Knight*, women (as well as men) seem actively to have revelled in the adventures of romance, much to the concern of Vives and Hyrd who reviled such 'ungracious books' as *Amadace*, *Tristan*, *Lancelot du Lac*, *Floris and Blancheflour*, *Parthenope*, *Generides*, *Guy*, *Bevis* and others – 'a woman should beware of all these books, likewise as of serpents or snakes' – and believed that it was better for her not to read at all.[120] Little wonder that maidens and women were tempted by such forbidden fruit, and besides it was only with the rise of such arch-conservatives in the sixteenth century that romance received strong condemnation.

The version of femininity presented in romance literature may be said to be purely fantastic, and neither derived from observation of 'real life' nor meant to have any impact on the ideals of its readers.[121] Where a didactic text like *The Book of the Knight* is a utopian narrative of femininity aimed at emulation in real life, romances present characters who were not necessarily read as exemplary in a literal sense, but who offered fantasies of social mobility, character and relationships between men and women which need never find absolute parallels in real life. Others have explored the genre's possibilities for modelling behaviour, though not suggesting anything as simplistic as a reflection of conduct, and a combination of these approaches is pursued here.[122] Romances evoked an idealised feudal past which bore little resemblance to contemporary social reality by the fifteenth century, and their appeal perhaps lay partly in their relatively expansive models of gender.[123]

In the romance *Guy of Warwick*, for example, the heroine Felice le Bel combines conventional femininity with talents that seem purely fantastic.[124] Her beauty is described in strictly conventional terms (white skin, long tresses, curved eyebrows, a well-shaped nose and mouth that invited kisses, grey eyes, a white neck and a shapely body) and her character is said to be 'gentle' (that is, well-bred) and 'demure', 'courteous' and 'free' (lines 65–79). However, she is also highly learned in the seven liberal arts, having been taught by scholars from Toulouse (lines 80–92). The ideals of beauty and character were certainly utopian, but they were not entirely impossible for individual women. But an education in the seven liberal arts, taught by university scholars from foreign lands, was infinitely beyond their reach. There is, though, the possibility that this fantasy had some connection with day-to-day notions of feminine roles and capabilities. Where conservative discourses fear and repudiate women's active participation in speaking authoritatively or writing, *Guy of Warwick* allows a female character into the active, privileged and powerful position of learnedness. This may not be purely fantastical but an exaggerated version of the authority which women had some access to. Not only were young women not all as meek and mild and quiet as didactic texts would like them to be, but authority in women was a quality that could be considered attractive, even an element of eligibility. Felice in the romance is visited by earls and dukes from across the world who sought to marry her, but she would have none (lines 95–8).

Felice also possesses a degree of power and authority over her aspiring lover, Guy, which is entirely conventional within courtly literature, and also seen in the romances *Ipomedon* and *The Squire of Low Degree*.[125] He adores her, and begs her to marry him, but she will not have him until he has proved himself in deeds of valour. Guy eventually wins her heart through his prowess, but it is she who has set the terms. It is for the man to beseech the woman, not the woman to beseech the man, she tells her maid when the latter takes pity upon Guy (lines 617–26). Debate over the representation of women in courtly narratives has swung from a literalist reading which saw the worship of the *domina* as representing a move towards a better social position for women, to feminist readings which argued that the woman on a pedestal is not empowered by her worship, because she remains little more than an object of men's desire.[126] Perhaps a more interesting reading is not to view such female characters as literally representative of 'women's position' in either a positive or negative way, but to see that through articulation of the possibility of such power romances offer a space in which women can be imagined by medieval readers as agents of authority.

Women's sexuality also receives substantially different treatment in romances from didactic literature. Rymenhild of *King Horn* is driven wild with desire for the hero, and Josian of *Bevis of Hampton* seeks out Bevis in his bed, and expresses desire for his bare body.[127] It may be significant that two of the most popular books among women readers, judging by testamentary evidence, were *Lancelot* and *Tristan*, whose heroines were passionate adulterers. Yet such passion does not go unpunished, leading to separation, exile, warfare, social decline and premature death. At the end of the fifteenth century Robert Henryson resurrected Chaucer's passionate Cresseid and infected her with leprosy, to make her pay for changing 'in filth all [her] femininity'.[128] And in the English courtship romances, as opposed to the French-derived adultery romances, women's passion and agency is ultimately channelled into the marriages which conclude the narratives.

The punishment of female characters or their containment in marriage should warn us against too simplistic a reading of romances, or too optimistic view of the role of female audiences in the construction of the text. The multiple messages of the genre are playfully encapsulated in a series of *bas de page* illustrations in the Taymouth Hours of *c.* 1330–40.[129] This book of hours contains, in addition to numerous illustrations dealing with biblical or hagiographic themes, a number of purely secular visual sequences. In addition to a remarkable series depicting women hunting, the book is noted for its scenes derived from *Guy of Warwick* and *Bevis of Hampton*. Perhaps most intriguing, though, is a series of images possibly derived from a lost tale, which to an extent confound some of the conventions of the romance genre.[130] It opens with a young lady and her damsels walking into a wood for their pleasure, when the lady is seized by a 'wodewose' or wild man, who attempts to ravish her. An 'old knight', Eneas, arrives upon the scene and rescues the damsel, only to be confronted by a 'young knight', who challenges him for the damsel. The old knight gives the damsel the choice between them and she chooses the young knight, but it is only when the young knight also challenges Eneas for his hound and the dog chooses to remain with his master, that a full conflict blows up. The young knight, angered, fights the old knight for the damsel and the dog, and is killed for his troubles. The tale ends with the damsel kneeling before the old knight, asking his forgiveness, but Eneas strides away with his hound, leaving her for her 'unnaturalness' (see Figures 6–8). The woman owner of this beautiful book, for it was almost certainly a woman, may have been amused by this variation on traditional themes, but may also have seen in it a wry reminder of the limitations of romance. The space which romance literature opens up for learnedness, authority and sexual agency within ideals of femininity is significant, and may be partly attributable to the role of women as readers, but should not be exaggerated. Despite the genre's capacity, in Susan Crane's words, to represent gender as 'unstable, open to question, and in danger of collapse', it closes off the possibilities which it has opened up by in the end reinforcing a conservative model of gender roles and characteristics. This tendency, always present in the genre, became stronger in the late fifteenth century, when a mood of gender conservatism (and possibly the greater influence of a mercantile audience) produced such virtuous and moralising romances as *Blanchardyn and Eglantine*, which Caxton published five years after his *Book of the Knight*.[131]

The social status of maidens reading *The Book of the Knight of the Tower* and Middle English romances was only a step up from that of the girls who left their provincial homes to take up apprenticeships with the famous silkwomen of London, and indeed the groups probably overlapped to a degree. Though they were entering an artisan world, their backgrounds were often respectable middle or upper-middle status, and the silkwomen were keen to emphasise the gentility of their milieu.[132] Katherine Nougle's brother John was a London haberdasher, while Eleanor Fincham's father Simon was described as a 'gentleman' of the county of Norfolk in her 1447 indenture and Elizabeth Eland's father John in 1454 was described as 'esquire' of Lincolnshire. For men of merchant and lower gentry standing to place their sisters and daughters in urban households, they must have been reassured that the girls would there be sheltered and learn virtue as well as a sound occupation. Such agreements, though, set the moral standards fairly low compared with the strictures laid down by the Knight of the Tower, and indicate that even if the background of apprenticed girls may not have been vastly different from that of Caxton's audience, the aspirations (or pretensions) of their guardians were miles apart. Girls from

6-8   The damsel refuses the old knight and takes off with the young one; the
two knights fight and the old knight kills the young; the old knight goes away
with his greyhound and leaves the damsel alone for her 'unnaturalness'

a range of rural and urban backgrounds left home in their early teens to go into service, often in households little better off than those they had left, but it seems they too were trained in conduct as well as in working life.

Three conduct texts for urban girls survive, and demonstrate the ways that notions of proper womanhood in working urban groups differ from those in aspirant or established groups. As with *The Book of the Knight of the Tower*, however, *The Good Wife Taught Her Daughter*, *The Good Wyfe Wold a Pylgremage* and *The Thewis off Gudwomen* should not be taken at face value as representative of social practice, but as attempts at engineering gender. Tauno F. Mustanoja notes that *The Good Wife Taught Her Daughter* (the earliest manuscript of which dates to before 1350) was, judging by the content, probably written by a man and probably a cleric, while Riddy goes further, basing her analysis on an examination of the manuscript contexts of the extant copies, and notes that two of the copies (including the earliest) are found in manuscripts which 'are at the interface between clerical and lay cultures', one a friar's handbook, and the others in household books.[133] The ostensible audience is composed of urban young women of middling rank, yet evidently male clerics and perhaps both male and female heads of households found it valuable. The evidence for the authorship and audience of *Pilgrimage*, dated to the second half of the fifteenth century, is more difficult to discern as there is no internal evidence and the poem survives in one manuscript only, which is of mixed contents, but its context probably did not differ too much from that of *Good Wife*, while *Thewis* is addressed to parents, especially fathers, and speaks of daughters in the third person, and was probably influenced by sermon literature.[134]

The conservative, clerical, masculine production of these poems gives these texts much in common with *The Book of the Knight*. Following standard exhortations to piety, the texts enumerate ideals of behaviour which differ little in type but somewhat in scene from the Knight's text, that is, the context shifts from noble houses, castles and courtly settings to the streets, taverns and family houses of the town. Women should not go to mystery plays without honest company, says the author of *Documenta*, where the Knight exhorts his daughters to keep friends and servants by them at feasts and dances.[135] Do not wear extravagant clothing, say the authors of all the texts,[136] and keep a steady countenance rather than looking around from side to side when in company or public.[137] Be modest, quiet and little of tongue, and do not argue or scold.[138] In particular, be meek and obedient with your husband, and play the peacemaker by calming his anger: 'Meekly him answer and not too attirling [venomously] / And so you may slake his mood and be his darling / Fair words wrath slakes.'[139] Be sweet and agreeable of manner.[140] Keep respectable company, and do not wander around in public.[141] These general rules of feminine conduct seem to span the social groups, though there are some differences of detail.

But there are more than small differences between the urban conduct books and *The Book of the Knight*. In three key areas the conservative authors of the four texts seek to define social differences and reinforce the notion of the superiority of the nobility, in order to keep bourgeois elements well defined and entrenched in their social position. The first pertains to concerns over dress. *Good Wife*, *Pilgrimage* and *Thewis* all exhort young women to be modest in dress and bearing, lest they get above, or fall below, their estate. 'With feigning fair not make over-much, / Not nice, proud nor over-delicate, / Nor counterfeit not over-high estate'; 'With rich robes and garlands and with rich things, / Counterfeit no lady as [if] thy husband were a king'; 'Show not thyself too proud, passing thine estate, / to make men look after thee and ask, "Who is that?" / A gentle-woman, or a harlot, men will deem thou art.'[142] Riddy discusses the occurrence of this idea in *Good Wife*, and reads it as a warning to young girls in towns to keep to their place within the bourgeois group, while at the same time helping the bourgeoisie to define themselves in a particular way.[143]

These thoughts on dress and status contrast with the Knight's anxieties about finery and vanity, which display a more religious than social gloss. In the Knight's text, extravagance in clothing is castigated as sinful, when the money spent there could be given to the poor instead.[144] Attention to fashion, moreover, may lead to the deadly sins of pride and lechery, and the Knight singles out such late fourteenth-century fashions as horned headdresses (like 'snails') and plucked eyebrows for particular opprobrium, echoing clerical writers.[145]

The second key difference is within the elements of respectability as defined for 'noble' and bourgeois maidens. Hard work and riches hold the key to happiness, the good wife tells her daughter: 'Go thou not to wrestling, nor shooting at cock, / As it were a strumpet or a gigelot. / Wone [remain] at home, daughter, and keep thine own wike [abode], / And so thou shalt, my lief [dear] child, soon wax rich.'[146] According to the author of *Thewis* a good woman is 'ever doing good in her house', does not play on work days, and does not lie long in bed in the morning, 'For mickle ill comes of idleness'.[147] Such sentiments, if found in a seventeenth-century text, would probably be labelled the 'Protestant work ethic' but are better seen as an aspect of Riddy's 'bourgeois ethos'. In contrast, the Knight's greater emphasis on devotional activities and on a religious sensibility guiding all actions implies a maidenly respectability tied firmly to the demands of piety. Work and prayer – these activities mark important differences in the ideals of femininity prescribed for bourgeois and gentle maidens.

The third difference is the idea, implicit yet present, that an awareness of interiority and a capacity for self-control are definitive of nobility and thus, when seen in women, are more indicative of the rank to which she (or her family) aspires than her gender. The theme of women's inconstancy is so pervasive throughout a wide range of discourses – from scientific to clerical to literary to legal genres – it is tempting to view it as a dominant discourse on femininity, and it found its way into the bourgeois conduct texts. The author of *Thewis*, announcing his reasons for writing the poem, says 'women's honour is tender and slyddir [frail], / and rather breaks by mickle thing / as fairest rose takes soonest fading'.[148] In the *Good Wife* women's inconstancy takes on a specifically sexual character, as it does in many other contexts, and the Good Wife counsels her daughter to have her own daughters married well and quickly, to keep them from temptation: 'Maidens be fair and amiable / but of their love full unstable, / My lief child.'[149] Yet the possibility for self-control through strength of will emerges much more clearly when the Knight writes about the virtues of chastity, taking as his model the virgin martyrs:

> as it is contained in their legends as of Saint Katherine, Saint Margaret, of Saint Christine, the eleven thousand virgins and of many others of which the great constance and fervent courage of them were too long to be recounted.... For many great and evil temptations shall befight and assail you. Be ye then strong and valiant to resist and overcome them and look and behold the place whereout ye be come of and what dishonour and shame might come to you thereof.[150]

Their strength of will is enabled primarily by social background ('the place whereout ye be come of'). In remembering their social and familial status his daughters could find the means to resist temptation. Control of the self, according to this aristocrat, was a quality to be found only within members of his own class.

In contrast, the chastity of lower-status girls was seen as the result not of self-*restraint* but of *constraint*. Not autonomously capable of resisting temptation, those maidens had simply to steer clear of it: 'Acquaint not with ilk a man thou meet in the street; / though he give him to thee, shortly you him greet. / Let him go by the way, by him thou not stand, / that he through no villainy thine heart nothing change.'[151] 'Sit not with no man alone, for oft in trust is treason. / Though thou think nothing amiss, yet fair words be gayssoun [deceitful].'[152] '[Do not let girls go to] clerk-plays nor pilgrimage / But there be with them wise folk of age.'[153]

Where the Knight gives young women credit for having the ability to face desires and temptation and withstand them, the books for urban maidens seek to reduce the chances of young women facing temptation in the first place. Their solution is physically to keep them away from it, either by limiting their contact with young men or keeping them away from places that might provoke temptation.

A number of Middle English lyrics offer similar images of lower-status maidens, focusing on their guilelessness and thoughtless enjoyment of sexual advances. They tell of the 'betrayed maiden', often a servant, who either takes part willingly in sexual high jinks, is seduced (usually by a cleric – 'Sir John', 'Joly Jack' or 'Jankin') and finds herself abandoned and pregnant. 'Alas, alas, the while – / that ever I could dance', is the lament of the maiden who 'led the dance at midsummer's day' and who was led astray by Jack, the holy-water clerk.[154] The girl who 'loved a child [lad] of this country' believed her lover when he told her 'he would be true' and 'therefore I let him have all his will', much to her later regret.[155] One maiden found the advances of her priest, Sir John, so pleasant that 'I have no power to say him nay', while another, raped by her Sir John, came to enjoy his attentions – 'we made as merry as flowers in May – / I was beguiled-ay'.[156]

These yokel maidens, whose simplicity is such that they have no defences against sexual advances nor any developed sense of sexual morality, are a common type in English and other European literatures, including the *chansons des femmes, pastourelles* and *fabliaux*.[157] The foolish maidens of the lyrics, though allowed to speak in the first person, are not presented as having fully formed subjectivities, and are carried away by their inherent weaknesses and sexual propensities. The Middle English lyrics have some-times been treated as evidence for the sexual activities of peasant maidens, and Bennett has recently explored their possibilities for representing the voices of maidens (though also the voices of clerics and mothers, among others), and is right in pointing out the possible connection between the lyrics and instances of maidens dancing and singing known from churchwarden's accounts.[158] Yet these representations had much more to do with a privileged group's fantasies about peasant girls, and could have been used as exempla of maidenly misfortune within a parish context.

Three of these *chansons des femmes* are found in Cambridge Caius College MS 383, a fifteenth-century commonplace book in Latin, French and English, consisting mostly of scribbled grammatical exercises and sample legal documents and which was probably a student's book.[159] This suggests that lyrics telling of simple, seduced peasant girls had a particular appeal to university students, certainly male and probably of middle to high status. The lyric in which the maiden tells of her rape by a priest ('Sir John') and curses him upon falling pregnant is especially interesting, as it is found in a manuscript which appears to have belonged to a parish priest, given its inclusion of several religiously themed pieces in Latin and English. These include *Directions to Parish Priests*, a piece on the seven deadly sins, a Latin piece on the day on which Christmas falls, and other items on Church festivals, the date of New Year and the seasons. The lyric at first seems to sit oddly in this company, but so do the *Tale of an Incestuous Daughter* and a *Tale of Robin Hood*.[160] This apparent incongruity offers a clue to a new understanding of the lyrics; they could have been used within the parish by the priest to teach local girls of the dangers of songs and dances, alongside other works which combined entertaining and edifying functions.[161] As already seen, concerns about girls singing and dancing were common in pastoral manuals. Some placed these activities alongside many other transgressions under the heading of 'Sins of [against] Work', including 'misspending of holy-days'.[162] The 'voice' of this first raped then 'beguiled' girl is actually the voice of the local priest, warning against exactly such an error. Though it might seem peculiar that a priest would enjoy a satirical poem about his profession, it is certainly possible that some clerics would see it as their duty, or an amusing exercise, to warn about the misdeeds of their fellows. They could have increased the power of the message by having actual maidens sing it on holidays. It is very likely that some girls may have cheerfully accepted the sentiments and been happy to sing about them, given their often conformist role in parish life.[163] In repeating these sentiments they spread the assumptions of a more elite group, that low-status women were sexually active, intellectually simple and lacking in the capacity for self-control. These simple maidens could not act in a conscious or controlled fashion, but were rather carried away by 'natural', uncontrollable desires and weaknesses. Likewise, the authors of bourgeois conduct literature were not interested in teaching young women to have an awareness of their own strength of character in facing moral challenges, but rather the necessity to avoid them altogether, and the contracts which maidens entering apprenticeship were bound by enforced, rather than encouraged, virtuous conduct on their part.

Conclusion

Early in this chapter the observation was made that we need a particular understanding of women's literacy. More than that, though, we need a particular understanding of the gendered nature of women's education – their upbringing, or leading out from childhood. In the contemporary West, education is more than anything else about the training of the mind, but the training of medieval maidens was ultimately an education of the body. Simone de Beauvoir's statement that at puberty the future 'takes residence in [a girl's] body' offers a view which Richard Hyrd would have heartily concurred with, though he pushed the age of bodily education back even into a girl's early childhood: 'Let the maid learn no uncleanly words, or wanton, or uncomely gesture and moving of the body', lest those habits be imprinted and lead to her later ruin.[164] Though his view was in some respects extreme compared with earlier authors, the theme of the disciplining of the maidenly body runs throughout their works. The edification of the mind had an important place, but was not an end in itself. The maiden's body was known as a site of desire, both as object and subject, and a tremendous effort was mounted to keep it from corruption even while it was upheld as a feminine ideal. It was educated in quietness of tongue, stillness of posture, and in keeping to relatively limited space. Differences between status groups and shifts over time, especially towards the more conservative sixteenth century, ensured some variation in this picture. We have seen, too, that there was some room for imagining alternative femininities, especially in virgin martyrs' lives and romance literature. And for the majority of maidens, but particularly those below the merchant class, education was also about the production of a working body. It is to work that we will now turn.

Notes

1 Simone de Beauvoir, *The Second Sex*, ed. and trans. H. M. Parshley (London, [1949] 1953), pp. 295, 351.
2 *Good Wife, Pilgrimage, passim.*
3 Marjorie Keniston McIntosh, *Controlling Misbehaviour in England, 1370–1600* (Cambridge, 1998); L. R. Poos, 'Sex, lies, and the Church courts of pre-Reformation England', *Journal of Interdisciplinary History*, 25 (1995), 585–607.
4 For example, contrast Caroline Barron's optimistic assessment of fifteenth-century London girls' schooling and literacy levels in 'The education and training of girls in fifteenth-century London', in D. E. S. Dunn (ed.), *Courts, Counties and the Capital in the Later Middle Ages* (Stroud, 1996), with Shannon McSheffrey's argument for very low levels of female reading literacy from evidence concerning

Lollard groups, 'Literacy and the gender gap in the late Middle Ages: women and reading in Lollard communities', in Lesley Smith and Jane H. M. Taylor (eds), *Women, the Book and the Godly* (Cambridge, 1995).

5 For example, Sandra Penketh, 'Women and books of hours', in Lesley Smith and Jane H. M. Taylor (eds), *Women and the Book: Assessing the Visual Evidence* (London, 1997), esp. pp. 266–70.

6 For example, Barron, 'Education and training of girls', p. 150; Sylvia L. Thrupp, *The Merchant Class of Medieval London [1300–1500]* (Ann Arbor, 1962), p. 171.

7 M. T. Clanchy, *From Memory to Written Record: England 1066–1307*, 2nd edn (Oxford, 1993), pp. 194–5; Paul Saenger, 'Books of hours and reading habits in the later middle ages', in Roger Chartier (ed.), *The Culture of Print: Power and the Uses of Print in Early Modern Europe*, trans. Lydia Cochrane (Oxford, 1989).

8 Clanchy, *From Memory*, pp. 226–30. To be *litteratus* was to understand Latin texts.

9 For a helpful discussion, see Wyn Ford, 'The problem of literacy in early modern England', *History*, 78 (1993), 22–37.

10 Clanchy, *From Memory*, brilliantly sums up modern scholars' biases towards literacy as a mark of culture or status, pp. 7–11.

11 *PL and P* 1, no. 362; see also nos. 287 and 363. Earlier editors of the Paston letters mistakenly identified her as Anne Haute, a damsel of Elizabeth Woodville, with whom John II had a long courtship.

12 Eleanor, daughter of Sir Robert Roos, was born probably *c.* 1440, was *domicella* to Margaret of Anjou in 1452–3 and 1453–4, and married first Robert Lovell, then Thomas Prout, squire to the king, by 1466–7, and Richard Haute in 1474. See Ethel Seaton, *Sir Richard Roos, c. 1410–1482: Lancastrian Poet* (London, 1961), pp. 52–3.

13 Now BL MS Royal 14.e.iii. For a transcript of the will see Seaton, *Sir Richard Roos*, pp. 547–8.

14 On French in the fifteenth-century court see M. B. Parkes, 'The literacy of the laity', repr. in *Scribes, Scripts and Readers: Studies in the Communication, Presentation and Dissemination of Medieval Texts* (London, 1991), pp. 289–90.

15 BL MS Royal 14.e.iii fols 1r and 162r.

16 T. H. Turner (ed.), 'Household roll of Eleanor, countess of Leicester, A. D. 1265', in *Manners and Household Expenses of England in the Thirteenth and Fifteenth Centuries*, Roxburgh Club (London, 1841), pp. 9, 24. Letters of *Domicella Alianor* are mentioned in the accounts of the same year, though the likelihood of her penning them seems slim, p. 18.

17 John Carmi Parsons (ed.), 'Liber garderobe', in *The Court and Household of Eleanor of Castile in 1290*, Studies and Texts – Pontifical Institute of Mediaeval Studies, 37 (Toronto, 1977), pp. 63–4.

18 Dorothy Gardiner, *English Girlhood at School: A Study of Women's Education through Twelve Centuries* (London, 1929), p. 73.

19 *PC*, no. 6. This letter is sometimes quoted as evidence for girls learning to write, but this appears to be the result of a misquotation in Eileen Power's *Medieval Women*, where 'hath near hand learned her sawter' was quoted as 'hath neat hand,

and learned her sawter' (Cambridge, repr. 1997), p. 77; see for example Sharon D. Michalove, 'The education of aristocratic women in fifteenth-century England', in Sharon D. Michalove and A. Compton Reeves (eds), *Estrangement, Enterprise and Education in Fifteenth-Century England* (Stroud, 1998), p. 130. The original mistake probably resulted from a misreading of Power's notes, perhaps by M. M. Postan when he edited her work for posthumous publication in 1975.

20 Eamon Duffy, *The Stripping of the Altars: Traditional Religion in England, c. 1400–c. 1580* (New Haven, 1992), p. 210; Christopher de Hamel, *A History of Illuminated Manuscripts* (Oxford, 1986), pp. 159–60.

21 *LL* 3 no. 539.

22 *LL* 3, no. 626.

23 Claire Donovan, *The de Brailes Hours: Shaping the Book of Hours in Thirteenth-Century Oxford* (Toronto, 1991), esp. pp. 23-4 on ownership.

24 Thrupp, *Merchant Class*, p. 162.

25 For urban incomes see Christopher Dyer, *Standards of Living in the Later Middle Ages* (Cambridge, 1989), pp. 193–6.

26 For the popularity of cheap primers among non-elite groups see Duffy, *Stripping of the Altars*, pp. 209–13.

27 Alexandra Barratt, 'Dame Eleanor Hull: a fifteenth-century translator', in Roger Ellis *et al.* (eds), *The Medieval Translator: The Theory and Practice of Translation in the Middle Ages* (Cambridge, 1989).

28 Barron, 'Education and training of girls', p. 150.

29 Moran, *Growth of English Schooling*, pp. 69–70; Thrupp, *Merchant Class*, p. 171; Barron, 'Education and training of girls', pp. 141-2, though Barron is optimistic about the possibility that some girls attended grammar schools despite the lack of evidence.

30 Anne M. Dutton, 'Passing the book: testamentary transmission of religious literature to and by women in England 1350-1500', in Smith and Taylor (eds), *Women, the Book and the Godly*, esp. p. 51.

31 Carol M. Meale, '"… alle the bokes that I haue of latyn, englisch, and frensch": laywomen and their books in late medieval England', in Meale (ed.), *Women and Literature*, esp. pp. 139–41.

32 *LL* 3, no. 588.

33 Juan Luis Vives, *De institutione foeminae Christianae* (Bruges, 1524); Rycharde Hyrd (trans.), *A Very Frutefull and Pleasant Boke Called the Instruction of a Christen Woman* (London, 1529). See also Foster Watson (ed.), *Vives and the Renascence Education of Women* (London, 1912), for edited extracts of further works of Vives and Hyrd, and Diane Bornstein (ed.), *Distaves and Dames: Renaissance Treatises for and about Women* (New York, 1978), for facsimile editions.

34 Barron, 'Education and training of girls'; Moran, *Growth of English Schooling*, pp. 69-70.

35 Cameron Louis (ed.), *The Commonplace Book of Robert Reynes of Acle: An Edition of Tanner MS 407* (New York, 1980). Reynes himself was married for eight years to Emma, who bore five sons, but no daughters are recorded, pp. 143, 175-7.

36 Steven Justice, *Writing and Rebellion: England in 1381* (Berkeley, 1994), pp. 32–66.

37 PRO C 47/4/1, fol. 11v.

38 Carol M. Meale, 'The manuscripts and early audience of the Middle English *Prose Merlin*', in Alison Adams *et al.* (eds), *The Changing Face of Arthurian Romance: Essays on Arthurian Prose Romances in Memory of Cedric E. Pickford* (Cambridge, 1986); Kate Harris, 'The origins and makeup of Cambridge University Library MS Ff.1.6', *Transactions of the Cambridge Bibliographical Society*, 8 (1983), 299–333.

39 *LL* 5, no. 1126; and 6, no. 1653.

40 *PL and P* 1, nos. 417–18, 420; 2, nos. 446, 500, 600, 724, also 545, 753, 820; *SL and P* 1, pp. xxvii, xlvii, nos. 70, 106, 120, 158; 2, nos. 168, 172, 175, 176, 180, 204, 306.

41 *SL and P* 2, no. 185.

42 Martha W. Driver, 'Pictures in print: late fifteenth- and early sixteenth-century English religious books for lay readers', in Michael G. Sargeant (ed.), *De cella in seculum: Religious and Secular Life and Devotion in Late Medieval England* (Cambridge, 1989), p. 243; Lesley Smith in her study of images of women writing in sources from across western Europe up to *c.* 1400 found St Bridget of Sweden to be exceptional in the large number of extant representations of her engaged in the act of writing, 'Scriba, femina', in Smith and Taylor (eds), *Women and the Book ... Visual Evidence*, p. 26.

43 *Book of the Knight*, cap. 89.

44 Clanchy, *From Memory*, p. 13; David Park, 'Form and content', in Christopher Norton, David Park and Paul Binski, *Dominican Painting in East Anglia: The Thornham Parva Retable and the Musée de Cluny Frontal* (Woodbridge, 1987), esp. pp. 50–3; Wendy Scase, 'St Anne and the education of the Virgin', in Nicholas Rogers (ed.), *England in the Fourteenth Century: Proceedings of the 1991 Harlaxton Symposium* (Stamford, 1993).

45 See Scott, *Later Gothic Manuscripts I*, plate 23, for a similar image.

46 The term is Brian Stock's, *The Implications of Literacy: Written Language and Models of Interpretation in the Eleventh and Twelfth Centuries* (Princeton, 1983), esp. p. 90.

47 Felicity Riddy, '"Women talking about the things of God": a late medieval sub-culture', in Meale (ed.), *Women and Literature*, esp. pp. 110–11; Ann M. Hutchinson, 'Devotional reading in the monastery and in the late medieval household', in Sargent (ed.), *De cella in seculum*, esp. pp. 225–6.

48 'Order and rules of the house of the Princess Cecill, mother of King Edward IV', in *Collection of Ordinances*, p. 37.

49 Andrew Taylor, 'Chivalric conversation and the denial of male fear', in Murray (ed.), *Conflicted Identities*; Felicity Riddy, 'Middle English romance: family, marriage, intimacy', in Roberta L. Krueger (ed.), *The Cambridge Companion to Medieval Romance* (Cambridge, 2000).

50 'Orders and rules ... Princess Cecill', p. 37.

51 BL MS Harl. 6815, fols 26r–v.

52 H. Leith Spencer, *English Preaching in the Late Middle Ages* (Oxford, 1993), pp. 71. 203, 207–16.

53 See essays by Mill, Lindenbaum, and Utley and Ward, 'Dramatic Pieces', in *Manual*, vol. 5. Mystery and miracle plays dramatised biblical and other Christian

narratives, morality plays dealt primarily with sin, penance and salvation, and folk drama presented popular lay and Christian tales.

54 French, *People of the Parish*, ch. 2.

55 See pp. 95–6.

56 *Good Wife, Pilgrimage*; *Documenta*; Hyrd (trans.), *Instruction of a Christen Woman*, II.xi.

57 *MED*, s.v. 'norture'.

58 W. A. Wright (ed.), *Femina*, Roxburgh Club (Cambridge, 1909), p. 1.

59 Walter de Bibbesworth, *Le Tretiz*, ed. William Rothwell, Anglo-Norman Text Society, Plain Texts series 6 (London, 1990). The text survives in sixteen manuscripts. For discussions see Clanchy, *From Memory*, pp. 197–200; Orme, *From Childhood to Chivalry*, pp. 8, 16, 80, 124.

60 F. D. Blackley and G. Hermansen (eds), *The Household Book of Queen Isabella of England for the Fifth Regnal Year of Edward II, 8th July 1311 to 7th July 1312* (Edmonton, 1971), pp. 102, 120.

61 *LL* 5, no. 1224.

62 On royal mistresses see Orme, *From Childhood to Chivalry*, esp. pp. 26–8; Margaret Sharp, 'The central administration system of Edward, the Black Prince', in T. F. Tout, *Chapters in the Administrative History of Mediaeval England*, 6 vols (Manchester, 1920–33), vol. 5, pp. 319–20. On *domicellae* see Chapter 3 of the present work.

63 Parsons, *Court and Household*, pp. 38–9.

64 Byerly and Byerly 1, pp. 171, 55.

65 Byerly and Byerly 2, p. 201.

66 Blackley and Hermansen (eds), *Household Book of Queen Isabella*, pp. xiv, 14, 142, 156, 172, 176.

67 Byerly and Byerly 2, p. 214. Mary had not only her own mistress, but her own tailor, carter, chamberlain, laundress, two sumptermen, and an outrider for her cart, p. xii. See also Parsons, *Court and Household*, p. 130.

68 C. D. Ross, 'The household accounts of Elizabeth Berkeley, countess of Warwick, 1420–1', *Transactions of the Bristol and Gloucestershire Archaeological Society*, 70 (1951), 81–105, esp. p. 89.

69 Benjamin Williams (ed.), *Chronique de la traïson et mort de Richart Deux Roy Dengleterre* (London, 1846), p. 246.

70 Froissart, *Chronicles*, vol. 4, pp. 659–60, 673–4.

71 Orme, *Childhood to Chivalry*, p. 27; *The Physician's Tale*, lines 72–92.

72 Wylie, *Henry the Fourth*, vol. 4, p. 222; vol. 2, pp. 437, 447; vol. 3, p. 242.

73 Power, *Medieval English Nunneries*, pp. 260–84.

74 Nicholas Orme, *Education in the West of England, 1066–1548* (Exeter, 1976), p. 204; *LL* 3, nos. 537, 539; 5, no. 1226.

75 Power, *Medieval English Nunneries*, p. 279.

76 C. M. Woolgar (ed.), *Household Accounts from Medieval England*, The British Academy Records of Social and Economic History, new series 17 and 18 (London, 1992), part 2, p. 671.

77 Four English girls' apprentice indentures are extant: WAM 5966; CLRO Misc.

MSS 1863; PRO E210/1176; NRO MS Hare 2091. I am indebted to Caroline Barron for these references. Riddy, 'Mother knows best', esp. pp. 71–85.

78 BIHR PR 2, fol. 407v.

79 Donovan, *de Brailes Hours*, pp. 42–104. As each book of hours was unique not all followed this narrative precisely, but the Hours of the Virgin did regularly follow the structure of the life of the Virgin.

80 R. N. Swanson, *Religion and Devotion in Europe, c. 1215–c. 1515* (Cambridge, 1995), p. 145.

81 Ross (ed.), *Middle English Sermons*, p. 248. See pp. 249, 251, on Mary as a model for all Christians.

82 *Book of the Knight*, caps 107–10.

83 Meredith (ed.), *Mary Play*, pp. 9–12.

84 Jeremy Goldberg, 'Craft guilds, the Corpus Christi Play and civic government', in Sarah Rees Jones (ed.), *The Government of Medieval York: Essays in Commemoration of the 1396 Royal Charter* (York, 1997), esp. pp. 145–8. J. A. Tasioulas, 'Between doctrine and domesticity: the portrayal of Mary in the N-Town plays', in Diane Watt (ed.), *Medieval Women in their Communities* (Cardiff, 1997), discusses the real-world appeal of Mary's characterisation in this play, and pp. 236–7 also considers she may have been played by a girl.

85 For some vernacular examples Beverley Boyd (ed.), *The Middle English Miracles of the Virgin* (San Marino, 1964).

86 Richard Beadle (ed.), *The York Plays* (London, 1982), 'The pewterers and founders', 'The hatmakers, masons and labourers', 'The marshals' and 'The spurriers and lorimers' (all for the Virgin Mary), 'The coopers' and 'The armourers' (for Eve), 'The fishers and mariners' (for Noah's wife), and 'The tapiters and couchers' (for Pilate's wife). See also 'The drapers' for the death of the Virgin and pledge of her role as intercessor and protector.

87 For example, T. F. Simmons and H. E. Nolloth (eds), *The Lay Folks' Catechism*, EETS os 118 (London, 1901); T. F. Simmons (ed.), *The Lay Folks' Mass Book*, EETS os 71 (London, 1879), and Henry Littlehales (ed.), *The Prymer, or Lay Folks' Prayer Book*, 2 vols, EETS os 105 and 109 (London, 1895–7).

88 Samuel Moore, 'Patrons of letters in Norfolk and Suffolk, *c.* 1450', 2 parts, *Proceedings of the Modern Language Association of America*, 27 (1912), 188–207 and 28 (1913), 70–105; A. S. G. Edwards. 'The transmission and audience of Osbern Bokenham's *Legendys of Hooly Wummen*', in A. J. Minnis (ed.), *Late Religious Texts and Their Transmission: Essays in Honour of A. I. Doyle* (Cambridge, 1994); Karen K. Jambek, 'Patterns of women's literary patronage: England, 1200–ca. 1475', in June Hall McCash (ed.), *The Cultural Patronage of Late Medieval Women* (Athens, GA, 1996); Karen A. Winstead, *Virgin Martyrs: Legends of Sainthood in Late Medieval England* (Ithaca, NY, 1997), pp. 118–23.

89 *Book of the Knight*, cap. 62, Christine de Pisan, *City of Ladies*, III.3.1. On virgin martyrs as role models for girls see Katherine J. Lewis, 'Model girls? Virgin-martyrs and the training of young women in late medieval England', in Lewis, Menuge and Phillips (eds), *Young Medieval Women*. Eamon Duffy, in contrast, emphasises their intercessory role: *Stripping of the Altars*, pp. 174–5.

90 See for example Wogan-Browne, 'Saints' lives and the female reader'.

91 Chaucer, *The Physician's Tale*, esp. lines 118–257. His probable source was the version in *The Romance of the Rose*, lines 5559–29, though versions also appeared in Boccaccio's *De claris mulieribus* and Gower's *Confessio amantis*, see Benson *et al.* (eds), *Riverside Chaucer*, pp. 901–2.

92 Wogan-Browne, 'Saints' lives and the female reader'; Lewis, *Cult of St Katherine*; Winstead, *Virgin Martyrs*.

93 The focus here is on pastoral or 'vices and virtues' literature, that is, versions of the *Manuel des péchés* and English versions of Lorens d'Orleans's thirteenth-century *Somme le roi*, or closely related works, and on some sermon material. For introductions to the pastoral texts see Robert R. Raymo, 'Works of religious and philosophical instruction', in *Manual*, vol. 7. On sermon content and lay audiences see Spencer, *English Preaching*, esp. ch. 5.

94 *Memoriale credencium*, from MS Harl. 2398 fol. 39v, quoted in G. R. Owst, *Literature and Pulpit in Medieval England* (Oxford, 1966), p. 119. For other versions of the tale see Sidney J. H. Herrtage (ed.), *The Early English Versions of the Gesta romanorum*, EETS ES 33 (London, 1879), p. 70, and *The Book of the Knight*, cap. 56.

95 On the dangers of singing and dancing see Arthur Brandeis (ed.), *Jacob's Well: An Englisht Treatise on the Cleansing of Man's Conscience*, EETS OS 115 (London, 1900), p. 158; *Gesta romanorum*, pp. 60-1, 93. Peter Biller notes that these concerns are found in both English and Italian pastoral manuals of the fourteenth and fifteenth centuries, 'Marriage patterns and women's lives: a sketch of pastoral geography', in Goldberg (ed.), *Women in Medieval English Society*, pp. 65–6.

96 *Jacob's Well*, pp. 80-1; F. J. Furnivall (ed.), *Robert of Brunne's 'Handlyng Synne'*, EETS OS 119 and 123 (London, 1901-3) pt. 1, pp. 113–15. See also Siegfried Wenzel (ed. and trans.), *Fasciculus morum: A Fourteenth-Century Preacher's Handbook* (University Park, 1989), pp. 50–4.

97 W. Nelson Francis (ed.), *The Book of Vices and Virtues*, EETS OS 217 (London, 1942), pp. 43–4. Versions of this passage are in *Jacob's Well*, pp. 158-9; Dan Michel, *Ayenbite of Inwyt*, ed. Richard Morris and Pamela Gradon, EETS OS 23 (London, 1965), p. 47; *Handlyng Synne* pt. 2, pp. 242-3. See also *Fasciculus morum*, pp. 650, 660.

98 *Book of the Knight*, cap. 56.

99 For an exploration of the disjuncture between these message see my article, 'Desiring virgins: maidens, martyrs and femininity in late medieval England', in Goldberg and Riddy (eds), *Youth in the Middle Ages*, forthcoming.

100 YMAH, Apprenticeship indenture, 1364; Maud Sellers (ed.), *York Memorandum Book*, 2 vols, Surtees Society 120 and 125 (Durham, 1912-15), vol. 1, pp. 54-5.

101 WAM 5966; CLRO Misc. MSS 1863; PRO E210/1176; NRO MS Hare 2091.

102 BL MS Add. 17716, fols 67–8. Caroline Barron alerted me to this interesting source also. She believes the book was probably compiled by London scrivener William Kingsmill in the early fifteenth century.

103 For conduct books for girls see Kathleen M. Ashley, 'Medieval courtesy literature and dramatic mirrors of female conduct', in Nancy Armstrong and Leonard

Tennenhouse (eds), *The Ideology of Conduct: Essays on Literature and the History of Sexuality* (New York, 1987), and Diane Bornstein, *The Lady in the Tower: Medieval Courtesy Literature for Women* (Hamden, 1983).

104 Nobert Elias, *The Civilizing Process: Sociogenetic and Psychogenetic Investigations*, trans. Edmund Jephcott, rev. edn (Oxford, [1939], 2000), pp. 85–6; Jonathan Nicholls, *The Matter of Courtesy: Medieval Courtesy Books and the Gawain Poet* (Woodbridge, 1985), pp. 70–4; Jorge Arditi, *A Genealogy of Manners: Transformations of Social Relations in France and England from the Fourteenth to the Eighteenth Century* (Chicago, 1998), p. 15; Mark Addison Amos, '"For manners make man": Bourdieu, de Certeau, and the common appropriation of noble manners in the *Book of Courtesy*', in Kathleen Ashley and Robert L. A. Clark (eds), *Medieval Conduct* (Minneapolis, 2001).

105 L. C. Hector and Barbara F. Harvey (eds), *The Westminster Chronicle 1381-1394* (Oxford, 1982), p. 192; *LL* 3, pp. 133–218.

106 On Caxton's audience see H. S. Bennett, *English Books and Readers, 1475–1557* (Cambridge, 1957), pp. 54–5; Lotte Hellinger, *Caxton in Focus: The Beginning of Printing in England* (London, 1982), pp. 101–2.

107 *Book of the Knight*, 'Introduction', pp. xi–xiii, xxxiv–xxxviii. The earlier translation, now BL MS Harl. 1764, a paper folio manuscript with moderate decoration, is not bound with any other works and bears no medieval annotation, making its purpose and audience difficult to deduce. For an edition see *The Book of the Knight of La Tour Landry*, ed. Thomas Wright, EETS os 33 (London, 1868). Caxton's edition is used here.

108 J. L. Grigsby, '*Le Miroir des bonnes femmes*', *Romania*, 82 (1961), 458–81, and 83 (1962), 30–51, and 'A new source of the *Livre de la Chevalier de la Tour Landry*', *Romania*, 84 (1963), 171–208; *Book of the Knight*, 'Introduction', pp. xxxiv–xliii, and caps 122–33.

109 John Fitzherbert, *Booke of Husbandrie*, facsimile of the 1598 London edition (Amsterdam, 1979), p. 178.

110 For example, Vives, *De institutione foeminae Christianae*; Hyrd (trans.), *Instruction of a Christen Woman*; Thomas Salter, *A Mirrhor Mete for All Mothers, Matrons, and Maidens, Intituled the Mirrhor of Modestie* (London, ?1579); William Lowth, *The Christian Man's Closet* (London, 1581); W. Averall, *A Dyall for Dainty Darlings* (London, 1581).

111 *Book of the Knight*, cap. 35.

112 *Book of the Knight*, cap. 12.

113 On courtly conversation see J. F. Kiteley, 'The *De arte honeste amandi* of Andreas Capellanus and the concept of courtesy in *Sir Gawain and the Green Knight*', *Anglia*, 79 (1961), 7–16; Felicity Riddy, 'The speaking knight: Sir Gawain and other animals', in Martin B. Shichtman and James P. Carly (eds), *Culture and the King: The Social Implications of the Arthurian Legend* (Albany, 1994).

114 *Book of the Knight*, caps 12–14.

115 *Book of the Knight*, cap. 17.

116 Cora Kaplan, 'Language and gender', repr. in Deborah Cameron (ed.), *The Feminist Critique of Language: A Reader* (London, 1990), p. 58.

117 Deborah Cameron, 'Introduction: why language is a feminist issue', in *Feminist Critique of Language*, pp. 3–4.

118 *Book of the Knight*, cap. 89; Hyrd (trans.), *Instruction of a Christen Woman*, I.iv.

119 Meale, '"alle the bokes"', pp. 138–142, and '"Gode men/ Wiues maydnes and alle men": romance and its audiences', in Carol M. Meale (ed.), *Readings in Medieval English Romance* (Cambridge, 1991), pp. 209–25; Gisela Guddat-Figge, *Catalogue of Manuscripts Containing Middle English Romances* (Munich, 1976), esp. p. 44

120 Hyrd (trans.), *Instruction of a Christen Woman*, I.v.

121 Eric Auerbach wrote that romance 'is not reality shaped and set forth by art, but an escape into fable and fairy tale', *Mimesis: The Representation of Reality in Western Literature*, trans. Willard R. Trask (Princeton, 1953), p. 138. Arlyn Diamond finds a social function for romances' fantasies of escape for those confined by feudal marriages, 'Unhappy endings: failed love / failed faith in late romances', in Meale (ed.), *Readings in Medieval English Romance*, pp. 70–1.

122 Felicity Riddy, *Sir Thomas Malory* (Brill, 1987), pp. 17–23; Carol M. Meale, 'The Middle English romance of *Ipomedon*: a late medieval "mirror" for princes and merchants', *Reading Medieval Studies*, 10 (1984), 136–91.

123 Kim M. Phillips, 'Bodily walls, windows and doors: the politics of gesture in late fifteenth-century English books for women', in Jocelyn Wogan-Browne *et al.* (eds), *Medieval Women: Texts and Contexts in Late Medieval Britain* (Turnhout, 2000).

124 *Guy of Warwick*, lines 65–92.

125 'Ipomedon' (selections) in Walter Hoyt French and Charles Brockway Hale (eds), *Middle English Metrical Romances*, 2 vols (New York, 1964), vol. 2, pp. 655–60; 'The squire of low degree', in Sands (ed.), *Middle English Verse Romances*, lines 115–278.

126 A feminist re-analysis is Toril Moi, 'Desire in language: Andreas Capellanus and the controversy of courtly love', in David Aers (ed.), *Medieval Literature: Criticism, Ideology and History* (Brighton, 1986).

127 'King Horn', in Sands (ed.), *Middle English Verse Romances*, lines 250–69; E. Kölbing (ed.), *The Romance of Sir Beves of Hamtoun*, EETS ES 46, 48, 65 (London, 1885–94), pp. 34–5, 53, 56–7. Sexuality in romances will be explored further in Chapter 4.

128 Robert Henryson, *Testament of Cresseid*, ed. Denton Fox (London, 1968), line 80. One contemporary understanding of leprosy saw it as a venereal disease: Fox's 'Introduction', pp. 27–8.

129 BL MS Yates Thompson 13. See Henry Yates Thompson, *Illustrations from One Hundred Manuscripts in the Library of Henry Yates Thompson*, 7 vols (London, 1907–18), vol. 4, pp. vi and 31, plate 51.

130 For the hunting scenes see fols 68r–83v, for Bevis of Hampton and Guy of Warwick see fols 8v–16r, and for the tale of the damsel and Eneas see fols 60v–68r. Linda Brownrigg, 'The Taymouth Hours and the Romance of *Beves of Hampton*', in Peter Beal and Jeremy Griffiths (ed.), *English Manuscript Studies 1100–1700*, vol. 1 (Oxford, 1989), esp. p. 238 for a transcription of the Anglo-Norman text accompanying the damsel and Eneas tale. I am most grateful to Tracy Adams for her help with translating this text.

131 Leon Kellner (ed.), *Caxton's Blanchardyn and Eglantine, c. 1489*, EETS es 58 (London, 1890); Phillips, 'Bodily walls, windows and doors', on the text's conservatism, and Jennifer R. Goodman, '"That women holde in ful greet reverence": mothers and daughters reading chivalric romances', in Smith and Taylor (eds), *Women, the Book and the Worldly*, on this text and the romances of BL MS Royal 14 E.iii (Eleanor Haute's book) as 'safe reading' for young women.

132 The classic account is M. K. Dale, 'The London silkwomen of the fifteenth century', *Economic History Review*, 4 (1933), 324–35. See Chapter 3 below.

133 Mustanoja (ed.), *Good Wife etc.*, 'Introduction', p. 126; Riddy, 'Mother knows best', pp. 70–3.

134 Mustanoja (ed.), *Good Wife etc.*, pp. 88–92, 131, 139. Note that one variant copy of *Thewis* was entitled *Documenta matris ad filiam*, and that version will be referred to when it substantially differs from *Thewis*. References to 'The good wife taught her daughter' will be to Mustanoja's 'Version E', unless otherwise stated. References to *Thewis* and *Documenta* will be to Girvan's editions.

135 *Documenta*, lines 83–4; *Book of the Knight*, cap. 24.

136 *Good Wife*, lines 100–6; *Pilgrimage*, line 16; *Thewis*, lines 29–38, 87–96; *Book of the Knight*, caps 20, 25, 26, 30, 48–51.

137 *Good Wife*, lines 33–45; *Pilgrimage*, lines 31–3; *Thewis*, lines 41, 109; *Book of the Knight*, caps 11–12.

138 *Good Wife*, lines 28–9, 42; *Pilgrimage*, lines 43–5; *Thewis*, lines 14–15, 25–6; *Book of the Knight*, caps 12–14, 21.

139 *Good Wife*, lines 25–7; *Book of the Knight*, cap. 17.

140 *Good Wife*, lines 28, 34; *Thewis*, lines 19, 41; *Book of the Knight*, cap. 10.

141 *Good Wife*, lines 46–51, 52–5, 59–62; *Pilgrimage*, lines 7–12, 39–40; *Thewis*, lines 16–18, 63–70, 109–18, 122–51, 160, 177–82, 187–202; *Book of the Knight*, caps 24, 56.

142 *Thewis*, lines 20–2; *Good Wife*, lines 100–1; *Pilgrimage*, lines 13–15.

143 Riddy, 'Mother knows best', pp. 77–8.

144 *Book of the Knight*, caps 51–2.

145 *Book of the Knight*, caps 48–53.

146 *Good Wife*, lines 59–62.

147 *Thewis*, lines 16, 86, 157–8.

148 *Thewis*, lines 8–10.

149 *Good Wife*, Version L, lines 185–91.

150 *Book of the Knight*, cap. 62.

151 *Good Wife*, lines 65–8.

152 *Pilgrimage*, lines 38–9.

153 *Doctrina*, lines 83–4.

154 Robbins (ed.), *Secular Lyrics*, pp. 22–4.

155 Robbins (ed.), *Secular Lyrics*, pp. 17–18.

156 Robbins (ed.), *Secular Lyrics*, pp. 19–20.

157 J. A. Burrow, *Medieval Writers and Their Work: Middle English Literature and Its Background 1100–1500* (Oxford, 1982), pp. 64–5; Kathryn Gravdal, *Ravishing Maidens: Writing Rape in Medieval French Literature and Law* (Philadelphia, 1991), pp. 104–21; John Hines, *The Fabliau in English* (London, 1993), pp. 43–65.

158 Hanawalt, *Ties that Bound*, pp. 192-3, 196-7; Judith M. Bennett, 'Ventriloquisms: when maidens speak in English songs, *c*. 1300-1550', in Ann Marie Rasmussen and Ann Klinck (eds), *Medieval Women's Song: Cross-Cultural Approaches* (Philadelphia, 2002). I am grateful to Professor Bennett for sending me a copy of this article before publication.

159 M. R. James, *A Descriptive Catalogue of the Manuscripts in the Library of Gonville and Caius College*, 3 vols (Cambridge, 1908), vol. 2, pp. 435-7; Julia Boffey, *Manuscripts of English Courtly Love Lyrics in the Later Middle Ages* (Woodbridge, 1985), p. 97.

160 C. Harwick *et al.*, *A Catalogue of the Manuscripts Preserved in the Library of the University of Cambridge*, 5 vols (Cambridge, 1857), vol. 2, pp. 505-9. Other lyrics are preserved in collections whose users are more difficult to discern, as they consist only of English songs: St John's College, Cambridge, MS 259, and BL MS Sloane 2593, are collections of carols and songs, the former containing one and the latter two *chansons des femmes*. See M. R. James, *A Descriptive Catalogue of the Manuscripts in the Library of St John's College, Cambridge* (Cambridge, 1913), pp. 294-6, and Edward J. L. Scott, *Index to the Sloane Manuscripts in the British Museum* (London, 1904), p. 427.

161 On *The Tale of an Incestuous Daughter* see Chapter 4 and on Robin Hood see Chapter 5.

162 Gustaf Holmstedt (ed.), *Speculum Christiani: A Middle English Religious Treatise of the 14th Century*, EETS OS 182 (London, 1933), pp. 87-91; Venetia Nelson (ed.), *A Myrour to Lewd Men and Women: A Prose Version of the Speculum vitae* (Heidelberg, 1981), pp. 126-7.

163 See Chapter 5, below.

164 Hyrd (trans.), *Instruction of a Christen Woman*, I.ii.

3

Work

The years leading up to marriage formed a crucial stage in a woman's economic or working life, as the teens and (often) early twenties were a time for learning the practical tasks of adult womanhood. Forms of 'work' were not reserved only to young women of the lower orders. Even within the gentry and aristocracy maidens frequently entered into positions of service which, though requiring hardly taxing labour, played a useful function in maintaining or improving their own and their families' economic and social position. At all levels, too, work had as much an educational purpose as economic, though especially in the upper ranks where maidens' service was not always rewarded with payments but rather held out the promise of a better economic future to girls through advantageous marriages or to their families through receiving favour. This and the previous chapter should therefore be seen as a natural pair, divided in this way only for greater readability. Both are concerned primarily with the training of young women.

A great deal of young women's work consisted of some kind of service. As Rosemary Horrox has put it so well, service has 'some claim to be considered the dominant ethic of the Middle Ages' in England, but she discusses only the roles of high-status men.[1] Her statement can be extended to women and all social groups. Even within a family, one's labour could be labelled 'service'. Whether a maiden was working as an agricultural labourer for her family or in the pay of another, as an apprentice or non-indentured servant in an artisan household, or in noble service to a greater lady, her labour aided the economic well-being and social status of others at least as much as herself.

Maidens' work should also be understood within the general context of women's work. As historians of women's labour for both the medieval and early modern periods have noted, women's work was notable for its low status, low pay, its standing as an accessory to male labour and the varied nature of the tasks women were required to perform.[2] Where a man could expect to be defined by his occupation if he were below the titled ranks, women were identified by their marital or familial status of daughter, wife or widow in the great majority of cases. Women were expected, in most cases, not to focus on a single occupational task but to turn their hand to whatever needed doing, often simultaneously. Goldberg has noted that ideologically loaded (but also socially accurate) visual portrayals of labour depict men undertaking one task such as digging while women perform a range of tasks simultaneously, such as spinning and childminding.[3] Young women, when they entered service, were being trained for this working future as secondary labourers: essential, but less important than male workers. The greatest exceptions to this rule were the London silkwomen, whose prestige as independent workers was such that they were able to operate their own workshops, indenture their own female apprentices, receive orders even from the royal court, and petition the Crown against perceived unfair competition from immigrant males. As Marion K. Dale wrote almost seventy years ago, they resembled master craftsmen in nearly every respect except in setting up their own guild.[4] Even this elite group among working women experienced increasing difficulties in defending their control over their craft by the later fifteenth century.

Noble service

Eleanor Roos was probably in her early or mid-teens when her father Sir Robert died in 1448, and she became a 'dauncell' or damsel in Queen Margaret of Anjou's household.[5] Such positions at court were highly valued and sought after, for daughters as well as sons, and with Eleanor's introduction to court society she was swept into exalted circles. She married, firstly, Robert Lovell probably around 1455, then by 1466–7 was wedded to Thomas Prout, squire to the new king Edward IV (and under her new name was listed among the damsels of Elizabeth Woodville),[6] and by 1474 had married Richard Haute, first cousin of the queen.[7] Her fortunes faded with the reign of Richard III, who executed her husband in 1483 for his role as one of the guardians of young Edward V, but she retained favour with the exiled queen and the two princesses, to one or all of whom she gave her treasured great book of romances.[8] Her loyalty to Princess Elizabeth was remembered with the rise of the Tudors and she was one of the ladies present at the christening of Prince Arthur in 1486.[9]

Entry to court in the years of maidenhood secured for Eleanor a place in high society through the ascendance and decline of three dynasties.

Eleanor's experience represents female service at the highest level in English society and gave her tremendous social privilege, though through the institution she shared something with maidens across the social spectrum. Daughters of great families, as much as peasant girls, counted service as useful experience, though the nature and rewards of their occupations differed markedly. Chief differences included the economic utility of their role, which for noble maidens often took a less direct form than for lower-status women, and the different kinds of tasks performed. Also, where the majority of the female population appear to have served in households outside those of their immediate family only while unmarried, women in royal and aristocratic service could retain their positions after marriage and even into old age. The wealth and position of great ladies allowed them to remain in service, delegating the tasks of running their households and raising their children to their own servants during the periods spent residing with their mistress. It was the ubiquity of the institution that so appalled a member of the Venetian diplomatic mission to England around 1500, who recorded the shocking practice of sending children into service, in which everyone 'however rich he may be', engaged.[10] What was shocking to the Venetian, because deemed little better than delivering one's daughter into prostitution in his home country, was honourable and prestigious even for daughters of the English nobility and for their families.[11]

Noble maidens' service has received less scholarly attention than that of lower-status girls. Indeed, because of the small numbers of female servants listed in the account books of great households compared with the enormous numbers of male staff in fifteenth-century great households in particular, historians have often relegated women servants to the background with a brief comment. For example, Kate Mertes's invaluable study of the members and operations of English noble households states that 'female household members were virtually nonexistent'.[12] While one cannot dispute the small numbers of women listed in household accounts (though such records probably underreport female servants as they were less likely to receive a wage or hold a position with an occupational title than male servants), their existence should not be ignored. The overlap between work and education also means that positions held by young women have been viewed often as part of the 'boarding out' system of female education, whereas their brothers, leaving home to take up positions as pages and other minor servants, are seen to be taking the first step on a career path. In 1465 Margaret Paston wrote to John III concerning his sister, probably Anne, 'I greet you well, letting you weet [know] that as for your sister's being with my lady, if your father will agree thereto I hold me right well pleased, for I would be right glad that she should do her service before any other'. Before 1466 Sir John Heveningham wrote to Margaret Paston requesting a place in her household for his kinswoman, 'I wrote unto you for my cousin Agnes Loveday to have been in your service'.[13] Taking a cue from the language of these letter writers, the experiences of these young women should be understood less as schooling than as service, which had the dual purpose of education and work.

Looking first at the lower levels of the nobility, it is surprisingly difficult to uncover the kinds of tasks performed by gentry girls serving families of the same status, yet enough fragments exist to begin to build up a picture. Maidens provided companionship for the lady of the house, especially important in this social group where a lady's husband was frequently absent and her own adolescent children likely to be in service elsewhere. This is apparent in a late fifteenth-century letter by Katherine Chatterton to her brother George Plumpton concerning her sister Isabell's loneliness: 'how such, [she] has neither woman nor maid with her, but herself alone'. She begs him to find a 'goodly young woman of her pay and body' of twenty-four or more.[14] Alice de Bryene's account book records that *ancillae* (maidservants) frequently accompanied their mistresses during visits to this gentlewoman's household.[15] Usually such women would have been expected to provide more than companionship, however, as a gentry household could have gained little benefit from keeping an idle girl in the house, and, moreover, her period in residence could provide valuable training in the skills she would need if she married. She would have been put to work with spinning, sewing, mending, cleaning garments, furs and linens, keeping vegetable and herb gardens, making potions for medicine and cosmetics and the rudiments of cooking. Most of these activities are explained in the Goodman of Paris's late fourteenth-century guide for his young wife, and though the work itself is not known to have had any circulation in England the similarities between these two cultures (unlike, for example, the great differences between England and northern Italy) make it likely that many or most of the tasks described were also expected of English knights' wives.[16] Elizabeth Stonor in a letter of 1476 made passing reference to the kerchiefs, smocks and small trinkets in the chest that 'Catherine my woman' had charge of, demonstrating female servants' tasks in looking after clothing, and Alice Crane, a gentlewoman in service, not only nursed her own lady during a long sickness but sent medicine to her acquaintance, Margaret Paston, in 1455.[17] Some of Alice de Bryene's maids may have been engaged to tend her poultry and herb garden.[18] In the early sixteenth century Vives's *Instruction of a Christian Woman*, the English translation of which was bound to have been aimed at a reasonably wide middle- and high-status audience, says in addition to reading and learning to work textiles, 'Let the maid also learn cookery, not that slubberyng and excess in meats to serve a great meinie [household], full of delicious pleasures and gluttony, which cooks meddle with, but sober and measurable, that she may learn to dress meat for her father, and mother, and brethren while she is a maid: and for her husband and children, when she is a wife'. She is better able, he says, to prepare pleasant food for her family than a servant can and no one, however great, should 'loathe the name of the kitchen'.[19] Dame Margery Salvin had a female cook, Elizabeth, to whom she bequeathed twenty pence in 1496 (though the small bequest may indicate a lower-status recipient), and the Cely household in Calais included a female servant called Alison who was paid during Lent 1482 to procure food and wine and was perhaps the cook.[20] Women of gentry rank and lower were probably not strangers to the kitchen, though they preferred to delegate food tasks to servants where possible.

When Margaret Paston sought a place for nineteen- or twenty-year-old Margery with the countess of Oxford or duchess of Bedford, feeling that her daughter was simply 'losing her time' at home and frustrated by her presence – 'we be either of us weary of other' – she was probably hoping for some practical training for her daughter. Equally, knowing the Pastons' predilection for upward mobility and their anxiety about Margery's romance with their bailiff Richard Calle, she was perhaps hoping to secure Margery a wealthy and suitable marriage.[21] In a great household such as the duchess of Oxford's or countess of Bedford's, a young woman would have generally had fewer general household duties imposed on her than if she had gone into a gentry home, but would have engaged in tasks linked closely to the lady and her young children. However, while household accounts and a small number of other sources offer a fair quantity of evidence concerning the roles and duties of *domicellae* or damsels in great and royal households, it is not often easy to discern the tasks of unmarried 'damsels' in particular, as both married and unmarried women were grouped under that term. Though it seems that many women entered the position of damsel while unmarried, they retained the title after marrying. An example is offered by Philippa de Roet, *domicella* to Philippa of Hainault, who in 1366 married Geoffrey Chaucer and yet continued to be referred to as a damsel, and in 1372 was recorded as *damoseyle* in the house of John of Gaunt.[22] An older, already married woman could become a damsel after completing other forms of service, as Alicia de la Legrave, formerly nurse to Edward II, became damsel to Queen Isabella alongside her own daughter, Cecily.[23] It is therefore only possible to identify maidens among a lady's 'damsels' where something is known of an individual's biography. For this reason, female service in aristocratic households will be considered in general terms, and distinctions between married and unmarried women made only where significant. Age and rank were more important than marital status.

The ladies and maidens of a great household formed a cluster of well-born women, of varying ages, at the core of an elite residence. At the beginning of our period, when such households were still peripatetic, they accompanied the lady on her progress from residence to residence, but by the mid-fourteenth century and thereafter that level of mobility had greatly decreased.[24] What remained constant was the proximity of the *domicellae* to their mistress and her needs. We saw in the previous chapter that female servants tended to take on child-care and educational duties towards the young children of the household, whether simply as 'rokkers' or cradle-tenders, or in the role of governess.[25] Maidens were less likely than married damsels to have been granted the latter task, but probably helped to tend the infants and toddlers of the household. Damsels were also expected to perform various duties attendant upon the lady's person. Before breakfast, according to the 'Harleian Regulations' of the late fifteenth century, one of the close gentlewomen of presence should bear her lady's train when the lord and lady entered their chapel for morning mass.[26] Another chief task was to aid with their mistress's dressing and toilette. The instructions for the coronation of a queen mention that the night before the coronation she would be led by two knights to her chamber, 'and there her ladies to change her anew, and alter her as it pleases her best'.[27] Accounts of maidens disarming and robing knights exist in romance literature, and while historical evidence for such intimacy between serving women and the lord of the household is lacking, the literary representation buttresses the sense of a broadly symbolic association of women servants with the intimate and bodily.[28] Even in households where no other female servants are evident, the task of laundering garments and linen always fell to a woman (though one of low status), and some evidence exists that laundresses could be called upon for such intimate tasks as washing a nobleman's head.[29]

Women servants dealt with their lady's bedding too, as in the 'Harleian Regulations', where the gentlewoman chamberer made the bed of estate with the aid of grooms of the chamber and a yeoman usher while the household was at morning mass. In the evening it was her duty, 'if the estate do lie with his feer', to bring the bedlinen and pillows to the bed, while the yeomen ushers made a fire and grooms placed lights in the bedchamber and smoothed the bed. The gentlewoman chamberer passed each item of linen to the grooms making up the bed, 'always kissing her hand when she delivers any of the sheet things to the grooms'.[30] In Henry VII's household, where the king and queen normally kept separate beds, male servants were responsible for making the king's bed and ladies and gentlewomen the queen's.[31]

The tasks of noblewomen in service were not restricted to such intimate matters, however. Damsels and gentlewomen could serve a political function, and were cultivated as useful advocates or go-betweens for ambitious men trying to gain the favour of a great lady. Sir John Paston and John Paston III used gifts to cajole Joan Rodon to 'labour' in Sir John's 'matters' with her mistress the duchess of Norfolk, and after Sir John's death John III looked to both Joan and another gentlewoman, Anne Montgomery, to smooth dealings for him.[32] Lady Honor Lisle asked her daughter Anne, who was in royal service in the 1530s and 40s, to intercede for her at court, though Anne tended to be uncooperative.[33] Other practical tasks included being entrusted with financial duties or errands by their ladies, but it was probably older or married ladies who were given the more responsible tasks or those requiring independent journeys. Eleanor of Castile charged Margerie de Haustede, one of her 'ladies', with the keeping of her jewels, and Edeline de Popiot made payments on behalf of the Crown for expenses concerning Eleanor's children.[34] Two of Isabella of France's *domicellae* rode to London on the queen's business in 1312, though as Isabella had many older married damsels it is likely that the damsels were two of these more mature women.[35] In the same year Alice de la Legrave, a married damsel, was sent with Lord William de Boudon, keeper of the queen's wardrobe, from London to Langley to Lady Christine de Marisco, 'to have a talk with her concerning certain affairs touching the queen herself'.[36] Although older damsels were entrusted with the greatest responsibilities, their training in the required codes of conduct while younger would have readied them for such tasks. They were certainly expected to acquit themselves responsibly and with humility, as Anne and Katherine Bassett were exhorted to 'be sober, sad, wise and discreet and lowly above all things' when applying for positions as maidens to Jane Seymour. 'Be obedient and governed and ruled by my Lady Rutland and my Lady Sussex [with whom the girls would stay at court], and Mrs Margery and such others as be your ladyship's friends here; and to serve God and be virtuous, for that is much regarded, to serve God well and to be sober of tongue.'[37] The emphasis on lowliness and restraint is found also in John Husee's letter of 1539, recommending his kinswoman Mary, daughter of John, Lord Hussee, for a position in the Lisle household, telling Lady Lisle that he hears 'so much of her good behaviour and honesty that there shall be no further enquiry. ... As far as I can learn she will use herself lowly and diligently.'[38] Inappropriate behaviour could result in dismissal or its threat for maidens, though unfortunately the letter writers are too discreet to supply details of the girls' faults. The Paston's kinsman Calthorp sought to remove Anne Paston from his household in 1470 for reasons unknown to her mother and brothers, while Anne Basset caused a flurry in 1537 when her behaviour irritated the countess of Sussex, who had to be pacified with letters and gifts from the solicitous Husee.[39]

Young *domicellae* served public or political roles in great households through less direct or obvious means. The wide cultural value of the maiden as a woman in 'perfect age' made young women welcome members of great households, for whom displays of splendour and beauty aided in their self-representation as strongholds of wealth and power. Though this emphasis on presentation grew much stronger towards the end of the Middle Ages, as aristocratic households reached their zenith and court life attained increasing complexity, some such concern may have been present even in the late thirteenth-century and early fourteenth-century courts, when queens and princesses were accompanied by retinues of ladies and maidens during their frequent travels and made some provision for their wardrobes.[40] In 1312 Queen Isabella gave her *domicella* Joan de Villers a cloth of gold, which could have been used for splendid self-presentation in the queen's service.[41] Aristocratic women of the fourteenth and fifteenth centuries also made a point of travelling with their female servants and often paid for items of clothing. When the widowed Lady Harington visited Elizabeth Berkeley's London home in June 1421 she was accompanied by three damsels, three esquires and eight valets, and when Elizabeth, Lady Dudley, came for dinner the following day she was escorted by two damsels, a chaplain, three esquires and six valets.[42] Elizabeth de Burgh had her female and male servants richly attired in cloth and furs.[43] Some ladies were not prepared to foot the bill for the clothing of maidens in their service yet could be angered if their presentation fell below expected standards, as the duchess of Suffolk threatened to expel Mary Barantyne and Elizabeth Stonor if they were not better arrayed.[44] In the early sixteenth century a good deal of attention was paid to maidens' dress at court, with Katherine and Anne Bassett advised to take two changes of 'honest' clothing, one of silk and one of damask, with them for their viewing by Jane Seymour as prospective maidens in 1537, and once Anne had been accepted to the position the queen ordered her to cease dressing in French fashions.[45] These concerns with appearances were no doubt partly prompted by aristocratic and royal desire to display their splendour (read power) to their peers, but at court also had a purpose within international diplomacy. Although the medieval use of damsels and ladies to provide an impressive court retinue did not reach the heights attained in the late sixteenth century by Elizabeth I who was inspired to dress her damsels in white, no doubt to provide a glittering backdrop to her own 'virginal' self-presentation,[46] the approving comments of official visitors such as Leo of Rozmital's secretary in the 1460s and Venetian ambassador Sebastian Giustinian in 1515 make explicit the effect the presence of beautiful young women could make upon foreign emissaries.[47] The symbolic value of the maiden as a woman of perfect age no doubt aided in her visual value as the medieval lady's equivalent of a modern businessman's 'arm candy', and through her cultural capital the youthful virgin reflected some of her glory back on the household which sustained her.

There was a clear gender division between the duties of young noble-men and women serving in great households. Damsels and gentlewomen were reserved for tasks concerning the lady's body, while male servants, employed extensively by women even where a queen or lady kept her own *familia* separate from her husband's, were on hand to attend to duties concerning food, fetching and carrying, and stewardship of domestic spaces. Not only queens' accounts, but also those of great noblewomen including Elizabeth Berkeley and Elizabeth de Burgh recorded the employ-ment of male servants within the lady's chambers, and noblewomen's wills include bequests to male servants.[48] The separation of tasks of male and female servants under everyday conditions became apparent under the extraordinary circumstances of royal childbirth, when the wish to preserve a purely female environment necessitated the adoption of masculine roles by women servants. The 1494 royal ordinances describe the beginning of a queen's confinement, when she is led to the birth chamber by men of the greatest estate who then must leave:

> Then all the ladies and gentlewomen to go in with her; and after that no man to come into the chamber where she shall be delivered, save women; and they to be made all manner of officers, as butlers, panters, sewers, carvers, cupbearers; and all manner of officers shall bring to

them all manner of things to the great chamber door and the women officers for to receive it in the chamber.[49]

The late fifteenth-century 'Beauchamp Pageant', illustrating the history of Richard Beauchamp, earl of Warwick, and his family, depicts just such a sex-segregated scene, representing the birth of Henry VI.[50]

Though Caroline Walker Bynum has written of the medieval association between food and the feminine, this association does not hold true for the highest-status households of late medieval England.[51] Women there neither cooked the food, worked within the kitchens, nor served it at table, nor when men performed these tasks were they engaged in non-masculine behaviour. The unpublished 'Harleian' ordinances for a late fifteenth-century household of a duke, marquess or earl lay out in great detail the choreography of meal times for the lord and his lady served in the great chamber. The grooms of the great chamber, the yeomen of the ewery, the cellar, the scullery, the buttery, and pantry, the gentlemen and yeomen ushers, the clerk of the kitchen, the carver, cupbearer, sewer (who oversaw the service of meals) and almoner all carry out highly specified tasks in setting up the tables, arraying table linen and dishes, carving and serving the food and carrying away the dishes and trestles at the end of the meal. Throughout the midday dinner, which by this period and in a household of such status was served separately in the chamber and hall, the lady's female servants play no practical role. The 'gentlewomen of presence' sit at the knight's board in the great chamber, that is, the lower of the two tables there (the lord and his lady are at the estate's board), alongside the gentleman ushers, and both are served by yeomen of the chamber. The chamberers and lady's gentlewomen sit at the next-ranked table, just outside the great chamber door, joined by the yeomen ushers once the latter have finished serving at the knight's board, and are served by grooms of the chamber. A similar seating arrangement was prescribed for the contemporary Percy household.[52] Royal ordinances support the impression of the gendered division of labour, with male servants responsible for bringing food to both lords and ladies: 'and she [the queen] to be served of her chamberlain, and of the greatest estate, like as the king is served.... And for the king's mother, to have a baron to bear her spice-plate, and a banneret to bear her cup.'[53] Even in such a powerfully feminine atmosphere as the churching feast of Elizabeth Woodville in 1465 which was described in some detail by the overawed Gabriel Tetzel in the retinue of the Bohemian emissary Leo of Rozmital, most impressed by the quantities of beautiful ladies and maidens present who knelt before the queen

117

throughout the meal, the food itself was apparently served by high-ranking men.[54]

Women servants sometimes played a role at meals and feasts, but one more closely bodily and intimate than the service of food. At Elizabeth of York's coronation feast two of her ladies, Dame Katherine Grey and Mistress Ditton, 'went under the table where they sat on either side [of] the Queen's feet all the dinner time'. It is difficult to see what purpose this could have served other than to convey an impression of feminine presence, but it is powerful as an expression of lowly but intimate service. Throughout the meal, served to the queen by Lord Fitzwater as sewer and by knights, the countess of Oxford and the countess of Rivers 'kneeled on either side of the Queen, and at certain times held a kerchief before her Grace', to collect her spittle and wipe her mouth.[55] A few decades later the countesses of Oxford and Worcester stood by Anne Boleyn at her coronation feast and intermittently 'did hold a fine cloth before the queen's face when she list to spit or do otherwise at her pleasure', and she too had two gentlewomen under the table at her feet.[56] The tasks of noblewomen servants at this elite level, then, reveal not a feminine association with food, but rather with intimate matters of their mistress's body. Male servants performed the same duties for their lords, thus eliminating the possibility of a straightforward interpretation of the women's tasks as, for example, 'unclean' and the men's as 'clean', but the exclusion of women from the symbolically powerful service of food and its associations with material wealth and status indicates an exclusion of noblewomen from the emblems of wealth and power, and a closer association with the body.

No medieval English equivalent of the 'courtesy book' – a guide to young men in service – exists for English noble maidens in service, and this makes it relatively difficult to piece together a picture of their duties.[57] But, given the evidence examined, it appears that English damsels were expected to perform the same kinds of tasks as the Aragonese *donzela* or French *damoisele*. En Amanieu de Sescas's late thirteenth-century *Ensenhamens de la donzela*, possibly the only European work extant aimed exclusively at this occupational group, describes how the *donzela* must rise before her mistress, help her to dress and be ready with needles and thread if necessary, to clean her nails, dress her hair, bring her water for her toilette and a mirror to check her appearance once finished.[58] Christine de Pisan's ladies and maidens-in-waiting are expected to be ever near their lady, 'waiting at hand to run to her if she sighs ever so slightly, ready on bended knee to provide service or obey orders at her word', and when she takes up some piece of handiwork 'will gather her handmaidens and ladies to do the same'.[59] Though young unmarried damsels were not idle, and their positions were invested with a fair degree of glamour, they lived in general a rather circumscribed existence. It is in romances that one finds youthful maidens performing more active, even adventurous, tasks, taking messages into battlefields or roaming far and wide on behalf of their mistresses.[60] Real maidens in aristocratic service reading of the exploits of their fictional counterparts must have vicariously enjoyed these tales of independent and intrepid damsels dashing across enemy territory or exotic lands, far from their own duties in making their mistress's bed, tending to her young children, paring her fingernails and wiping away her spittle.

Economically, gentry and other noble maidens were subsumed within the great financial machine of their immediate and extended families. Their work in service, therefore, was not always undertaken for their direct or individual economic benefit, and was often not rewarded by a salary. Frequently their parents had even to help pay the board of their daughters in other people's households. When Elizabeth Paston was with Lady Pole her mother Agnes reminded herself to send 26s. 8d. to cover the board, just as Margaret Paston was prepared to help with the funding of Margery, and John II was ready to meet his sister Anne's expenses of one hundred shillings a year though she was not his daughter.[61] On the other hand, Calthorp claimed that he wished Anne Paston out of his house because of problems in receiving money from tenants and the resulting necessity to reduce his household and live more thriftily, while a main-tenance indenture from 1383 within the Lestrange family revealed that the household included a squire and damsel at the cost of 4d. a day in lodging.[62] Some householders paid for the shoes or clothes of resident maidens,[63] though as already noted, mistresses as high-placed as the duchess of Suffolk were not always prepared to pay for the girls' clothing and Dorothy Plumpton in 1506 asked her father to send a hat and some cloth for kerchiefs.[64] Lady Lisle's correspondence with Anne and Mary Basset and their French hostesses largely concerned their petty expenses and requests for clothing.[65] Even at court some queens were unwilling to supply damsels with necessities. Jane Seymour would not pay for Anne Bassett's clothing or bedding, which Lady Lisle was obliged to provide. Anne was however paid a respectable salary of £10 per annum, and maidens in aristocratic households sometimes received wages.[66] There is no apparent consistency to the way in which maidens in service were dealt with financially. Although it seems that sometimes the unmarried damsels received less than married servants, as in Elizabeth of York's account where the unmarried Anne Percy does not appear on the wages list alongside her married counterparts nor is recorded as receiving clothing, at others they were more generously treated than married women, as in Eleanor of Castile's court.[67] This variety of financial circumstances makes clear that although money was of some consideration for both parents and mistresses in the employment of damsels, noble maiden's service was aimed more to procure an indirect than a direct economic reward. This came about primarily through the advantageous marriages which service helped noble girls towards (either because they met their future husbands in service or their mistress or other contacts aided in finding them an appropriate match), but also for the girls' families, through the extension or strengthening of networks through daughters' service which could eventually lead to improvements in the family's standing as a whole. Noble girls in service, then, were part of something much larger than themselves, and for the same reason they had no real economic autonomy during maidenhood. Though they were privileged, noble maidens' lives were not their own.

Town and country

Adolescent women constituted a highly visible and vital part of economic life in medieval English towns and the countryside. Work, often in some kind of 'service', formed as central a role in the life cycle of urban and rural maidens as secondary schooling has come to play in the lives of modern adolescent girls. Medieval families and employers, as in many recent and contemporary economies, found many benefits for themselves in using such cheap, usually low-skilled, non-organised workers. In addition to their activities in apprenticeships, service and within the family unit, young unmarried women took on wider economic functions as heiresses, recipients of property by various *inter-vivos* means, and participants in court cases involving property transfer or disputes. But what kind of status did they possess as workers and economic agents, and what degrees of autonomy were open to them? To what extent were maidens of middle and low status better off than the wives and widows they would become?

It has become a common perception that maidens in towns and the countryside enjoyed a higher degree of independence and self-determination than was possessed by women at other life-cycle phases, and that unmarried young women possessed legal abilities and economic autonomy far exceeding what was available to wives and, in terms of rights if not actual circumstances, even approaching those of men. The notion of women's greater independence during adolescence has taken two different, though in some respects overlapping, forms among historians. Judith Bennett has argued for women's greater legal and economic autonomy while young and single than when married, even though in general and over a *longue durée* women's work was low-status and low-paid compared with men's. Young unmarried women on the manor of Brigstock before the Black Death engaged in land transactions (mostly as receivers) and participated in civil pleas in the manorial court in a manner comparable to – though in numbers smaller than – adolescent sons, while merchet payments on the Ramsey manor from 1398 to 1458 suggest that peasant maidens enjoyed a degree of economic autonomy in the post-Plague period too, as one-third of merchets over that period were paid in the bride's name. These women probably earned money to pay merchets through their own wage labour.[68] In their recent collection on premodern European singlewomen, Bennett and Froide note that although 'life-cycle singlewomen' were not entirely free from the regulation of elders and possessed only a little wealth, 'they found adolescence to be a time of exceptional autonomy'.[69] Jeremy Goldberg, who has undertaken the most sustained studies of young single-women's work in late medieval England, places greater emphasis on change over time and the impact of the Black Death. He argues that in the period from the Black Death to around the mid-fifteenth century young women found spaces opening up for them in the labour market which enabled them to leave the natal home, migrate to other villages and towns where they could engage in waged labour (usually as servants), save for their own marriages and exert a greater degree of choice over their marital partner, away from the prying eyes of family members. 'The institution of service [in this period] provides for a high degree of emotional and even economic independence from parents and family at an early age.'[70] This window of opportunity began to close in the second half of the fifteenth century. Caroline Barron's work on women in London also contends that the period from the mid-fourteenth to mid- or late fifteenth century offered improved conditions for working women, though she focuses more on married and widowed women than maidens.[71]

Although in fundamental respects their views oppose one another, Bennett and Goldberg share the view that young unmarried women at certain times during our period had relatively strong opportunities to pursue independent ways of living in the years before marriage, and it is implied that such independence was desirable or advantageous in the eyes of the young women themselves. Others have offered a similar perspective. Richard Smith compares evidence on post-plague English female service with its Tuscan equivalent, and suggests that in England service did not indicate a 'marginal' status for women, nor was it necessarily an undesirable second-best option (where early marriage did not occur), but rather could be 'a context which [young women] themselves desired'.[72]

Independence, autonomy, desirable choices – these are all attractive terms to modern scholars and readers sympathetic to the aspirations of late twentieth-century feminism. The mental image of 'those spirited and daring girls who left their villages and went to work in the towns; who lived together in cheap lodgings, drank in alehouses, told jokes in church, paraded in the street, chatted to young men; who got themselves into various kinds of trouble with the law; who led risky, unconventional, and adventurous lives', is almost irresistible.[73] But may it be slightly romanticised? Moreover, does the available evidence support this perspective? This section will attempt to synthesise the now substantial body of evidence on maidens' economic activity and labour, adding a small amount of new material, and query whether recent scholars have been too quick to understand medieval maidens' economic participation through the lens of modern feminism's notion of work as a form of liberation for women.

It is not difficult, when examining any set of medieval records dealing with property and civil disputes, to find examples of women described as 'daughter of'. Daughters made wills, charters, received land through inheritance or other means, and acted on their own behalf in manorial, borough and common-law courts.[74] In some instances, 'daughters' are even more common than women described as 'formerly wife of'. The rolls of the Wakefield manor court and tourn in two sample years of the early fourteenth century, which in almost 75 per cent of instances describe women by relationship to another as 'daughter', 'sister', 'wife', 'widow' or 'maid' of rather than by name alone, record a high proportion of the women involved in land transactions as daughters.[75] Of the 122 land transactions involving women, including payments of heriot and merchet by women, 45 per cent involve women described as 'daughters'.[76] Widows act in just under 19 per cent of the transactions, women of unknown household status in just under 16 per cent of instances, married women act alongside their husbands in just under 15 per cent, and women described as 'wife' and acting alone in just under 6 per cent of transactions.

Daughters in early fourteenth-century Wakefield were more active in landholding activity than women at other life phases, and this, like Bennett's evidence for Brigstock, would seem to demonstrate the unmarried woman's ability to act under her own name in the law. It does not necessarily indicate autonomy, however, as a bald quantitative exercise such as this does little to indicate the extent to which daughters' landholding was bound up in the activities of a wider kin network. It may also result in an overly optimistic assessment of unmarried women's economic activity if that is not compared with male patterns. As Bennett notes, in pre-Plague Brigstock wider gender patterns of landholding applied among sons and daughters: as women overall made up 21 per cent of participants in the land market, so one daughter granted or received land for every four sons. Sons were more likely to receive land as heirs, while daughters relied on parental gifts, or *inter-vivos* transactions. Also, as women were generally more likely to act jointly or intrafamilially than men, so daughters were more likely to act alongside partners or family members than sons were.[77] Bennett's study of the Brigstock singlewoman, Cecilia Penifader who took up her first piece of land at twenty and added many more holdings to that throughout her life, demonstrates landholding daughters' dependence on family members in the absence of a husband, as Cecilia took up plots near those of her brothers and the siblings probably worked together to tend the lands and animals.[78] On a more technical note, 'daughter' is not a guaranteed indicator of maiden status. Older women who had not married might be so described, as indeed might women who were in fact wives or widows.[79] On the manor of Havering in 1235, Beatrice, daughter and heiress of Osbert of the Beme, sold some land and appended her seal identifying herself as Osbert's daughter to the deed of sale, and fourteen years later, though by now married, was still using the same seal and identity of daughter.[80] In addition, some of the women identified by name only may have been maidens, though they could equally have been older singlewomen, wives or widows.[81]

While it is important not to overstate the extent to which young unmarried women were able to act independently in the rural land market in pre-Plague rural England, it is also worth noting that the numbers of 'daughters' taking up holdings went into significant decline after the Black Death in a number of districts. First, let us consider women's chances of inheritance in general terms. It has been calculated that in a stable medieval population, roughly 60 per cent of landowners left at their death one or more sons, roughly 20 per cent left daughters only, and roughly 20 per cent left no children. Under the simplest circumstances then (which probably rarely existed in reality), one could expect daughters to inherit estates in about 20 per cent of families in which primogeniture prevailed, as among the late-medieval English nobility under common law. It was never actually this simple, as for example the offspring of dead sons would sometimes be preferred as heirs over remaining surviving sons or daughters. Still, the 20:20:60 ratio offers a basic guide. Jack Goody has calculated that in periods of demographic crisis the percentage of families leaving sons could drop dramatically to around 35 per cent while the percentage leaving only daughters would remain constant, and the percentage with no surviving heirs could rise to as high as 45 per cent. Estates in the last instance could pass either to male or female collaterals, and the net result would be a rise in the number of estates in female hands.[82] Simon Payling has found that among the landed aristocracy, rates of female inheritance under common law varied dramatically from 1236 to 1496, with direct female heirs in as few as 6.8 per cent of cases in 1327–35 to as many as 18.1 per cent in middle of the post-Plague population slump in 1370–7. One of his arguments is that despite the availability of strategies to reduce female inheritance through the use and tail male by this time, demographic factors were allowed to prevail and female rates of inheritance rose sharply.[83] Among the nobility, then, female inheritance rose substantially in the decades following the Black Death, but was this also the case within peasant communities?

Calculating the proportion of peasant holdings which one would expect to pass into daughters' hands is even more complicated, because systems of inheritance within peasant society did not straightforwardly follow the model of primogeniture. Although it is possible to discern the emergence of unigeniture systems – such as primogeniture and ultimogeniture – within English peasant society from the twelfth century onwards, these never entirely supplanted older structures of partible inheritance which were designed to secure the welfare of the whole sibling group.[84] Younger (or, in the case of ultimogeniture, older) sons and daughters (where any sons were present) could and often would be provided for by a range of other provisions, especially forms of *inter-vivos* transfer.[85] In the case of daughters, one would expect to find such transfers in dowries or premarital gifts of land. In sum, were fourteenth- and fifteenth-century English peasant inheritance patterns to operate in a strictly rational fashion according to the systems of devolution which manorial society devised for itself, one would expect to find families with daughters in control of holdings and parts of holdings in excess of the minimum 20 per cent expected under primogeniture and common law.

This was not the case. Moreover, the demographic catastrophe of the Black Death seems to have lessened, rather than improved, daughters' chances of holding land in English peasant society. No historian has attempted to undertake a sustained study of patterns of daughters' landholding before and after 1348, though some have begun to trace *women's* tenancies more generally.[86] What follows therefore is a necessarily tentative case for the decline of daughter's access to property after the mid-fourteenth century, based on fragments gathered from a range of manorial studies carried out over the last two decades or so, and future studies will no doubt cast a clearer light on this subject.

On the Suffolk manor of Redgrave, daughters were relatively visible participants in the land market before 1348. While this may to an extent mirror their general visibility in other manors before the Black Death, such as Brigstock and Wakefield, Poos and Smith have located a 'striking increase' in female participation during several crisis periods: the early 1270s, early 1280s, mid- to late 1290s, and 1310–19 – all eras of harvest failures, subsequent food shortages, and deaths of male heirs.[87] The appearance of women at this time probably indicates sales of property which they inherited as a result of the lack of male siblings. In the period 1315–19, Smith has also suggested an expansion in parents' gifts of land to daughters among wealthier tenant families.[88] That is, girls in this group were being granted larger dowries and other premarital gifts, during these famine years. This is what one would generally expect: at times of demographic crisis a larger proportion of male heirs fails, and land is more strongly concentrated into female hands.

On the Essex manor of Havering, McIntosh also notes fairly strong patterns of female tenancy in the mid-thirteenth century (though she does not give figures for the crisis years as Poos and Smith do). In 1251, 42 out of 367 tenants and subtenants (11.5 per cent) were widows and singlewomen (wives were included as co-tenants only under their husbands' names). Of these 42 women, 20 were singlewomen, and at least some of these presumably maidens (14 were listed under their own name only, and 6 as 'daughters'). She also notes that thirteenth-century families, even the poor, tended to grant their daughters dowries in land. The total number of female tenants and subtenants rose slightly but significantly to 17 per cent in 1352/3. More to the point, while the proportion of widows among female tenants had been over half in 1251, by the mid-fourteenth century it had dropped to 15 per cent. In contrast, 38 of the 86 female tenants (44 per cent) were listed in their own name, and 35 (41 per cent) were described as 'daughters'. In Havering, at least, one immediate effect of the Plague was that a great many more tenancies were in the hands of singlewomen, many of them probably maidens whose brothers had died or abandoned the manor. It is worth noting, though, that in 1352/3, as in 1251, singlewomen's holdings were regularly smaller than men's.[89]

Daughters' relative prosperity did not last long at Havering, though. In 1405/6, women holding land on their own constituted only 1.5 per cent of tenants, and by 1444/5 no women at all held tenancies alone (6 per cent and 2 per cent of tenancies were held by wives alongside their husbands in 1405/6 and 1444/5 respectively). McIntosh explains this rapid change in women's fortunes as a result of strong patterns of migration (that is, migration of men) onto the manor after 1352/3.[90] The situation in Havering after the plague, therefore, offers interesting points of similarity to Redgrave. In the latter, Smith has noted that daughters after the Black Death did not inherit at the rate one would expect, based on demographic factors, and while wives and widows benefited from *inter-vivos* transactions, daughters were not so favoured. Early-fifteenth-century evidence 'shows little favour bestowed upon their daughters by men as they arranged for the dispersal of property after their death. What is more, dowries in land to daughters ... were at this date an increasingly rare event.'[91] The declining incidence of dowries in land granted to girls has also been noted by Mate in Sussex, where thirteenth- and fourteenth-century dowries were either in land or money, and often in land following the Black Death, but by the fifteenth century were almost always in money or chattels.[92]

Although other historians of manorial landholding have paid less attention to women than Smith and McIntosh, it is possible to detect comparable patterns elsewhere in England. At Kibworth Harcourt in Leicestershire, the steward, Simon Pakenham, responded with remarkable swiftness to the crisis of 1348–9. Forty-four landholders died over this time, leaving only a small proportion of holdings unaffected. By the end of 1349 only four of the forty-four holdings were without a tenant, the great majority distributed by Pakenham to sons (many of them minors), brothers, and nephews, other relatives or affines, and widows. In Howell's words, 'There was no need for daughters to inherit'.[93] As waves of plague recurred through the century and families became extinct in the male line, holdings passed to sons-in-law, adopted sons and nephews.[94] Although at Kibworth Harcourt the rights of widows were strong, the almost complete exclusion of daughters from holdings during such a crisis, with even minors preferred as tenants, seems extraordinary. Moreover, daughters did not benefit much from *inter-vivos* transactions, as dowries in land were modest or non-existent on the manor.[95] At Cuxham in Oxfordshire (where again widows were favoured heirs), daughters seem not to have been seen as the solution to vacant tenancies in the wake of the Plague either, despite the mortality rate of around 66 per cent. Holdings were filled, slowly, by 1355, and all the new villeins were apparently migrants from outside the manor.[96] The Berkshire manor of Englefield, examined by Rosamund Faith, shared more in common with Havering in Essex, with a large proportion of tenancies in female hands immediately following the first wave of plague (32 per cent in 1349), but dropping sharply away thereafter, with 4 per cent in 1402, 8 per cent in 1441, and no female tenants at all in the listings for 1474 and 1496.[97] Faith lists numbers of female tenants on eight other Berkshire manors, and while it is difficult to discern definite trends one pattern which does seem common is the decline in female tenancy by the end of the fifteenth century. Dyer notes that in Whitstones in the West Midlands, in 1538, customary tenants claimed they had never known a man's daughter to become an heir under customary tenure, though investigation of the court rolls shows daughters in fact inheriting as late as 1462.[98]

Though further investigation, and a closer focus on daughters, will be necessary before any conclusions may be stated with certainty, some trends emerge from these studies. Daughters, though they might be expected to take up a larger proportion of peasant holdings at times of demographic crisis, frequently did not, and they nowhere experienced great benefit in the longer term towards the end of the fifteenth century. Even in those instances where they held a larger proportion of land than usual immediately after the first wave of plague, this quickly disappeared, presumably because they married immigrants to the manor and control of the holding passed to their new husbands, and thence to male heirs. In some instances, as in Kibworth Harcourt and perhaps Cuxham, there appears to have been a concerted effort to keep land out of the hands of daughters. This is perhaps hardly surprising, as independent female tenure of land was undesirable, in most cases, as medieval agricultural activity required the labour of a family group. Indeed, a good deal of evidence regarding daughters' taking-up of holdings must be hidden to the historian, as it would often have shortly preceded or followed her marriage, and her husband would answer for it. Yet the fact that women, including daughters, are seen to take up land and act independently with regard to it in numerous districts before the Plague, and appear to do so less and less in the years following, must be significant. The post-Plague era, often seen as something of a golden age for the English peasantry and as ringing the death-knell of serfdom, was no halcyon era for young women on the land. It is as though the waves of death so shocked the populace – both lords and tenants – that male control of property had to be asserted with greater force than ever. Alternatively, the sheer mass of land lying unoccupied was unprecedented, and far more visible than even at earlier moments of demographic crisis, and men who would traditionally have had to remain landless saw and seized the chance to take up holdings on a scale not witnessed before. Faced with the choice of single women, or male relatives with lesser claims and migrant males arriving on their doorstep, lords and their stewards opted for the latter groups as a safer bet.

If rural daughters had decreasing opportunities to make their living from landholding after the Black Death, did migration to towns or other villages and taking up work in service nevertheless offer young women a degree of economic independence? There has been considerable debate over this question in recent years.[99] The view offered here is that because evidence on young women's work in service before the Plague has been little explored, and indeed little may be available, the matter of whether young women's opportunities to find positions improved after the Black Death must, for the time being, be laid aside. Specialist studies may well in the future offer a clearer perspective on whether young women's opportunities were in decline by the late fifteenth century.[100] What can be achieved, at this point, is some sense of how attractive and advantageous young single women's work was for maidens themselves, in rural and urban areas.

Though it is not possible to measure proportions, many rural maidens clearly stayed at home with their natal families for some or all of this life-cycle phase. These girls worked for the benefit of their families, as indeed they would have done since early in childhood. The 1379 Poll Tax returns for Howden and Howdenshire, which purport to list all inhabitants of sixteen years and over, are unusual in designating the occupations of daughters (*filiae*) living within the household. Of 115 daughters who appear to be living in their natal homes, 79 (69 per cent) are listed as 'servant', 17 (15 per cent) are called 'labourer', 5 (4 per cent) are called 'webster', 2 (nearly 2 per cent) are 'brewsters', and 12 (10 per cent) are not given any occupations. These 115 daughters were listed within the homes of 'husbandmen' or 'labourers' in 63 instances (55 per cent), within brewing households in 16 instances (14 per cent), within other craft or skilled households (tailors, smiths, wrights, websters, millers and clerks) in 17 instances (15 per cent), and in the homes of servants (some of whom seem to have been single females, possibly widows) in 9 instances (8 per cent).[101]

As most of these daughters were resident in households whose living was based primarily on agrarian and labouring work, and the great majority of these girls were listed as servant or labourer, the kinds of work which they engaged in would have been varied but essentially in low-skilled domestic and agricultural tasks. While these sixteen-year-old and older girls would have shared in some of the tasks of their younger sisters (and brothers), including childminding, fetching water, wood, nuts and fruit, they would also have been taking on adult women's tasks around the house such as brewing and baking, making cheese and butter, spinning, carding, sewing and weaving, tasks nearby the house such as sheep-shearing, milking cows and sheep, feeding and tending poultry, growing vegetables and laundering, and tasks which took them out into the fields such as weeding crops, reaping, gleaning and winnowing.[102] A few jobs, such as carting and ploughing, were usually the preserve of men, but while there was some notion of a gendered division of labour, this did not constitute a separation of spheres, and it would not have been thought unusual or unseemly for young women to work near or alongside men.[103] It was only the incidence of accidental death which was unusual in the case of Cecily, a servant of John de Saltewells in a Bedfordshire village, who in 1274 went in a cart with William, son of William de Burtone, looking for sheaves of dredge, and who died when the cart turned over in a ditch and her neck was broken.[104]

Girls in Howdenshire may have found it easier to find enough work to support them within their home villages than young women in some other parts of the country, as it was a predominantly pastoral area, and thus offered more in the way of 'women's work' such as sheep-washing and shearing, carding, spinning and weaving, milking sheep and cows, and making butter and cheese, than more strongly arable regions did.[105] Unmarried daughters across the country, however, did not always find adequate economic opportunities available to them in their home villages. As it was not the nature of peasant families, except perhaps the wealthier ones, easily to absorb excess labour and hungry mouths, these daughters looked beyond the home village for work. Whether they remained in their own village or moved to another, many young women would have been engaged in waged labour, especially during harvest and haymaking seasons when labour was in strong demand. At such times rural maidens had the opportunity to earn something of an independent income for themselves, but, as Sandy Bardsley has shown in a sophisticated recent study, women's average earnings would often be considerably less than men's. In pre-Plague Ebury and the post-Plague East Riding, the highest women's wages reached parity only with the lowest men's wages: thus the ablest women were often paid the same as the weakest men (the old, young or disabled). Adolescent women and girls, given this pattern, were probably paid less than the best-paid women.[106]

Away from home, in villages and towns, young women found themselves employed usually as maids of all work, whether in agrarian, craft, trade or mercantile households, rather than in specialised occupations.

Goldberg, Smith and others have portrayed this movement into service as motivated as much out of desire as necessity, but the working conditions Goldberg and others describe seem often far from enticing. As adults, especially as widows, women were found as household heads within a few major industries and trades. Poll Tax evidence shows female heads concentrated into the occupational categories of textiles, victualling and clothing. Spinsters and hucksters (petty retailers), were the most often recorded, and shepsters (dressmakers), laundresses, brewers, tapsters and hostillers appeared in smaller numbers, alongside a number of other industries.[107] There was nothing elite, lucrative, or even necessarily comfortable about the status of these occupations, yet these were the occupations in which adult women might expect to secure an independent income, as married *femmes soles*, as singlewomen or as widows. An intriguing point about Goldberg's findings is that the kinds of households that were most commonly open to women as independent workers were not the households in which we most often find female servants. While textiles and clothing accounted for between 48 and 68 per cent of independent women workers (depending on the region), these industries employed only 6 to 20 per cent of female servants. And conversely, while mercantile households were hardly ever headed by women, they employed a large proportion of female servants. As he goes on to point out, only infrequently 'can women have set themselves up in trades for which they had received formal training within service', although many would have gained informal training in tasks such as needlework and washing from an early age, no matter what kind of household they worked in.[108] This insight provides a useful modification to a straightforward notion of life-cycle service as a form of female 'education' or occupational training. In most cases, young women in service were engaged in dead-end kinds of work which held little promise of a future in a skilled trade. Service did, of course, offer vocational training of a sort, but only occasionally in the kinds of trades which could sustain independent women. The exceptional case of silk-workers will be considered shortly.

Girls left home to enter service at an apparently minimum age of twelve, and there seems to have been some attempt to protect girls from entering service earlier than this.[109] Though younger girls were no doubt occasionally found in service, such as 'little' Margaret, *ancilla* to Agnes de Kyrketon who bequeathed the girl ten marks 'if she lives to the age of discretion',[110] girls below the canonical age of consent were generally not perceived to be old enough to leave home. This is not surprising when one considers the often transient and insecure nature of their occupation.

Servants in York and Exeter were usually contracted for the term of one year, though evidence for longer periods of employment can be found.[111] The practice of yearly hiring is usually seen by historians as advantageous, rather than fundamentally insecure, to the employee in this post-Plague environment, as it offered workers the opportunity to move to more attractive work environments year by year. But there is no direct evidence that young unmarried female servants gained a great deal from this supposedly labour-friendly environment. Goldberg's suggestion that service was an attractive institution in freeing girls from the influence of their natal families, allowing them to work for wages and so build up savings towards their own marriages and thus be at greater liberty to choose the marital partner of their own preference, is to an extent countered by his evidence on wages. While some kindly and well-off employers bequeathed money and household goods to their maids, not all servants would have experienced the death of their mistress or master while in their employ, as Goldberg notes.[112] And wages for female servants were small – often half the male rate or less. In 1391–2 in Oxford mean female servants' wages were 4s. 10d., compared with 13s. 2d. for males. Frequently, the wages were non-existent. As was common in the early modern era, young female servants seem often to have worked for their food, lodging and clothes.[113] Even if some young women managed well, it is difficult to see how such harsh working conditions could have in general held a high degree of economic and emotional independence for young women.

What work opportunities awaited adolescent women in towns, other than the low-status and lowly remunerative work of service? The classically 'feminine' trades of brewing, prostitution and silkwork all held a place, but little prestige or financial comfort, for young unmarried female workers. Although young singlewomen tended not to become brewsters in their own right, given the time and capital outlay required, maiden brewsters were not unheard of, but would have brewed only occasionally rather than on any large or regular scale.[114] Moreover, daughters and servants would have helped with the brewing process while working in their parents' or others' households, as is apparent from the Howdenshire evidence. Robert Belamy's daughter Amice was working in the brewhouse of Lady Juliana de Beauchamp in Staplehoe in Bedfordshire, around three o'clock one October afternoon in 1270, when her feet slipped and she fell into the boiling vat and the tub of grout she and another maidservant carried between them fell on top of her, and she was fatally scalded.[115] This example provides a glimpse of a task probably common among daughters and young female servants.

Certainly, adolescent women were found among the prostitutes, or 'common women', of late-medieval England. Women of different types, young and middle-aged, single and married, were involved in prostitution – which often provided casual rather than full-time work, for women in poverty needing to supplement their meagre incomes – and maidens already living within precarious economic circumstances were sometimes drawn into this world.[116] Service and apprenticeship sometimes provided the route into commercial sexual activity for adolescent women – by their consent, by coercion, or by force. In London in 1385 the court of the mayor, aldermen and sheriffs heard the case against Elizabeth Moring, who had allegedly taken one Johanna into her household as an apprentice embroiderer, alongside a number of other women, but incited Johanna and the others 'to live a lewd life, and to consort with friars, chaplains, and all other such men as desired to have their company ... and used to hire them out to the same friars, chaplains, and other men, for such stipulated sum as they might agree upon, as well in her own house as elsewhere'.[117] Ruth Karras discusses a number of well-documented cases from the London courts in which young women, living away from their natal families, were coerced into commercial sex, sold as sex-slaves or procured for rape, and Hanawalt also examines London evidence which emphasises the sexual vulnerability of young women living far away from home.[118] Such tales are balanced out, on the other hand, by examples of employers, masters or mistresses of female servants and apprentices, taking on quasi-parental roles in relation to the adolescent women living under their roofs, such as John Bown, a cordwainer, enforcing marriage upon his servants Margaret Barker and John Waryngton when he found them in compromising circumstances in his house in York in 1417. He ordered John Waryngton to thus do 'honour' to Margaret, clearly seeing her as the vulnerable and injured party.[119] While no single example can sum up the experiences of either abuse or paternalism, exploitation or protection, meted out by employers to maidens under their roofs, clearly some young women away from home were exploited targets or willing subjects for sexual experiences, some of which were commercially oriented.

It was no doubt with a sense of the potentially sceptical eye which male governing elites would cast upon households of independent women workers and their youthful female assistants that the 'silkwomen' of London repeatedly petitioned the Crown in the second half of the fifteenth century, to protect their industry against the competition from foreign men moving into London. The petitions cast the silkwomen as virtuous dames and damsels in economic distress, neatly employing three key devices in the petition of 1455 to aid their case: the virtuous and worshipful character of the women, the rightness of keeping the craft in the hands of women of English nation and blood above allowing it to fall into the hands of Lombard interlopers, and the evils of the 'great idleness amongst young gentlewomen and other apprentices of the same crafts within the said city' should the silkwoman's share of the industry fail. Eight years later the same tactics were employed, but in 1482, the stakes were raised, and the petition speaks not only of silkwomen but of 'the king's woeful men and women' of the craft (and reiterates the phrase 'as well men as women' thereafter), claims that the threat from foreigners comes not only from the 'Lombards' of earlier petitions but from 'Jews and Saracens', and from worrying about enforced idleness moves to bemoaning a vision of unemployed silk-workers cast into a life of crime and ruin.[120] The first and second petitions' anxiety to convey an image of 'many good households' full of gentlewomen learning the craft 'full virtuously, unto the pleasance of God, whereby afterward they have grown to great worship', and the third's inclusion of male workers among those wronged, was perhaps seen as necessary in an era when other cities were beginning to express anxiety about women living away from the control of men.[121] It is notable that when the grievance had earlier been brought before the London mayor and aldermen in 1368 the silkwomen's case was presented in much more straightforward language of financial disadvantage.[122]

The London silk industry was the only one to apprentice girls in a widespread and organised manner. There are only scattered references to female apprentices in cities outside London, such as Isabella de Wakefield who is called apprentice to seamstress Christiana de Knarisburgh in a York cause paper of 1402, a handful of other girls under apparently informal apprenticeships including one to a York armourer, and Joan Blakhay 'servant and apprentice' to a male weaver in Exeter in 1380.[123] In London, female apprenticeship was so firmly connected with the silk industry that the sample female indenture in William Kingsmill's early fifteenth-century formulary book chose 'silkwoman' as the occupation for the imagined girl's putative mistress.[124] Of the four surviving girls' inden-tures, two were apprenticed to silk throwsters, one to a silkwoman, and one to a tent or canopy maker, while another London girl apprentice worked for a corseweaver.[125] Where female servants were generally required to be over the age of twelve, it appears that apprentices needed to be at least fourteen. In 1417 the mayor of London found that Katherine Lightfoot, who had been bound by Thomas Blounvyle and his wife as an apprentice to themselves, against her will and her father's, should be exonerated from her contract as the court found her to be 'still under fourteen years of age'.[126] While female apprentices were supposed to be formally enrolled by the City, and contracted for seven years, the substantial numbers of mistresses and masters of girls appearing before the mayor's court to answer why they had not properly enrolled them suggests that female apprenticeship was more common and *ad hoc* than available records indicate, and many girls may have served for only a short time, providing craft households with useful and financially attractive labour (apprenticeships were not waged: they had to be paid *for*). After all, the silkwomen had no guild, and could not receive the freedom of the City, so there was little official advantage for girls in serving full terms.[127]

Like the petitions to the Crown, the silkworker-apprenticeship indentures present a fiction of hard-working, highly respectable bourgeois households. In addition to their promises not to commit fornication, mentioned in the previous chapter, girls promised not to frequent taverns, play unseemly games, or marry without their permission. The experiences of girls such as Johanna, apprenticed to embroiderer and procuress Elizabeth Moring, indicate that the virtuous households were sometimes less reputable than the fiction maintains, and a number of cases brought before the mayor involving the excessive beating of female apprentices suggests a degree of abuse or exploitation within some households.[128] Although they tended to come from well-off backgrounds, the vulnerability of some girls was perhaps heightened by the fact that many of them were orphans. Katherine Nougle and Eleanor Fincham were probably orphans (in the contemporary sense that they had lost their fathers), as their brothers rather than their fathers undertook to place them in apprenticeships. Of the nineteen cases concerning female apprentices found in the printed plea and memoranda rolls, fifteen were probably orphans as their fathers were not mentioned in the proceedings, and the remaining four had fathers alive.[129] Of the twelve appearances of female apprentices in the Letter Books of 1335 to 1436 all were orphans, though this is slightly deceptive as their appearance in court reflects the mayor and aldermen's duty to oversee the girls' wardships.

It is hoped that the present study does not paint an unremittingly grim picture. No doubt individual maidens – those with kindly and generous employers or mistresses, those from nurturing and better-off family backgrounds, and those who were fortunate enough to earn and save money – had reasonably positive experiences. No doubt many expected little, and were grateful for the chance to make their living. But the established accounts of independent and fortunate young women enjoying the fruits of the post-Plague economy, or enjoying a strong degree of autonomy during their years of maidenhood, seem too rosy when the evidence is examined more broadly.

Conclusion

The labouring lives and economic experiences of maidenhood prepared young women for fundamental aspects of their futures as adult women. The work and service most would perform throughout their lives would be piecemeal, often unskilled or low skilled, supplementary to the main work of household, without high status (except for those few at the highest social levels), and lowly paid if at all. Daughters of gentry and aristocratic families found service a rather more comfortable experience, but independence had little if any part to play. Work and service during maidenhood provided excellent education and preparation for the less attractive aspects of life as a wife. Combined with the ideological messages circulating throughout the culture, it set young women up for future usefulness, and an expectation of secondary status.

Notes

1 Rosemary Horrox, 'Service', in Rosemary Horrox (ed.), *Fifteenth Century Attitudes: Perceptions of Society in Late Medieval England* (Cambridge, 1994), p. 61.

2 See, for example, Judith M. Bennett, *Ale, Beer, and Brewsters in England: Women's Work in a Changing World, 1300–1600* (New York, 1996), esp. pp. 145–57; Olwen Hufton, *The Prospect before Her: A History of Women in Western Europe, Volume One, 1500–1800* (London, 1997), pp. 152–72.

3 P. J. P. Goldberg, 'Delvers and spinsters: gender and work in late medieval English towns' (unpublished paper, Leeds International Medieval Congress, 11 July 2000).

4 Dale, 'London silkwomen'.

5 A. R. Myers (ed.), 'The household of Queen Margaret of Anjou, 1452–3', in A. R. Myers, *Crown, Household and Parliament in the Fifteenth Century* (London, 1985), p. 184. Though Myers notes that the Eleanor Roos listed is difficult to identify, Seaton easily marks her as the daughter of Sir Robert, *Sir Richard Roos*, p. 52.

6 Myers (ed.), 'The household of Queen Elizabeth Woodville, 1466–7', in *Crown, Household, and Parliament*, p. 289.

7 For grants to Eleanor and Richard Haute see *CPR 1467–77*, pp. 90, 460–1.

8 See above, p. 64.

9 Seaton, *Sir Richard Roos*, pp. 52–5.

10   C. A. Sneyd (ed.), *A Relation, or Rather a True Account, of the Island of England c. 1500*, Camden Society os 37 (London, 1847), pp. 24–5.

11   Christiane Klapisch-Zuber, 'Women servants in Florence during the fourteenth and fifteenth centuries', in Barbara A. Hanawalt (ed.), *Women and Work in Preindustrial Europe* (Bloomington, 1986); Michael E. Goodich, '*Ancilla Dei*: the servant as saint in the late Middle Ages', in Julius Kirshner and Suzanne F. Wemple (eds), *Women of the Medieval World* (Oxford, 1985); Smith, 'Geographical diversity'.

12   Kate Mertes, *The English Noble Household, 1250–1600: Good Governance and Politic Rule* (Oxford, 1988), pp. 42–3, 57–8; also C. M. Woolgar, *The Great Household in Late Medieval England* (New Haven, 1999), pp. 34–6; Ward, *English Noblewomen*, pp. 52–4.

13   *PL and P* 1, no. 186; and 2, no. 723.

14   *PC*, p. xxxix.

15   M. K. Dale (ed.), Vincent Redstone (trans.) and J. M. Ridgard (postscript), *The Household Book of Dame Alice de Bryene of Acton Hall, Suffolk, September 1412 to September 1413*, Suffolk Institute of Archaeology and History, 2nd edn (Bungay, 1984).

16   Eileen Power (trans.), *The Goodman of Paris* (London, 1928). The Goodman or *Ménagier* was certainly a knight, and was possibly Guy de Montigny: see Nicole Crossley-Holland, *Living and Dining in Medieval Paris: The Household of a Fourteenth-Century Knight* (Cardiff, 1996), pp. 3–9, 185–211.

17   *SL and P* 2, no. 172; *PL and P* 2, no. 711.

18   ffiona Swabey, *Medieval Gentlewoman: Life in a Widow's Household in the Later Middle Ages* (Stroud, 1999), p. 117.

19   Hyrd (trans.), *Instruction of a Christen Woman*, I.iii.

20   *TE* 4, pp. 116–17; Alison Hanham, *The Celys and their World: An English Merchant Family of the Fifteenth Century* (Cambridge, 1985), pp. 271–2.

21   *PL and P* 1, no. 201. On Margery Paston and Richard Calle see Chapter 4 below.

22   Martin M. Crow and Clair C. Olson (eds), *Chaucer Life Records* (Oxford, 1966), pp. 67–93.

23   Blackley and Hermansen (eds), *Household Book of Queen Isabella*, pp. xiv, 14, 142, 156, 172, 176.

24   Woolgar, *Great Household*, pp. 46–9.

25   See above, pp. 74–5.

26   BL MS Harl. 6815, fol. 26v.

27   'Articles ordained … Henry VII', in *Collection of Ordinances*, p. 123.

28   For example, Wheatley (ed.), *Merlin*, pp. 225, 466, 499 and 607; *Blanchardyn and Eglantine*, p. 50.

29   Margaret Wade Labarge, *Women in Medieval Life: A Small Sound of the Trumpet* (London, 1986), p. 68, finds a payment to Bogo de Clare's laundress for washing his head in the accounts for 1234–6, and wonders if some laundresses, especially those associated with military campaigns, may have doubled as prostitutes. Ruth Mazo Karras finds clear connections, *Common Women: Prostitution and Sexuality in Medieval England* (New York, 1996), pp. 54–5.

30 BL MS Harl. 6815, fols 26v–27r, 37v.
31 'Articles ordained … Henry VII', in *Collection of Ordinances*, pp. 121, 127.
32 *PL and P* 1, nos. 270, 271, 354, 383.
33 *LL* 5, no. 1513.
34 Parsons, *Court and Household*, p. 29; Byerly and Byerly 1, p. 55, 2, p. 201.
35 Blackley and Hermansen (eds), *Household Book of Queen Isabella*, p. 48.
36 Blackley and Hermansen (eds), *Household Book of Queen Isabella*, p. 142.
37 *LL* 4, no. 887.
38 *LL* 5, no. 1382.
39 *PL and P* 1, no. 206; *LL* 4, no. 906.
40 Byerly and Byerly 1, p. 23; 2, p. 57; Blackley and Hermansen *Household Book of Queen Isabella*, pp. 60, 120, 156, 176.
41 Blackley and Hermansen (eds), *Household Book of Queen Isabella*, p. 236.
42 Ross, 'Accounts of Elizabeth Berkeley', p. 95.
43 Ward, *English Noblewomen*, p. 56.
44 *SL and P* 2, no. 172.
45 *LL* 4, nos. 887, 896.
46 On Elizabeth's ladies' and damsels' white dresses see Arthur Collins (ed.), *Letters and Memorials of State in the Reigns of Queen Mary, [etc.]*, (London, 1746), vol. 2, pp. 171–2; Paul Hentzner, *A Journey into England in the Year MDXCVIII*, ed. Horace Walpole, Aungervyle Society Reprints, ser. 1 (Edinburgh, 1881), p. 32; E. K. Chambers, *The Elizabethan Stage*, 4 vols (Oxford, 1923), vol. 1, p. 45.
47 Malcolm Letts (ed. and trans.), *The Travels of Leo of Rozmital through Germany, Flanders, England, France, Spain, Portugal and Italy 1465–1467*, Hakluyt Society ser. 2, 108 (Cambridge, 1957), p. 47; Rawdon Brown (ed.), *Four Years at the Court of Henry VIII: Selection of Despatches Written by the Venetian Ambassador Sebastian Guistinian*, 2 vols (London, 1854), vol. 1, pp. 79, 81.
48 For Eleanor of Castile see Parsons (ed.), 'Liber garderobe', in *Court and Household*, and Byerly and Byerly 1 and 2; for Isabella of France see Blackley and Hermansen (eds), *Household Book of Queen Isabella*; for Joan of Navarre, Margaret of Anjou and Elizabeth Woodville see Myers's editions in *Crown, Household and Parliament*, and for Elizabeth of York see Nicholas Harris Nicolas (ed.), *Privy Purse Expenses of Elizabeth of York: Wardrobe Accounts of Edward the Fourth* (London, 1830). For Elizabeth de Burgh see Ward, *English Noblewomen*; for Elizabeth Berkeley see Ross, 'Household accounts of Elizabeth Berkeley'; and for a range of other noblewomen with *domicellae*, gentlewomen, chamberers and maidens see *TE* 1, pp. 151, 293, 382–3; 2, p. 122; 4, pp. 6, 189, 258; 5, pp. 51, 202, 297 (I have not included the abundant references to female servants as *serviens*, *ancilla* or *famula* as these probably indicate lower-status women). For male servants in noblewomen's wills see Ward (ed. and trans.), *Women … Gentry and Nobility*, pp. 189, 225.
49 'Articles ordained … Henry VII', in *Collection of Ordinances*, p. 125.
50 Viscount Dillon and W. H. St John Hope (eds), *The Pageant of the Birth, Life and Death of Richard Beauchamp, Earl of Warwick, K. G. 1389–1439* (London, 1914), plate 44.

51 Caroline Walker Bynum, *Holy Feast and Holy Fast: The Religious Significance of Food to Medieval Women* (Berkeley, 1987).

52 BL MS Harl. 6815, fol. 31v; *NHB*, p. 301.

53 'Articles ordained ... Henry VII', in *Collection of Ordinances* p. 110. See also pp. 111–12, 121.

54 This point is not at all clear in Malcolm Letts's translation, which is somewhat abbreviated compared with Myers's extract: A. R. Myers (ed.), *English Historical Documents 1327–1485* (London, 1969), p. 1169; cf. Letts (ed. and trans.), *Leo of Rozmital*, p. 47.

55 John Leland, *Antiquarii de rebus Britannicus collectanea*, ed. Thomas Hearn, 6 vols (London, 1774), vol. 4, pp. 226–7.

56 James Gairdner (ed.), *Letters and Papers, Foreign and Domestic, of the Reign of Henry VIII* (London, 1882), vol. 6, no. 601.

57 See Chapter 2, p. 83 on the distinction between courtesy and conduct books.

58 A summary of de Sescas's text may be found in Alice A. Hentsch, *De la littérature didactique du Moyen Âge, s'adressant spécialement aux femmes* (Cahors, 1903), pp. 95–6.

59 Christine de Pizan, *A Medieval Woman's Mirror of Honour: The Treasury of the City of Ladies*, trans. Charity Cannon Willard, ed. Madeleine Pelner Cosman (New York, 1989), pp. 72, 96–7.

60 For example, J. Douglas Bruce (ed.), *Le Morte Arthur: A Romance in Stanzas of Eight Lines*, EETS ES 88 (London, 1903), lines 2048–85, 2608–715; W. Aldis Wright (ed.), *Generydes: A Romance in Seven-Line Stanzas*, EETS OS 55 and 70 (London, 1873–78), lines 5596–702.

61 *PL and P* 1, nos. 29, 201, 270.

62 *PL and P* 1, no. 206; Nigel Saul, *Knights and Esquires: The Gloucestershire Gentry in the Fourteenth Century* (Oxford, 1981), p. 12.

63 *SL and P* 2, no. 234; T. H. Turner (ed.), 'Expenses of Sir John Howard, Knight, from A.D. 1462 to A.D. 1469', in *Manners and Household Expenses*, pp. 312–13, 582; Woolgar (ed.), *Household Accounts*, part 1, p. 239; part 2, pp. 586, 662.

64 *PC*, no. 201.

65 *LL* 3, pp. see esp. pp. 213–14 for Mary's account, payable upon her departure.

66 *LL* 4, nos. 887, 895; *NHB*, pp. 46, 256; Turner (ed.), 'Expenses of Sir John Howard', p. 222, 267; Woolgar (ed.), *Household Accounts*, part 2, p. 671

67 Nicolas (ed.), *Privy Purse Expenses of Elizabeth of York*; Parsons, *Court and Household*, p. 29.

68 Bennett, *Women in the Medieval English Countryside*, pp. 76–82; 'Medieval peasant marriage', passim. She has made the case for the continuity of the poor status of women's work in a number of works. See, for example, 'Medieval women, modern women: across the great divide', in David Aers (ed.), *Culture and History 1350–1600: Essays on English Communities, Identities and Writing* (London, 1992), and *Ale, Beer, and Brewsters in England: Women's Work in a Changing World, 1300–1600* (Oxford, 1996), ch. 8.

69 Bennett and Froide, 'A singular past', p. 8.

70 Goldberg, *Women, Work, and Life Cycle*. Quote at p. 327. A shorter version is in

his 'Female labour, service and marriage in the late medieval urban North', *Northern History*, 22 (1986), 18–38.

71 Barron, '"Golden age"'.

72 Smith, 'Geographical diversity', esp. pp. 41-6, quote at p. 42.

73 Riddy, 'Mother knows best', p. 86.

74 For example, for York wills of 'daughters' see BIHR PR 1, fol. 45; PR 2, fols 13, 155, 247v, 407v, 414v, 557v, 637; PR 3, fols 35, 535, 543, 563; PR 4, fols 3, 32, 147v, 175; PR 4c, fol. 149; PR 5, fols 18, 168, 171, 393v.

75 This is based on two samples taken from the printed rolls, each covering the records of manor court for a year: William Paley Baildon (ed.), *Court Rolls of the Manor of Wakefield*, Yorkshire Archaeological Society Publications 36 (Leeds, 1906), pp. 52–114 (October/November 1306–September 1307), and John Lister (ed.), *Court Rolls of the Manor of Wakefield*, Yorkshire Archaeological Society Publications 57 (Leeds, 1917), pp. 1–68 (October 1313 to September 1314). From a total of 702 appearances by women, 516, or 73.5 per cent, are defined by relationship with another individual. For women in Wakefield after the Plague see Helen M. Jewell, 'Women at the courts of the manor of Wakefield, 1348–1350', *Northern History*, 26 (1990), 59–81.

76 Payments of heriot are included in the sample because they indicate land passing to the heir(ess) on the death of the former tenant. Merchet payments are included because although they were ostensibly fines allowing a servile woman to marry, historians including Eleanor Searle have argued that they acted as a tax on dowry for better-off peasant girls, for whom dowry was a form of pre-mortem inheritance. Dowry reserved part of the family holding for use of a daughter and her husband upon marriage. One consequence of this was a reduction in the proportion of chattels to which the lord would be entitled as heriot upon the death of the tenant of the family holding. Thus merchet, argues Searle, acted as compensation for such foreseen reduction in the lord's entitlement. See the debate between Jean Scammell and Eleanor Searle carried out in *Economic History Review*, ser. 2, 27 (1974), 523–37; 29 (1976), 482–6, and 487–90; also Searle, 'Seigneurial control of women's marriage: the antecedents and function of merchet in England', *Past and Present*, 82 (1979), 3–43; Paul A. Brand and Paul R. Hyams, 'Debate: seigneurial control of women's marriage', *Past and Present*, 99 (1983), 123–60, including contributions by Brand and Hyams, Rosamund Faith, and Searle.

77 Bennett, *Women in the Medieval English Countryside*, pp. 81–2.

78 Judith M. Bennett, *A Medieval Life: Cecilia Penifader of Brigstock, c. 1295–1344* (Boston, 1999), esp. pp. 80–1.

79 For some examples see C. W. Shickle (ed.), *Ancient Deeds Belonging to the Corporation of Bath XIII–XVI Centuries*, Bath Records Society Publications (Bath, 1921), pp. 8, 11–12, 23.

80 Marjorie Keniston McIntosh, *Autonomy and Community: The Royal Manor of Havering, 1200–1500* (Cambridge, 1986), p. 170.

81 Problems of identifying women by marital status are discussed by Bennett in her *Ale, Beer, and Brewsters*, pp. 166–70. For Flemish parallels see Ellen E. Kittell,

'The construction of women's social identity in medieval Douai: evidence from identifying epithets', *Journal of Medieval History*, 25 (1999), 215–27.

82 E. A. Wrigley, 'Fertility strategy for the individual and the group', in Charles Tilly (ed.), *Historical Studies of Changing Fertility* (Princeton, 1978); Paul Brand, 'Family and inheritance, women and children', in Chris Given-Wilson (ed.), *An Illustrated History of Medieval England* (Manchester, 1996), esp. p. 75; S. J. Payling, 'Social mobility, demographic change, and landed society in late medieval England', *Economic History Review*, 45 (1992), 51–73; Jack Goody, 'Strategies of heirship', *Comparative Studies in Society and History*, 15 (1973), 3–20.

83 Payling, 'Social mobility', esp. pp. 51–62.

84 Cicely Howell, 'Peasant inheritance customs in the midlands, 1280–1700', in Jack Goody, Joan Thirsk and E. P. Thompson (eds), *Family and Inheritance: Rural Society in Western Europe, 1200–1800* (Cambridge, 1976), pp. 113–19.

85 For the methods available by the fourteenth century to tenants to transfer land to their heirs and other children see Lloyd Bonfield and L. R. Poos, 'The development of deathbed transfers in medieval English manor courts', in Zvi Razi and Richard M. Smith (eds), *Medieval Society and the Manor Court* (Oxford, 1996). For changes in property entitlements as they affected women in particular, but mostly wives and widows rather than daughters, see Richard M. Smith, 'Women's property rights under customary law: some developments in the thirteenth and fourteenth centuries', *Transactions of the Royal Historical Society*, ser. 2, 36 (London, 1986), 165–94.

86 For example, Smith, 'Women's property rights', and 'Coping with uncertainty: women's tenure of customary land in England *c.* 1370–1430', in Jennifer Kermode (ed.), *Enterprise and Individuals in Fifteenth-Century England* (Stroud, 1991).

87 L. R. Poos and Richard M. Smith, '"Legal windows onto historical populations"? Recent research on demography and the manor court in medieval England', repr. in Razi and Smith (eds), *Medieval Society and the Manor Court*, p. 304.

88 Richard M. Smith, 'Families and their land in an area of partible inheritance: Redgrave, Suffolk 1260–1320', in Richard M. Smith (ed.), *Land, Kinship and Life-Cycle* (Cambridge, 1984), pp. 160–1.

89 McIntosh, *Autonomy and Community*, pp. 171–3.

90 McIntosh, *Autonomy and Community*, p. 173.

91 Smith, 'Coping with uncertainty', p. 62.

92 Mate, *Daughters, Wives and Widows*, p. 25.

93 Howell, *Land, Family and Inheritance*, p. 242.

94 Howell, *Land, Family and Inheritance*, pp. 42–3, and 242–3.

95 Howell, *Land, Family and Inheritance*, pp. 258–61.

96 P. D. A. Harvey, *A Medieval Oxfordshire Village: Cuxham 1240 to 1400* (Oxford, 1965), pp. 123, 135–7.

97 Rosamund Faith, 'Berkshire: fourteenth and fifteenth centuries', in P. D. A. Harvey (ed.), *The Peasant Land Market in Medieval England* (Oxford, 1984), p. 161, table VII.

98 Christopher Dyer, 'Changes in the size of peasant holdings in some West Midland villages 1400–1540', in Smith (ed.), *Land, Kinship and Life-Cycle*, pp. 291–2.

99 Goldberg, *Women, Work, and Life Cycle*; cf. Bailey, 'Demographic decline'. For an introduction to aspects of the debate see Mavis E. Mate, *Women in Medieval English Society* (Cambridge, 1999), pp. 27–61.

100 This is not to underestimate the importance of such questions. It is because of their importance, and because of the inconclusive state of the debate at this point, that premature conclusions are avoided here.

101 'Assessment roll of the poll-tax for Howdenshire, etc., in the second year of the reign of King Richard II (1379)', *Yorkshire Archaeological Journal*, 9 (1886), 129–62. The other 8 per cent were scattered across a range of households.

102 Hanawalt, *Ties that Bound*, pp. 159–61, and her 'Peasant women's contribution to the home economy in late medieval England', in Barbara A. Hanawalt (ed.), *Women and Work in Preindustrial Europe* (Bloomington, 1986); Goldberg, *Women, Work, and Life Cycle*, pp. 139–49; Helena Graham, '"A woman's work …": labour and gender in the late medieval countryside', in Goldberg (ed.), *Women in Medieval English Society*.

103 Hanawalt has argued for a clear division of spatial spheres, with 'women's chief sphere of work as the home and men's as the fields and forests, *Ties that Bound*, p. 145, but Goldberg has made the case that the coroners' rolls of Hanawalt's focus indicate not so much a separation of spheres as of tasks, 'The public and the private: women in the pre-Plague economy', in Peter R. Coss and S. D. Lloyd (eds), *Thirteenth Century England III* (Woodbridge, 1991), pp. 75–8.

104 R. F. Hunnisett (ed.), *Bedfordshire Coroners' Rolls*, Bedfordshire Historical Society Publications, 41 (Streatley, 1961), p. 63.

105 Goldberg, *Women, Work, and Life Cycle*, pp. 139–40, 282–94.

106 Sandy Bardsley, 'Women's work reconsidered: gender and wage differentiation in late medieval England', *Past and Present*, 165 (1999), 3–29.

107 Goldberg, *Women, Work, and Life Cycle*, pp. 86–104, provides full details.

108 Goldberg, *Women, Work, and Life Cycle*, pp. 98–9, 186–9.

109 For an example see Sellers (ed.), *York Memorandum Book*, vol. 2, p. 29. See also Goldberg, *Women, Work, and Life Cycle*, pp. 168–73, and Mate, *Daughters, Wives and Widows*, p. 28.

110 Goldberg, *Women, Work, and Life Cycle*, p. 182.

111 Goldberg, *Women, Work, and Life Cycle*, pp. 173–6; Maryanne Kowaleski, 'Women's work in a market town: Exeter in the late fourteenth century', in Hanawalt (ed.), *Women and Work*, p. 153.

112 Goldberg, *Women, Work, and Life Cycle*, p. 182.

113 Goldberg, *Women, Work, and Life Cycle*, pp. 185–6; Mate, *Daughters, Wives and Widows*, p. 46.

114 Bennett, *Ale, Beer, and Brewsters*, pp. 39–42.

115 Charles Gross (ed.), *Select Cases from the Coroners' Rolls, A. D. 1265–1413*, Selden Society Publications 9 (London, 1896), pp. 14–15.

116 On the frequently casual and supplementary nature of work in prostitution see Karras, *Common Women*, pp. 53–4; P. J. P. Goldberg, 'Pigs and prostitutes: streetwalking in comparative perspective', in Lewis, Menuge and Phillips (eds), *Young Medieval Women*, pp. 176–9.

117 Henry Thomas Riley (ed.), *Memorials of London and London Life in the XIIIth, XIVth and XVth Centuries* (London, 1868), pp. 484–6.
118 Karras, *Common Women*, pp. 57–61; Hanawalt, *Growing Up*, pp. 122–3.
119 BIHR CP F 127. See P. J. P. Goldberg, 'Masters and men in later medieval England', in Hadley (ed.), *Masculinity in Medieval Europe*.
120 John Strachey and Edward Upham (eds.), *Rotuli parliamentorum*, 7 vols (London, 1832), vol. 5, pp. 325, 506; vol. 6, pp. 222–3.
121 Mary Dormer Harris (ed.), *The Coventry Leet Book*, EETS, os 134, 135, 138, 146 (London 1907–13), vol. 2, pp. 545, 568.
122 *CPM* 1, pp. 99–107.
123 BIHR CP F 22 (and see Goldberg, *Women, Work, and Life Cycle*, p. 191); Heather Swanson, *Medieval Artisans: An Urban Class in Late Medieval England* (Oxford, 1989), pp. 71, 116; Kowaleski, 'Women's work in a market town', p. 163, n. 56.
124 BL MS Add. 17716, fol. 68. The sample boy's indenture places the youth in apprenticeship to a scrivener – a natural choice for Kingsmill; fol. 67.
125 Katherine Nougle of London was apprenticed to a silk throwster in 1392, and Eleanor Fincham to another in 1447, CLRO Misc. MS 1863 and NRO MS Hare 2091. Elizabeth Eland of Lincolnshire was apprenticed to a silkwoman in 1454, PRO E/210/1176; and Margaret Bishop from near Lewes was apprenticed to a 'teldemakere' in 1378, WAM 5966. Ellen Semy was apprenticed to a corseweaver in 1445, *CPM* 5, p. 65.
126 *CPM* 4, pp. 229, see also pp. 53–4.
127 Hanawalt, *Growing Up*, pp. 142–4.
128 See for example, *CPM* 2, p. 107; *CPM* 4, pp. 42–3; *CPM* 4, pp. 53–4; and *CPM* 5, p. 63.
129 Those four cases are *CPM* 2, p. 107; *CPM* 4, pp. 42–3, 53–4, 229.

4

Sexualities

Late medieval English priests liked to tell exemplary stories as part of their Sunday sermons. Such tales, which they did not invent but took from a widely available and now almost forgotten stock of stories, were endowed with a strong moral flavour by the priestly teller and sometimes explained as allegories of the relationship of humanity with the Trinity and the Virgin Mary. Despite their moralising conclusions, the stories were at times very earthy in subject matter, and would have played an important role in educating lay audiences about licit and illicit forms of sexuality even while the very explicitness of the tales attracted listeners' attention.

One widely repeated tale was that of *The Incestuous Daughter*.[1] An extraordinary (to modern eyes) saga of sex, murder and redemption, it told of a Spanish man who had one beautiful daughter. He loved and cherished her greatly, and when she came to the age of fourteen or fifteen, fell into the sin of fornication with her. They maintained their sinful relationship for some years, and the daughter bore her father three children, murdered each baby, and buried them in the dungheap. At last the girl's mother found her husband and daughter together, and the girl killed her to keep her quiet. The father, horrified at these murders, resolved to abandon his sins, but his daughter took an axe and killed him while he slept. She left the house and went to a far-away city, and became a common woman, refusing the advances of no man – monks or friars, clerks or 'lewd' men. Finally a day came when she observed people going into a church and followed them in, and hearing the sermon preached there of God's infinite mercy she repented of her sins, and cried out her guilt in the middle of the sermon. So overcome with sorrow that her heart burst, she died, but because of her repentance was at once carried up to heaven.

Ostensibly, the story preaches the promise of redemption for even the most deplorable sinners, exemplified here through the incestuous, murderous and prostituted daughter. At another, more literal, level, it preaches a message on illicit forms of sexuality: for this young woman, incest and whoredom. But at the same time the tale performs the less edifying function of catching the listeners' interest through titillation – through making the obscene the centre of attention. There is no reason to suppose that maidens would have been excluded from the audience of such a sermon. Some of the edifying tales repeated in *The Book of the Knight of the Tower* were, if anything, more explicit, and that was a text aimed directly at inculcating virtues in young women.[2] Nor should this incest narrative be seen as nothing more than a bizarre one-off. Stories of father–daughter, brother–sister, and occasionally mother–son incest are found scattered throughout contemporary literatures of piety and of entertainment.[3] Incest taboos were of course central to the Church's teaching on sexuality and marriage, as an institution which had built up some of the most elaborate regulations against incest seen in any culture.[4] While the more extreme prohibitions on sex within four degrees of blood, affine and spiritual kinship were constantly broken in practice, sex within the first degree of kinship was at once railed against, and a subject for horrified (or excited) fascination.

This discussion of sexuality and maidenhood begins with this popular incest tale because in order to understand past cultures' constructions of sexuality it is helpful to emphasise their strangeness. One of the impediments to comprehension of past sexual practices and subjectivities has been the assumption that modern concepts and behaviours hold good for other cultures. The most recent scholarship on the subject emphasises the dangers of anachronism, and the helpfulness of studies of sexuality in overcoming such presentism. 'Few topics are more likely to challenge us to think differently than past sexualities, since we often assume what Peter Brown calls a "certain knowingness", a smug confidence that we already know it', write the editors of *Constructing Medieval Sexuality*.[5] Though much valuable work has been undertaken for several years on the subject of medieval sexuality, a large proportion of such studies presume that they know what 'it' – sexuality – is, and focus their attention on the various attitudes to it in different sources, especially those of learned discourses such as theology, canon law and medicine or natural philosophy.[6] The major challenge to presentist approaches came first from historians of 'homosexuality', making brilliant observations on ancient Greek society among others. Then slowly, though lagging somewhat behind, analyses of past forms of 'heterosexuality' have begun to emerge: what James A.

Schultz aptly terms 'heterosexuality before heterosexuality'.[7] It is within the latter field of study that this chapter aims to make a contribution. For while medieval maidens were taught by their families, their communities, their religion and their culture to be broadly speaking 'heterosexual', that is, to focus their desires on men rather than other potential sexual objects, they were not taught to be heterosexual in the same ways that young women of the twentieth and early twenty-first century have been.

An important factor is the comparative lack of importance of 'lesbianism' or female same-sex sexuality in late medieval English culture.[8] Technically speaking, such acts should have been deemed a species of lechery by confessors and a form of immorality to be punished by the ecclesiastical courts, but English manuals on the vices and virtues make no explicit mention of it and no case of female same-sex acts has yet been found in the records of the English ecclesiastical courts.[9] Indeed, concerted efforts on the part of a number of historians have to date turned up only about a dozen individual women punished for sexual relationships with other women, from across Europe, for the entire medieval period.[10] English literary works rarely address the subject either, with oblique exceptions such as Gower's adaptation of the tale of Iphis and Iante in *Confessio amantis*,[11] and some scholars have resorted to slightly strained readings of texts in an effort to identify female homoeroticism.[12] The clearest warnings against female-to-female sex acts are contained in some works concerning nuns, such as the *Ancrene Riwle* and Lollard denunciation of the abuses of the Church – though ambiguously in the latter – and in such instances the anxiety is about perverse female sexuality in general rather than singling same-sex acts out for particular condemnation.[13] No evidence has come to light to indicate that lay maidens were commonly warned against or titillated by public discussion of lesbian sexuality. No doubt women who loved and desired other women lived and had relationships with one another in later medieval England. The point is that their activities were not deemed threatening, appalling or exciting enough to warrant much explicit attention within texts, sermons or legal systems.

Without the opposite pole of lesbianism against which to be defined, medieval female heterosexuality needs to be understood in relationship to other categories of sexual subjectivity and activity. Concerns about social status played a strong role in constructing young women's sexuality, as did incest anxieties, and the oppositions of young and old, Christian and heathen, and of lay and cleric. While these categories established the borderlines between licit and illicit acts, they sat alongside the powerful constructions of the virgin and the whore, which condemned any kind of sexual act for unmarried women. It is also important to see, though, that between the poles of approved and proscribed sexualities lay the realm of the intriguing or titillating. This third group consists of sexualities forbidden in practice, but not absolutely unthinkable in fantasy or humour. Acknowledging the existence of this third category should help us to understand more fully the complexity of constructions of young women's sexuality.

Sexual boundaries

Sex, more than any other single factor, defined medieval maidenhood (especially, but not exclusively, elite maidenhood). Its simultaneous presence, in the maiden's maturing body and her idealisation as perfect femininity, and absence, in her virginity, were what marked her out most clearly from women at other stages of life.[14] The ambiguity and tension inherent within this conception indicate the wider ambiguity of maidens' sexuality. Although physical virginity was central to a maiden's identity, that did not render her an entirely asexual being either as an object or subject of desire. Throughout the period of her maidenhood she underwent preparation for her future life as a sexually active woman (if not among the handful destined for the convent) – as a wife, mother and member of a specific social group, and evidence from both court and parish life indicates that the display of maidens was culturally valuable, given their unique possession of sexual and virginal attractions. The construction of young women's sexuality was therefore complicated and many layered.

The chief and most obvious sexual borderline governing the lives of maidens was the boundary between virginity and its loss. However, that is not to say that loss of premarital virginity was everywhere of equal concern, nor that all social groups found maidens' defloration impossible to accommodate. In theory, in any culture, daughters' premarital sexual activity should be of most concern amongst status groups which have a tradition of passing property down a patrilineal line, and where a wife's fidelity is required to ensure that a landholder's offspring are truly his own. The premarital activity of unmarried daughters has the potential to disrupt the patrilineage, either because her behaviour while young forbodes future adultery, or because it may result in illegitimate offspring who could pose a rival claim to property. Perhaps even more significant, once the material or economic concerns linking property to female sexuality have been long established within a social group they become embedded in the cultural outlook of that group, with the result that control over wives' and daughters' sexuality becomes an integral aspect of masculine identity and male honour. This may have particularly important implications for groups in which daughters are offered as items of exchange or 'gift' between men. At this point, the cultural aspect of the perceived necessity to control women's sexuality may take on a life of its own, and endure even where no concerns about property prevail. What survives is a notion that the behaviour of daughters is intimately linked to and may reflect badly on masculine, especially paternal, identity.[15]

We saw in Chapter 1 that the belief that first intercourse at too early an age causes excessive libidinousness in a woman in later years dates at least to Aristotle's *Politics*, and received circulation within late medieval English intellectual culture in Giles of Rome's *De regimine principum*, and also in vernacular gynaecological texts.[16] Yet how widespread were concerns about daughters' chastity? One might expect to find the greatest level of concern within the aristocracy and gentry, some within mercantile and upper peasant groups, and the least in artisan and lower peasant groups. This is based on evidence regarding the importance of vertical lineage connections to those groups, judging from data regarding concepts of 'family property' and its transference from one generation to another, and the adoption of patrilineal surnames.[17] Yet investigation of a range of sources turns up a more complex picture.

By the second quarter of the thirteenth century, loss of virginity had gained a central place in common-law perceptions of the felony of rape. During the twelfth century common law had described rape in terms of generalised violence against a woman's body, whether she was a virgin or not, both in treatises and the language of court records. But with the composition of 'Bracton's' treatise of 1218–29 and in the records of subsequent cases before the royal courts, the question of whether or not the alleged victim had been a virgin before the crime had been committed gained prominence. This shift may have been due to the growing role of lay members of the gentry and aristocracy in the framing and practice of common law by the time of Henry III's minority, with the law on rape shaped better to reflect lay elite concerns about possession of daughters' sexuality.[18] Though rape law was formed by the interests of high-status groups, however, it was mostly used by victims of lower status, who seem often to have resorted to bringing appeals of rape (despite the astoundingly low non-conviction rate of alleged rapists) not so much to secure a conviction as a compensatory payment for their defilement.[19] Further complicating the picture, the development of Parliament as a legislative body, and the influence of lay gentlemen and aristocrats there, contributed to a third shift in common law's conception of rape, with the increasing

147

conflation of the felony of rape and the trespass of abduction in the statutes of 1275, 1285, 1382 and culminating in 1487's declaration that abduction of women constituted a felony.[20]

The development and practice of common law on rape, and the importance there placed upon defloration, offer in microcosm a glimpse of the complexities encountered in attempting to evaluate the extent to which familial concern about daughters' premarital virginity varied across the social spectrum. One key point to emerge is that it was by no means only the highest-status groups who shared anxiety about daughters' chastity. Given the practical, and possibly emotional, difficulties of pursuing an appeal of rape in the common-law courts and the extreme unlikelihood that it could result in conviction, daughters of poor families may only have troubled to take such action when it had the benefit of helping to clear their reputation and in some instances to be compensated by money payments. Indeed, one reason such a large proportion of victims never appeared in court to follow up their appeals must have been that the matter had been settled out of court, and this is sometimes recorded: 'The jurors testify that [Agnes Mason and Adam Turner] have come to an agreement', is the record of one outcome, and in another 'afterwards [Alice Stanchard] confessed … that Thomas, Simon's son, had undertaken to make amends to her for it'.[21] Ascertaining the socio-economic status of the women is difficult, but the fairly low levels of compensation sometimes recorded indicate that some of the victims who pursued compensation fit Robert Mannyng's picture of 'poor maidens' who, upon ravishment, deserved to be paid damages: 'If thou ravish a maiden poor / Thou art held to her succour, / And that shall be at her will / For as she will, thou shalt fulfil. / For thou hast done her a treason: / Thou hast stolen her waryson [gift, treasure].'[22]

A small number of cases have to date come to light which indicate that some young women, perhaps because they were of slightly higher status, were able to secure compensation for defloration without pursuing appeals of rape. In giving evidence to the York consistory court in 1453 John Russell deposed that he had heard Sir John Collom (vicar of Garton-on-the-Wolds) say that Robert Chew had deflowered Isabella Alan, a blood relative of the vicar, and because of the deflowering had left her twenty marks from his purse to spend.[23] The virginity of Isabella Alan (who seems along with other participants in the case to have belonged to the relatively well-off peasantry or yeomanry),[24] valued at £13 6s. 8d., was of a price far above the likely income of a yeoman farmer or skilled craftsman (at £5 per annum), and above even a minimum income for a gentleman (at £10 per annum).[25] As Robert Chew was not about to make an honest woman of Isabella, and instead went on to marry her kinswoman Agnes Cosyn,[26] he did (or was compelled to do) what he no doubt felt was the decent thing and provided her with a compensatory sum which she could use as her dowry which would improve her presumably reduced chances of marriage.

The chance survival of this transaction – which would never have been recorded, had Chew's marriage not come to be contested – may reveal a glimpse of a broader social practice. In the mid-fifteenth century Robert Trenender, a brazier of Bristol, and his wife Isabel made a petition to the court of Chancery, complaining that Philip Rychard had defiled their daughter and neglected to pay the damages assessed by arbitrators of the ward at a pipe and a half of woad or £20.[27] Given the size and type of the payment, Rychard was more likely to have been a trader in dyes than a humble dyer. From fifteenth-century London, Hanawalt has found a record of a man required to pay the substantial sum of £40 to be kept in trust by the city chamberlain for his young victim, while in late fourteenth-century Paris a small number of cases also record dowry contributions as compensation for defloration, or provision of maintenance upon the birth of an illegitimate child.[28] Although the evidence is patchy, the casualness of John Russell's remark, the evident grievance felt by the Trenenders, the involvement of civic officials in Bristol and London and Robert Mannyng's directives indicate that compensation for defloration of lower-middle- and middle-status maidens was common and expected in England, if lacking the regulation of Paris.

Already, it seems that to link concern with daughter's premarital virginity strictly to contexts in which strong concern for lineage prevailed is too simplistic. Evidently, some girls of poor backgrounds and some of middling urban status, as well as well-off peasantry, were subject to such concerns. It would be a mistake to imagine that servile or other lowly rural families never paid attention to their daughters' conduct. In 1366 the villein John Dogeson, father-in-law to Alice Redyng, told the York consistory court how he found John Boton and Alice in bed together, Alice naked and John partially so, and ordered John to espouse Alice on the spot.[29] John refused, while Alice claimed they were already betrothed. Others have found that often it was the young female partner who insisted on the existence of a marriage contract between herself and her lover, no doubt to preserve her reputation as well as financial security.[30]

Still, low-status rural daughters were probably subject to less pressure to remain chaste than those of other groups. Given that in early modern England bridal pregnancy was a common phenomenon, and given too that medieval English society found ways to accommodate bastards without too much difficulty (though without giving them the status of legitimate children), it seems unlikely that prohibitions on premarital sex were always as strong in practice as in ideals.[31] Lacking such riches as registers of births and marriages, historians have had little in the way of evidence for calculating levels of premarital sexual activity among lower-status peasant women, though presentments for leyrwite (a fine for female fornication imposed on servile women) and childwite (a fine for illegitimate birth) in manor courts can give us some notion of practice.[32] The highly erratic recording of leyrwite fines – with only some manors enforcing it, and then very inconsistently – suggests that the high numbers of fines in a given year may tell us more about a lord's need for funds than about fornication rates, and after the mid-fourteenth century the fine began to disappear altogether. One point which emerges, nonetheless, is that poorer girls in Halesowen and Redgrave were more likely to be amerced for leyrwite or childwite than daughters of better-off villagers.[33] This could indicate greater sexual experimentation and less control over daughters of the poorer levels of villein society, a view substantiated by the evidence that, in Yorkshire at least, suits brought by the ecclesiastical court to enforce marriage upon couples who had failed to cease sexual relations after being ordered by the court to do so were largely brought against members of lower peasant society.[34]

Horizontal bonds of household relationships, as well as vertical ones of kinship relations, also influenced perspectives on maidens' chastity. In urban artisan society notions of lineage were relatively weak,[35] yet a good deal of anxiety was expressed about young women's chastity. Some ecclesiastical court cases record parental enforcement of marriage to shore up a daughter's reputation, as in William Rote's 1475 London claim that his marriage was made under force and fear, when the father of his lover, Agnes Wellys, threatened him with a knife: 'You have violated Agnes, my daughter, and have known her carnally. You will contract marriage with her if I have to force you and you will be sorry.' When William ran away down the street Agnes and her mother both ran after him, calling 'Hold the thief'.[36]

Concern about maidens' chastity seems to have been just as strong, if not more so, among their employers, masters and mistresses, and wider members of the community. Given that many young unmarried women in towns were living away from the natal family, mostly as household servants and sometimes as apprentices, this is perhaps unsurprising. We have seen how female-apprenticeship indentures forbade sexual activity more strictly

than indentures for boys did, by barring them from any fornication within
the house or outside of it,[37] while employers of servants could enforce
marriage of male and female servants found in compromising circumstances within their master's home.[38] The community's role in sexual
policing is apparent in the 1497 London case concerning Joan Rokker's
alleged defamation of Joan Sebar. A witness told of how he had seen Rokker
in the street, scolding Sebar who was standing in a nearby doorway, calling
her 'Thou strong whore and strong harlot', throwing a piece of bread at
Sebar's head, and shouting, 'Go home thou strong whore and bid thy
dame ordain the clouts [cloths to use as nappies or swaddling]; an ever I
had child in my belly thou hast one. Here wert thou dight [an appropriate
translation might be 'screwed'], and here lay thy legs and here thy feet',
pointing to the next-door doorway. Deponents agreed that the defamatory
words would have a very deleterious effect on Sebar's reputation, and ruin
her marriage prospects.[39] Larry Poos and Marjorie McIntosh have undertaken extensive studies of late-medieval English defamation suits and
turned up clear patterns of the sexual double standard, where women were
far more likely than men to be defamed sexually, and men far more likely
than women to be slandered as thieves or for dishonesty (thus making
sense of the case concerning William Rote, above). Moreover, Poos has
demonstrated that (as in the Rokker and Sebar case), it is usually other
women who defame women sexually, and McIntosh has pointed to patterns
of ideological change in the later fifteenth century, with prosecutions for
sexual offences (among other forms of social deviance) increasing at this
time.[40]

Girls' premarital chastity, then, was important not only where concerns
of lineage were present, but also where notions of respectable reputation
across the household or the community were central to the control of
residents' behaviour. Within the households and communities so far
examined, there was only minor difference between the social status of
master and servant. Concerns about female residents' conduct were therefore all the greater, because of the bond of social identity between
employer and servant, or among local inhabitants. Such bonds are missing
in a letter concerning a servant's seduction and pregnancy in a gentry
household, from William Wittcars to Sir Robert or to William Plumpton:

> Right worshipful Master Plumpton, as heartily as I can recommend me
> unto you, desiring you to be a good master unto this poor woman, the
> bearer hereof. Sir, it is so that a servant of yours hath gotten a child with
> her, the which is lost for lack of keeping, as God knows. She hath kept it

as long as she may, whilst she hath not a cloth to her back but which I have given her, since she came to my service. And if it would please you to hear this poor woman speak, I trust to God ye will be good master to her and rather the better for my sake. And if I had not been, she would have run her way; and all this while I keep the child of my own proper cost, and will do till I hear some word from you.[41]

The role of the head of the gentry household as financial guardian of his *familia* is evident here, but there is no sense of moral outrage. The woman is to be pitied and offered charity, rather than seen as bringing down the reputation of the household by her transgression. Artisanal concern for the reputation of the whole household seems to be stronger by the fifteenth century than earlier, and the circulation of conduct texts such as *The Good Wife Taught Her Daughter* and *The Good Wyfe Wold a Pylgremage* seem to be responding to this desire for 'bourgeois respectability'.[42]

Within mercantile families, records of flirtation and courtship indicate a highly controlled level of interaction. Richard Cely had brief opportunity to cast his eyes over young Miss Dalton for the benefit of his brother George, when she took breakfast with him in the company of her mother, commenting favourably on her fairness, 'well-bodied' physique, serious manner and good height.[43] The following year Richard made an effort to form an acquaintance with Elizabeth Limerick, whom he inspected during and after Matins in Northleach Church in the Cotswolds and while sharing a drink in the afternoon (reporting later to his brother that she was agreeably young, 'little', well favoured and intelligent in conversation), her stepmother present all the while.[44] The soberness and carefully chaperoned nature of such encounters fits with the messages of the printed conduct books which were beginning to appear at the close of the Middle Ages. *The Book of the Knight of the Tower*, one of Caxton's earliest printed works, was simply the first in what would be a long line of printed works aimed at a respectable mercantile and gentle audience, and advocating increasingly strict limitations on maidens' contact with men. *The Book of the Knight* retains elements of its aristocratic French authorship, but its clerically inspired messages introduced a level of dourness to the text, making it of limited interest to audiences until the later fifteenth century, when its appearance in print was surely calculated to appeal to the respectable merchant class of which Caxton himself was a member. The Knight's book warns young women against interaction with young men, especially at such dangerous functions as feasts, dances and jousts, and a long rhetorical debate between the Knight and his wife over whether maidens should take courtly paramours ends with victory for his wife, who fervently argues that they should not.[45] The inclusion of courtly scenes of feasting, tournaments, dancing and licit flirtation with paramours, though they are ultimately warned against, reveals *The Book of the Knight* as a transitional text – marking the beginnings of a shift for merchant or lower-noble classes from courtly to more bourgeois ideals of conduct. By the mid-sixteenth century a stricter standard is evident in the appearance in print of numerous conduct books which have their origins in Spanish or Italian culture.[46]

A double standard was certainly present in the *Book of the Knight*, and in mercantile life too. The Knight advises his daughters not to show jealousy if upon marrying they find their husbands to be adulterous, but rather to win back their hearts through courtesy and obedience.[47] The Cely boys had their dalliances before marriage. George kept a French or Flemish woman called Clare at a house in Calais around 1479, while in 1482 begat a child (possibly his second with her) on a Calais cook called Margery (the baby girl later died).[48] Also in 1482 a woman called Em bore Richard Cely an illegitimate child.[49] Female servants living in mercantile houses were expected to resist such pressures. In 1401 Emma, wife of Henry Preston, a prominent York merchant, stated in her will that Alice Stede should have five marks towards her marriage 'if she will stay and remain an honest virgin and of good repute until she have a husband', but 'in the event that ignorantly or heedlessly she shall commit fornication or adultery, that she shall have only two marks and 6s. 8d.', suggesting that some mercantile households shared with artisanal ones a tendency to identify the sexual reputation of all female residents with the reputation of the household.[50]

Evidence so far examined indicates a desire to ensure young women's premarital virginity across a wide social range, though with slightly less emphasis among the lower ranks of rural society. Thus the theoretical model outlined at the beginning of this section offers a useful way into the topic, but must not be applied too strictly. The link between masculine honour and young women's sexuality in some instances prevailed where no concerns with property or lineage were relevant, such as between employer and servant. The limitations of the model are also apparent when attitudes within aristocratic society are considered. This group should have been more concerned than any other with daughters' chastity, given their obsession with lineage and the family name, and concern for familial honour and reputation. And indeed parents of aristocratic and gentry girls living either at home or in service at court or another great household took care to ensure their daughters were chaperoned, as Anne and Katherine Bassett were placed under the guidance of Lady Sussex and

Lady Rutland at court, and younger damsels and maids-in-waiting would generally have been under the supervision of older ladies-in-waiting in great households.[51] Yet, as will be elaborated later, flirtation and 'parasexual' interaction were common elements of life within elite households, and sometimes spilled over into full-blown affairs, which were not always treated with the simple outrage one might suspect. Families of higher rank had numerous ways to demonstrate their prestige and pedigree, so safeguarding daughters' virginity was perhaps not so pressing.

For men of the court, straightforward sexual encounters met with subdued or little condemnation. Thirteenth- and fourteenth-century royal ordinances indicate both a concern about the presence of women and prostitutes at court, and an acknowledgement that their presence was inevitable. In 1318 it was ordered that no member of the court should keep his wife or any *femme de fol vie* at court, and any such prostitute was to be banished from court, branded on the forehead if found a second time, and imprisoned for forty days on the third offence. A treatise of 1370 seems more resigned to their presence and includes serjeantry of the prostitutes among the clerk of the market's duties.[52] Chronicles indicate that noblemen's use of prostitutes or concubines at court or on campaign was simply normal. In an episode from the Hundred Years War, Froissart tells of how Philip von Artaveld took a damsel from Ghent with him on campaign 'as his sweetheart', and dispassionately describes how she rose from the tent where he lay sleeping one night and raised the alarm when she heard the French army massing to attack nearby.[53] The romantic exploits of Edward III, John of Gaunt and Edward IV are well known. But was tolerance of elite male sexuality no more than an example of the double standard, with their paramour's conduct condemned?

To an extent, the answer is yes. That several of the most celebrated royal concubines, such as Alice Perrers, Katherine Swynford and Elizabeth Shore were married or widowed suggests that maidens at court were often protected or excluded from sexual affairs. Yet such affairs did occur, and the examples of two other great late-fourteenth-century scandals suggest that even in these affairs it was mainly matters beyond the innocence of the girls that offended elite sensibilities. In 1387 when John of Gaunt's daughter Elizabeth Lancaster was sent to court 'to study the behaviour and customs of courtly society', she apparently learnt them too well. Though betrothed seven years earlier at sixteen to the then seven-year-old earl of Pembroke, the engagement seems to have been broken by the time that Elizabeth made close acquaintance with the king's constable Sir John Holland. He fell 'violently in love with her at first sight', according to the Westminster

Chronicler, and pursued her doggedly, until Elizabeth was found to be pregnant with Holland's child. Gaunt agreed that the pair should be married, and showed the constable no ill-feeling in accepting him as a travel companion on an important journey to Spain after the wedding.[54] Neither Henry Knighton nor the Westminster Chronicler dwell on the shocking nature of the event – indeed Knighton does not even allude to the seduction or pregnancy, only to the marriage – though it must have occasioned a good deal of gossip in its day and was considered by both newsworthy enough for inclusion in the chronicles. The lack of emphasis on ill-effects to Elizabeth's reputation is striking. Holland suffered not at all (for this misdemeanour at any rate) and a year later was created earl of Huntingdon, with an income of £1000 per annum, in 1389 was made admiral and keeper of the town and castle of Brest, and in 1390 appointed as the king's chamberlain.[55]

Later in 1387 Robert de Vere, duke of Ireland, rocked the court by procuring a divorce from his wife Lady Philippa de Coucy, and 'copulated in nefarious marriage' with Agnes Lancecron, a Bohemian *domicella* of the queen.[56] Agnes, it seems, did not consent, given the evidence that two of de Vere's followers abducted her.[57] The disgust expressed in polite circles regarding the duke's actions was not in response to the abduction but partly out of sympathy with the abandoned wife – de Vere's own mother expressed her devotion to Philippa and condemnation of her son – and there was also a powerful sense that codes of class conduct within sexual relations had been breached. This is fervently expressed by the monastic chronicler Thomas Walsingham:

> It happened in those days that Robert de Vere, elevated by the honours which the king gave out inexhaustibly, repudiated his young wife, who was noble, and also beautiful, born of the illustrious King Edward's daughter Isabella, and took another, who came with Queen Anne from Bohemia (it is said), daughter of a certain cellarer of that country; in a word, ignoble, and even disgusting (*ignobilem prorsus atque foedam*).[58]

It is that last phrase which is so startling. Agnes, the daughter of a Bohemian cellarer, is not only of ignoble birth but is *foeda* – foul, filthy, vile, loathsome, disgraceful, disgusting. Walsingham is noted for intemperate outbursts, but still it is revealing to consider what so appalled him. Agnes was not deemed so *foeda* that she could not occupy a position as lady-in-waiting, and was hardly the first such maiden to have an affair with a nobleman: before his relationship with Swynford, John of Gaunt had had a son by Marie de Saint Hilaire, one of Queen Philippa's maidens.[59] It was not so much the sexual affair which the court and commentators could not tolerate, but the marriage. In Froissart's account of Gaunt's marriage to Swynford the duke's peers said 'he had sadly disgraced himself by thus marrying his concubine', and was a 'doting fool'.[60] The disgrace for Katherine, in Froissart's eyes, seems not in being the mistress of a great man, for at court 'she was a lady accustomed to honours', but in getting above her 'base-born' station by presuming to marry the man she slept with. Similarly, in the case of Edward III's affair with Alice Perrers, outrage was not so much with the affair as the influence reputedly Alice gained over her lover.[61] In Lancecron's case, as in Swynford's, it was in marriage that her social standing suddenly became of acute importance: Swynford became 'base-born', and Lancecron 'foul'.

The importance of consciousness of rank as a defining factor in the construction of medieval sexualities has been paid little attention, which is perhaps surprising when one remembers that social status played as great a role or greater than biological sex in creating categories of licit and illicit sexualities in other cultures obsessed with hierarchy, such as ancient Athens.[62] Medieval English culture did not impose strict taboos on sexual and marital relations between individuals of slightly different status. Indeed, the fluidity of late medieval English society was a key factor which prevented English status groups from ever becoming rigid castes, and hypergamy (women marrying up) in particular had important practical functions.[63] Any notion that licit sexuality was closely tied to concerns about status should not be overstated, then, but neither should it be ignored. English elite society was materialistic and pragmatic enough to tolerate marriages between merchant and gentry, or gentry and aristocratic, groups, if worldly ambitions were served thereby, but powerful taboos, born out of intense class consciousness, lurked just below the surface.

This awareness enables us to read some of the most famous correspondence concerning a late medieval English marriage in a new light. The anger of Margery Paston's brothers and mother over her clandestine marriage to their bailiff Richard Calle has been read largely as frustration over a wasted social opportunity – especially given the Pastons' exceptional avidity for social climbing.[64] But the depth of horror expressed by Margery's mother Margaret, in particular, inspires a closer consideration. Margery was after all just one of seven children, and the five brothers at least seem to have played along with their parents' ambitions without great demur (though her younger sister Anne was also romantically involved with a servant, John Pampyng).[65] In strictly practical terms, then, the 'waste' of a daughter's marriage was an inconvenience, but hardly deserved the extremity of the family's reaction to this 'ungracious sister', fated 'to sell candle and mustard in Framlingham'.[66] Margaret offers the most detail, telling how the bishop 'put her [Margery] in remembrance how she was born, what kin and friends that she had, and should have more if she were ruled and guided after them; and if she did not, what rebuke and shame and loss it should be to her'. She ordered her servants not to receive her in the house, spoke of Margery's behaviour and the whole matter as 'lewd', and comforted her son not to take it pensively, though it went so near their hearts, because 'we have lost of her but a brethel [wretch]'.[67]

The strength of language, incomprehension, anger and genuine anguish expressed here all demonstrate that more than practical considerations were at stake. Margery's family were deeply embarrassed, indeed appalled and ashamed, that she could have stooped to marrying a servant. It is not the language of simple sexual disgust which is employed here (Margery is not called a whore), rather a kind of revulsion against cross-class sex. The terms 'brethel', and 'lewd', indicate a sense of proper status divisions having been breached.[68] The only response possible was to cast her out of the family for ever, even while retaining Calle in their employ.

These examples move us to another level in understanding the construction of medieval sexuality for young women. They were subject not only to varying degrees of concern not to breach the boundary between virgin and whore, but also boundaries of social status, religion, kinship and age. Among the lower social ranks, ecclesiastical court cases sometimes indicate that perceptions of disparity in status or wealth could affect choices of marriage partners. Sometimes this has little to do with anything which could be labelled a cultural taboo on cross-status sexual interaction. The record of the disputed marriage of Alice Redyng to John Boton, which came before the York consistory court in 1366, makes much mention of Alice's servile birth (her father was a serf, though her mother was free), with witnesses disagreeing over whether or not Alice had been manumitted and whether John (a 'merchant') was much wealthier than Alice (a servant, who supplemented her annual income with harvest work).[69] The issue, however, seems to have been Alice's financial motives for pursuing her claim of marriage to John, rather than any sense of breach of social propriety. In a York case from 1394 one deponent states that Margaret Greystanes initially demurred when Thomas del Dale proposed marriage to her, claiming to be a pauper with no goods to bring to the marriage, and thus an unsuitable match for him.[70] A greater sense of cultural, rather than practical unease, however, seems to guide deponents in the London case concerning the marriage of Robert Smyth and Rose Langtoft in 1472, where one witness claimed that Rose, though a servant, came of a wealthier background than Robert, and others disagreed over whether it would therefore be 'suitable' for Robert to marry her.[71] In a London case from 1487 the groom, John Ely, was concerned about what his neighbours would think of his betrothal to a servant, Agnes Whittingdon, to the point that he ordered that she never be seen carrying laundry to the Thames as part of her servant's duties. If her master threatened to dismiss her for refusing to carry the laundry, John was prepared to take her in and maintain her until their wedding.[72] Some echo of the potential shame in marrying below one's status for these representatives of middling urban society comes through these sources.

In moving from anxieties over daughters' loss of virginity before marriage to matters of sex within the appropriate status group, we begin to see that the construction of sexuality for medieval maidens consisted of more than just concern about defloration. Cross-class sexual relations leading to marriage resembled a mild kind of miscegenation (the illicit mating of different human types), which raises another matter increasingly of interest to historians; that is, the degree to which concepts of race and/or religion had a role in constructions of licit sexualities. The term 'race' is not entirely appropriate – as modern notions of racial identity are as inapplicable to a medieval context as modern notions of sexual identity – so the focus here is on religious difference, noting that the latter often had an element of something like race.[73] Members of non-Christian religions were thought to look different from Christians, live separately and under their own laws and customs, and were perceived as essentially different types of beings from Christians. English society lacked any strong expression of concern over inter-religious sexual relations. Although canon-legal theory explicitly forbade intermarriage of Christians and non-Christians, the minor nature of this impediment in an English context is apparent from its non-appearance in annulment claims brought before Church courts.[74] This lack of interest results from the near-uniformity of religious identity in contemporary England (heretics excepted), following Edward I's expulsion of the Jews by 1290 and absence of any substantial Muslim community. Inter-religious marriage was chiefly a concern in European regions with large multi-cultural communities, such as the Crusader states and the Spanish kingdoms. We will see in a moment, though, that such relationships were a popular element in literary fantasies.

The distinction of lay and cleric offered a further binary to aid the construction of sexualities. Sex was forbidden for members of monastic orders, and always had been, while priests in holy orders had been prevented from marrying or taking concubines since the reforms of the eleventh and twelfth centuries.[75] In practice, however, the enforcement of clerical celibacy was always limited. Priests and other clergy in orders often kept concubines and are known to have been among the most regular clients of prostitutes, while clergy in minor orders (such as parish clerks) were not forbidden to marry.[76] 'Priest's whore', 'monk's whore' or 'friar's whore' were common insults hurled at women, according to the records of defamation litigation, and Church courts regularly prosecuted women for acts of fornication with members of the clergy.[77] Alice Ridyng, before the bishop of Lincoln's court in 1517, was charged with having conceived a child by Thomas Denys, a chaplain, and in a startling echo of the tale of *The Incestuous Daughter* immediately killed the baby by suffocation and buried him in her father's garden beneath the dungheap.[78] The sexual division between lay and cleric was therefore not as clear-cut as might be presumed, although sexual interaction between the groups, or between clerics, was frowned upon.

More strongly forbidden in practice, though without perhaps the depth of anxiety with which it is surrounded in the present day, was the sexuality of children or adult/child contact. The canon law on the age of consent set the lowest age for licit sexuality with reasonable strictness, while as we have seen in practice many parents and others preferred a delay until the mid-teens or later for young people to begin sexual relationships.[79] The contempt or ridicule greeting marriages involving a large age discrepancy is apparent from the satirical theme of the 'May–January' marriage, explored in *The Merchant's Tale* and its analogues,[80] and it caused Thomas Betson some sleepless nights in contemplating his imminent marriage to the pubescent Katherine Ryche.[81] But these deal with the spectacle of young women married to old men, rather than adults and children.

There is, however, some indication that where in the present day it is usually unthinkable even to mention 'children' and 'sexuality' in the same breath (the discipline of psychology offering a major exception to the rule), a slightly more relaxed attitude existed in the medieval context. In some cases where the marriages of underage children took place for diplomatic purposes, a symbolic 'consummation' was enacted – doubtless to enhance the indissolubility of the match (though canon lawyers would probably have been unimpressed by such pseudo-consummations). In the 1380s Princess Beatrice of Portugal was betrothed to John, son of the earl of Cambridge, both aged ten. The betrothal ceremony was completed with a great feast, with all great barons and prelates of the realm present, and then, 'young as the married couple were, they were both laid in the same bed'.[82] In a subsequent Portuguese–English alliance, John of Gaunt arranged for the marriage of his daughter Philippa to the king of Portugal. Anxious to seal the coveted match without delay, the wedding vows were first exchanged in Santiago with a proxy acting for the king, and after the ceremony 'the archbishop of Braganza and the lady Philippa were courteously laid beside each other, on a bed as married persons should lie'.[83] In this case the bride was an adult, at twenty-six, and the example reveals more about attitudes to lay–cleric than adult–child sex, but one has only to consider likely present-day responses to the spectacle of a Catholic archbishop lying publicly in bed with a young woman for the purposes of consummation, however symbolic, to realise the depth in shift from medieval to modern sexual sensibilities.

To gain a sense of the teachings on sexual boundaries available to maidens across the social spectrum, homiletic tales repeated both in books and oral teaching offer the best perspective. The tales collected in versions of the *Gesta romanorum*, for example, give an indication of the major sexual concerns.[84] The most often mentioned sex offence is adultery, with ten examples, of which a woman was the sexual initiator in nine instances. Tales of rape are the next most numerous, with eight tales of the defloration of virgins, and simple fornication and incest comprising four examples each, with a woman taking the initiative in one fornication tale and one incest tale. Two tales tell of desire of a Christian for a heathen (in one instance, unusually, the lust-object is a Jewish maiden), and in both instances the initiator is a clergyman. These two tales plus one concerning the lust of a bishop add up to three tales of clerical lechery. Finally, procuring and prostitution appear in one tale each, with a woman initiating the sin in both cases. Thus of thirty-three instances of sexual transgression, married female characters take the initiative in thirteen cases and virginal maidens are corrupted in ten cases (all the rape tales and two of the fornication tales). The adulterous wife and the violated virgin constitute two key exemplary figures in these homiletic narratives, offering warnings to maidens of both active transgression and the perils of premarital contact with men. In general, the sermon tales support the view that the mode of licit sexuality modelled for women was primarily marital, consensual and monogamous, and also exogamous. The messages were reinforced through other cultural manifestations. The maidens of certain West Midlands villages had the chance to view dramatic representations of the seduction, lechery, repentence and penitence of Mary Magdalene, for example, while East Anglian daughters watched the play of *Dux Moraud* and its depiction of father–daughter incest.[85] Penitential texts and manuals for priests bound up anxieties about incest with concerns about sex in childhood and the sexual looseness which would ensue in later life, recommending that brothers and sisters should not be allowed to sleep in the same bed after the age of seven.[86]

Theologians' and canon lawyers' pronouncements on licit and illicit sexuality have been deliberately set aside up to this point, as those have so heavily dominated the existing scholarship and it seemed important to focus more closely on the actual experiences of young women and on texts they would have read or which circulated more broadly. Some kind of comparison with ecclesiastical concepts may now be offered. Theologians discussing the vice of lechery frequently divided the sin into varying degrees of seriousness, with fornication the least serious, followed by adultery, incest, varieties of rape (violation alone or with abduction), and finally the vice against nature (the latter consisting of any sexual act from which procreation could not result, including oral or anal sex, masturbation, use of contraceptives and abortifacients, bestiality, and all forms of same-sex sex).[87] Vernacular penitential literature, which is more likely to have had a direct impact on women's sexual education, frequently distinguished however between *fourteen* degrees of lechery of the body: 1. fornication between single man and woman; 2. fornication of man with common woman; 3. single man with widow; 4. married man with single woman; 5. married man with married woman; 6. unnatural or non-procreative sex of a man with his wife; 7. man with spiritual kin; 8. man with his own blood kin; 9. man with his wife's kin (or vice versa); 10. woman with a hooded clerk; 11. layman with woman in religious life; 12. male religious with female religious; 13. prelates with anyone; and 14. the unmentionable vice – that practised in Sodom and Gomorrah.[88] While the precise nature of 'sodomy' is no clearer here than most medieval texts, it is interesting that these vernacular sources, more than Latin discussions, distinguish between illicit sex within marriage and other forms of the vice against nature. It is also notable that lesbian sex is not explicitly commented upon.

Ecclesiastical courts regulated sexual contact partly through prosecutions for fornication, adultery and prostitution, but also through making certain kinds of marriage forbidden: where one or both parties were underage, where the marriage transgressed prohibited degrees (of consanguinity, affinity or spiritual kinship), where the male proved impotent, where the parties had previously been guilty of adultery, where a previous contract existed, or where it could be demonstrated that the marriage had been made through force and fear.[89] While the last two impediments concern matters of consent and legality rather than sexual taboos, the others, taken together with the teachings on lechery, add up to essential Church dogma on sexual practice: marital, monogamous, procreative sex between consenting lay adults who were unrelated through blood or spiritual kinship or by previous sexual relationships.

The examination of social practices and literary representations undertaken here demonstrates that while these broad strictures were held to in practice, taken alone they cannot adequately account for the teachings on sexuality which would have shaped a young woman's understanding. Some elements which are of great interest to modern commentators and interested clerical authors to an extent – such as the vices against nature – were of relatively minor importance. On the other hand, taboos on sexual contact between individuals of widely divergent social status, not mentioned by ecclesiastics, could have a profound effect on young women's lives. Moreover, by paying attention chiefly to ecclesiastical strictures on sexuality we risk missing the subtle shadings of attitude actually present in the culture. Premarital sex, while never openly approved for young women, was regarded more leniently, or could at least be accommodated, in some social groups and under certain circumstances (for example, where status taboos governing marriage were not breached) than among others. Some forms of sexuality remained more deeply taboo (for example, sex across a wide class gulf, between Christians and Jews, or involving children), or were a virtual non-issue (for example, lesbian sexuality). Yet imaginative literature offered a space for contemplating the loosening of some sexual boundaries, with cross-religious desire, lay–clerical sex, adultery, rape and (to a lesser extent) sex across small class divides explored for their exotic, humorous or titillating qualities.

Flirtation and fantasy

Any culture's construction of sexuality consists of more than drawing the boundaries between licit and illicit behaviour. Between those two lies the realm of flirtatious interaction, playfulness, humour and titillation. The sexualities which gain a foothold in this interim level are those which are generally proscribed in practice, but are not so utterly condemned as to close down all representation. In modern 'Anglo' cultures the spectacle of a man in woman's clothing, or the young woman dressed as a schoolgirl, fit common stereotypes of naughty humour or sexiness respectively. While all levels of the medieval social hierarchy would have had their own expressions of cheekiness or sauciness, difficulty in obtaining sources for 'popular culture' require, for now, a focus on flirtation and fantasy within the social elites – aristocracy, gentry and merchant groups.

A most useful tool for analysing the flexibility inherent in sexuality for daughters of the upper nobility is supplied by Peter Bailey's concept of 'parasexuality': 'sexuality that is deployed but contained, carefully channelled rather than fully discharged; in vulgar terms, it might be represented as "everything but"'.[90] Everything but actual sexual physical contact, that is. In the great noble and royal households young men and women mingled, flirted and courted, but under controlled circumstances. Young men and women of great households spent their days, though not their nights, in visual and physical proximity to one another within an architecture that at once fostered and contained their levels of contact. Some historians and archaeologists have overlooked this proximity, claiming sex segregation as a feature of castle and manor-house life.[91] While ladies and their attendants may have slept in all-female chambers at night, those rooms were rearranged during the day for eating, socialising, working and business. Men came and went there in their official capacities as household servants, performing duties which female servants did not perform except on such exceptional occasions as during childbirth.[92] High-placed male and female servants often dined at the same tables at both feasts and in day-to-day life, as shown for example in the Northumberland Household Book and the Harleian Regulations, and they danced together after dinner.[93]

Records such as chronicles and accounts of state functions suggest that low levels of sexual interaction were not only tolerated at court, they were central to court culture. The tournament or joust was a ritual which required and celebrated this atmosphere of contained yet festive sexuality. Froissart tells of a tournament in 1390 hosted by Richard II in London, opened with a parade of sixty ladies on palfreys, each lady leading a knight with a silver chain, a playful inversion of power roles and a representation of the courtly sexual bonds of knights and ladies.[94] A narrative account of the marriage of Richard, duke of York with Ann of Norfolk in January 1478 describes the joust which followed the wedding, where the great lords competed under the appraising gaze of the ladies. Then followed a great feast and dancing for 'all ladies, and gentlewomen, lords, knights, and esquires', and Ann and her ladies took counsel together and made awards to the competitors who had shown the greatest prowess.[95] While the tournament provided an important opportunity for men to display manly prowess to each other, it was also a chance for women to view and assess their attributes. Though in this case the 'marriage' was of two minors (Ann was either four or six, and Prince Richard just six), the usual sexual symbolism of the dance, the joust and the judgement of the ladies were considered appropriate for their wedding. The charged atmosphere of tournaments in general, with their ritualised forms of flirtation between men and women, led many clerical authors to fulminate against their temptation to lechery, echoed by the Knight of the Tower and Richard Hyrd.[96]

The semi-erotic implications of the joust were only tolerated so long as they were contained within certain boundaries of propriety and ritual. Knighton's *Chronicle* includes a tale of women appearing at tournaments, attired

> as though they were a company of players, dressed in men's clothes of striking richness and variety, to the number of forty or fifty such damsels, all very eye-catching and beautiful, though hardly of the kingdom's better sort. ... And thus they paraded themselves at tournaments on fine chargers and other well-arrayed horses, and consumed and spent their substance, and wantonly and with disgraceful lubricity displayed their bodies, as the rumour ran. And thus, neither fearing God nor abashed by the voice of popular outrage, they slipped the traces of matrimonial restraint.

God punished them, with visitations of great storms and tempests wherever they appeared.[97] The women (whether real or purely fantastic) transgressed their natural roles in many ways, from financial extravagance to cross-dressing, and in exploiting the quasi-theatrical space of the tournament to display their bodies lubriciously they stepped over the boundaries of both the licit sexuality of marriage and the contained parasexuality of the tournament.

Court culture and the tournament in particular offered a space for maidens in service in royal or other great households to view and play with heterosexual desire, without breaching the boundaries between physical virginity and its loss, or between gulfs in social status. Romances and other literary works such as the works of Chaucer widened that space still further, allowing many practices subject to social taboo to be viewed voyeuristically, for pleasure or amusement. Cross-class sexual relations had strong potential to intrigue medieval audiences, lying in that third realm between the licit and the utterly proscribed. The French genre of the *pastourelle*, with its tales of wandering knights encountering shepherd maidens and raping them, provides one such example of socially prohibited sexual practices turned to titillating uses in contemporary France.[98] The form seems not to have taken off among English audiences, however, as Middle

English examples of the genre are very rare. Indeed, English literary audiences do not seem to have had a particular taste for sexual scenes involving individuals from *widely* divergent status groups, though sex across more closely associated groups was sometimes viewed salaciously. Chaucer's *The Miller's Tale* describes Alison as an object of desire 'For any lord to leggen in his bedde,/ Or yet for any good yeman to wedde' (lines 3269–70), indicating an element of titillation in a fairly small, if significant, distinction of social groups. Alison as a carpenter's wife is of middling status: she is no serf. The Griselda legend, best known in *The Clerk's Tale*, does tell of marriage between a great lord and very lowly peasant girl, but there is nothing salacious or erotic in the tale. A small number of romances, such as *Guy of Warwick*, *The Squire of Low Degree* and *Ipomedon* play with the theme of attraction between a great lady and more lowly knight or squire – which after all was basic to the original French *fin amour* genre – but the degree to which such erotic attraction transgressed social boundaries was minor compared with the *pastourelle*.[99] Sexual relations between the nobility and peasantry seem then, in English culture, to have been proscribed to the point of the unthinkable. The taboos surrounding such interaction could be seen as guided by an ideology similar to the modern taboo of miscegenation, which expresses profound anxiety about the sexual mingling of groups of humans seen as fundamentally distinct from one another.

However, inter-religious sexual attraction was a frequently recurring theme in romance literature, though we must distinguish between perceptions of Jews and Muslims. Representations of Jews were almost invariably harsh caricatures and attempts at demonisation, with Chaucer's *The Prioress's Tale* offering the best-known example. Depictions of Muslims, on the other hand, were more complex, and though not without negative elements often held strong romantic and orientalist connotations. One example of virulently anti-Muslim mentality is contained in the fourteenth-century romance of *Richard Coer de Lion*, which was apparently quite popular given its survival in seven manuscripts and printing in 1509 by Wynken de Worde. An episode set in Acre sees King Richard ill and longing for pork. A Saracen's head is boiled for him, and unsuspectingly he devours it with relish. Laughing upon being told the source of his 'pork', he later dines on another head, commenting that no Christian need starve so long as any Saracen is left.[100] This cannibalistic episode reveals a notion of Muslims as almost a different species from Christians. Several romances depict attraction and courtship between Christian and Saracen lovers, including Bevis and Josian (of *Bevis of Hampdon*), Guy of Burgundy and Floripas (of *The Sowdon of Babylon*), Florentyn and the Sultan's daughter (in *Octavian*), yet in each of these cases the heathen party renounces Islam and undergoes Christian baptism before the couple marry and consummate their desire. The results of interbreeding are horribly illustrated in the early fourteenth-century tale of *The King of Tars*, in which a Christian princess marries a heathen sultan to bring peace to their peoples. Their son is born a formless lump of flesh, but is transformed into a handsome boy upon baptism. His Saracen father, thus inspired to convert to Christianity, is transformed in the baptismal water from black flesh to white.[101] Love *between* heathens could be treated without censure, as in the tale of Generydes – a knight born of the king of India and the fairy-like queen of Syria, who falls in love with and marries Clarionas, daughter of the Persian sultan.[102] Such tales give no hint of the perception of heathens as another species: indeed, the exotic settings of *Generydes* seem designed simply to lend eastern glamour to an otherwise conventional courtly narrative. In summary, true miscegenation was condemned in literature as in law, but parasexual courtship and desire between Christian and Muslim was a favoured topic among romance authors. Thus Malory's pagan knight Palomides and his hopeless and unrequited yearnings for La Beale Isoud are made palatable, indeed, fascinating, for medieval readers, while maintaining the message that sex and marriage across religions were forbidden.[103]

Literary works such as *fabliaux* played with the prohibition on sex between clergy and laity, often in a satirical manner partly aimed at critiquing the corruption of the clergy, though also with the lighter purpose of bawdy entertainment. The prominence of such stories among Chaucer's *Canterbury Tales*, with the *Reeve's*, *Shipman's*, and *Summoner's* tales all telling of unchaste clerks, indicates both the popularity of the theme and the relative mildness of the transgression. Lay–clerical sexual contact was the subject for humour in the literature read by elite groups, rather than deep anxiety or savage condemnation, suggesting that while the boundaries of licit sexuality excluded such contact it was not so generally reviled as to deserve the strongest denunciation. At lower social levels, the message is less clearly humorous and apparently more caution-ary. Songs told of the woes of parish maidens who could not resist the charms of clerks and priests and fell pregnant by them.[104] It was suggested in Chapter 2 that these had the dual function of amusing the university students and clerics who copied them down, and of teaching young women of the parish the dangers of trusting men in holy orders.

Rape stories, some of which tell of virgins' defloration, are fairly common in Middle English literature – including Chaucer's *The Wife of Bath's Tale*, *The Franklin's Tale*, and his retellings of the rapes of Philomela and Lucrece in *The Legend of Good Women*, Gower's account of Philomela in *Confessio amantis*, the rape of the princess in *Sir Degaré*, and the many tellings of the Dinah legend. Like the *chansons des femmes* these tales bore a range of moralising messages and cautionary messages for young women, though for elements of their audience they could also have offered a sensationalising and prurient form of entertainment.[105] In contrast, children's sexuality or child–adult sexuality was not generally a topic for parasexual, salacious or humorous interest. The contempt or ridicule greeting marriages involving a large age discrepancy is apparent from the satirical theme of the 'May–January' marriage. The romance of *Floris and Blancheflour* comes closest to exploring the child sexuality, though obliquely and without clear attempts at humour or titillation.

Conclusion

Because the great majority of medieval maidens, rich and poor, led an existence shaped by the expectation of marriage and procreation, sexuality played an important role in their young womanhood. This was, usually, a heavily monitored, contained and limited form of sexuality, which was supposed to stop short of a sexual act, but that lack does not remove sex from the picture of young women's lives entirely. However, medieval sexuality in its dominant form was not simply modern heterosexuality transposed in time and with greater social and ideological strictures built around it. Nor was it the same for women of all social groups. The sexuality of aristocratic daughters was not subject to straightforward repression but was instead turned to public uses of display and flirtatious interaction, especially within court society with its playful parasexuality in both daily life and the set-piece occasions of feasts and jousts. Gentry daughters would have taken part in this when they entered service in the greater households. Maidens of all these groups were taught not only to desire and make themselves desirable to *men*, but to ensure that serious sexual intentions were entertained only for men of or near their status. Broader social teachings on consensual sex, and prohibitions on cross-religious and lay–cleric sexuality, were simultaneously reinforced and subverted in the literatures of romance and *fabliaux*, where uses of illicit sexual interaction for titillation or amusement offered a socially safe way for variations on the prescribed erotic norm to be explored. Daughters of the higher peasantry and artisan families experienced increasing pressures

from families, employers and communities to refrain from sexual experimentation by the fifteenth century, and some also experienced pressure
not to transgress class-sex taboos. Poor peasant maidens' sexual encounters
were perhaps less strictly controlled, even though they were sometimes
taxed by manorial lords. Lacking good sources for medieval English popular
culture, we cannot really know how maidens below the elite explored
alternatives to prescribed norms: no doubt they told and listened to bawdy
stories, dirty jokes and sang songs of illicit fornication, but we will never
know about them. The almost total absence of discussion of lesbianism fits
the broader gender framework which lay maidens' upbringing placed
them within. Young laywomen were taught to live in subordinate relationship to men, and therefore sexuality was defined phallocentrically. But
gender differences were not the only concern, with the boundaries of
social status, religious identity and age also important.

One recurrent theme in this chapter has been that of exterior control:
control and construction of maidens' sexuality by families, communities,
employers and by the Church. But the culture was not utterly repressive.
Within certain limits, there was room for flirtation, playfulness, salacious-
ness and laughter. Moreover, maidens themselves played some small role
in this construction. Some young women actively joined in with their
families or communities in forcing their lovers to the church door, aware
no doubt of the damage to their reputations otherwise. Wealthy maidens'
choice of reading material, perhaps most importantly their preference for
romances, blurred the space between the illicit and the approved. Some
young women appear to have fended off pressures to marry, temporarily at
least, preferring flirtation and perhaps premarital encounters. John Paston
II joked in a letter to John III about the unlikelihood of the latter securing
the hand of Katherine Dudley, as she counted him as merely one of her
admirers: 'She recketh not how many gentlemen love her – she is full of
love.... She answered me that she will [wishes for] no [husband] these two
years, and I believe her, for I think she has the life that she can hold
her[self] content with. I trow [believe] she will be a sore labouring woman
these two years for meed [reward] of her soul.'[106] Whether Mistress Dudley
wore out her confessor during those two years with simple tales of lust and
flirtation, or anything more mortally sinful, is of minor importance.
Medieval maidens may have been subject to widespread sexual control,
and even to an extent deemed as sexual possessions by families and
manorial lords, but there was room in their culture for them to take up
constructions of their own sexuality in sometimes fearful, but at other
times knowing and playful, ways.

Notes

1   Herrtage (ed.), *Gesta romanorum*, pp. 390–2. Versions are also edited in Brandeis (ed.), *Jacob's Well*; Mary MacLeod Banks (ed.), *An Alphabet of Tales: An English 15th Century Translation of the* Alphabetum narrationum, EETS os 126 (London, 1904), pp. 145–6.

2   *Book of the Knight*, e.g. caps 35–6. For incest see cap. 55.

3   For example, *Gesta romanorum*, pp. 250–61, 388–90; *Alphabet of Tales*, pp. 11, 317–18; *Jacob's Well*; 'Dux Moraud', in Norman Davis (ed.), *Non-Cycle Plays and Fragments*, EETS ss 1 (London, 1970); Edith Rickert (ed.), *The Romance of Emaré*, EETS es 99 (London, 1908); *Sir Degaré*, in French and Hale (eds), *Middle English Metrical Romances*. For a sample of the growing work on incest in Middle English literature see Elizabeth Archibald, 'Gold in the dungheap: incest stories and family values in the Middle Ages', *Journal of Family History*, 22 (1997), 133–49; Anne Savage, 'Clothing paternal incest in *The Clerk's Tale*, *Emaré*, and the *Life of St Dympna*', in Wogan-Browne *et al.* (eds), *Medieval Women.*

4   Jack Goody, *The Development of the Family and Marriage in Europe* (Cambridge, 1983); David Herlihy, 'Making sense of incest: women and the marriage rules of the early Middle Ages, in *Women, Family and Society in Medieval Europe: Historical Essays, 1978–1991* (Providence, 1995).

5   'Introduction', to Karma Lochrie, Peggy McCracken and James A. Schultz (eds), *Constructing Medieval Sexuality* (Minneapolis, 1997), p. ix, citing Peter Brown, *The Body and Society: Men, Women, and Sexual Renunciation in Early Christianity* (New York, 1988), p. xviii. Brown is actually quoting Foucault.

6   Brundage, *Law, Sex, and Christian Society*; Pierre J. Payer, *The Bridling of Desire: Views of Sex in the Later Middle Ages* (Toronto, 1993); Cadden, *Meanings of Sex Difference*; Vern L. Bullough and James A. Brundage (eds), *Handbook of Medieval Sexuality* (New York, 1996) – to name only some of the most important works.

7   The literature on constructions of sexuality is now far too vast to list here. For an overview see Kim M. Phillips and Barry Reay, 'Introduction: sexualities in history', in their *Sexualities in History: A Reader* (New York, 2002); also Robert A. Nye (ed.), *Sexuality* (Oxford, 1999); and Jeffrey Weeks, *Making Sexual History* (Malden, MA, 2000). For heterosexuality see James A. Schultz, 'Bodies that don't matter: heterosexuality before heterosexuality in Gottfried's *Tristan*', in Lochrie, McCracken and Schultz (eds), *Constructing Medieval Sexuality*, which is valuably innovative though very narrow in focus. Good ideas can be gleaned from Jonathan Ned Katz, *The Invention of Heterosexuality* (New York, 1995), though he mystifyingly skips the entire medieval period, and John d'Emilio and Estelle B. Freedman, *Intimate Matters: A History of Sexuality in America*, 2nd edn (Chicago, 1997).

8   Welcome recent additions to scholarship on medieval lesbianism include Francesca Canadé Sautman and Pamela Sheingorn (eds), *Same Sex Love and Desire among Women in the Middle Ages* (New York, 2001), but none of the essays in the volume deals with a specifically English context.

9   Explicit references to female same-sex acts are absent in English penitential texts.

Richard M. Wunderli in his study of later fifteenth- and early sixteenth-century London Church court material found no cases of female homosexual acts (indeed only one accusation of male sodomy out of 21,000 defendants from 1470 to 1516, and only one case of imputed homosexuality in a defamation suit): *London Church Courts and Society on the Eve of the Reformation* (Cambridge, MA, 1981), pp. 83–4. Ruth Mazo Karras has found no clear indication of lesbian acts in her researches into the secular and ecclesiastical courts of fourteenth- and fifteenth-century England: *Common Women*, p. 174, n. 67, and p. 185, n. 9.

10 Judith M. Bennett, '"Lesbian-like" and the social history of lesbianisms', *Journal of the History of Sexuality*, 9 (2000), 1–24, see p. 3. For medieval 'lesbianism' in general see Jacqueline Murray, 'Twice marginal and twice invisible: lesbians in the Middle Ages', in Bullough and Brundage (eds), *Handbook of Medieval Sexuality*.

11 Carolyn Dinshaw, *Getting Medieval: Sexualities and Communities, Pre- and Postmodern* (Durham, NC, 1999), pp. 10–11; Diane Watt, 'Behaving like a man? Incest, lesbian desire, and gender play in "Yde et Olive"', *Comparative Literature*, 50 (1998), 265–85.

12 For example, Kathy Lavezzo, 'Sobs and sighs between women: the homoerotics of compassion in *The Book of Margery Kempe*, in Louise Fradenburg and Carla Freccero (eds), *Premodern Sexualities* (New York, 1996). A subtler reading of Margery Kempe as 'queer' is Dinshaw, *Getting Medieval*, pp. 143–65.

13 See Dinshaw, *Getting Medieval*, pp. 87–94.

14 See Chapter 1.

15 Though they do not adhere to any of the following exactly, these conclusions are influenced by readings of Frederick Engels, *The Origin of the Family, Private Property and the State* (London, [1884] 1972), ch. 2; Gerda Lerner, *The Creation of Patriarchy* (New York, 1986), ch. 2; Gayle Rubin, 'The traffic in women: notes on the "political economy" of sex', repr. in Scott (ed.), *Feminism and History*; Sherry Ortner, 'The virgin and the state', *Feminist Studies*, 4 (1978), 19–37; and Sherry Ortner, 'Gender and sexuality in hierarchical societies: the case of Polynesia and some comparative implications', in Sherry B. Ortner and Harriet Whitehead (eds), *Sexual Meanings: The Cultural Construction of Gender and Sexuality* (Cambridge, 1981).

16 See above, p. 26.

17 Unfortunately there is not space to lay out all the steps leading to this point, but various sources of evidence point to relative lack of interest in lineage among urban artisans in particular. Maryanne Kowaleski argues that English artisanal families were characterised by 'fluidity and instability', and 'extended family structures are almost never found in English towns', 'The history of urban families', *Journal of Medieval History*, 14 (1988), 47–63, esp. p. 58. Heather Swanson's study of York artisans found that few owned any property, and a quarter of those who bequeathed holdings in their wills gave them to the Church: *Medieval Artisans*, pp. 159–60. Both points indicate the weakness of lineage notions. It is also noteworthy that in Oxfordshire, at least, patrilineal surnames (which were spreading from use among the nobility to lower social groups by the mid-fourteenth century) were taken up later in towns than rural areas. See Richard A.

McKinley, *The Surnames of Oxfordshire*, English Surnames Series 3 (London, 1977), pp. 7-25, 29-30. See also McKinley's *Norfolk and Suffolk Surnames in the Middle Ages*, English Surnames Series 2 (Chichester, 1975), pp. 3-30.

On peasant familial attachment to property, see Zvi Razi, 'Intrafamilial ties and relationships in the medieval village: a quantitative approach employing manor court rolls', in Razi and Smith (eds), *Medieval Society and the Manor Court*, esp. p. 371. There is no agreement among scholars on this issue though, as others including Christopher Dyer have argued for weakening of peasant family–land bonds in the post-Black Death era, with the greater availability of land. For an introduction to the debates see R. M. Smith, 'Some issues concerning families and their property in rural England 1250–1800' in Smith (ed.), *Land, Kinship and Life Cycle*, and the essays by Dyer and Razi in the same volume. For fourteenth-century rural families' adoption of patrilineal surnames see McKinley, *Surnames of Oxfordshire*, pp. 7-25, and *Norfolk and Suffolk Surnames*, pp. 3-30.

18 *Glanvill*, p. 175; *Bracton* 2, pp. 344-5, 403, 414-18; Kim M. Phillips, 'Written on the body: reading rape from the twelfth to fifteenth centuries', in Noël James Menuge (ed.), *Medieval Women and the Law* (Woodbridge, 2000), and see the cases cited there.

19 Ruth Kittel, 'Rape in thirteenth-century England: a study of the common-law courts', in D. Kelly Weisberg (ed.), *Women and the Law: A Social-Historical Perspective*, 2 vols (Cambridge, MA, 1982), vol. 2, esp. pp. 107-8; J. B. Post, 'Ravishment of women and the Statutes of Westminster', in J. H. Baker (ed.), *Legal Records and the Historian* (London, 1978), esp. pp. 152-3. For a similar argument though in an earlier context see Roger D. Groot, 'The crime of rape *temp.* Richard I and John', *Journal of Legal History*, 9 (1988), 324-34.

20 *The Statutes of the Realm*, 12 vols (London, repr. 1963), vol. 1, 29, c. 13; vol. 1, 87, c. 34; vol. 2, 27, c. 6; vol. 3, 512, c. 2/3; Phillips, 'Written on the body', pp. 135-8; Post, 'Ravishment of women'; J. B. Post, 'Sir Thomas West and the Statute of Rapes, 1382', *Bulletin of the Institute for Historical Research*, 53 (1980), 24-30; E. W. Ives, '"Agaynst taking awaye of Women": the inception and operation of the Abduction Act of 1487', in E. W. Ives, R. J. Knecht and J. J. Scarisbrick (eds), *Wealth and Power in Tudor England* (London, 1978).

21 Alan Harding (ed.), *The Roll of the Shropshire Eyre of 1256*, Selden Society 96 (London, 1980), p. 258; Doris Mary Stenton (ed.), *Rolls of the Justices in Eyre Being the Rolls of Pleas and Assizes for Lincolnshire, 1218-19*, Selden Society 53 (London, 1934), pp. 579-80.

22 Kittel, 'Rape in thirteenth-century England', p. 108; *Handlyng Synne*, lns. 2185-90.

23 BIHR CP F 189. Jeremy Goldberg kindly directed me to this case.

24 There is no direct evidence for the social status of the participants, but it may be inferred that they are agriculturalists because of their places of residence (villages near Driffield on the Yorkshire wolds), and that they are relatively well off because of the large sum paid to Isabella, and by the evidence that the family of Robert Chew's bride have a bakehouse on their property (see deposition of Robert Kirkeby).

25 Dyer, *Standards of Living*, pp. 31-2.

26 Illicitly, given his previous sexual relationship with Isabella. The only reason we have any record of the twenty marks compensation is that Robert was accused in the York court of making an invalid marriage with Agnes, related as she was in the fourth degree to Isabella.

27 PRO C1 45/24. I am grateful to Cordelia Beattie for alerting me to this entry.

28 Barbara A. Hanawalt, 'Whose story was this? Rape narratives in medieval English courts', in *'Of Good and Ill Repute': Gender and Social Control in Medieval England* (New York, 1998), p. 133. J.-P. Lévy, 'L'Officialité de Paris et les questions familiales à la fin du XIV siècle', in *Études d'histoire du droit canonique dédiées à Gabriel le Bras*, 2 vols (Paris, 1965), vol. 2, p. 1283. I owe the latter reference to Peter Biller.

29 BIHR CP E 92, deposition of John Dogeson of Scampston.

30 Charles Donahue Jr, 'Female plaintiffs in marriage cases in the court of York in the later Middle Ages: what can we learn from numbers?', in Sue Sheridan Walker (ed.), *Wife and Widow in Medieval England* (Ann Arbor, 1993).

31 On fornication and pregnant brides in seventeenth-century England see Martin Ingram, *Church Courts, Sex and Marriage in England, 1570–1640* (Cambridge, 1987). On illegitimacy in medieval England see Alice Curteis and Chris Given-Wilson, *The Royal Bastards of Medieval England* (London, 1984), esp. pp. 42–54; Peter Laslett, 'Introduction: comparing illegitimacy over time and between cultures', in Peter Laslett, Karla Oosterveen and Richard Smith (eds), *Bastardy and Its Comparative History: Studies in the History of Illegitimacy and Marital Nonconformism in Britain, France, Germany, Sweden, North America, Jamaica, and Japan* (London, 1980); Hanawalt, *Ties that Bound*, pp. 72–3.

32 F. W. Maitland and William P. Baildon (eds), *The Court Baron*, Seldon Society 4 (London, 1891), p. 102; Scammell and Searle debate, 1974–1983; Razi, *Life, Marriage and Death*, pp. 64–6 (though most other commentators have disagreed with his equation of leyrwite and illegitimate pregnancy); Jack Ravensdale, 'Population changes and the transfer of customary land on a Cambridgeshire manor in the fourteenth century', in Smith (ed.), *Land, Kinship and Life Cycle*, pp. 211–12, 218, 222–3; Tim North, 'Legerwite in the thirteenth and fourteenth centuries', *Past and Present*, 111 (1986), 3–16.

33 Poos and Smith, '"Legal windows"', pp. 320–2.

34 Goldberg, *Women, Work, and Life Cycle*, pp. 208–9; also his 'Debate: fiction in the archives: the York cause papers as a source for later medieval social history', *Continuity and Change*, 12 (1997), 425–45, esp. p. 434.

35 See note 17 above.

36 Shannon McSheffrey (ed. and trans.), *Love and Marriage in Late Medieval London* (Kalamzoo, 1995), pp. 81–2.

37 See p. 83.

38 BIHR CP F 127. For a translation see Goldberg (ed. and trans.), *Women in England*, pp. 110–14.

39 McSheffrey (ed. and trans.), *Love and Marriage*, pp. 86–7.

40 Poos, 'Sex, lies and the Church courts'; McIntosh, *Controlling Misbehavior*.

41 *PC*, p. 109 (not dated by the editor except to the reign of Henry VII).

42 Riddy, 'Mother knows best'. As she points out, although the texts speak of

'mothers' and 'daughters', 'mistresses' and 'servants' were probably key components of their audience.

43 *CL*, no. 117.

44 *CL*, no. 165.

45 *Book of the Knight*, caps 24, 122–33.

46 Including Hyrd (trans.), *Instruction of a Christen Woman*; Salter, *Mirrhor of Modestie*; Lowth, *Christian Man's Closet*; Averall, *Dyall for Dainty Darlings*.

47 *Book of the Knight*, cap. 16.

48 *CL*, nos. 49, 54, 92,105, 141, 142, 181, 188.

49 *CL*, no. 169; Hanham, *The Celys and Their World*, pp. 266, n. 43, 269.

50 Goldberg, *Women in England*, p. 126. For a brief biography of Henry Preston see Jenny Kermode, *Medieval Merchants: York, Beverley and Hull in the Later Middle Ages* (Cambridge, 1998), p. 342.

51 *LL* 4, no. 887. See pp. 114–15 above. Among Princess Mary's retinue upon her marriage to Louis XII of France in 1514 was Lady Jane Guildford, whom the princess called 'Mother Guldeford' and who probably played a protective role towards the younger maidens as well as the seventeen-year-old princess: Henry Ellis (ed.), *Original Letters, Illustrative of English History*, 11 vols (London, 1825), ser. 1, vol. 1, pp. 113–19. See also de Pizan, *Treasury of the City of Ladies*, pp. 126–9.

52 T. F. Tout, 'The household ordinance of Westminster, 13th November 1279', in *Chapters*, vol. 2, p. 162; T. F. Tout (ed.), 'The household ordinances of Edward II', in Hilda Johnstone (ed.) *The Place of the Reign of Edward II in English History*, rev. edn (Manchester, 1936), p. 280; Chris Given-Wilson, *The Royal Household and the King's Affinity: Service, Politics and Finance in England, 1360–1413* (New Haven, 1986), p. 60.

53 Froissart, *Chronicles*, vol. 2, p. 630. Admittedly this is an example from the Low Countries, but it indicates elite attitudes which probably crossed national boundaries.

54 Hector and Harvey (eds), *Westminster Chronicle*, p. 192. See also G. H. Martin (ed. and trans.), *Knighton's Chronicle* (Oxford, 1995), p. 342.

55 Hector and Harvey (eds), *Westminster Chronicle*, pp. 294, 392–4, 414. He was executed in 1400, but not because of his marriage.

56 Hector and Harvey (eds), *Westminster Chronicle*, pp. 188–90.

57 *CPR 1388–92*, p. 20.

58 Thomas Walsingham, *Historia Angliae*, ed. H. T. Riley, 2 vols (London, 1863–4), vol. 2, p. 160. Froissart does not pass such strong judgement on Agnes, but his account also emphasises the illustrious birth of Philippa de Coucy: *Chronicles*, vol. 3, pp. 463–4.

59 F. George Kay, *Lady of the Sun: The Life and Times of Alice Perrers* (London, 1966), pp. 78–9.

60 Froissart, *Chronicles*, vol. 4, pp. 472–3.

61 V. H. Galbraith (ed.), *The Anonimalle Chronicle 1333 to 1381* (Manchester, 1927), pp. 87, 91, 92.

62 E.g. David M. Halperin, *One Hundred Years of Homosexuality and Other Essays on Greek Love* (New York, 1990).

63 E.g. Peter Fleming, *Family and Household in Medieval England* (Houndmills, 2001), pp. 31–4.

64 H. S. Bennett, *The Pastons and Their England: Studies in an Age of Transition* (Cambridge, 1922), pp. 42–6; Ann S. Haskell, 'The Paston women on marriage in fifteenth-century England', *Viator*, 4 (1973), 459–71, esp. pp. 467–8; Keith Dockray, 'Why did fifteenth-century English gentry marry?: The Pastons, Plumptons and Stonors reconsidered', in Michael Jones (ed.), *Gentry and Lesser Nobility in Late Medieval Europe* (Gloucester, 1986).

65 *PL and P* 1, no. 283.

66 *PL and P* 1, no. 332.

67 *PL and P* 1, no. 203.

68 *MED*, s. v. 'leued', 'brethel'.

69 BIHR CP E 92.

70 BIHR CP E 215.

71 McSheffrey (ed. and trans.), *Love and Marriage*, pp. 59–65.

72 McSheffrey (ed. and trans.), *Love and Marriage*, pp. 56–9.

73 Insightful examinations of these issues are found throughout the articles collected in *Journal of Medieval and Early Modern Studies*, 31, no. 1 (2001).

74 Brundage, *Law, Sex, and Christian Society*, examines canon condemnation of miscegenation through developments in the law from the high to late Middle Ages, pp. 195–6, 207, 238, 244, 267, 340, 361, 379–80. Helmholz, however, does not find miscegenation among the impediments to marriage recognised by English ecclesiastical courts, *Marriage Litigation*, pp. 76–100.

75 On the papal crackdown on clerical sex see the summary in James A. Brundage, 'Sex and canon law', in Bullough and Brundage (eds), *Handbook of Medieval Sexuality*, pp. 36–7.

76 Goldberg, 'Pigs and prostitutes', pp. 175–6; Karras, *Common Women*, pp. 30, 45, 76; P. H. Cullum, 'Clergy, masculinity and transgression in late medieval England', in Hadley (ed.), *Masculinity in Medieval Europe*, esp. pp. 192–3.

77 For example, see Poos, 'Sex, lies and the Church courts', p. 602; Goldberg (ed. and trans.), *Women in England*, p. 230.

78 Goldberg (ed. and trans.), *Women in England*, p. 119, and pp. 120–2 for further examples.

79 See Chapter 1, above.

80 For analogues see Benson (ed.), *Riverside Chaucer*, p. 884; Burrow, *Ages of Man*, pp. 156–62.

81 See pp. 41–2.

82 Froissart, *Chronicles*, vol. 2, p. 506.

83 Froissart, *Chronicles*, vol. 3, p. 378.

84 The editions used here are those in Herrtage (ed.), *Gesta romanorum*, which collects tales from three separate redactions.

85 Donald C. Baker, John L. Murphy and Louis B. Hall (eds), *The Late Medieval Religious Plays of Bodleian MSS Digby 133 and e Museo 160*, EETS OS 283 (Oxford, 1982); Davis (ed.), *Non-Cycle Plays*.

86 Myrc, *Instructions for Parish Priests*, p. 7; *Handlyng Synne*, lines 1663–76, 7657–60.

87 On the degrees of lechery see Payer, *Bridling of Desire*, p. 9, and his 'Confession and the study of sex in the middle ages', in Bullough and Brundage (eds), *Handbook of Medieval Sexuality*, p. 12.

88 For example, *Ayenbite of Inwit*, pp. 48–50.

89 Helmholz, *Marriage Litigation*, pp. 74–100

90 Peter Bailey, 'Parasexuality and glamour: the Victorian barmaid as cultural prototype', *Gender and History*, 2 (1990), pp. 148–72, quotation at p. 148. Although Bailey draws this concept from his reading of a modern phenomenon, his insights are extremely useful for anyone wishing to examine the 'middle ground' of sexuality, including flirtation and courtship, and the public display of attractive women and men. I have elsewhere used his ideas to examine the messages of virgin martyrs' lives: see 'Desiring virgins', in Goldberg and Riddy (eds), *Youth in the Middle Ages* (forthcoming).

91 Orme, *From Childhood to Chivalry*, pp. 31–2; Roberta Gilchrist, 'Medieval bodies in the material world: gender, stigma and the body', in Sarah Kay and Miri Rubin (eds), *Framing Medieval Bodies* (Manchester, 1993); Roberta Gilchrist, *Gender and Material Culture: The Archaeology of Religious Women* (London, 1994), pp. 167–9.

92 See pp. 116–17.

93 *NHB*, p. 301; BL MS Harl. 6815, fols 28v–29r, 31v; 'The r ecord of Bluemantle Pursuivant', in Myers (ed.), *English Historical Documents*, pp. 1176–7; and William Henry Black (ed.), 'Narrative of the marriage of Richard Duke of York with Ann of Norfolk, the "matrimonial feast" and the grand justing, A.D. 1477 [1478]', in *Illustrations of Ancient State and Chivalry from Manuscripts Preserved in the Ashmolean Museum*, Roxburgh Club (London, 1840), p. 31. For dancing see BL MS Harl. 6815, fol. 33r; Letts (ed.), *Travels of Leo of Rozmital*, p. 47; Orme, *From Childhood to Chivalry*, pp. 170–4.

94 Froissart, *Chronicles*, vol. 3, pp. 228–32.

95 Black (ed.), 'Marriage of Richard duke of York with Ann of Norfolk', pp. 32–40.

96 Juliet R. V. Barker, *The Tournament in England, 1100–1400* (Woodbridge, 1986), pp. 72–3; *Book of the Knight*, cap. 24; Hyrd (trans.), *Instruction of a Christen Woman*, I.v.

97 *Knighton's Chronicle*, pp. 92–4.

98 William D. Paden (ed. and trans.), *The Medieval Pastourelle*, 2 vols (New York, 1987); Gravdal, *Ravishing Maidens*.

99 Zupitza (ed.), *Guy of Warwick*; 'The squire of low degree', in Sands (ed.), *Middle English Verse Romances*; 'Ipomedon' (selections), in French and Hale (eds), *Middle English Metrical Romances*, vol. 2. Ipomedon, however, was a king's son in disguise, so any cross-class sexual tension in the text would have been muted.

100 'Richard Coer de Lion', in Henry W. Weber (ed.), *Metrical Romances of the Thirteenth, Fourteenth and Fifteenth Centuries*, 3 vols (Edinburgh, 1810), vol. 2.

101 Judith Perryman (ed.), *The King of Tars* (Heidelberg, 1980).

102 Wright (ed.), *Generydes*. The version in Cambridge Trinity College MS O.5.2 was probably owned by Anne Knevet, a young Norfolk gentlewoman, at the time of her marriage: Derek Pearsall, 'Notes on the manuscript of Generydes', *The Library*, 5th ser., 16 (1961), 205–10.

103 Thomas Malory, *Works*, ed. Eugène Vinaver and P. J. C. Field, 3 vols (Oxford, 1990), books 9 and 10.

104 Robbins (ed.), *Secular Lyrics*, pp. 18–24.

105 Alastair Minnis views Chaucer's *Legend of Good Women* as a poem which contemporaries may have read, in part, for amusement: A. J. Minnis, with V. J. Scattergood and J. J. Smith, *Oxford Guides to Chaucer: The Shorter Poems* (Oxford, 1995), pp. 440–1. On French rape tales as entertainment see Evelyn Birge Vitz, 'Rereading rape in medieval literature: literary, historical, and theoretical reflections', *Romanic Review*, 88 (1997), 1–26.

106 *PL and P* 1, no. 248.

5

Voices

When feminist theorists claim that gender is the cultural interpretation
of sex or that gender is culturally constructed, what is the manner or
mechanism of this construction? If gender is constructed, could it be
constructed differently, or does its constructedness imply some form
of social determinism, foreclosing the possibility of agency and
transformation?[1]

The greatest difficulty in assessing the means by which young
medieval women were socialised in femininity is to account for the
role of maidens themselves in the process. English women of the late
thirteenth to early sixteenth centuries are notorious, among those who
attempt to study their lives, for the few records they have left which could
be said with confidence to represent their own voices, and the problems of
interpreting sources and of female literacy (in the sense of the ability to
write) are always immense stumbling blocks. Even where documents such
as wills or letters are signed in a woman's name, in the great majority of
cases the document was produced by a male scribe, and items such as wills,
deeds or charters adhere with slight variations to prescribed formulae. All
the usual frustrations of seeking women's voices, though, are enormously
compounded when seeking the voices of maidens. The chief problem in
seeking to discover the words, much less thoughts or aspirations, of
maidens is that there are very few records in existence even purporting to
represent their point of view. The common problem of women's silence is
magnified by the silences of young people in general and of the lower
orders who formed the vast majority of the medieval population.

Still, the desire to reach, or at least approach, the individual personalities and sensibilities of young medieval women remains compelling.
Despite the paucity of material and its bias towards elite or wealthy groups,

despite the challenge of taking into account the specific circumstances of authorship and audience in the production of texts, and the requirements of formulae or discursive registers, and despite the shaping of our reading by our own politics and contexts, without at least seeking the perspectives of some maidens our understanding will be too narrowly limited to the voices of their fathers, mothers, employers and priests. To answer Butler's question posed above and to return to Morwenna Griffiths' metaphor, young women did have some agency in spinning webs of their own making within limits imposed from outside themselves.

One point to acknowledge is that while all historical sources are vexed by problems of interpretation, they are not all vexed in exactly the same way or to the same degree. The nature and purpose of the item in question significantly affects its ability to help with certain questions. So, for example, to say that 'medieval legal records' never represent anything close to the sensibilities of the participants would be too heavy-handed. While it is true that many or most of the records of common law practised in the court of King's Bench, for example, have severe limitations for this purpose because of the formulaic nature of legal *narrationes*, the use of professional attorneys and the abbreviated and summarised nature of the record produced by the clerk for the future use of the judge, records from the 'Year Books' make more of an attempt to record fragments of speech exchanged in court.[2] Records from ecclesiastical courts differ again, with their sometimes lengthy transcriptions of deponents' statements, and concerted effort on occasion to record the exact words spoken (using the vernacular where necessary).[3] Letters exchanged between family members offer a more reliable (though never simple) source than wills, to take another example. And even where no words have been recorded, one can derive some level of understanding from young women's actions, which might sometimes even speak louder than words. Although one should not underestimate the difficulties entailed in such an exercise, it is not a hopeless endeavour. If the following readings of maidens' recorded voices and actions cannot ultimately be definitive, one virtue that they have is to illustrate the variety found between individuals and status groups concerning maidens' experiences of and attitudes towards their socialisation, and to show that prescriptive accounts of maidenhood are far more limited than the range of young women's sensibilities and experiences suggest.

'Send more clothes'

At the end of our period, during the first rumblings of the English
Reformation, Arthur Plantagent, viscount Lisle (who was an illegitimate
son of Edward IV) was told in March 1533 that he had been appointed
Lord Deputy of Calais and moved across the Channel with his wife, Lady
Honor Lisle. In April 1540 Thomas Cromwell abruptly summoned him
back to London on charges of conspiracy, implicating him in the fiendishly
complicated struggle over power and religion which would see Cromwell
himself executed within months. The details of Lisle's fall are not the issue
here, but the event accounts for the preservation of an extraordinary body
of documents, the Lisle Letters, which were seized by the Crown along
with all other family papers at the time of Lisle's arrest. Among those
letters are a number from Honor Lisle's daughters from her first marriage,
most from Anne and Mary Basset who were sent to board with the aristocratic de Riou and de Bours households in northern France in late 1533
and 1534 respectively.[4] These provide a rare glimpse into the responses of
young aristocratic women to the shaping of their own femininity.

Anne Basset moved to the de Riou household at Pont de Remy on the
Somme in November 1533, aged twelve or nearly thirteen. It was the first
step towards a career which would see her enter royal service as a maiden-
in-waiting to Jane Seymour in 1537, and after a period with the countess of
Sussex return to court as maiden to Anne of Cleves, Katherine Howard
and Katherine Parr. She could be described as an aristocratic career girl,
whose youth was directed to setting her up for the most dazzling preferment
available, and who delayed marriage as a result of her concentration on
service. She was finally married at about thirty-four to Walter Hungerford,
a baron's son twelve years her junior (and with an amazingly sordid family
history), and died three years later. Similarly her sister Katherine, who was
turned down for a place at court, entered the service of the countess of
Rutland in 1537 and from 1540 spent seven years with Anne of Cleves (no
longer queen), marrying an esquire in 1547 at about twenty-eight or
perhaps thirty.[5]

Anne's upbringing, then, was aimed at promoting her family's interests
not immediately through marriage (though probably her mother and
stepfather fantasised about the potential matches to be made from court
contact) but through royal service. Some of Lady Lisle's correspondence
with Anne at court reveals the political uses a royal maid-in-waiting could
be put to, though Anne was not always cooperative.[6] Anne's socialisation
in gender was not aimed primarily at making her a good wife, but at

fitting her for an active, quasi-public role at the highest rung of the social ladder.

Anne's letters to her mother from the de Riou household, written from the age of about twelve to about sixteen, reveal a prickly character. Compared with those of her sisters they are abrupt and haughty, and display only one chief interest: clothes. This is apparent from her first letter, of May 1534:

> Madame, an it might please you, I would heartily desire you to send me some demi-worsted for a gown, and a kirtle of velvet, and also some linen to make smocks, and some hosen and shoes. I send you back again the gold ornaments which I brought with me, because I know not how to make use of them here. I heartily beseech you that it may please you to send me some others. I have need of three ells of red cloth to make me a cloak, with a hood of satin.[7]

An even more brusque communication came in August 1535:

> Madame, I would most earnestly entreat you that if I am to pass the winter in France I may have some gown to pass it in, as I am out of apparel for every day. Madame, I know well that I am very costly unto you, but it is not possible to do otherwise, there are so many little trifling things which are here necessary which are not needed in England, and one must do as others do.[8]

Tempting though it might be to read these extracts as amusing evidence for perennial adolescent anxiety about fashion and peer approval, it is more useful to see Anne's concerns in contemporary context. Appearances were of tremendous importance in high society, and especially at court. When Jane Seymour agreed to examine Katherine and Anne as prospective maid-in-waiting in July 1537 she ordered that they should come to court so she might 'know their manners, fashions and conditions', and that they should each bring an outfit of satin and another of damask.[9] Following Anne's appointment the queen issued further directives concerning her clothing, including her wish that Anne give up her French fashions, while in 1538 a furious domestic squabble arose over Anne's rather graceless ingratitude towards her mother who had sent her sixscore pearls – an inadequate number for the needs of court dress.[10] Anne was probably chosen over Katherine partly for her appearance. In 1540, when Lady Lisle was once more trying to place Katherine at court and asked Anne to look into it, Anne replied that she had spoken to the king, but he was willing to accept only those who were 'fair, and as he thought meet for the room'.[11] Sceptical though one might be about the king's preference for attractive damsels, his partiality was shared by the queen and court circle.

If scholarly achievements, accomplishments and a warm personality had been valued at court, Anne's sister Mary would have been a far better contender. Both girls learned to speak French during their years of boarding, but Anne's scholarly abilities were limited. All the letters in her name contained within the collection, whether in English or French, were produced by a scribe, and in response to her mother's irritation at her low level of correspondence in 1538 Anne retorted, 'where your ladyship doth think that I can write English, in very deed I cannot, but that little I can write is French'.[12] Her mother was very annoyed when on one occasion in 1539 Anne even let her scribe sign a letter for her, and Anne explained 'I cannot write nothing myself but mine own name; and as for that, when I had haste to go up to the Queen's chamber, my man did write it which did write my letter'.[13] Mary, however, from understanding no French on her arrival at the de Bours's house in August 1534 had by that November learned enough with the aid of a schoolmaster to scribe several of her own letters.[14] She also learned to play musical instruments and to embroider, and if Anne also gained these talents no mention is made of them.[15] Though Mary too made requests for clothing, they seemed to be more out of need than a wish to be fashionable (apart from a request for pearls), and she apologised on occasion for the expense she incurred. She also seems to have been more truly interested in the well-being and needs of others (where Anne makes only formulaic enquiries) requesting gifts for others, including servants, sending gifts herself, and composing genuinely warm letters to her elder sister Philippa and increasingly anxious ones to her mother when no news of the latter's pregnancy was forthcoming.[16] Where Anne and Lady Lisle had an often strained relationship, Honor Lisle's only concern about Mary seems to have been her penchant for gambling, though she might have been more worried had she known about the romance between Mary and her hostess's son, Gabriel de Montmorency.[17]

In looks, some felt Mary to be more attractive than Anne, so the Lisles' decision to push Anne and Katherine forward must have been based on more than natural beauty.[18] Anne's self-assurance and sense of style, as well as her haughtiness, self-absorption and imperious manner even with her own mother – traits which make her appear less appealing to modern eyes – fit her well for a specific form of contemporary femininity. For maidens of the high aristocracy, royal service was a higher calling than the more commonly espoused role of the good wife. It is ironic that the de Riou family, from which Anne received her head-start, were connected by marriage to a descendant of Geoffrey, Knight of la Tour Landry, as it seems unlikely that she would have enjoyed his homilies on the importance of maidenly virtue and wifely obedience.[19] Though the frequent tiffs with her mother and a serious breach with Lady Sussex while in her service demonstrate that Anne had a rather aggressive character, it was not her path in life which she was rebelling against.[20] From the evidence preserved in her letters, Anne Basset embraced the part of the high-flying career maiden, and pursued it with determination.

'Marry me'

A great contrast in styles and personalities is revealed by comparing Anne Basset's letters with those of a young gentlewoman, Margery Brews of Norfolk, to her future husband John Paston III. Despite the differences, though, these too tell us something about how a young woman responded to and used constructions of femininity to her own ends.[21] Written in February 1477, Margery's two letters of courtship are illustrative of the uses to which a young woman could put conventions of appealing maidenhood, and the influence that could be gained through them when no other method was available. Margery draws upon models of ideal femininity to present a certain kind of character – the eligible young gentlewoman. Whether she employed these models consciously or unconsciously is not knowable, and perhaps irrelevant. The letters seem to have been crafted carefully with a view to persuading John III that marriage to Margery was a most attractive proposition, regardless of financial difficulties with her father. There is a problem of possible scribal intervention, as Norman Davis identified the letter as written in the hand of Thomas Kela, Thomas Brews's clerk. But as it was common practice (especially amongst women) to have a secretary scribe one's letters, that alone is no reason to suppose that Kela was in any sense the author of the letter, though he may have helped Margery with the composition. Kela did act as Margery's advocate in the 'matter', writing to John III in another letter from February 1477, but in an entirely different tone from Margery's open and exuberant style.[22] It is possible that Margery drafted a rough copy which Kela then neatly transcribed. Margery appended subscriptions and signatures in her own hand to two letters in 1481, showing that she could write a little.[23]

The first of the letters is dated to February 1477. Its timing, along with Dame Elizabeth Brews's note of the same month referring to 'Saint

Valentines Day', when 'every bird chooses him[self] a mate',[24] immediately places it within the discourse of love and courtship, and Margery's greeting to 'my right well-beloved Valentine' leaves no doubt about the letter's genre. Margery employs a number of literary conventions of love and courtship in her overtures. Enquiring after John III's health, she remarks of her own 'I am not in good health of body nor of heart, nor shall be till I hear from you', alluding to the trope of love as, if not an illness, at least a physical dis-ease.[25] She shifts into verse to dramatise the depth of her longing: 'For there weets [knows] no creature what pain I endure, / And for to be dead I dare it not discover.' Her claims of secret suffering are melodramatically exaggerated, as is clear from the lines following which speak of her mother's efforts with her father on her behalf, and Dame Elizabeth's own complaint to John that 'You have made her such [an] advocate for you that I may never have rest night nor day for calling and crying upon to bring the said matter to effect'.[26]

Margery follows her couplet with a brief mention of the 'matter' and her mother's failure to prise any more dowry money out of her father, but moves swiftly from such mundane matters back to the business of love, this time as a bargaining tool: 'if that you love me, as I trust verily that you do, you will not leave me therefore: for if that you had not half the livelihood that you have, for to do the greatest labour that any woman on live [alive] might, I would not forsake you.' Flirting with emotional blackmail, Margery knows she cannot win John III by simply practical means and instead attempts to talk him into being in love with her. Six further lines of awkward verse crank the message of devotion up a gear, Margery pledging to respect his commands even above her own family's wishes, and the missive ends with a typical lover's request that it be kept hidden from all but the lover's eyes.

Margery's attempts to persuade John to respond in kind to her devotion rely little on rational argument and greatly on casting herself as a feminine object of desire. She is therefore less direct than Cicely Daune had been in courting John II a decade or more earlier, who also attempted to use the promise of love to overcome financial difficulties but ultimately argued that marrying her would be a sensible decision: 'me seems [I think] wedding would have good advisement'.[27] Like Margery Brews, she had little material incentive to offer Paston (to the point that she was reduced to pleading with him to pay for new clothing to see her through the winter), but lacked Margery's gift for portraying herself as a woman who is loving, patient, forgiving, humble, devoted and charming – that is, as an ideal bride.

Margery's second letter was less romantic, more concerned with practical considerations, and more urgent. John's reply to her valentine note was apparently fairly brisk. Margery repeats the sense of his communication, that he would arrive shortly at her parents' house in Topcroft to conclude the matter with her father, and that if the prospects looked no better for him he would not put her father and mother to further 'cost nor business'. Thus Margery makes one last desperate attempt, yet couched in rather passive language. She avoids promising that *he* will be made happy by marriage, but perseveres with girlish charm: 'If that you could be content with that good [i.e. her dowry] and my poor person, I would be the merriest maiden on ground.' Although she seems to release him from pressure or expectations within the marriage, for simply by accepting her he would fulfil her dreams, the element of emotional persuasion is still strong. Margery calls John her 'valentine' twice in this second letter, and signs it with the same word, implying that the romantic bond between them is a given and that they are equal in this regard. Clearly, though, they are not. Another woman lurks in the background: '[If] you might have much more good, as I have understood by you afore, good, true, and loving Valentine ... let it [the matter] pass, and never more to be spoken of as I may be your true lover and bedewoman [servant] during my life.' John, that good, true and loving valentine, has informed her that he can do better elsewhere. Perhaps Margery is having a slight dig at John III for his materialism, or cunningly, through flattery, opening up a space for him to slip into. He has only to play along with the role of the lover she has cast him in.

The letters provide a rare glimpse of a young woman who ardently wished to marry but was relatively powerless – as not only a woman, but the daughter of a gentleman – to bring it about. The marital negotiations, so delicately yet revealingly termed 'the matter', seem to be controlled by John III and her father: she calls them 'the matter betwixt my father and you'. There is a chain of command in action. Margery talks to her mother, her mother to her husband, and both parents, but mainly her father, talk to John. Margery has found a way to bypass the obstacles and conduct her own negotiations, on separate terms. Margery was not the only young woman represented in the Paston letters who had specific hopes for her marital career, though others seem to have been less successful. John II wrote to John III in 1474 of Stockton's daughter, who was to be wedded in haste to a man called Skeerene, and how she had confided in Sir John's silkmaid (who was to make part of her wedding outfit) that her heart was broken and 'she should [wished she could] have had Master Paston'. She told the silkmaid a tall tale of how this Master Paston had come with twenty men to take her away but had failed. John II, in his inimitable manner, replied that he would not have had her for 3000 marks.[28] Elisabeth Clere's celebrated letter to John I in around 1449 tells of Elizabeth Paston's decision to take Stephen Scrope as her husband, despite his 'simple person' (he was apparently disfigured), as then 'men should have the more dainty [esteem] of her if she rule her to him as she ought to do'. She fought so hard with her mother over this that Agnes locked her up and beat her about the head sometimes twice a day. Yet, writes Mistress Clere, 'she will have him, whether that her mother will [wishes] or will not'.[29] This desire of Elizabeth's to marry this unappealing suitor, a fifty-year-old disabled widower, has seemed so unlikely to modern readers that for decades many have read the letter as evidence for parental attempts to enforce an unwanted marriage upon a hapless daughter.[30] It is difficult for some readers to accept that what would seem unbearable for a modern young woman would have had many attractive advantages for a medieval girl. The desirability of secure wedlock for some young women should not be underestimated.

Where Elizabeth Paston, Stockton's daughter and Cecily Daune failed in their courtship endeavours, Margery Brews finally triumphed in securing her man. Through casting herself as an affectionate, undemanding, easy to please, vivacious and agreeable woman, she asserted her own eligibility. Though such feminine roles would generally have a limiting function, in this instance they helped Margery gain that which she so desired.

'Ave Maria'

Moving away from the upper social ranks, the possibilities for 'hearing' maidens' voices become still thinner. Yet there are avenues awaiting exploration, and records from the Church courts, which were more concerned in some instances to record the precise words spoken by deponents than other legal venues such as the royal courts, could be cautiously examined. But in the widespread absence of reported voices, one way forward is to examine what maidens *did*. Although individuals' actions cannot be shown to be always true to what they thought or felt in their 'innermost selves', they, like the letters by noble girls, can be said to demonstrate the identity which maidens felt would be acceptable to their communities. For urban and village girls, especially from artisan families, churchwardens' accounts are an invaluable source for allowing us closer to a few lower-status maidens.

In 1531, in the rural parish of Morebath in Devon, it was recorded that

Johanna Hucly, '*puella* and *filia* [of] Richard Hucly', had given a candlestick with five branches to stand before a new image of the Virgin. The candlestick cost her father 8*s*. 5*d*., and she also gave 4*d*. to pay for the alms light.[31] Johanna, who had died prematurely, with this final gesture signalled both her own commitment to parish life, but also her involvement not as an individual but as a family member, and in particular as the daughter of a prominent local man. A further, more detailed, entry, clarifies that Johanna had donated some money herself but her gift had been twenty shillings short of the price, so Richard had made up the difference rather than see the installation of the candlestick delayed.[32] Johanna and Richard Hucly were members of one of the more active families in the parish, mentioned in numerous entries concerning gifts to the church and also in a range of offices from 1526 to 1540. Richard, a farmer, was twice churchwarden during this time, and in other years was warden of the stores of St Anthony and St George, while John Hucly was also very active and twice in the period served as churchwarden.[33] The younger family members took part too, with Alison Hucly chosen as one of the wardens of the maidens' guild in 1530, as was another Johanna Hucly in 1533, while a younger Richard Hucly was young men's warden in 1534.[34]

The involvement of whole family groups, including unmarried daughters, in parish life and worship is a feature of medieval communal life that is only now beginning to be fully appreciated.[35] The extensive involvement of women and adolescent male and female children alongside husbands and fathers makes the parish a much more fruitful focus for the study of the intersection of familial and communal interests than possibly any other source for urban and village life (though because few accounts are extant from before the mid-fifteenth century they can be revealing only of very late medieval parish activities).[36] The values and social sensibilities represented by parish society are not easy to pin down. On one hand, its semi-liberalism is signalled by its respect for democratic processes in electing officials and in sometimes allowing women to be officials, including a handful of widows serving as churchwardens.[37] On the other, parishes seem to have held to sets of values which could be labelled 'conservative' or 'traditional', though in a form particular to them and partly divorced from the more obviously powerful and institutionalised values of the Church and secular elite. Perhaps they bear most in common with the respectable working classes of the nineteenth and first half of the twentieth centuries: hardworking, churchgoing, family-focused and community-spirited, and with their own distinctive culture. Parish organisation was dominated by families of the better-off and more reputable trades, such as brewers, tailors, barbers, goldsmiths, weavers and smiths, or by mercers and merchants, rather than by local gentry or by the lower trades or small landholders.[38]

Certainly, the pre-Reformation churchwardens' accounts bear testament to the enthusiasm of at least some ordinary parishioners for orthodox religious life, with their regular donations of money and goods to their church, involvement in fund-raising activities, and willingness to give up their time to act as church officials.[39] But the enormous range of activities controlled by the parish make it far more than a religious grouping. Beat Kümin traces the development of parish organisation from the mid-twelfth century (though on a very small scale until the mid-fourteenth century and after), as churchgoers grew frustrated with the centralised Church's often inadequate provision and maintenance of church buildings, vessels, images, ornaments and liturgical books. By the mid-fourteenth century some parishes attempted to keep communal funds and property out of the incumbent's grasp.[40] Local participation in the Church's affairs not unnaturally led to the development of organised groups, with officials appointed each year to take on specific responsibilities, and this created the necessity for account-keeping. It seems to have been by the fifteenth century that parishioners extended their influence from financial matters to moral and spiritual ones, monitoring the behaviour of the parish priest to ensure 'conscientious performances of spiritual services at an affordable price' (thus for example setting tariffs for priestly services such as churchings and marriages) and policing and laying complaints about negligent or absent incumbents.[41] Parish officials also sometimes took on a regulatory function within the secular community, such as monitoring church attendance and behaviour during services, and enforcing payment of church dues, and wider aspects of social control such as keeping the peace, monitoring strangers and condemning brothels and fornication.[42]

It is within this climate of local independence combined with anxiety about morality and respectability that one must place the activities of local maidens. Young unmarried women had a prominent role within the fund-raising, spiritual and festive activities of many parishes, often alongside the 'young men' or 'yonglings' of the parish. We find them acting as individuals or within a family setting, as Johanna Hucly did in making her donations, but also sometimes as a recognised grouping with their own responsibilities and funds. Morebath had an exceptionally active maidens' guild, with responsibility for raising money for a light to stand before the image of the Virgin their main activity, though at times they also contributed to the lights before the high cross and the images of Christ and of St

Sidwell, and in 1533 aided in providing for the gilding of 'our Lady of pity'.[43] The maidens of St Ewen's in Bristol, contemporaries of the peace-making merchant's wife Elizabeth Sharp with whom this book began, also collected money for their Lady light,[44] and French's extensive study of extant pre-Reformation accounts has revealed that of the eleven parishes with recorded activities by maidens' guilds, four or five were dedicated to the Virgin (as were seven of the fifteen wives' guilds studied, indicating that devotion to the Virgin was a life-long form of feminine worship). St Margaret was the only other saint with a maidens' guild's dedication in her study (at Margaret's Church in Southwark), and the dedications of the remaining five maidens' guilds are unknown.[45] Maidens displayed devotion to other holy figures, as already seen with the examples of St Sidwell and Christ at Morebath, and French mentions the maidens' veneration of Henry VI at Walberswick in Suffolk,[46] but maidens' and wives' particular devotion to the Virgin does strongly indicate an association of respectable femininity with the peace-weaving and intercessory role of the Virgin within these ranks of upright village and urban society.[47]

In addition to their regular collections for lights and images the young women and girls could rally with the rest of the parish to make occasional contributions to help with major parish projects, as two separate 'virgins' guilds' in Bodmin did in 1469 and 1472 to aid in the building of the church.[48] A revealing example comes from the Morebath accounts for 1534, when a thief took a ladder and broke into the church through the belfry, broke the coffers and stole a chalice. In response the maidens' and young men's guilds 'drew themselves together and with their gifts and provision they bought in another chalice without any charges of the parish'. The young people's contribution was seen as so noteworthy that each name was recorded along with the corresponding donation. 'Johanna Hucly' was one of thirty-four maidens, and 'John Hucly' was among sixty-seven young men.[49] This list was probably meant for recitation by the priest before the congregation on a Sunday, as frequently happened with bede rolls, and demonstrates young people's incorporation into parish life and the value of the collection as an opportunity to receive public approval from their elders.[50]

Social or festive occasions also provided a stage for the maidens, where their symbolic associations with both sexuality and virginity made them especially welcome. St Martin's Church in Leicester made special provision for the 'virgins' in its annual procession through the town to the church on Whitsunday.[51] Whitsuntide was a season suited to maidens, as a celebration of the culmination of spring blossoming and first hints of summer flowering, and St Edmund's in Salisbury collected money from dances at this time, while at London's St Mary at Hill maidens held a collection on St Barnabas's Day (June 11), for which rose garlands were made.[52] Maidens of the parish of St Margaret's in Southwark also raised money from dancing, as did those of St Ewen's (see Figure 9).[53] Whitsun could also provide an occasion for the maidens to hold an ale, as it did in Croscombe in 1547, and in the St Ewen's accounts for 1473–4 Margaret Nancothan, evidently active in the maidens' guild and dances, was among those who sold ale, possibly at Whitsun.[54] Popular imagination usually associates maidens with May Day celebrations, however. May Day ales were held, as at Allhallows, London Wall, in 1510, and as the use of May poles spread in the late fifteenth century and after, maidens were among the dancers.[55] A window at Betley Hall, Staffordshire, from the time of

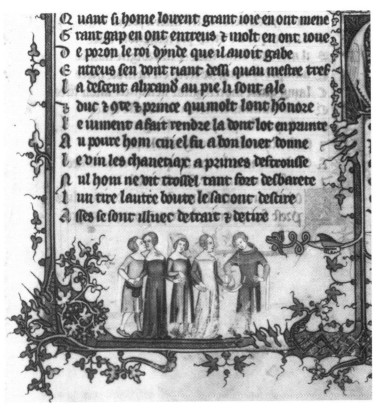

9   The perils of dancing

Edward IV, depicts eleven male May dancers and one female figure, the May Queen, crowned and holding a flower.[56] The staging of the Robin Hood play which was a feature of May time festivities in parishes including Croscombe in Devon, where the Robin Hood guild was an important source of income, may have involved young women, as it did in St Laurence's parish in Reading, where payments were made for the maidens' banner at the play in 1502 and for Maid Marion's coat in 1529. Likewise, Kingston upon Thames paid for a 'gown for the lady' at the Robin Hood's play in 1504 and St Andrew Hubbard collected 13s. 4d. from 'Mistress Marian' from the play in 1538–40.[57] Though spring and early summer were the most apt for maidens' involvement they took part in less obviously appropriate festivals too, as in St Mary Woolnoth in 1539 where the virgins wore garlands and played harps on Allhallows' Day.[58]

Hocking has received a good deal of recent attention by historians as a parish activity in which women played an essential role, and though most accounts simply record the 'women's' or 'wives'' hock money some also record maidens' involvement.[59] The hockday rituals which occurred (more often in urban than rural contexts and mostly in southern and central England, on the second Monday and Tuesday after Easter), required women on Hock Monday and men on Hock Tuesday lightheartedly to threaten members of the opposite sex with being bound by a rope, unless they paid a forfeit. The money collected was given to the churchwarden. As French calculates, hocking could provide an important source of parish income, and the women invariably raised more money than the men [60] (the most obvious reason for which is that men are likely to have had more ready money to pay in forfeit, though perhaps men were more willing to submit to the threat of binding given its hint of sexual play and implications of violence, however playfully expressed). Maidens or daughters took part in hocking in certain parishes, including St Edmund's and St Thomas's in Salisbury, and Croscombe was unusual in reserving Hocktide celebrations to the young men and maidens' guilds.[61] The more usual association between married women and hocking, though, and the fact that frequently it was women of some standing in the parish who took charge of the collection (as at Allhallows in London, where names of fifteenth- and early sixteenth-century hockmoney collectors include 'Butler's wife', 'Pratt's wife' and 'Webb's wife', all wives of men who were churchwardens at various times, St Mary the Great in Cambridge where the money was collected by Mistress Sabyn, Mistress Butt and Mistress Halhed in 1518, all sharing surnames with prominent and active members of the parish, or Lambeth where 'Bever's wife' who was one of the collectors from 1517 to 1519 was wife of a man several times churchwarden), suggest that this was an activity considered too potentially risqué or compromising of female virtue to be generally appropriate for maidens.[62] Indeed, even by the mid-fifteenth century a good deal of ecclesiastical disquiet was being expressed about this 'noxious corruption' and these 'unsuitable pastimes', early signs of official dissent which would crescendo with the banning of the practice in most parishes from the mid-sixteenth century.[63]

The example of hocking and its repression offers up the possibility of reading the churchwarden-account evidence regarding women slightly differently from usual, and suggests that the later fifteenth and early sixteenth centuries were not so much a period of heightened expression of women's involvement in local seasonal customs as the beginning of their containment and ultimate suppression. The problem with sustaining such a reading is lack of evidence for the practices before the widespread habit of keeping accounts in the fifteenth century, but it is offered here as a plausible alternative interpretation. No one knows the origins of the ritual of hocking.[64] The first records of its practice are from 1406, from the first of a series of London ordinances which attempted to prohibit the practice, and in 1416 in Coventry the 'Hox Tuesday' revels begin to be recorded, but the earliest known use of 'Hocktide' to denote a date is from c. 1175.[65] It is quite likely that the practice predated its recording. The emergence of hocking in the accounts as a conveniently profitable and socially respectable custom – the nice ladies of the parish letting their hair down for a day – more likely marks its envelopment and containment by the parish than its appearance as a 'new holiday'.[66] It is too easy to conflate the first appearance of an activity in the historical record with its actual inception. In the case of hocking, an old, rather indecorous, practice was coming under scrutiny by the fifteenth century, appearing in records almost simultaneously as cause for concern about public morals and as a welcome source of revenue raising. For the latter to be tolerated, hocking needed to be taken in hand by the Mistress Butlers, Mistress Sabyns and Mistress Bevers of the neighbourhood before its ultimate repression in the later sixteenth century.

It is within such a late medieval climate of social transition and tightening control that the parish activities of maidens can be at least partly understood. For while examples examined so far demonstrate the happy, even enthusiastic, participation of maidens, evidence exists for the limitations of this involvement, and its direction by parish leaders, usually male. This is glimpsed partly in the records of the names of the wardens of the maidens' guilds. In Morebath over the period from 1527 to 1538, twenty-three out of the twenty-four maiden wardens (two were appointed each year) share a surname with churchwardens over the period 1526 to 1540. Of these, Christina Morris in 1536 and Johanna at Come in 1538 are noted as the daughters of William Morris and William at Come, members of prominent families.[67] The list of the hundred and one young men and maidens who donated money for the new chalice at Morebath in 1534 comprises thirty-eight different surnames, of which twenty-one are surnames shared with churchwardens. The remaining seventeen surnames were spread out over twenty individuals (with only one donation per name in most cases, two per name in three cases), while the dominant surnames covered eighty-one individuals, clearly showing that a substantial minority of families dominated the life of the parish.[68] The choice of maiden wardens from within the prominent families indicates a likely degree of influence of the men of those families over the activities of the maidens' guild.

Similar, though not so decisive, results emerge from examining the names of the maiden wardens at Croscombe. Of the thirteen different maiden wardens whose names are recorded from 1477 to 1503 (in some years and after 1503 the names are not recorded, in most only one of the names is mentioned, and some maidens serve more than one year), six clearly share surnames with churchwardens over the period 1475 to 1560, when the record ends, and two more could be counted if Joan 'Bayle' is a member of the busy Bole family, and Isabel 'Hoper' is among the active Harpers. Joan Hill, described as 'Morris's servant' and maiden warden in 1480 and possibly 1483, has two connections to churchwardens from the high-profile Hill and Morris families. Of the remaining five maidens with no clear connection to the churchwardens, Margaret Smith and Elizabeth Joyce share surnames with men who are listed a number of times for their donations to the parish, and indeed all the men who share names with maiden wardens appear frequently in the records for their donations and wardenship of minor guilds. Only Agnes Beke, Margaret Elme and Joan Knap have no obvious connection to prominent men of the parish.[69]

Such detail is not always available, but signs that older, especially male, parishioners, kept an eye on maidens' activities and in particular on their financial dealings are visible in a number of parishes. The names of the maiden wardens in Morebath in 1527 are recorded by their editor as 'John Tywell' and 'John Rumbelow', and if this is correct it indicates direct male control of the guild.[70] At St Ewen's in the accounts for 1464–5 John Nancothan paid 10s. 1d. 'of old dancing money left in his daughter's hands', his daughter probably the Margaret Nancothan who was among two women and two men to pass over the dancing money three years later.[71] In the same parish in 1481–2 the parson paid over 2*s*. 2*d*. as 'the maidens' money which rested with him in keeping for our lady taper'.[72] At Croscombe, although in the majority of instances one of the maiden wardens herself received the 'stoke' from the wardens to pay for the wax and making of tapers for the year, on three occasions it was taken by William Branch and on one by William Carpenter, churchwardens on those occasions. William Branch also took charge of the money from the 'wife's dancing' in 1483.[73] In Peterborough, though the church is not known to have had a maidens' guild, men often took charge of daughters', wives', sisters' and female servants' payments to the great bell and other offerings, paying them over on the women's behalf.[74] Though there were occasions when a woman took charge of maidens' money, as in the parish of Allhallows, London Wall, in 1512, when the 'goodwife Webb' paid the gathering of twelvepence 'of virgins' money',[75] and probably the hock money in the charge of goodwives in many instances included maidens' contributions, usually the watchfulness maintained over the maidens was masculine.[76]

Such control began to be exerted within the physical space of the parish church by the early sixteenth century. Though the extent of the segregation of women from men within the church by this time has been perhaps exaggerated at the expense of considerations of status and family groupings, some parishes did begin to seat maids separately.[77] In 1524–5 in St Mary at Hill in London, payments were made for pews for Mistress Roche's maidens and Mistress Russell's maids, while at St Andrew Hubbard in Eastcheap payment was made between 1500 and 1503 'for a pew making in the loft for the maidens', indicating the placement of young women up high out of harm's reach, and in full view.[78]

The picture that emerges from this evidence is slightly ambiguous. Maidens showed agency in playing an economically important and symbolically attractive role in parish life, but by the end of our period were often kept under the watchful eye of their elders. They were active within the parish, but in a limited way. As French has put it, parish roles gave women 'more visibility, but also paradoxically affirmed and reinforced what were deemed to be appropriate female behavior and interests'.[79] They, like the maid of Elizabeth Sharp who carried the cake with candles into St Ewen's on a January morning in 1464, were learning the active docility desired of daughters and wives. Their cultural valency as embodiments of both fertility and virginity made them desired participants especially in the festivities of late spring and early summer, and to a lesser and more controlled extent in the more risqué pastime of hocking. But the roles created for them were overseen by the town and village worthies who controlled parish social life and worship, and reinforced through the choice of churchwardens' daughters or kinswomen as maiden wardens.

How, then, can the activities outlined here possibly stand in any way for 'maidens' voices'? Certainly, they represent only a visible subsection of parish maidens. The young women who were chosen as maiden wardens and the likes of Johanna Hucly were probably distinguished from the kinds of young women who by the sixteenth century were being seated together under watchful eyes. These records are dominated by the doings of good girls. Like the churchwardens and other active parishioners they were so often linked to, they were probably from respectable and moderately well-off artisan and some merchant households, rather than from the poorest farming or artisan groups or from village or urban elites. They represent a lower-middle to middle social group for whom the forces of convention were as strong, in their own way, as those for the higher levels. Churchwardens' accounts suggest that the unmarried daughters of this group shared their elders' values, or at least recognised the advantages of being seen to do so. When the virgins of Bodmin gathered funds for the building of their church, or the Morebath maidens joined the young men to raise funds for the new chalice, or any individual young woman gave of her time, money or goods to the benefit of the church, they were expressing both a depth of religious conviction and pride in their communal identity. It is to other kinds of records we need to turn for girls who cared less for the acquisition of active docility.

Restive voices

'Don't call me lass', is a close approximation of the words of Agnes Cosyn, a young woman of well-off farming background who objected to marrying Robert Chew in Yorkshire in 1453. We have already met Robert Chew, as the man whose premarital liaison with Isabella Alan led to his payment of twenty marks compensation for deflowering her. Agnes was working in the bakehouse on her family's holding at Eastburn in the wolds, when Robert Chew arrived to seal their contract with her father William. Robert Kirkeby, a relative of Robert Chew, was present and asked her why she would not take Robert as a husband though her father preferred him to all other suitors and everyone believed them already contracted. She replied, 'sub hac forma', 'I never contracted with him except under the condition that he should remain as free and unbound (liber et solutus) on his part as I on mine'. But, continues Kirkeby, she said the main reason for refusing Robert was that his relatives called and named her 'lass'.[80]

It is difficult to be sure of precisely what Agnes was objecting to in either instance. It is tempting to read her wish that the pair retain a certain level of independence in marriage as an exuberant outburst against the inequalities inherent in medieval matrimony, but this may be breaching Page duBois's warning to historians not to make women of their study too closely resemble themselves.[81] Perhaps she was referring to some specific matter, such as property arrangements. One point seems clear – Agnes had a strong sense of her own interests. Her objection to being called lass seems to have come from a dislike of being demeaned. This northern word derived from an Old Norse term for an unmarried woman, *lösk kona*, *lösk* in turn possibly deriving from *löskr*, idle or weak (perhaps, by extension, also indicating lesser or inadequate status).[82] 'Lass' seems in any case to have retained some negative overtones in north-east England by the mid-fifteenth century, judging by Agnes's reaction, though Robert's family may have used it neutrally. It could have held connotations of low social status, or regional inferiority. Agnes Cosyn had a strong sense of herself, and no tolerance for being belittled.

No less defiant, though with very different motivations, were villein daughters on the manor of Halesowen during the insurgent decades of the late thirteenth century. Though others, in particular Zvi Razi, have written of the general uprising of villein tenants at Halesowen against their monastic landlords in the 1270s, 1280s and 1290s, women's involvement has been little recognised.[83] Yet young villein women were visible participants. By November 1279 enough tenants were running away from the manor for the abbey to launch an enquiry, and in January 1280 Matilda de Leche was recorded as one who had fled.[84] Matilda de Hiddeley was in January 1280 accused of verbally abusing the abbot in her mother's home, and though her words have not been recorded, the emotion behind them seems clear.[85] Women are the majority of those recorded for burning the lord's hedges, particularly during the conflict that raged in the 1290s.[86] Whether they burned the hedges *in situ*, or broke them up to use for firewood at home, the act represents a destruction of the lord's property. And in a most telling example of young women joining in the general rebellion against the manor, in late 1293 Amice Green and Julian and Christina, daughters of Roger of Honeford, went to the place were the abbot's bailiffs had erected gallows and Christina knocked the scaffold to the ground. The young women must then have run away from the manor, as they could not be found by the time the case came before the court.[87] It is likely that the landlord's use of leyrwite at Halesowen during the 1280s, 90s and early 1300s was aimed in part at shaming and quelling particular young women and their families, as many of the women fined for the misdemeanour during that period were daughters of or otherwise related to key male instigators of the uprising.[88] Once again, although we hear no actual voices of maidens from late thirteenth-century Halesowen, their active participation within villein society in resisting the excessive impositions of their landlords indicates a notion of belonging within a specific social grouping and in sharing the values of that group. There was little that was docile or otherwise conventionally 'feminine' about their behaviour. On the other hand, though, if the abbot's use of leyrwite as a shaming tactic were to have any effect, the young women and/or their families must have shared with the wider culture a notion of the centrality of maidens' chastity to the maintenance of their own and their families' good names.

Conclusion

Vexed with difficulties though any attempt to recover the 'voices' or sensibilities of medieval English maidens will always be, there are distinct advantages to trying the exercise. Perhaps the greatest advantage is that it turns up such a range of viewpoints. These stand out clearly when set beside the teachings of the conduct books for maidens of varying status. Those books' attempts to homogenise the behaviour and values of young women within their social classes are shown to be two-dimensional compared with the range of perspectives actually held. Medieval maidens have the capacity to surprise us.

But another important point which arises is the absence of any sense among maidens that they shared any particular disadvantage as young women, as a result of their socialisation in femininity. Though many, such as Anne Bassett, Elizabeth Paston and Agnes Cosyn, struggled against aspects of their personal circumstances, these seem to have been individualised forms of resistance. Where more communal forms of resistance occurred, as at Halesowen, the young women were energised by the needs of their status group and community. In other contexts, such as in parish society, young women seem to have taken an active part in conventional society, and gone along with their training in active docility. Some maidens struggled against elements of their culture, such as young gentlewomen's attempts to overcome their enforced passivity in marital negotiations, yet by the same token embraced conventional elements of their socialisation in femininity, such as the desire to become a wife. If any junior Wives of Bath lurked in the villages and towns of medieval England they have not yet turned up in the records. That is not to say they could not have existed.

But it does appear that many maidens, across the social spectrum, wove webs of selfhood which took unique individual forms, yet were always strongly shaped by the circumstances of their weaving.

Notes

1 Judith Butler, *Gender Trouble: Feminism and the Subversion of Identity* (New York, 1990), p. 11.

2 See Sayles (ed.), *Select Cases in the Court of King's Bench*, 6 vols; Maitland *et al.* (eds), *Year Books of Edward II*, 27 vols.

3 For some translated extracts see Goldberg, (ed. and trans.), *Women in England*; McSheffrey (ed. and trans.), *Love and Marriage*.

4 *LL* 3, pp. 133–219.

5 For Katherine, Anne and Mary's later experiences see *LL* 6, pp. 276–80.

6 For example, *LL* 5, no. 1513.

7 *LL* 3, no. 571.

8 *LL* 3, no. 578.

9 *LL* 4, no. 887.

10 *LL* 4, nos. 895–6; 5, nos. 1136a., 1137, 1154, 1155.

11 *LL* 6, no. 1653.

12 *LL* 5, no. 1126.

13 *LL* 5, no. 1513, and 6, no. 1653.

14 *LL* 3, nos. 574, 575, 587, 622a, 623a., 624.

15 *LL* 3, nos. 583a., 587, 620.

16 *LL* 3, 575, 587, 588, 590, 597a., 609, 615, 617, 619, 620, 622a., 623a., 624.

17 *LL* 3, no. 583a. For the clandestine affair see *LL* 6, pp. 138–51.

18 *LL* 3, no. 574; 4, no. 899.

19 *LL* 3, p. 134.

20 *LL* 4, no. 906.

21 *PL and P* 1, nos. 415–16.

22 *PL and P* 2, no. 792.

23 *PL and P* 1, nos. 417–18.

24 *PL and P* 2, no. 791.

25 Mary Frances Wack, *Lovesickness in the Middle Ages: The* Viaticum *and its Commentaries* (Phildelphia, 1990).

26 *PL and P* 2, no. 791.

27 *PL and P* 2, no. 753.

28 *PL and P* 1, no. 287. Davis suggests this was possibly the same woman as the Mistress Agnes John III courted in the same year, no. 362, though it seems unlikely given that Stockton's daughter was apparently more interested in John II.

29 *PL and P* 2, no. 446.

30 For example, Bennett, *Pastons and Their England*, pp. 29–31; Haskell, 'Paston women on marriage', pp. 466–7. Cf. Dockray, 'Why did fifteenth-century English gentry marry?', pp. 72–3, and Colin Richmond, 'Elizabeth Clere: friend of the

Pastons', in Wogan-Browne *et al.* (eds), *Medieval Women*, p. 253.

31 J. Erskine Binney (ed.), *The Accounts of the Wardens of the Parish of Morebath, Devon 1520-1573* (Exeter, 1904), p. 25. Eamon Duffy's important new study of sixteenth-century Morebath, *The Voices of Morebath: Reformation and Rebellion in an English Village* (New Haven, 2001), came into my hands only in the final stages of revising my manuscript, and I have therefore not been able to acknowledge his work as fully as I would otherwise have done.

32 Binney (ed.), *Morebath*, p. 35. She also donated some beads to the image of St Sidwell, but the wardens recorded that they had been lost, p. 30.

33 Binney (ed.), *Morebath*, pp. 3, 20, 26, 27, 41-2, 99.

34 Binney (ed.), *Morebath*, 14, 44, 54.

35 Recent important studies include Beat A. Kümin, *The Shaping of a Community: The Rise and Reformation of the English Parish c. 1400-1560* (Aldershot, 1996); Katherine L. French, Gary G. Gibbs and Beat A. Kümin (eds), *The Parish in English Life 1400-1600* (Manchester, 1997); Katherine L. French, '"To free them from binding": women in the late medieval English parish', *Journal of Interdisciplinary History*, 27 (1997), 387-412; French, 'Maidens' lights and wives' stores: women's parish guilds in late medieval England', *Sixteenth Century Journal*, 29 (1998), 399-425; French, *People of the Parish*; Duffy, *Voices of Morebath*.

36 See especially the works of Katherine French for women's involvement at all ages.

37 Kümin, *Shaping of a Community*, pp. 28-9. On tolerance for female church-wardens, all known examples of which are from the west of England, see French, 'Maidens' lights and wives' stores', p. 405, and 'To free them from binding', p. 395. For a more pessimistic view of parish women's opportunities see Judy Ann Ford, 'Marginality and the assimilation of foreigners in the lay parish community: the case of Sandwich', in French, Gibb and Kümin (eds), *Parish in English Life*, p. 214.

38 Kümin, *Shaping of a Community*, provides a table of churchwardens' occupations, p. 38, noting that eligibility was determined by factors including residency, administrative and financial experience, and some level of economic independence (as demands could be made on the warden's private purse), and concludes that the parish was dominated by a reasonably broad but also socially middling sort of class, pp. 32-41.

39 For a survey of the fund-raising activities of Somerset parishes, which were mirrored by those of parishes throughout the country, see Katherine L. French, 'Parochial fund-raising in late medieval Somerset', in French, Gibb and Kümin (eds), *Parish in English Life*.

40 Kümin, *Shaping of a Community*, pp. 17-26.

41 Kümin, *Shaping of a Community*, p. 43.

42 Kümin, *Shaping of a Community*, pp. 50-2, and for their involvement in an extraordinary range of other duties see pp. 53-64.

43 Binney (ed.), *Morebath*, e.g. pp. 52, 70, 80.

44 Masters and Ralph (eds), *St Ewen's*, pp. 94, 110, 129.

45 French, 'Maidens' lights and wives' stores', pp. 421-2.

46 French, 'Maidens' lights and wives' stores', p. 409; 'To free them from binding', p. 395.

47 The other saints French finds wives' particular devotion to are two references to St Anne, and one each to Katherine, Ursula, Peter and John the Baptist, 'Maidens' lights and wives' stores', pp. 421–2.

48 The 'virgins of Forestreet' and the 'virgins of Borestreet' together contributed 5s. 11d. in 1469, a sum far lower than any other contribution from the thirteen other religious fraternities, the highest sum of £9 13s. 4d. coming from the guild of John the Baptist, John James Wilkinson (ed.), *Receipts and Expenses in the Building of Bodmin Church A.D. 1469 to 1472*, Camden Miscellany 7, Camden Society new series 14 (London, 1875), p. 5. In 1470 the virgins contributed 6s. 17d. altogether, p. 10, see also p. 33.

49 Binney (ed.), *Morebath*, pp. 64-5. See Duffy, *Voices of Morebath*, pp. 82–3.

50 Ford, 'Marginality and the assimilation of foreigners', pp. 212–13; Duffy, *Stripping of the Altars*, pp. 153–4, 335–6.

51 Thomas North (ed.), *The Accounts of the Churchwardens of S. Martin's, Leicester. 1489–1844* (Leicester, 1884), pp. 3, 70; Thomas North, *A Chronicle of the Church of S. Martin in Leicester During the Reigns of Henry VIII. Edward VI. Mary, and Elizabeth with Some Account of its Minor Altars and Ancient Guilds* (London, 1866), pp. 70, 73, 139.

52 Henry James Fowle Swayne (ed.), *Churchwardens' Accounts of S. Edmund and S. Thomas, Sarum, 1443–1702, with Other Documents*, Wiltshire Record Society 1 (Salisbury, 1896), pp. 73, 76, 81, 110, though the involvement of 'wives' is shown p. 83; Henry Littlehales (ed.), *The Medieval Records of a London City Church (St Mary at Hill) A.D. 1420–1589*, 2 vols, EETS os 125, 128 (London, 1904-5), p. 283.

53 J. Payne Collier (ed.), 'St Margaret's, Southwark', *The British Magazine*, 32 (1847), p. 488; Masters and Ralph (eds), *St Ewen's*, pp. 68, 77.

54 Edmund Hobhouse (ed.), *Churchwardens' Accounts of Croscombe, Pilton, Patton, Tintinhull, Morebath, and St Michael's Bath, Ranging from A.D. 1349 to 1560* , Somerset Record Society 4 (London, 1890), p. 44; Masters and Ralph (eds), *St Ewen's*, pp. 68, 77, 93.

55 Charles Welch (ed.), *The Churchwardens' Accounts of the Parish of Allhallows, London Wall, in the City of London. 33 Henry VI to 27 Henry VIII (A.D. 1455–A.D. 1536)* (London, 1912), p. 48; J. Charles Cox, *Churchwardens' Accounts from the Fourteenth Century to the Close of the Seventeenth Century* (London, 1913), p. 66; Hutton, *Merry England*, pp. 30, 56–7.

56 Cox, *Churchwardens' Accounts*, p. 65.

57 Hobhouse (ed.), *Croscombe, passim*; Cox, *Churchwardens' Accounts*, pp. 282–4. Note that Hutton believes that by the Elizabethan period, at least, men played the part of Maid Marian: *Merry England*, pp. 117–18. Many would say the same of the fifteenth century.

58 Cox, *Churchwardens' Accounts*, p. 277.

59 Among the many valuable recent studies of hocking see Sally Beth MacLean, 'Hocktide: a reassessment of a popular Pre-Reformation Festival', in Meg Twycross (ed.), *Festive Drama* (Cambridge, 1996); French, 'To free them from binding';

Christopher Humphrey, 'The dynamics of urban festal culture in late medieval England' (D.Phil. thesis, University of York, 1997), pp. 144–62.

60 French, 'To free them from binding', pp. 401–7.

61 Swayne (ed.), *S. Edmund and S. Thomas*, pp. 50, 273–4; Hobhouse (ed.), *Croscombe*, pp. 1–43; French, 'To free them from binding', p. 404.

62 Welch (ed.), *Allhallows*, pp. 4, 20, 55; J. E. Foster (ed.), *Churchwardens' Accounts of St Mary the Great Cambridge from 1504 to 1635*, Cambridge Antiquarian Society, ser. 8, 35 (London, 1905), p. 34; Charles Drew (ed.), *Lambeth Churchwardens' Accounts 1504–1645 and Vestry Book 1610*, 4 vols, Surrey Record Society 18 (Lambeth, 1941), vol. 2, pp. 29–30, 35. On the relatively high status of women hockmoney collectors see French, 'To free them from binding', pp. 408–9; Humphrey, 'Dynamics of urban festal culture', pp. 157–60.

63 French, 'To free them from binding', p. 390; Hutton, *Merry England*, pp. 87, 119.

64 Tradition is divided over whether the festival commemorates the death of Harthacnut on 8 June 1042 or a defeat of the Danes on 13 November 1002. The first is said to fit the holiday's date better, but the second event was legendary in medieval times for women's part in the battle against the Danes. See R. W. Ingram (ed.), *Records of Early English Drama: Coventry* (Manchester, 1981), p. lxiii; Thomas Sharp, *A Dissertation on the Pageants or Dramatic Mysteries Anciently Performed at Coventry* (Wakefield, [1825] 1973), pp. 130–2. Hutton thinks hocking was a fifteenth-century invention, *Merry England*, pp. 59–60.

65 French, 'To free them from binding', p. 390, n. 6; Sharp, *Dissertation*, p. 125.

66 French, 'To free them from binding', p. 412.

67 Binney (ed.), *Morebath*, pp. 1–114.

68 Binney (ed.), *Morebath*, pp. 64–5.

69 Hobhouse (ed.), *Croscombe*, esp. pp. 1–26

70 Binney (ed.), *Morebath*, p. 6.

71 Masters and Ralph (eds), *St Ewen's*, pp. 68, 77.

72 Masters and Ralph (eds), *St Ewen's*, p. 110.

73 Hobhouse (ed.), *Croscombe*, pp. 12, 13, 17, 21, 22. William Branch, who was probably father of the Johanna Branch who was maiden warden in 1492, dominated Croscombe parish to an unusual extent among contemporary parishes, serving twenty-five terms as churchwarden between 1478 and 1506, surpassed only by Edward Bole or Middle who served thirty-three times between 1506 and 1556. William Carpenter was warden three times, 1494–7, each time with William Branch. On Croscombe and neighbouring Tintinhull's unusual status as parishes obviously dominated by a handful of families see Kümin, *Shaping of a Community*, p. 32.

74 W. T. Mellows (ed.), *Peterborough Local Administration: Parochial Government before the Reformation: Churchwardens' Accounts 1467–1573, with Supplementary Documents 1107–1488*, Northamptonshire Record Society 9 (Kettering, 1939), pp. 1–35, 67, 101. Note that they sometimes also made payments on behalf of parents, once a widow paid for her daughter (p. 103), and on a couple of occasions wives made offerings for their husbands, but such payments do not seem to have been made on behalf of sons.

75 Welch (ed.), *Allhallows*, p. 53. For her payment of the hock money the following year see note 62.

76 See French, 'Maidens' lights and wive's stores', p. 412, though she prefers to call this 'guidance' and 'supervision' rather than 'watchfulness' and 'control'.

77 Margaret Aston, 'Segregation in church', in Sheils and Wood (eds), *Women in the Church*. Records like those of St Edmund's, Salisbury, make references to the 'wives' pews', but also mention pews apparently shared by husband and wife: Swayne (ed.), *S. Edmund and S. Thomas*, e.g. pp. 64, 50.

78 Littlehales (ed.), *St Mary at Hill*, vol. 1, pp. 323, 328; vol. 2, p. lxxv. That the pews at St Mary at Hill were enclosed with doors is indicated by a reference to the door to 'Mr Roche's' pew, p. 323. On young men's and maidens' galleries in the London churches of St Botoloph Aldersgate and St Michael in the 1570s, some of which were in the choir behind the preacher, and on employment of poor and disabled women to oversee their behaviour, see Claire S. Schen, 'Women and the London parishes', in French, Gibb and Kümin (eds), *Parish in English Life*, pp. 258–9.

79 French, 'Maidens' lights and wives' stores', p. 401, see also p. 420.

80 BIHR CP. F 189.

81 See above, p. 10.

82 *MED*, s.v. 'las(se)'.

83 Amphlett (ed.), *Hales Court Rolls I*; Razi, 'Struggles between the abbots of Halesowen and their tenants'; Peter Franklin, 'Politics in manorial court rolls: the tactics, social composition, and aims of a pre-1381 peasant movement', in Razi and Smith (eds), *Medieval Society and the Manor Court*, p. 188.

84 Amphlett (ed.), *Hales Court Rolls I*, pp. 116–17, 121.

85 Amphlett (ed.), *Hales Court Rolls I*, p. 122.

86 Amphlett (ed.), *Hales Court Rolls I*, pp. 232, 247, 257, 261, 270–1, 325, 348.

87 Amphlett (ed.), *Hales Court Rolls I*, p. 245.

88 Kim M. Phillips, 'Four virgins' tales: sex and power in medieval law', in Anke Bernau, Ruth Evans and Sarah Salih (eds), *Medieval Virginities* (Cardiff, forthcoming).

CONCLUSION

If the separate spheres ideology of the mid-nineteenth to mid-twentieth centuries gave women anything, it was a sense of common experience and common identity. The separation of the roles and realms of men and women had many negative implications for women, relegated as they were to the 'private' sphere of home and family, denied independent incomes, and generally excluded from varied opportunities in working and personal life. But it was the widespread sense of having been denied the options and advantages more often available to men that gave rise to the second wave of the feminist movement, of the 1960s, 1970s and 1980s. The feeling of exclusion endowed a sense of unity among the women involved. The unity was rather fleeting, however, and was partly illusory in the first place – as socialist and black feminists or critics of feminism were quick to point out. The divisions between women were remarked upon, and since the partial breakdown of separate spheres has begun those divisions are felt more keenly, with feminist feelings of commonality dissipating. How do Western women define themselves now? By their occupation, race or ethnicity, nationality, social class, sexual orientation, age and marital status, and only partially by their gender.

In late medieval England, centuries before the development of the ideology of separate spheres, women also viewed their identity through a number of lenses, and a notion of gender identity was only one of these. The aristocrat Anne Basset and her courtly ilk were profoundly aware of their social status, and the need to 'perform' their rank through clothing, conduct, personal demeanour and forms of address and interaction above all other considerations, for the furtherance of career and standing. The young gentlewoman Margery Brews wanted more than anything to marry, and to be the kind of woman a Paston would want for a wife, in letters which emphasise her level of devotion to her future husband and a charming nature which would minimise the disadvantages of her small dowry. Parish maidens of respectable backgrounds across rural and urban England fitted themselves within the framework of their familial and communal contexts, joining in the devotional, fund-raising and social activities of the parish which enabled them to mingle with other girls their own age as well as with boys, but in activities controlled by parental and community intervention. The daughters of insurgent servile tenants in late thirteenth-century Halesowen joined in the resistance mounted by their fathers, brothers and mothers, displaying common cause with their kinsfolk and their class. Some young women such as the yeoman's daughter Agnes Cosyn indicate a sense of self as individuals, with perhaps some awareness of their own status as women and a desire not to be constrained or demeaned by their gender, but it is rather difficult to find such young women in the sources.[1] Others, such as Katherine Dudley, appear to have spent their youths revelling in flirtatious femininity and refusing to be subdued by the models of maidenly virtue and chastity which were so constantly iterated by those who wished to shape youthful femininity according to their own ideals – authors, parents, employers, priests, siblings and communities.

Medieval maidenhood existed as a female life-cycle stage with its own distinct attributes of bodily, mental and spiritual development, and was experienced by most girls across the social spectrum, though sometimes for shorter periods in the nobility. In many respects it differed from the adolescence of contemporary boys, but especially in the representation of maidenhood as an ideal or peak of femininity. Yet it was also a time of learning the roles of adult women, of learning femininity, which constituted the major part of their 'education' and experiences of work and service. Much of their upbringing, training and experience was aimed at making them uncomplaining members of the useful secondary sex. Medieval maidens did not conform to the kinds of autonomy-seeking young women, resisting socialisation in gender, that it is to tempting to imagine them to have been, any more than they entirely complied with the models of chaste, quiet, obedient, docile yet useful maidens which so many of their contemporaries wished them to be. As a group or as individuals, they cannot be easily labelled as either acquiescent or rebellious. They might conform to gender roles while resisting the authority of parents, or the strictures of unfree peasant status.

It is possible that some existing accounts of young medieval womanhood are influenced, however unconsciously, by modern narratives of girls growing up and the trials and joys of becoming women. Many twentieth-century women's memoirs and autobiographies employ common themes in recounting their experience of adolescence and moving towards womanhood.[2] The authors remember their adolescent and early adult years as a time of chafing against the constraints of their upbringing, or of a vague feeling of restlessness and urge to escape. Burgeoning sexuality poses common problems, as in the memoirs of Lorna Sage and Doris Lessing, as does conflict with mothers, often over maternal incomprehension of their daughters' intellectual ambitions or political beliefs, as in the autobiographies of Margaret Forster, Simone de Beauvoir and Lessing. Margaret Forster resolved never to imitate the perpetual martyrdom of her mother's life, and to seek fulfilment in study and career instead. Janet Frame felt so trapped by the gulf between the vivid life of her imagination and the mundane narrowness of her daily existence that she attempted suicide, was diagnosed as mentally ill and committed to an asylum. The transition to full adult womanhood, signalled by Frame's and Lessing's ocean journeys and first successes in print, and Sage's, Forster's and de Beauvoir's flight into intellectual life via university, represents an escape from increasingly claustrophobic adolescence and early adulthood. No longer bound so tightly by the limitations of youthfulness, according to this narrative, young women in modernity have found themselves freed as they approach adulthood to fulfil themselves, following paths they beat for themselves. The image of the autonomous medieval maiden differs from such accounts in that a brief period of youthful independence was followed by marriage and the closing down of options for self-governance, yet the link between young womanhood and a greater degree of independence is strong in both models.

But these are twentieth-century stories, and tell of the lives of young women profoundly shaped by the gender upheaval of the middle decades of that century. Such narratives will not suffice for young medieval women, although we can glimpse occasional similarities in experience and response. No matter what their background, young medieval women had to live lives strongly shaped by community and social status, as well as by expectations of gender. Nor does the narrative of fleeting autonomy or independence really account for young medieval women's upbringing and experiences. A desire for security, in different roles, is easier to trace than any longing for liberation. These young women cannot be relegated to the role of mere ciphers, used to demonstrate some currently favoured perspective, and the lives of modern young women do not provide an adequate framework. Ultimately, as has become clear through the variety of perspectives uncovered in this book, medieval maidens need stories of their own.

Notes

1 See also Rigby, *English Society*, pp. 278–81.
2 Simone de Beauvoir, *Memoirs of a Dutiful Daughter*, trans. James Kirkup (Harmondsworth, [1958] 1963); Margaret Forster, *Hidden Lives: A Family Memoir* (London, 1995); Janet Frame, *An Angel at My Table: Autobiography 2* (London, 1984); Doris Lessing, *Under My Skin: Volume One of My Autobiography, to 1949* (London, 1994); Lorna Sage, *Bad Blood* (London, 2000).

BIBLIOGRAPHY

Manuscript sources

Borthwick Institute for Historical Research, York
    CP E 23, 71, 76, 89, 92, 159, 215
    CP F 22, 127, 189, 280
    PR vols 1–5
British Library, London
    Additional Manuscripts 12195, 17716
    Harleian Manuscripts 1764, 6815
    Royal Manuscripts 14 E.iii, 18 A.vi
    Sloane Manuscripts 5, 249, 421A, 2463
    Yates Thompson Manuscript 13
Corporation of London Record Office, London
    Miscellaneous Manuscript 1863
Norfolk Record Office
    Hare Manuscript 2091
Public Record Office, Kew
    C 1/45/24
    C 47/4/1
    E 210/1176
York Merchant Adventurer's Hall
    Apprenticeship indenture, 1364

Printed primary sources

Albertus Magnus, *Quaestiones super* De animalibus, ed. Ephrem Filthaut, vol. 12 of *Opera Omnia*, ed. Bernhard Geyer, Münster, 1955.

Amphlett, John, Sydney Graves Hamilton and R. A. Wilson (eds), *Court Rolls of the Manor of Hales 1272–1307*, 3 vols, Worcestershire Historical Society, Oxford, 1910–33.

Andrew, Malcolm, and Ronald Waldron (eds), *The Poems of the Pearl Manuscript*, Exeter, 1987.

Aquinas, Thomas, *Summa theologiae*, London, 1973.

Aristotle, *Politics*, ed. and trans. H. Rackham, Cambridge, MA, 1932.

Aristotle, *Generation of Animals*, trans. A. L. Peck, London, 1943.

Asloan, John, 'The spectacle of luf', in W. A. Craigie (ed.), *The Asloan Manuscript: A Miscellany in Verse and Prose*, 2 vols, Scottish Text Society ser. 2, 14–16, Edinburgh, 1923–5.

'Assessment roll of the poll-tax for Howdenshire, etc., in the second year of the reign of King Richard II (1379)', *Yorkshire Archaeological Journal*, 9 (1886), 129–62.

Averall, W., *A Dyall for Dainty Darlings*, London, 1581.

Baildon, William Paley and John Lister (eds), *Court Rolls of the Manor of Wakefield*, Yorkshire Archaeological Society Publications 36 and 57, Leeds, 1906–17.

Baker, Donald C., John L. Murphy and Louis B. Hall (eds), *The Late Medieval Religious Plays of Bodleian MSS Digby 133 and e Museo 160*, EETS os 283, London, 1982.

Banks, Mary MacLeod (ed.), *An Alphabet of Tales: An English 15th Century Translation of the* Alphabetum narrationum, EETS os 126, London, 1904.

Barratt, Alexandra (ed.), *Women's Writing in Middle English*, London, 1992.

Barratt, Alexandra (ed.), *The Knowing of Woman's Kind in Childing: A Middle English Version of Material Derived from the Trotula and Other Sources*, Turnhout, 2001.

Bateson, Mary (ed.), *Borough Customs*, 2 vols, Selden Society 18 and 21, London, 1904–6.

Beadle, Richard (ed.), *The York Plays*, London, 1982.

Benson, Larry D. (ed.), *The Riverside Chaucer*, 3rd edn, Oxford, 1987.

Bickley, Francis B.(ed.), *The Little Red Book of Bristol*, 2 vols, Bristol, 1900.

Binney, J. Erskine (ed.), *The Accounts of the Wardens of the Parish of Morebath, Devon 1520–1573*, Exeter, 1904.

Black, William Henry (ed.), 'Narrative of the marriage of Richard duke of York with Ann of Norfolk, the "matrimonial feast" and the grand justing, A.D. 1477 [1478]', in *Illustrations of Ancient State and Chivalry from Manuscripts Preserved in the Ashmolean Museum*, Roxburgh Club, London, 1840.

Blackley, F. D., and G. Hermansen (eds), *The Household Book of Queen Isabella of England for the Fifth Regnal Year of Edward II, 8th July 1311 to 7th July 1312*, Edmonton, 1971.

Boccaccio, Giovanni, *Eclogues*, trans. Janet Levarie Smarr, New York, 1987.

Bokenham, Osbern, *Legendys of Hooly Wummen*, ed. Mary S. Serjeantson, EETS os 206, London, 1938.

Bornstein, Diane (ed.), *Distaves and Dames: Renaissance Treatises for and about Women*, New York, 1978.

Boyd, Beverley (ed.), *The Middle English Miracles of the Virgin*, San Marino, 1964.

Brandeis, Arthur (ed.), *Jacob's Well: An Englisht Treatise on the Cleansing of Man's Conscience*, EETS OS 115, London, 1900.

Brie, Friedrich W. D. (ed.), *The Brut, or The Chronicles of England*, EETS OS 131, 136, London, 1906–8.

Brook, G. L. (ed.), *The Harley Lyrics: The Middle English Lyrics of Ms. Harley 2253*, Manchester, 1968.

Brown, Rawdon (ed.), *Four Years at the Court of Henry VIII: Selection of Despatches Written by the Venetian Ambassador Sebastian Guistinian*, 2 vols, London, 1854.

Bruce, J. Douglas (ed.), *Le Morte Arthur: A Romance in Stanzas of Eight Lines*, EETS ES 88, London, 1903.

Byerly, Benjamin F., and Catherine Ridder Byerly (eds), *Records of the Wardrobe and Household, 1285–1286*, London, 1977.

Byerly, Benjamin F., and Catherine Ridder Byerly (eds), *Records of the Wardrobe and Household, 1286–1289*, London, 1986.

Byrne, Muriel St Clare (ed.), *The Lisle Letters*, 6 vols, Chicago, 1981.

Calendar of Patent Rolls, London, 1891–1986.

Carpenter, Christine (ed.), *Kingsford's Stonor Letters and Papers, 1290–1483*, Cambridge, 1996.

Carpenter, John, and Richard Whitington (eds), *Liber albus: The White Book of the City of London*, trans. Henry Thomas Riley, London, 1861.

Caxton, William (trans.), *The Book of the Knight of the Tower*, ed. M. Y. Offord, EETS SS 2, London, 1971.

Christine de Pisan, *The Book of the City of Ladies*, trans. Earl Jeffrey Richards, London, 1983.

Christine de Pisan, *A Medieval Woman's Mirror of Honour: The Treasury of the City of Ladies*, trans. Charity Cannon Willard, ed. Madeleine Pelner Cosman, New York, 1989.

Collier, J. Payne (ed.), 'St Margaret's, Southwark', *The British Magazine*, 32 (1847).

Collins, Arthur (ed.), *Letters and Memorials of State in the Reigns of Queen Mary, [etc.]*, London, 1746.

Crow, Martin M., and Clair C. Olson (eds), *Chaucer Life Records*, Oxford, 1966.

Dale, M. K. (trans.) and Vincent B. Redstone (ed.), with J. M. Ridgard, *The Household Book of Alice de Bryene of Acton Hall, Suffolk, September 1412 to September 1413*, Suffolk Institute for Archaeology and History, 2nd edn, Bungay, 1984.

Dan Michel, *Ayenbite of Inwyt*, ed. Richard Morris and Pamela Gradon, EETS OS 23, London, 1965.

Davis, Norman (ed.), *Non-Cycle Plays and Fragments*, EETS SS 1, London, 1970.

Davis, Norman (ed.), *The Paston Letters and Papers of the Fifteenth Century*, 2 vols, Oxford, 1971–6.

Dillon, Viscount, and W. H. St John Hope (eds), *The Pageant of the Birth, Life and Death of Richard Beauchamp, Earl of Warwick, K. G. 1389–1439*, London, 1914.

Drew, Charles (ed.), *Lambeth Churchwardens' Accounts 1504–1645 and Vestry Book 1610*, 4 vols, Surrey Record Society 18, Lambeth, 1941.

Ellis, Henry (ed.), *Original Letters, Illustrative of English History*, 11 vols, London, 1825.

Fisher, John, 'Mornynge remembraunce had at the moneth mynde of the noble Prynces Margarete Countesse of Rychmonde and Darbye', in John E. B. Mayor (ed.), *The English Works of John Fisher*, part 1, EETS ES 27, London, 1876.

Fitzherbert, John, *Booke of Husbandrie*, facsimile of the 1598 London edition, Amsterdam, 1979.

Foster, J. E. (ed.), *Churchwardens' Accounts of St Mary the Great Cambridge from 1504 to 1635*, Cambridge Antiquarian Society, ser. 8, 35, London, 1905.

Fowler, David C., Charles F. Briggs, and Paul G. Remley (eds), *The Governance of Kings and Princes: John Trevisa's Middle English Translation of the De regimine principum of Aegidius Romanus*, New York, 1997.

Francis, W. Nelson (ed.), *The Book of Vices and Virtues*, EETS OS 217, London, 1942.

French, Walter Hoyt, and Charles Brockway Hale (eds), *Middle English Metrical Romances*, 2 vols, New York, 1964.

Friedberg, E. (ed.), *Corpus iuris canonici*, 2 vols, Leipzig, 1879.

Froissart, Jean, *Chronicles of England, France and the Adjoining Countries*, trans. Thomas Johnes, 5 vols, n.p., 1803.

Furnivall, F. J. (ed.), *The Babees Book: Manners and Meals in Olden Time*, EETS OS 32 , London, 1868.

Furnivall, F. J. (ed.), *Robert of Brunne's 'Handlyng Synne'*, 2 vols, EETS OS 119 and 123, London, 1901–3.

Gairdner, James (ed.), *Letters and Papers, Foreign and Domestic, of the Reign of Henry VIII*, London, 1882.

Galbraith, V. H. (ed.), *The Anonimalle Chronicle 1333 to 1381*, Manchester, 1927.

Galen, *On the Usefulness of the Parts of the Body*, trans. Margaret Tallmadge May, 2 vols, Ithaca, NY, 1968.

Geoffrey de la Tour Landry, *The Book of the Knight of La Tour Landry*, ed. Thomas Wright, EETS OS 33, London, 1868. See also Caxton.

Geoffrey of Vinsauf, *The Poetria nova*, translated in Ernest Gallo, *The Poetria nova and Its Sources in Early Rhetorical Doctrine*, The Hague, 1971.

Girvan, R. (ed.), *Ratis Raving and Other Early Scots Poems on Morals*, Scottish Text Society, ser. 3, 2, Edinburgh, 1937.

Goldberg, P. J. P. (ed. and trans.), *Women in England, c. 1275–1525* Manchester, 1995.

Gordon, E. V. (ed.), *Pearl*, Oxford, 1953.

Gower, John, *Confessio amantis*, ed. Russell A. Peck, New York, 1968.

Green, Monica H. (ed. and trans.), *The* Trotula: *A Medieval Compendium of Women's Medicine*, Philadelphia, 2001.

Gross, Charles (ed.), *Select Cases from the Coroners' Rolls, A. D. 1265–1413*, Selden Society 9, London, 1896.

Hall, G. D. G. (ed. and trans.) with guide to further reading by M. T. Clanchy, *The Treatise on the Laws and Customs of the Realm of England Commonly Called Glanvill*, Oxford, 1993.

Hallaert, M. R. (ed.), *The 'Sekenesse of Wymmen'*, Scripta: Mediaeval and Renaissance Texts and Studies 8, Brussels, 1982.

Hanham, Alison (ed.), *The Cely Letters, 1472–1488*, EETS OS 273, London, 1975.

Harding, Alan (ed.), *The Roll of the Shropshire Eyre of 1256*, Selden Society 96 London, 1980.

Harris, Mary Dormer (ed.), *The Coventry Leet Book*, EETS OS 134, 135, 138, 146, London 1907–13.

Hector, L. C., and Barbara F. Harvey (eds), *The Westminster Chronicle 1381–1394*, Oxford, 1982.

Henryson, Robert, *Testament of Cresseid*, ed. Denton Fox, London, 1968.

Hentzner, Paul, *A Journey into England in the Year MDXCVIII*, ed. Horace Walpole, Aungervyle Society Reprints, ser. 1, Edinburgh, 1881.

Herrtage, Sidney J. H. (ed.), *The Early English Versions of the* Gesta romanorum, EETS ES 33, London, 1879.

Hobhouse, Edmund (ed.), *Churchwardens' Accounts of Croscombe, Pilton, Patton, Tintinhull, Morebath, and St Michael's Bath, Ranging from A.D. 1349 to 1560*, Somerset Record Society 4, London, 1890.

Holmstedt, Gustaf (ed.), *Speculum christiani: A Middle English Religious Treatise of the 14th Century*, EETS OS 182, London, 1933.

Howarth, Lisa (ed.), 'Þe knowyng of womans kynde in chyldyng', in 'The practice of midwifery in late medieval England', unpublished MA dissertation, University of York, 1995.

Hunnisett, R. F. (ed.), *Bedfordshire Coroners' Rolls*, Bedfordshire Historical Society 41, Streatley, 1961.

Hunnisett, R. F. (ed.), *Calendar of Nottingham Coroners' Inquests, 1485–1558*, Thoroton Society 25, Leeds, 1969.

Hyrd, Richard (trans.), *A Very Frutefull and Pleasant Boke called the Instruction of a Christen Woman*, London, 1529.

Ingram, R. W. (ed.), *Records of Early English Drama: Coventry*, Manchester, 1981.

Jacobus de Voragine, *Legenda aurea vulgo historia Lombardica*, ed. Thomas Graesse, Osnabrück, 1969.

Jacobus de Voragine, *The Golden Legend: Readings on the Saints*, trans. William Granger Ryan, 2 vols, Princeton, 1993.

Kellner, Leon (ed.), *Caxton's Blanchardyn and Eglantine, c. 1489*, EETS ES 58, London, 1890.

Kölbing, E. (ed.), *The Romance of Sir Beves of Hamtoun*, EETS ES 46, 48, 65, London, 1885–94.

Lawn, Brian (ed.), *The Prose Salernitan Questions*, Auctores Britannici Medii Aevi 5, London, 1979.

Leland, John, *Antiquarii de rebus Britannicus collectanea*, ed. Thomas Hearn, 6 vols, London, 1774.

Letts, Malcolm (ed. and trans.), *The Travels of Leo of Rozmital through Germany, Flanders, England, France, Spain, Portugal and Italy 1465–1467*, Hakluyt Society ser. 2, 108, Cambridge, 1957.

Lewis, J., *Life of John Fisher*, 2 vols, London, 1855.

Littlehales, Henry (ed.), *The Medieval Records of a London City Church (St Mary at Hill) A.D. 1420–1589*, EETS OS 125, 128, London, 1904–5.

Littlehales, Henry (ed.), *The Prymer, or Lay Folks' Prayer Book*, 2 vols, EETS OS 105 and 109, London, 1895–7.

Louis, Cameron (ed.), *The Commonplace Book of Robert Reynes of Acle: An Edition of Tanner MS 407*, New York, 1980.

Lowth, William, *The Christian Man's Closet*, London, 1581.

Lyndwood, William, *Provinciale (seu constitutiones Angliae)*, Oxford, 1679.

Maitland, F. W., *et al.* (eds), *Year Books of Edward II*, 27 vols, Selden Society 17–104, London, 1903–88.

Maitland, F. W., and William P. Baildon (eds), *The Court Baron*, Seldon Society 4, London, 1891.

Malory, Thomas, *Works*, ed. Eugène Vinaver and P. J. C. Field, 3 vols, Oxford, 1990.

Manzalaoui, M. A. (ed.), *Secretum secretorum: Nine English Versions*, EETS OS 276, London, 1977.

Martin, G. H. (ed. and trans.), *Knighton's Chronicle*, Oxford, 1995.

Maskell, William (ed.), *Monumenta ritualia ecclesiae Anglicanae*, 3 vols, London, 1846–7.

Masters, Betty R., and Elizabeth Ralph (eds), *The Church Book of St Ewen's, Bristol, 1454–1584*, Bristol and Gloucestershire Archaeological Society 6, Gloucester, 1967.

Matthew of Vendôme, *The Art of Versification*, trans. Aubrey E. Galyon, Ames, 1980.

McSheffrey, Shannon (ed. and trans.), *Love and Marriage in Late Medieval London*, Kalamazoo, 1995.

Meech, S. B., and H. E. Allen (eds), *The Book of Margery Kempe*, EETS OS 212 London, 1940.

Mellows, W. T. (ed.), *Peterborough Local Administration: Parochial Government before the Reformation: Churchwardens' Accounts 1467–1573, with Supplementary Documents 1107–1488*, Northamptonshire Record Society 9, Kettering, 1939.

Meredith, Peter (ed.), *The Mary Play from the N Town Manuscript*, London, 1987.

Millett, Bella, and Jocelyn Wogan-Browne (eds), *Medieval English Prose for Women: Selections from the Katherine Group and Ancrene Wisse*, Oxford, 1990.

Mustanoja, Tauno F. (ed.), *The Good Wife Taught Her Daughter, The Good Wyfe Wold a Pylgremage, The Thewis of Gud Women*, Helsinki, 1948.

Myers, A. R. (ed.), *The Household of Edward IV: The Black Book and the Ordinance of 1478*, Manchester, 1959.

Myers, A. R. (ed.), *English Historical Documents 1327–1485*, London, 1969.

Myers, A. R. (ed.), 'The captivity of a royal witch: the household accounts of Queen Joan of Navarre, 1419–21', in A. R. Myers, *Crown, Household and Parliament in the Fifteenth Century*, London, 1985.

Myers, A. R. (ed.), 'The household of Queen Elizabeth Woodville, 1466–7', in A. R. Myers, *Crown, Household and Parliament in the Fifteenth Century*, London, 1985.

Myers, A. R. (ed.), 'The household of Queen Margaret of Anjou, 1452–3', in A. R. Myers, *Crown, Household and Parliament in the Fifteenth Century*, London, 1985.

Myers, A. R. (ed.), 'The jewels of Queen Margaret of Anjou', in A. R. Myers, *Crown, Household and Parliament in the Fifteenth Century*, London, 1985.

Myrc, John, *Instructions for Parish Priests*, ed. Edward Peacock, EETS OS 31 London, 1868.

Neilson, N. (ed.), *Year Books of Edward IV. 10 Edward IV and 49 Henry VI, A.D. 1470*, Selden Society 47, London, 1930.

Nelson, Venetia (ed.), *A Myrour to Lewd Men and Women: A Prose Version of the Speculum vitae*, Heidelberg, 1981.

Nicolas, Nicholas Harris (ed.), *Privy Purse Expenses of Elizabeth of York: Wardrobe Accounts of Edward the Fourth*, London, 1830.

North, Thomas (ed.), *The Accounts of the Churchwardens of S. Martin's, Leicester. 1489–1844*, Leicester, 1884.

Paden, William D. (ed. and trans.), *The Medieval Pastourelle*, 2 vols, New York, 1987.

Parsons, John Carmi (ed.), 'Liber garderobe', in *The Court and Household of Eleanor of Castile in 1290*, Studies and Texts – Pontifical Institute of Mediaeval Studies 37, Toronto, 1977.

Percy, Thomas (ed.), *The Regulations and Establishment of the Household of Henry Algernon Percy at His Castles of Wreshill and Likinfield in Yorkshire* (a.k.a. *Northumberland Household Book*), London, 1827.

Perryman, Judith (ed.), *The King of Tars*, Heidelberg, 1980.

Power, Eileen (trans.), *The Goodman of Paris*, London, 1928.

Pronay, Nicholas, and John Cox (eds), *The Crowland Chronicle Continuations, 1459–1486*, London, 1986.

Pseudo-Albertus Magnus, *Women's Secrets: A Translation of Pseudo-Albertus Magnus'* De secretis mulierum, ed. and trans. Helen Rodnite Lemay, Albany, 1992.

Raine, J., *et al.* (eds), *Testamenta Eboracensia: A Selection of Wills from the Registry at York*, 6 vols, Surtees Society 4, 30, 45, 53, 79, 106, Durham, 1836–1902.

Rickert, Edith (ed.), *The Romance of Emaré*, EETS ES 99, London, 1908.

Riley, Henry Thomas (ed.), *Liber albus in munimenta Gildhallae Londoniensis*, Rolls Series 12, 3 vols, London, 1859–62.

Riley, Henry Thomas (ed.), *Memorials of London and London Life in the XIIIth, XIVth and XVth Centuries*, London, 1868.

Robbins, Rossell Hope (ed.), *Secular Lyrics of the XIVth and XVth Centuries*, Oxford, 1955.

Ross, Woodburn O. (ed.), *Middle English Sermons*, EETS OS 209, London, 1940.

Rowland, Beryl (ed.), *Medieval Woman's Guide to Health: The First English Gynecological Handbook*, London, 1981.

Rychner, Jean (ed.), *Les Lais de Marie de France*, Paris, 1966.

Sacrosancta concilia, 15 vols, Paris, 1671.

Salter, Thomas, *A Mirrhor Mete for All Mothers, Matrons, and Maidens, Intituled the Mirrhor of Modestie*, London, ?1579.

Sands, Donald (ed.), *Middle English Verse Romances*, Exeter, 1986.

Sayles, G. O. (ed.), *Select Cases in the Court of King's Bench*, 6 vols, Selden Society 55, 57, 58, 74, 76, 82, London, 1936–65.

Sellers, Maud (ed.), *York Memorandum Book*, 2 vols, Surtees Society 120 and 125, Durham, 1912–15.

Seymour, M. C., *et al.* (eds), *On the Properties of Things: John Trevisa's Translation of Bartholomaeus Anglicus* De proprietatibus rerum. *A Critical Text*, 2 vols, Oxford, 1975.

Sharpe, Reginald R. (ed.), *Calendar of Letter Books of the City of London*, 11 vols, London, 1899–1912.

Sharpe, Reginald R. (ed.), *Calendar of Coroners' Rolls of the City of London, A.D. 1300–1378*, London, 1913.

Shickle, C. W. (ed.), *Ancient Deeds Belonging to the Corporation of Bath XIII–XVI Centuries*, Bath Records Society Publications, Bath, 1921.

Simmons, T. F. (ed.), *The Lay Folks' Mass Book*, EETS OS 71, London, 1879.

Simmons, T. F. and H. E. Nolloth (eds), *The Lay Folks' Catechism*, EETS OS 118, London, 1901.

Sneyd, C. A. (ed.), *A Relation, or Rather a True Account, of the Island of England c. 1500*, Camden Society OS 37, London, 1847.

Society of Antiquaries of London (ed.), *A Collection of Ordinances and Regulations for the Government of the Royal Household*, London, 1790.

Stapleton, Thomas (ed.), *The Plumpton Correspondence*, Camden Society OS 4, London, 1839.

The Statutes of the Realm, 12 vols, London, repr. 1963.

Stenton, Doris Mary (ed.), *Rolls of the Justices in Eyre Being the Rolls of Pleas and Assizes for Lincolnshire, 1218–19*, Selden Society 53, London, 1934.

Stone, E. D. (ed.), *Norwich Consistory Court Depositions, 1499–1512 and 1518–30*, Norfolk Record Society 10, Norwich, 1938.

Strachey, John, and Edward Upham (eds), *Rotuli parliamentorum*, 7 vols, London, 1832.

Swayne, Henry James Fowle (ed.), *Churchwardens' Accounts of S. Edmund and S. Thomas, Sarum, 1443–1702, with Other Documents*, Wiltshire Record Society 1, Salisbury, 1896.

Thomas, A. H. (ed.), *Calendar of Early Mayor's Court Rolls, Preserved among the Archives of the Corporation of the City of London at the Guildhall, A.D. 1298–1307*, Cambridge, 1924.

Thomas, A. H. and Philip E. Jones (eds), *Plea and Memoranda Rolls of the City of London, 1323–1482*, 6 vols, Cambridge, 1926–61.

Tolhurst, J. B. L. (ed.), *The Ordinale and Customary of the Benedictine Nuns of Barking Abbey*, Henry Bradshaw Society 65 and 66, London, 1927–8.

Tout, T. F. (ed.), 'The household ordinance of Westminster, 13th November 1279', in T. F. Tout, *Chapters in the Administrative History of Mediaeval England*, 6 vols Manchester, 1920–33, vol. 2.

Tout, T. F. (ed.), 'The household ordinances of Edward II', in Hilda Johnstone (ed.), *The Place of the Reign of Edward II in English History*, rev. edn, Manchester, 1936.

Turner, T. H. (ed.), *Manners and Household Expenses of England in the Thirteenth and Fifteenth Centuries*, Roxburgh Club, London, 1841.

Vergil, Polydore, *Three Books of Polydore Vergil's English History, Comprising the Reigns of Henry VI, Edward IV, and Richard III*, ed. Henry Ellis, Camden Society OS 29, London, 1844.

Vincent of Beauvais, *De eruditione filiorum nobilium*, ed. Arpad Steiner, Cambridge, MA, 1938.

Vives, Juan Luis, *De institutione foeminae Christianae*, Bruges, 1524.

Walsingham, Thomas, *Historia Angliae*, ed. H. T. Riley, 2 vols, London, 1863–4.

Walter de Bibbesworth, *Le Tretiz*, ed. William Rothwell, Anglo-Norman Text Society, Plain Texts series 6, London, 1990.

Ward, Jennifer C. (ed. and trans.), *Women of the English Nobility and Gentry, 1066–1500*, Manchester, 1995.

Watson, Foster (ed.), *Vives and the Renascence Education of Women*, London, 1912.

Weber, Henry W. (ed.), *Metrical Romances of the Thirteenth, Fourteenth and Fifteenth Centuries*, 3 vols, Edinburgh, 1810.

Welch, Charles (ed.), *The Churchwardens' Accounts of the Parish of Allhallows, London Wall, in the City of London. 33 Henry VI to 27 Henry VIII (A.D. 1455–A.D. 1536)*, London, 1912.

Wenzel, Siegfried (ed. and trans.), *Fasciculus morum: A Fourteenth-Century Preacher's Handbook*, University Park, 1989.

Wheatley, Henry B. (ed.), *Merlin, or The Early History of King Arthur*, EETS os 10, 21, 36, 112, London, 1865–99.

Whittaker, W. J. (ed.), *The Mirror of Justices*, Selden Society 7, London, 1893.

Wilkinson, John James (ed.), *Receipts and Expenses in the Building of Bodmin Church A.D. 1469 to 1472*, Camden Miscellany 7, Camden Society new series 14, London, 1875.

Williams, Benjamin (ed.), *Chronique de la traïson et mort de Richart Deux Roy Dengleterre*, London, 1846.

Williams, C. H. (ed.), *Year Books of Henry VI. 1 Henry VI, A.D. 1422*, Selden Society 50, London, 1933.

Woodbine, G. E. (ed.), and Samuel E. Thorne (trans.), *Bracton on the Laws and Customs of England*, 4 vols, Cambridge, MA, 1968.

Woolgar, C. M. (ed.), *Household Accounts from Medieval England*, The British Academy Records of Social and Economic History, new series 17 and 18, London, 1992.

Wright, W. A. (ed.), *Femina*, Roxburgh Club, Cambridge, 1909.

Wright, W. Aldis (ed.), *Generydes: A Romance in Seven-Line Stanzas*, EETS os 55 and 70, London, 1873–78.

Zupitza, Julius (ed.), *The Romance of Guy of Warwick*, EETS es 42, 49 and 59, London, 1883–91.

Secondary sources

Alexandre-Bidon, Danièle, and Didier Lett, *Children in the Middle Ages: Fifth–Fifteenth Centuries*, trans. Jody Gladding, Notre Dame, 1999.

Amos, Mark Addison, "'For manners make man": Bourdieu, de Certeau, and the common appropriation of noble manners in the *Book of Courtesy*, in Kathleen Ashley and Robert L. A. Clark (eds), *Medieval Conduct*, Minneapolis, 2001.

Amundsen, Darrel W., and Carol Jean Diers, 'The age of menarche in medieval Europe', *Human Biology*, 45 (1973), 363–9.

Archibald, Elizabeth, 'Gold in the dungheap: incest stories and family values in the Middle Ages', *Journal of Family History*, 22 (1997), 133–49.

Arditi, Jorge, *A Genealogy of Manners: Transformations of Social Relations in France and England from the Fourteenth to the Eighteenth Century*, Chicago, 1998.

Ariès, Philippe, *Centuries of Childhood*, trans. Robert Baldick, New York, [1960] 1962.

Ashley, Kathleen M., 'Medieval courtesy literature and dramatic mirrors of female conduct', in Nancy Armstrong and Leonard Tennenhouse (eds), *The Ideology of Conduct: Essays on Literature and the History of Sexuality*, New York, 1987.

Aston, Margaret, 'Segregation in church', in W. J. Sheils and Diana Wood (eds), *Women in the Church*, Studies in Church History 27, Oxford, 1990.

Attreed, Lorraine C., 'From Pearl maiden to tower princes: towards a new history of medieval childhood', *Journal of Medieval History*, 8 (1983), 131–43.

Auerbach, Eric, *Mimesis: The Representation of Reality in Western Literature*, trans. Willard R. Trask, Princeton, 1953.

Bailey, Mark, 'Demographic decline in late medieval England: some thoughts on recent research', *Economic History Review*, 49 (1996), 1–19.

Bailey, Peter, 'Parasexuality and glamour: the Victorian barmaid as cultural prototype', *Gender and History*, 2 (1990), 148–72.

Baker, J. H., *Introduction to English Legal History*, 3rd edn, London, 1990.

Bardsley, Sandy, 'Women's work reconsidered: gender and wage differentiation in late medieval England', *Past and Present*, 165 (1999), 3–29.

Barker, Juliet R. V., *The Tournament in England, 1100–1400*, Woodbridge, 1986.

Barratt, Alexandra, 'Dame Eleanor Hull: a fifteenth-century translator', in Roger Ellis *et al.* (eds), *The Medieval Translator: The Theory and Practice of Translation in the Middle Ages*, Cambridge, 1989.

Barron, Caroline M., 'The "Golden Age" of women in medieval London', *Reading Medieval Studies*, 15 (1989), 35–58.

Barron, Caroline M., 'The education and training of girls in fifteenth-century

London', in D. E. S. Dunn (ed.), *Courts, Counties and the Capital in the Later Middle Ages*, Stroud, 1996.

Barron, Caroline M., and Anne F. Sutton (eds), *Medieval London Widows, 1300–1500*, London, 1994.

Beattie, Cordelia, 'Meanings of singleness: the single woman in late medieval England', D.Phil. thesis, University of York, 2001.

Ben-Amos, Ilana Krausman, *Adolescence and Youth in Early Modern England*, New Haven, 1994.

Bennett, H. S., *The Pastons and Their England: Studies in an Age of Transition*, Cambridge, 1922.

Bennett, H. S., *English Books and Readers, 1475–1557*, Cambridge, 1957.

Bennett, Judith M., 'Medieval peasant marriage: an examination of marriage license fines in *Liber gersumarum*', in J. A. Raftis (ed.), *Pathways to Medieval Peasants*, Toronto, 1981.

Bennett, Judith M., *Women in the Medieval English Countryside: Gender and Household in Brigstock Before the Plague*, Oxford, 1987.

Bennett, Judith M., 'Medieval women, modern women: across the great divide', in David Aers (ed.), *Culture and History 1350–1600: Essays on English Communities, Identities and Writing*, London, 1992.

Bennett, Judith M., *Ale, Beer, and Brewsters in England: Women's Work in a Changing World, 1300–1600*, New York, 1996.

Bennett, Judith M., *A Medieval Life: Cecilia Penifader of Brigstock, c. 1295–1344*, Boston, 1999.

Bennett, Judith M., '"Lesbian-like" and the social history of lesbianisms', *Journal of the History of Sexuality*, 9 (2000), 1–24.

Bennett, Judith M., 'Ventriloquisms: when maidens speak in English songs, c. 1300–1550', in Ann Marie Rasmussen and Ann Klinck (eds), *Medieval Women's Song: Cross-Cultural Approaches*, Philadelphia, 2002.

Bennett, Judith M., and Amy M. Froide, 'A singular past', in Judith M. Bennett and Amy M. Froide (eds), *Singlewomen in the European Past, 1250–1800*, Philadelphia, 1999.

Biller, Peter, '"Demographic thought" around 1300 and Dante's Florence', in John C. Barnes and Cormac Ó Cuilleanáin (eds), *Dante and the Middle Ages: Literary and Historical Essays*, Dublin, 1995.

Biller, Peter, 'Marriage patterns and women's lives: a sketch of pastoral geography', in P. J. P. Goldberg (ed.), *Women in Medieval English Society*, Stroud, 1997.

Bishop, Ian, *'Pearl' in Its Setting*, Oxford, 1968.

Boffey, Julia, *Manuscripts of English Courtly Love Lyrics in the Later Middle Ages*, Woodbridge, 1985.

Bonfield, Lloyd, and L. R. Poos, 'The development of deathbed transfers in medieval English manor courts', in Zvi Razi and Richard M. Smith (eds), *Medieval Society and the Manor Court*, Oxford, 1996.

Bornstein, Diane, *The Lady in the Tower: Medieval Courtesy Literature for Women*, Hamden, 1983.

Brand, Paul, 'Family and inheritance, women and children', in Chris Given-Wilson (ed.), *An Illustrated History of Medieval England*, Manchester, 1996.

Brand, Paul A., and Paul R. Hyams, 'Debate: seigneurial control of women's marriage', *Past and Present*, 99 (1983), 123–60.

Brewer, D. S., 'The ideal of feminine beauty in medieval literature, especially "Harley Lyrics", Chaucer, and some Elizabethans', *Modern Language Review*, 50 (1955), 257–69.

Briggs, C. F., 'Manuscripts of Giles of Rome's *De regimine principum* in England, 1300–1500: a handlist', *Scriptorium*, 47 (1993), 60–73.

Brownrigg, Linda, 'The Taymouth Hours and the Romance of *Beves of Hampton*', in Peter Beal and Jeremy Griffiths (ed.), *English Manuscript Studies 1100–1700*, vol. 1, Oxford, 1989.

Brundage, James A., *Law, Sex, and Christian Society in Medieval Europe*, Chicago, 1987.

Brundage, James A., *Medieval Canon Law*, London, 1995.

Brundage, James A., 'Sex and canon law', in Vern L. Bullough and James A. Brundage (eds), *Handbook of Medieval Sexuality*, New York, 1996.

Bullough, Vern L., and James A. Brundage (eds), *Handbook of Medieval Sexuality*, New York, 1996.

Burrow, J. A., *Medieval Writers and Their Work: Middle English Literature and Its Background 1100–1500*, Oxford, 1982.

Burrow, J. A., 'Chaucer's *Knight's Tale* and the three ages of man', in *Essays in Medieval Literature*, Oxford, 1984.

Burrow, J. A., *The Ages of Man: A Study in Medieval Writing and Thought*, Oxford, 1986.

Butler, Judith, *Gender Trouble: Feminism and the Subversion of Identity*, New York, 1990.

Bynum, Caroline Walker, *Holy Feast and Holy Fast: The Religious Significance of Food to Medieval Women*, Berkeley, 1987.

Bynum, Caroline Walker, *The Resurrection of the Body in Western Christianity, 200–1336*, New York, 1995.

Cadden, Joan, *Meanings of Sex Difference in the Middle Ages: Medicine, Science and Culture*, Cambridge, 1993.

Cameron, Deborah, 'Introduction: why language is a feminist issue', in Deborah Cameron (ed.), *The Feminist Critique of Language: A Reader*, London, 1990.

Camille, Michael, *The Gothic Idol: Ideology and Image-Making in Medieval Art*, Cambridge, 1989.

Carter, Angela, 'I could have fancied her', *London Review of Books*, 16 (February, 1989).

Chamberlayne, Joanna L., 'Crowns and virgins: queenmaking during the Wars of the Roses', in Katherine J. Lewis, Noël James Menuge and Kim M. Phillips (eds), *Young Medieval Women*, Stroud, 1999.

Chamberlayne, Joanna L., 'English queenship, 1445–1503', D.Phil. thesis, University of York, 1999.

Chambers, E. K., *The Elizabethan Stage*, 4 vols, Oxford, 1923.

Chojnacki, Stanley, 'Measuring adulthood: adolescence and gender in Renaissance Venice', *Journal of Family History*, 17 (1992), 371–95.

Clanchy, M. T., *From Memory to Written Record: England 1066–1307*, 2nd edn, Oxford, 1993.

Clark, Elaine, 'City orphans and custody laws in medieval England', *American Journal of Legal History*, 34 (1990), 168–87.

Clark, Kenneth, *The Nude: A Study of Ideal Art*, London, 1956.

Clark, Kenneth, *Feminine Beauty*, London, 1980.

Cox, J. Charles, *Churchwardens' Accounts from the Fourteenth Century to the Close of the Seventeenth Century*, London, 1913.

Crane, Susan, *Gender and Romance in Chaucer's* Canterbury Tales, Princeton, 1994.

Crawford, Sally, *Childhood in Anglo-Saxon England*, Stroud, 1999.

Crossley-Holland, Nicole, *Living and Dining in Medieval Paris: The Household of a Fourteenth-Century Knight*, Cardiff, 1996.

Cullum, P. H., 'Clergy, masculinity and transgression in late medieval England', in D. M. Hadley (ed.), *Masculinity in Medieval Europe*, London, 1999.

Cunningham, Hugh, *Children and Childhood in Western Society Since 1500*, London, 1995.

Cunnington, Phillis, and Catherine Lucas, *Costumes for Births, Marriages and Deaths* London, 1972.

Curry, Walter Clyde, *The Middle English Ideal of Personal Beauty; As Found in the Metrical Romances, Chronicles, and Legends of the XIII, XIV, and XV Centuries*, Baltimore, 1916.

Curteis, Alice, and Chris Given-Wilson, *The Royal Bastards of Medieval England* London, 1984.

Dale, M. K., 'The London silkwomen of the fifteenth century', *Economic History Review*, 4 (1933), 324–35.

Danbury, Elizabeth, 'Images of English queens in the later Middle Ages', *The Historian*, 46 (1995), 3–9.

de Beauvoir, Simone, *The Second Sex*, ed. and trans. H. M. Parshley, London, [1949] 1953.

de Beauvoir, Simone, *Memoirs of a Dutiful Daughter*, trans. James Kirkup, Harmondsworth, [1958] 1963.

de Hamel, Christopher *A History of Illuminated Manuscripts*, Oxford, 1986.

d'Emilio, John, and Estelle B. Freedman, *Intimate Matters: A History of Sexuality in America*, 2nd edn, Chicago, 1997.

Diamond, Arlyn, 'Unhappy endings: failed love / failed faith in late romances', in Carol M. Meale (ed.), *Readings in Medieval English Romance*, Cambridge, 1991.

Dinshaw, Carolyn, *Getting Medieval: Sexualities and Communities, Pre- and Postmodern*, Durham, NC, 1999.

Dockray, Keith, 'Why did fifteenth-century English gentry marry?: The Pastons, Plumptons and Stonors reconsidered', in Michael Jones (ed.), *Gentry and Lesser Nobility in Late Medieval Europe*, Gloucester, 1986.

Donahue, Charles, Jr, 'What causes fundamental legal ideas? Marital property in England and France in the thirteenth century', *Michigan Law Review*, 78 (1979), 59–88.

Donahue, Charles, Jr, 'Female plaintiffs in marriage cases in the court of York in the later Middle Ages: what can we learn from the numbers?', in Sue Sheridan Walker (ed.), *Wife and Widow in Medieval England*, Ann Arbor, 1993.

Donovan, Claire, *The de Brailes Hours: Shaping the Book of Hours in Thirteenth-Century Oxford*, Toronto, 1991.

Dove, Mary, *The Perfect Age of Man's Life*, Cambridge, 1986.

Driver, Martha W., 'Pictures in print: late fifteenth- and early sixteenth-century English religious books for lay readers', in Michael G. Sargeant (ed.), *De cella in seculum: Religious and Secular Life and Devotion in Late Medieval England*, Cambridge, 1989.

duBois, Page, 'The subject in antiquity after Foucault', in David H. Larmour, Paul Allen Miller and Charles Platter (eds), *Rethinking Sexuality: Foucault and Classical Antiquity*, Princeton, 1998.

Duffy, Eamon, 'Holy maydens, holy wyfes: the cult of women saints in fifteenth- and sixteenth-century England', in W. J. Sheils and Diana Wood (eds), *Women in the Church*, Studies in Church History 27, Oxford, 1990.

Duffy, Eamon, *The Stripping of the Altars: Traditional Religion in England, c. 1400–c. 1580*, New Haven, 1992.

Duffy, Eamon, *The Voices of Morebath: Reformation and Rebellion in an English Village*, New Haven, 2001.

Dutton, Anne M., 'Passing the book: testamentary transmission of religious literature to and by women in England 1350–1500', in Lesley Smith and

Jane H. M. Taylor (eds), *Women, the Book and the Godly*, Cambridge, 1995.

Dutton, Anne M., 'Women's use of religious literature in late medieval England', University of York, D.Phil. thesis, 1995.

Dyer, Christopher, 'Changes in the size of peasant holdings in some West Midland villages 1400–1540', in Richard M. Smith (ed.), *Land, Kinship and Life-Cycle*, Cambridge, 1984.

Dyer, Christopher, *Standards of Living in the Later Middle Ages*, Cambridge, 1989.

Earl, James W., 'Saint Margaret and the Pearl Maiden', *Modern Philology*, 70 (1972), 1–8.

Edwards, A. S. G., 'The transmission and audience of Osbern Bokenham's *Legendys of Hooly Wummen*', in A. J. Minnis (ed.), *Late Religious Texts and their Transmission: Essays in Honour of A. I. Doyle*, Cambridge, 1994.

Elias, Nobert, *The Civilizing Process: Sociogenetic and Psychogenetic Investigations*, trans. Edmund Jephcott, rev. edn, Oxford, [1939] 2000.

Elliott, Dyan, 'Dress as mediator between inner and outer self: the pious matron of the high and later Middle Ages', *Mediaeval Studies*, 53 (1991), 279–308.

Engels, Frederick, *The Origin of the Family, Private Property and the State*, London, [1884] 1972.

Erler, Mary C., 'Margery Kempe's white clothes', *Medium Ævum*, 62 (1993), 78–83.

Esmein, A., *Le Mariage en droit canonique*, 2 vols, New York, [1891] 1968.

Faith, Rosamund, 'Berkshire: fourteenth and fifteenth centuries', in P. D. A. Harvey (ed.), *The Peasant Land Market in Medieval England*, Oxford, 1984.

Farmer, David Hugh (ed.), *The Oxford Dictionary of Saints*, Oxford, 1992.

Fisher, J. D. C., *Christian Initiation: Baptism in the Medieval West*, Alcuin Club Collections 47, London, 1965.

Fleming, Peter, *Family and Household in Medieval England*, Houndmills, 2001.

Ford, Judy Ann, 'Marginality and the assimilation of foreigners in the lay parish community: the case of Sandwich', in Katherine L. French, Gary G. Gibbs and Beat A. Kümin (eds), *The Parish in English Life 1400–1600*, Manchester, 1997.

Ford, Wyn, 'The problem of literacy in early modern England', *History*, 78 (1993), 22–37.

Forster, Margaret, *Hidden Lives: A Family Memoir*, London, 1995.

Frame, Janet, *An Angel at My Table: Autobiography 2*, London, 1984.

Franklin, Peter, 'Politics in manorial court rolls: the tactics, social composition, and aims of a pre-1381 peasant movement', in Zvi Razi and Richard M. Smith (eds), *Medieval Society and the Manor Court*, Oxford, 1996.

French, Katherine L., 'The legend of Lady Godiva and the image of the female body', *Journal of Medieval History*, 18 (1992), 3–19.

French, Katherine L., 'Parochial fund-raising in late medieval Somerset', in Katherine L. French, Gary G. Gibbs and Beat A. Kümin (eds), *The Parish in English Life 1400–1600*, Manchester, 1997.

French, Katherine L., '"To free them from binding": women in the late medieval English parish', *Journal of Interdisciplinary History*, 27 (1997), 387–412.

French, Katherine L., 'Maidens' lights and wives' stores: women's parish guilds in late medieval England', *Sixteenth Century Journal*, 29 (1998), 399–425.

French, Katherine L., *The People of the Parish: Community Life in a Late Medieval English Diocese*, Philadelphia, 2001.

Gardiner, Dorothy, *English Girlhood at School: A Study of Women's Education Through Twelve Centuries*, London, 1929.

Giddens, Anthony, *The Constitution of Society: Outline of the Theory of Structuration*, Cambridge, 1984.

Gilchrist, Roberta, 'Medieval bodies in the material world: gender, stigma and the body', in Sarah Kay and Miri Rubin (eds), *Framing Medieval Bodies*, Manchester, 1993.

Gilchrist, Roberta, *Gender and Material Culture: The Archaeology of Religious Women*, London, 1994.

Given-Wilson, Chris, *The Royal Household and the King's Affinity: Service, Politics and Finance in England, 1360–1413*, New Haven, 1986.

Given-Wilson, Chris, *The English Nobility in the Late Middle Ages*, London, 1987.

Goldberg, P. J. P., 'Female labour, service and marriage in the late medieval urban north', *Northern History*, 22 (1986), 18–38.

Goldberg, P. J. P., 'Women in fifteenth-century town life', in John A. F. Thompson (ed.), *Towns and Townspeople in the Fifteenth Century*, Gloucester, 1988.

Goldberg, P. J. P., 'The public and the private: women in the pre-Plague economy', in Peter R. Coss and S. D. Lloyd (eds), *Thirteenth Century England III*, Woodbridge, 1991.

Goldberg, P. J. P., *Women, Work, and Life Cycle in a Medieval Economy: Women in York and Yorkshire, c. 1300–1520*, Oxford, 1992.

Goldberg, P. J. P., 'Girls growing up in later medieval England', *History Today* (June, 1995), 25–32.

Goldberg, P. J. P., 'Craft guilds, the Corpus Christi Play and civic government', in Sarah Rees Jones (ed.), *The Government of Medieval York: Essays in Commemoration of the 1396 Royal Charter*, York, 1997.

Goldberg, P. J. P., 'Debate: fiction in the archives: the York cause papers as a source for later medieval social history', *Continuity and Change*, 12 (1997), 425-45.

Goldberg, P. J. P., 'Marriage, migration and servanthood: the York cause paper evidence', and 'For better, for worse: marriage and economic opportunity for women in town and country', in P. J. P. Goldberg (ed.), *Women in Medieval English Society*, Stroud, 1997.

Goldberg, P. J. P., 'Pigs and prostitutes: streetwalking in comparative perspective', in Katherine J. Lewis, Noël James Menuge and Kim M. Phillips (eds), *Young Medieval Women*, Stroud, 1999.

Goldberg, P. J. P., 'Masters and men in later medieval England', in D. M. Hadley (ed.), *Masculinity in Medieval Europe*, London, 1999.

Goldberg, P. J. P., 'Delvers and spinsters: gender and work in late medieval English towns', unpublished paper, Leeds International Medieval Congress, 11 July 2000.

Goodich, Michael E., '*Ancilla Dei*: the servant as saint in the late Middle Ages', in Julius Kirshner and Suzanne F. Wemple (eds), *Women of the Medieval World*, Oxford, 1985.

Goodich, Michael E., *From Birth to Old Age: The Human Life Cycle in Medieval Thought 1250-1350*, Lanham, MD, 1989.

Goodman, Anthony, *John of Gaunt: The Exercise of Princely Power in Fourteenth Century Europe*, Harlow, 1992.

Goodman, Jennifer R., '"That women holde in ful greet reverence": mothers and daughters reading chivalric romances', in Lesley Smith and Jane H. M. Taylor (eds), *Women, the Book and the Worldly*, Cambridge, 1995.

Goody, Jack, 'Strategies of heirship', *Comparative Studies in Society and History*, 15 (1973), 3-20.

Goody, Jack, *The Development of the Family and Marriage in Europe*, Cambridge, 1983.

Grabar, André, *Christian Iconography: A Study in its Origins*, London, 1969.

Graham, Helena, '"A woman's work ...": labour and gender in the late medieval countryside', in P. J. P. Goldberg (ed.), *Women in Medieval English Society*, Stroud, 1997.

Gransden, Antonia, 'Childhood and youth in mediaeval England', *Nottingham Medieval Studies*, 16 (1972), 3-19.

Gravdal, Kathryn, *Ravishing Maidens: Writing Rape in Medieval French Literature and Law*, Philadelphia, 1991.

Green, Mary Ann Everett, *Lives of the Princesses of England from the Norman Conquest*, 6 vols, London, 1849-55.

Green, Monica H., 'Women's medical practice and health care in medieval Europe', *Signs*, 14 (1989), 434–74.

Green, Monica H., 'Obstetrical and gynecological texts in Middle English', in *Women's Healthcare in the Medieval West: Texts and Contexts*, Aldershot, 2000.

Griffiths, Morwenna, *Feminisms and the Self: The Web of Identity*, London, 1995.

Griffiths, Paul, *Youth and Authority: Formative Experiences in England 1560–1640*, Oxford, 1996.

Grigsby, J. L., '*Le Miroir des bonnes femmes*', *Romania*, 82 (1961), 458–81, and 83 (1962), 30–51.

Grigsby, J. L., 'A new source of the *Livre de la Chevalier de la Tour Landry*', *Romania*, 84 (1963), 171–208.

Groot, Roger D., 'The crime of rape *temp*. Richard I and John', *Journal of Legal History*, 9 (1988), 324–34.

Guddat-Figge, Gisela, *Catalogue of Manuscripts Containing Middle English Romances*, Munich, 1976.

Hadley, D. M. (ed.), *Masculinity in Medieval Europe*, London, 1999.

Hajnal, John, 'European marriage patterns in perspective', in D. V. Glass and D. E. C. Eversley (eds), *Population in History: Essays in Historical Demography*, London, 1965.

Halperin, David M., *One Hundred Years of Homosexuality and Other Essays on Greek Love*, New York, 1990.

Hanawalt, Barbara A., 'Peasant women's contribution to the home economy in late medieval England', in Barbara A. Hanawalt (ed.), *Women and Work in Preindustrial Europe*, Bloomington, 1986.

Hanawalt, Barbara A., *The Ties that Bound: Peasant Families in Medieval England*, Oxford, 1986.

Hanawalt, Barbara A., 'Historical descriptions and prescriptions for adolescence', *Journal of Family History*, 17 (1992), 341–51.

Hanawalt, Barbara A., *Growing Up in Medieval London: The Experience of Childhood in History*, Oxford, 1993.

Hanawalt, Barbara A., 'Whose story was this? Rape narratives in medieval English courts', in '*Of Good and Ill Repute*': *Gender and Social Control in Medieval England*, New York, 1998.

Hanham, Alison, *The Celys and their World: An English Merchant Family of the Fifteenth Century*, Cambridge, 1985.

Harris, Kate, 'The origins and makeup of Cambridge University Library MS Ff.1.6', *Transactions of the Cambridge Bibliographical Society*, 8 (1983), 299–333.

Hartung, Alfred E. and Jonathan Burke Severs (eds), *Manual of the Writings in Middle English*, 9 vols, New Haven, 1967–.

Harvey, P. D. A., *A Medieval Oxfordshire Village: Cuxham 1240 to 1400*, Oxford, 1965.

Harwick, C., *et al.*, *A Catalogue of the Manuscripts Preserved in the Library of the University of Cambridge*, 5 vols, Cambridge, 1857.

Haskell, Ann S., 'The Paston women on marriage in fifteenth-century England', *Viator*, 4 (1973), 459–71.

Hellinger, Lotte, *Caxton in Focus: The Beginning of Printing in England*, London, 1982.

Helmholz, R. H., *Marriage Litigation in Medieval England*, Cambridge, 1974.

Hentsch, Alice A., *De la littérature didactique du Moyen Age, s'adressant spécialement aux femmes*, Cahors, 1903.

Herlihy, David, *Medieval Households*, Cambridge, MA, 1985.

Herlihy, David, 'Making sense of incest: women and the marriage rules of the early Middle Ages', in *Women, Family and Society in Medieval Europe: Historical Essays, 1978–1991*, Providence, 1995.

Herlihy, David, and Christiane Klapisch-Zuber, *Tuscans and Their Families: A Study of the Florentine Catasto of 1427*, New Haven, 1985.

Hines, John, *The Fabliau in English*, London, 1993.

Holdsworth, William, *A History of English Law*, 16 vols, London, 1942.

Hollander, Anne, *Seeing through Clothes*, New York, 1975.

Hollingsworth, T. H., 'A demographic study of the British ducal families', in D. V. Glass and D. E. C. Eversley (eds), *Population in History: Essays in Historical Demography*, London, 1965.

Horrox, Rosemary, 'Service', in Rosemary Horrox (ed.), *Fifteenth Century Attitudes: Perceptions of Society in Late Medieval England*, Cambridge, 1994.

Howell, Cicely, 'Peasant inheritance customs in the midlands, 1280–1700', in Jack Goody, Joan Thirsk and E. P. Thompson (eds), *Family and Inheritance: Rural Society in Western Europe, 1200–1800*, Cambridge, 1976.

Howell, Cicely, *Land, Family and Inheritance in Transition: Kibworth Harcourt 1280–1700*, Cambridge, 1983.

Hudson, Barbara, 'Femininity and adolescence', in Angela McRobbie and Mica Nava (eds), *Gender and Generation*, Houndmills, 1984.

Hufton, Olwen, *The Prospect before Her: A History of Women in Western Europe, Volume One, 1500–1800*, London, 1997.

Humphrey, Christopher 'The dynamics of urban festal culture in late medieval England', D.Phil. thesis, University of York, 1997.

Husband, Timothy, with Gloria Gilmore, *The Wild Man: Medieval Myth and Symbolism*, New York, 1988.

Hutchinson, Ann M., 'Devotional reading in the monastery and in the late medieval household', in Michael G. Sargeant (ed.), *De cella in seculum: Religious and Secular Life and Devotion in Late Medieval England*, Cambridge, 1989.

Hutton, Ronald, *The Rise and Fall of Merry England: The Ritual Year 1400–1700*, Oxford, 1994.

Ingram, Martin, *Church Courts, Sex and Marriage in England, 1570–1640*, Cambridge, 1987.

Ives, E. W., '"Agaynst taking awaye of Women": the inception and operation of the Abduction Act of 1487', in E. W. Ives, R. J. Knecht and J. J. Scarisbrick (eds), *Wealth and Power in Tudor England*, London, 1978.

Jacquart, Danielle, and Claude Thomasset, *Sexuality and Medicine in the Middle Ages*, trans. Matthew Adamson, Princeton, 1988.

Jambek, Karen K., 'Patterns of women's literary patronage: England, 1200–ca.1475', in June Hall McCash (ed.), *The Cultural Patronage of Late Medieval Women*, Athens, GA, 1996.

James, M. R., *A Descriptive Catalogue of the Manuscripts in the Library of Gonville and Caius College*, 3 vols, Cambridge, 1908.

James, M. R., *A Descriptive Catalogue of the Manuscripts in the Library of St John's College Cambridge*, Cambridge, 1913.

Jewell, Helen M., 'Women at the courts of the manor of Wakefield, 1348–1350', *Northern History*, 26 (1990), 59–81.

Johnson, Elizabeth A., 'Marian devotion in the Western Church', in Jill Raitt (ed.), *Christian Spirituality: High Middle Ages and Reformation*, New York, 1987.

Jones, Michael K., and Malcolm G. Underwood, *The King's Mother: Lady Margaret Beaufort, Countess of Richmond and Derby*, Cambridge, 1992.

Justice, Steven, *Writing and Rebellion: England in 1381*, Berkeley, 1994.

Kaplan, Cora, 'Language and gender', repr. in Deborah Cameron (ed.), *The Feminist Critique of Language: A Reader*, London, 1990.

Karras, Ruth Mazo, *Common Women: Prostitution and Sexuality in Medieval England*, New York, 1996.

Katz, Jonathan Ned, *The Invention of Heterosexuality*, New York, 1995.

Kay, F. George, *Lady of the Sun: The Life and Times of Alice Perrers*, London, 1966.

Kelso, Ruth, *Doctrine for the Lady of the Renaissance*, Urbana, 1956.

Kermode, Jenny, *Medieval Merchants: York, Beverley and Hull in the Later Middle Ages*, Cambridge, 1998.

Kirby, Joan W., 'Women in the Plumpton correspondence: fiction and reality', in Ian Wood and G. A. Loud (eds), *Church and Chronicle in the Middle Ages*, London, 1991.

Kiteley, J. F., 'The *De arte honeste amandi* of Andreas Capellanus and the concept of courtesy in *Sir Gawain and the Green Knight*, *Anglia*, 79 (1961), 7–16.

Kittell, Ellen E., 'The construction of women's social identity in medieval Douai: evidence from identifying epithets', *Journal of Medieval History*, 25 (1999), 215–27.

Kittel, Ruth, 'Women under the law in medieval England 1066–1485', in Barbara Kanner (ed.), *The Women of England from Anglo-Saxon Times to the Present: Interpretive Bibliographical Essays*, London, 1979.

Kittel, Ruth, 'Rape in thirteenth-century England: a study of the common-law courts', in D. Kelly Weisberg (ed.), *Women and the Law: A Social-Historical Perspective*, 2 vols, Cambridge, MA, 1982.

Klapisch-Zuber, Christiane, 'Women servants in Florence during the fourteenth and fifteenth centuries', in Barbara A. Hanawalt (ed.), *Women and Work in Preindustrial Europe*, Bloomington, 1986.

Knight, Stephen, 'The social function of the Middle English romances', in David Aers (ed.), *Medieval Literature: Criticism, Ideology and History*, Brighton, 1986.

Kowaleski, Maryanne, 'Women's work in a market town: Exeter in the late fourteenth century', in Barbara A. Hanawalt (ed.), *Women and Work in Preindustrial Europe*, Bloomington, 1986.

Kowaleski, Maryanne, 'The history of urban families', *Journal of Medieval History*, 14 (1988), 47–63.

Krueger, Roberta L., 'Transforming maidens: singlewomen's stories in Marie de France's *Lais* and later French courtly narratives', in Judith M. Bennett and Amy M. Froide (eds), *Singlewomen in the European Past, 1250–1800*, Philadelphia, 1999.

Kümin, Beat A., *The Shaping of a Community: The Rise and Reformation of the English Parish c. 1400–1560*, Aldershot, 1996.

Labarge, Margaret Wade, *Women in Medieval Life: A Small Sound of the Trumpet* London, 1986.

Laslett, Peter, 'Age at sexual maturity in Europe since the Middle Ages', in *Family Life and Illicit Love in Earlier Generations: Essays in Historical Sociology*, Cambridge, 1977.

Laslett, Peter, 'Introduction: comparing illegitimacy over time and between cultures', in Peter Laslett, Karla Oosterveen and Richard Smith (eds), *Bastardy and Its Comparative History: Studies in the History of Illegitimacy and Marital Nonconformism in Britain, France, Germany, Sweden, North America, Jamaica, and Japan*, London, 1980.

Lavezzo, Kathy, 'Sobs and sighs between women: the homoerotics of compassion in *The Book of Margery Kempe*, in Louise Fradenburg and Carla Freccero (eds), *Premodern Sexualities*, New York, 1996.

Lea, H. C., *A History of Auricular Confession and Indulgences in the Latin Church*, 3 vols, New York, 1896.

Lees, Clare A., with the assistance of Thelma Fenster and Jo Ann McNamara (eds), *Medieval Masculinities: Regarding Men in the Middle Ages*, Minneapolis, 1994.

Lerner, Gerda, *The Creation of Patriarchy*, New York, 1986.

Lessing, Doris, *Under My Skin: Volume One of My Autobiography, to 1949*, London, 1994.

Levi, Giovanni, and Jean-Claude Schmitt (eds), *A History of Young People*, vol. 1, *Ancient and Medieval Rites of Passage*, trans. Camille Naish, Cambridge, MA, 1997.

Lévy, J.-P., 'L'Officialité de Paris et les questions familiales à la fin du XIV siècle', in *Études d'histoire du droit canonique dédiées à Gabriel le Bras*, 2 vols, Paris, 1965.

Lewis, Katherine J., 'Model girls? Virgin-martyrs and the training of young women in late medieval England', in Katherine J. Lewis, Noël James Menuge and Kim M. Phillips (eds), *Young Medieval Women*, Stroud, 1999.

Lewis, Katherine J., *The Cult of St Katherine of Alexandria in Late Medieval England*, Woodbridge, 2000.

Loengard, Janet Senderowitz, '"Legal history and the medieval English-woman" revisited', in Joel T. Rosenthal (ed.), *Medieval Women and the Sources of Medieval History*, Athens, GA, 1990.

Lutrell, C. A., 'The medieval tradition of the Pearl virginity', *Medium Ævum*, 31 (1962), 194–200.

McIntosh, Marjorie Keniston, *Autonomy and Community: The Royal Manor of Havering, 1200–1500*, Cambridge, 1986.

McIntosh, Marjorie Keniston, *Controlling Misbehavior in England, 1370–1600*, Cambridge, 1998.

McKinley, Richard A., *Norfolk and Suffolk Surnames in the Middle Ages*, English Surnames Series 2, Chichester, 1975.

McKinley, Richard A., *The Surnames of Oxfordshire*, English Surnames Series 3 London, 1977.

MacLean, Sally Beth, 'Hocktide: a reassessment of a popular pre-Reformation festival', in Meg Twycross (ed.), *Festive Drama*, Cambridge, 1996.

McSheffrey, Shannon, 'Literacy and the gender gap in the late Middle Ages: women and reading in Lollard communities', in Lesley Smith and Jane H. M. Taylor (eds), *Women, the Book and the Godly*, Cambridge, 1995.

McSheffrey, Shannon, '"I will never have none ayenst my faders will": consent and the making of marriage in the late medieval diocese of London', in Constance M. Rousseau and Joel T. Rosenthal (eds), *Women, Marriage and Family in Medieval Christendom*, Kalamazoo, 1998.

Marwick, Arthur, *Beauty in History: Society, Politics and Personal Appearance c. 1500 to the Present*, London, 1988.

Mate, Mavis E., *Daughters, Wives and Widows after the Black Death: Women in Sussex, 1350–1535*, Woodbridge, 1998.

Mate, Mavis E., *Women in Medieval English Society*, Cambridge, 1999.

Mead, Margaret, *Coming of Age in Samoa: A Study of Adolescence and Sex in Primitive Societies*, Harmondsworth, 1943.

Meale, Carol M., 'The Middle English romance of *Ipomedon*: a late medieval "mirror" for princes and merchants', *Reading Medieval Studies*, 10 (1984), 136–91.

Meale, Carol M., 'The manuscripts and early audience of the Middle English *Prose Merlin*', in Alison Adams *et al.* (eds), *The Changing Face of Arthurian Romance: Essays on Arthurian Prose Romances in Memory of Cedric E. Pickford*, Cambridge, 1986.

Meale, Carol M., '"… alle the bokes that I haue of latyn, englisch, and frensch": laywomen and their books in late medieval England', in Carol M. Meale (ed.), *Women and Literature in Britain, 1150–1500*, 2nd edn, Cambridge, 1996.

Meale, Carol M., '"Gode men / Wiues maydnes and alle men": romance and its audiences', in Carol M. Meale (ed.), *Readings in Medieval English Romance*, Woodbridge, 1994.

Menuge, Noël James, 'Female wards and marriage in romance and law: a question of consent', in Katherine J. Lewis, Noël James Menuge and Kim M. Phillips (eds), *Young Medieval Women*, Stroud, 1999.

Menuge, Noël James, *Medieval English Wardship in Romance and Law*, Woodbridge, 2001.

Mertes, Kate, *The English Noble Household, 1250–1600: Good Governance and Politic Rule*, Oxford, 1988.

Metz, René, 'La Couronne et l'anneau dans la consécration des vierges', *Revue des sciences religieuses*, 28 (1954), 113–32.

Michalove, Sharon D., 'The education of aristocratic women in fifteenth-century England', in Sharon D. Michalove and A. Compton Reeves (eds), *Estrangement, Enterprise and Education in Fifteenth-Century England*, Stroud, 1998.

Miles, Margaret R., 'The Virgin's one bare breast: female nudity and religious meaning in Tuscan early Renaissance culture', in Susan Rubin Suleiman (ed.), *The Female Body in Western Culture: Contemporary Perspectives*, Cambridge, MA, 1986.

Miles, Margaret R., *Carnal Knowing: Female Nakedness and Religious Meaning in the Christian West*, Boston, 1989.

Minnis, A. J., with V. J. Scattergood and J. J. Smith, *Oxford Guides to Chaucer:*

The Shorter Poems, Oxford, 1995.

Mirrer, Louise (ed.), *Upon My Husband's Death: Widows in the Literature and Histories of Medieval Europe*, Ann Arbor, 1992.

Mitterauer, Michael, *A History of Youth*, trans. Graeme Dunphy, Oxford, 1992.

Moi, Toril, 'Desire in language: Andreas Capellanus and the controversy of courtly love', in David Aers (ed.), *Medieval Literature: Criticism, Ideology and History*, Brighton, 1986.

Moi, Toril, 'What is a woman? Sex, gender, and the body in feminist theory', in *What is a Woman? And Other Essays*, Oxford, 1999.

Moore, Samuel, 'Patrons of letters in Norfolk and Suffolk, *c.* 1450', 2 parts, *Proceedings of the Modern Language Association of America*, 27 (1912), 188–207 and 28 (1913), 70–105.

Moran, Jo Ann Hoeppner, *The Growth of English Schooling, 1340–1548: Learning, Literacy, and Laicization in Pre-Reformation York Diocese*, Princeton, 1985.

Murray, Jacqueline, 'Twice marginal and twice invisible: lesbians in the Middle Ages', in Vern L. Bullough and James A. Brundage (eds), *Handbook of Medieval Sexuality*, New York, 1996.

Murray, Jacqueline (ed.), *Conflicted Identities and Multiple Masculinities: Men in the Medieval West*, New York, 1999.

Nader, Laura, 'The anthropological study of law', *American Anthropologist*, 67 (1965), 3–32.

Naz, Raoul (ed.), *Dictionnaire de droit canonique*, 7 vols, Paris, 1935–65.

Newhauser, Richard, 'Sources II: scriptural and devotional sources', in Derek Brewer and Jonathan Gibson (eds), *A Companion to the Gawain-Poet*, Cambridge, 1997.

Newman, Barbara, 'Flaws in the golden bowl: gender and spiritual formation in the twelfth century', *Traditio*, 45 (1989–90), 111–46.

Nicholls, Jonathan, *The Matter of Courtesy: Medieval Courtesy Books and the Gawain Poet*, Woodbridge, 1985.

North, Thomas, *A Chronicle of the Church of S. Martin in Leicester during the Reigns of Henry VIII. Edward VI. Mary, and Elizabeth with Some Account of Its Minor Altars and Ancient Guilds*, London, 1866.

North, Tim, 'Legerwite in the thirteenth and fourteenth centuries', *Past and Present*, 111 (1986), 3–16.

Nye, Robert A. (ed.), *Sexuality*, Oxford, 1999.

Oliva, Marilyn, 'Aristocracy or meritocracy? Office-holding patterns in late medieval English nunneries', in W. J. Sheils and Diana Wood (eds), *Women in the Church*, Studies in Church History 27, Oxford, 1990.

Onclin, W., 'L'Âge requis pour le mariage dans la doctrine canonique médiévale', in Stephan Kuttner and J. Joseph Ryan (eds), *Proceedings of the Second International Congress of Medieval Canon Law*, Vatican City, 1965.

Orme, Nicholas, *English Schools in the Middle Ages*, London, 1973.

Orme, Nicholas, *Education in the West of England, 1066–1548*, Exeter, 1976.

Orme, Nicholas, *From Childhood to Chivalry: The Education of the English Kings and Aristocracy, 1066–1530*, London, 1984.

Orme, Nicholas, 'Children and the Church in medieval England', *Journal of Ecclesiastical History*, 45 (1994), 563–87.

Ortner, Sherry B., 'The virgin and the state', *Feminist Studies*, 4 (1978), 19–37.

Ortner, Sherry B., 'Gender and sexuality in hierarchical societies: the case of Polynesia and some comparative implications', in Sherry B. Ortner and Harriet Whitehead (eds), *Sexual Meanings: The Cultural Construction of Gender and Sexuality*, Cambridge, 1981.

Owst, G. R., *Literature and Pulpit in Medieval England*, Oxford, 1966.

Park, David, 'Form and content', in Christopher Norton, David Park and Paul Binski, *Dominican Painting in East Anglia: The Thornham Parva Retable and the Musée de Cluny Frontal*, Woodbridge, 1987.

Parkes, M. B., 'The literacy of the laity', repr. in *Scribes, Scripts and Readers: Studies in the Communication, Presentation and Dissemination of Medieval Texts*, London, 1991.

Parsons, John Carmi, 'Mothers, daughters, marriage, power: some Plantagenet evidence, 1150–1500', in John Carmi Parsons (ed.), *Medieval Queenship*, Stroud, 1994.

Parsons, John Carmi, 'Ritual and symbol in English medieval queenship to 1500', in Louise Olga Fradenburg (ed.), *Women and Sovereignty*, Edinburgh, 1992.

Payer, Pierre J., *The Bridling of Desire: Views of Sex in the Later Middle Ages*, Toronto, 1993.

Payer, Pierre J, 'Confession and the study of sex in the middle ages', in Vern L. Bullough and James A. Brundage (eds), *Handbook of Medieval Sexuality*, New York, 1996.

Payling, S. J., 'Social mobility, demographic change, and landed society in late medieval England', *Economic History Review*, 45 (1992), 51–73.

Pearsall, Derek, 'Notes on the manuscript of Generydes', *The Library*, 5th ser., 16 (1961), 205–10.

Pearsall, Derek, 'The development of Middle English romance', *Mediaeval Studies*, 27 (1965), 91–116.

Penketh, Sandra, 'Women and books of hours', in Lesley Smith and Jane H. M. Taylor (eds), *Women and the Book: Assessing the Visual Evidence*, London, 1997.

Phillips, Kim M., 'Maidenhood as the perfect age of woman's life', in

Katherine J. Lewis, Noël James Menuge and Kim M. Phillips (eds), *Young Medieval Women*, Stroud, 1999.

Phillips, Kim M., 'Bodily walls, windows and doors: the politics of gesture in late fifteenth-century English books for women', in Jocelyn Wogan-Browne *et al.* (eds), *Medieval Women: Texts and Contexts in Late Medieval Britain*, Turnhout, 2000.

Phillips, Kim M., 'Written on the body: reading rape from the twelfth to fifteenth centuries', in Noël James Menuge (ed.), *Medieval Women and the Law*, Woodbridge, 2000.

Phillips, Kim M., 'Desiring virgins: maidens, martyrs and femininity in late medieval England', in P. J. P. Goldberg and Felicity Riddy (eds), *Youth in the Middle Ages*, York, forthcoming.

Phillips, Kim M., 'Four virgins' tales: sex and power in medieval law', in Anke Bernau, Ruth Evans and Sarah Salih (eds), *Medieval Virginities*, Cardiff, forthcoming.

Phillips, Kim M., and Barry Reay (eds), *Sexualities in History: A Reader*, New York, 2002.

Plucknett, T. F. T., *A Concise History of the Common Law*, 5th edn, London, 1956.

Pollock, F., and F. W. Maitland (eds), *The History of English Law before the Time of Edward I*, 2 vols, Cambridge, [1895] 1968.

Pollock, Linda, *Forgotten Children: Parent–Child Relations from 1500 to 1900*, Cambridge, 1993.

Poos, L. R., 'Sex, lies, and the church courts of pre-Reformation England', *Journal of Interdisciplinary History*, 25 (1995), 585–607.

Poos, L. R., and Richard M. Smith, '"Legal windows onto historical populations"? Recent research on demography and the manor court in medieval England', repr. in Zvi Razi and Richard M. Smith (eds), *Medieval Society and the Manor Court*, Oxford, 1996.

Post, J. B., 'Ages at menarche and menopause: some mediaeval authorities', *Population Studies*, 25 (1971), 83–7.

Post, J. B., 'Ravishment of women and the Statutes of Westminster', in J. H. Baker (ed.), *Legal Records and the Historian*, London, 1978.

Post, J. B., 'Sir Thomas West and the Statute of Rapes, 1382', *Bulletin of the Institute for Historical Research*, 53 (1980), 24–30.

Power, Eileen, *Medieval English Nunneries, c. 1275–1535*, Cambridge, 1922.

Power, Eileen, *Medieval People*, London, 1924.

Power, Eileen, *Medieval Women*, Cambridge, [1977] 1997.

Ravensdale, Jack, 'Population changes and the transfer of customary land on a Cambridgeshire manor in the fourteenth century', in Richard M. Smith (ed.), *Land, Kinship and Life Cycle*, Cambridge, 1984.

Razi, Zvi, *Life, Marriage and Death in a Medieval Parish: Economy, Society and Demography in Halesowen 1270–1400*, Cambridge, 1980.

Razi, Zvi, 'The struggles between the abbots of Halesowen and their tenants in the thirteenth and fourteenth centuries', in T. H. Aston *et al.* (eds), *Social Relations and Ideas: Essays in Honour of R. H. Hilton*, Cambridge, 1983.

Razi, Zvi, 'Intrafamilial ties and relationships in the medieval village: a quantitative approach employing manor court rolls', in Zvi Razi and Richard M. Smith (eds.), *Medieval Society and the Manor Court*, Oxford, 1996.

Reyerson, Kathryn L, 'The adolescent apprentice/worker in medieval Montpellier', *Journal of Family History*, 17 (1992), 353–70.

Richmond, Colin, 'The Pastons revisited: marriage and the family in fifteenth-century England', *Bulletin of the Institute for Historical Research*, 58 (1985), 25–36.

Richmond, Colin, *The Paston Family in the Fifteenth Century: The First Phase*, Cambridge, 1990.

Richmond, Colin, *The Paston Family in the Fifteenth Century: Fastolf's Will*, Cambridge, 1996.

Richmond, Colin, 'Elizabeth Clere: friend of the Pastons', in Jocelyn Wogan-Browne *et al.* (eds), *Medieval Women: Texts and Contexts in Late Medieval Britain*, Turnhout, 2000.

Riddy, Felicity, *Sir Thomas Malory*, Brill, 1987.

Riddy, Felicity, 'The speaking knight: Sir Gawain and other animals', in Martin B. Shichtman and James P. Carly (eds), *Culture and the King: The Social Implications of the Arthurian Legend*, Albany, 1994.

Riddy, Felicity, 'Mother knows best: reading social change in a courtesy text', *Speculum*, 71 (1996), 66–86.

Riddy, Felicity, '"Women talking about the things of God": a late medieval sub-culture', in Carol M. Meale (ed.), *Women and Literature in Britain, 1150–1500*, 2nd edn, Cambridge, 1996.

Riddy, Felicity, 'Middle English romance: family, marriage, intimacy', in Roberta L. Krueger (ed.), *The Cambridge Companion to Medieval Romance*, Cambridge, 2000.

Rigby, S. H., *English Society in the Later Middle Ages: Class, Status and Gender*, Houndmills, 1995.

Riley, Denise, 'Does sex have a history?', in *Am I That Name? Feminism and the Category of 'Women' in History*, London, 1988.

Rosenthal, Joel T., 'Aristocratic marriage and the English peerage, 1350–1500: social institutional and personal bond', *Journal of Medieval History*, 10 (1984), 181–94.

Ross, C. D., 'The household accounts of Elizabeth Berkeley, countess of Warwick, 1420-1', *Transactions of the Bristol and Gloucestershire Archaeological Society*, 70 (1951), 81–105.

Rubin, Gayle, 'The traffic in women: notes on the "political economy" of sex', repr. in Joan Wallach Scott (ed.), *Feminism and History*, Oxford, 1996.

Rubin, Miri, 'A decade of studying medieval women, 1987–1997', *History Workshop Journal*, 46 (Autumn, 1998), 213–39.

Saenger, Paul, 'Books of hours and reading habits in the later middle ages', in Roger Chartier (ed.), *The Culture of Print: Power and the Uses of Print in Early Modern Europe*, trans. Lydia Cochrane, Oxford, 1989.

Sage, Lorna, *Bad Blood*, London, 2000.

Sandler, Lucy Freeman, *Gothic Manuscripts 1285–1385*, 2 vols, in J. J. G. Alexander (general ed.), *A Survey of Manuscripts Illuminated in the British Isles*, London, 1986.

Saul, Nigel, *Knights and Esquires: The Gloucestershire Gentry in the Fourteenth Century*, Oxford, 1981.

Sautman, Francesca Canadé, and Pamela Sheingorn (eds), *Same Sex Love and Desire among Women in the Middle Ages*, New York, 2001.

Savage, Anne, 'Clothing paternal incest in *The Clerk's Tale, Emaré*, and the *Life of St Dympna*', in Jocelyn Wogan-Browne *et al.* (eds), *Medieval Women: Texts and Contexts in Late Medieval Britain*, Turnhout, 2000.

Scammell, Jean, 'Freedom and marriage in medieval England', *Economic History Review*, 2nd ser. 27 (1974), 523–37.

Scammell, Jean, 'Wife-rents and merchet', *Economic History Review*, 2nd ser. 29 (1976), 487–90.

Scase, Wendy, 'St Anne and the education of the Virgin', in Nicholas Rogers (ed.), *England in the Fourteenth Century: Proceedings of the 1991 Harlaxton Symposium*, Stamford, 1993.

Schen, Claire S., 'Women and the London parishes', in Katherine L. French, Gary G. Gibbs and Beat A. Kümin (eds), *The Parish in English Life 1400–1600*, Manchester, 1997.

Schlegel, Alice, and Herbert Barry III, *Adolescence: An Anthropological Inquiry*, New York, 1991.

Schultz, James A., 'Medieval adolescence: the claims of history and the silences of German narrative', *Speculum*, 66 (1991), 519–37.

Schultz, James A., *The Knowledge of Childhood in the German Middle Ages, 1100–1350*, Philadelphia, 1995.

Schultz, James A., 'Bodies that don't matter: heterosexuality before heterosexuality in Gottfried's *Tristan*', in Karma Lochrie, Peggy McCracken and James A. Schultz (eds), *Constructing Medieval Sexuality*, Minneapolis, 1997.

Scott, Edward J. L., *Index to the Sloane Manuscripts in the British Museum*, London, 1904.

Scott, Joan Wallach (ed.), *Feminism and History*, Oxford, 1996.

Scott, Kathleen L., *Later Gothic Manuscripts*, 2 vols, in J. J. Alexander (general ed.), *A Survey of Manuscripts Illuminated in the British Isles*, London, 1996.

Searle, Eleanor, 'Freedom and marriage in medieval England: an alternative hypothesis', *Economic History Review*, 2nd ser. 29 (1976), 482–6.

Searle, Eleanor, 'Seigneurial control of women's marriage: the antecedents and function of merchet in England', *Past and Present*, 82 (1979), 3–43.

Sears, Elizabeth, *The Ages of Man: Medieval Interpretations of the Life Cycle*, Princeton, 1986.

Seaton, Ethel, *Sir Richard Roos, c. 1410–1482: Lancastrian Poet*, London, 1961.

Segal, Lynne, *Why Feminism?: Gender, Psychology, Politics*, Cambridge, 1999.

Shah, Mazhar H., *The General Principles of Avicenna's* Canon of Medicine, Karachi, 1966.

Shahar, Shulamith, *Childhood in the Middle Ages*, London, 1990.

Sharp, Margaret, 'The central administration system of Edward, the Black Prince', in T. F. Tout, *Chapters in the Administrative History of Mediaeval England*, 6 vols Manchester, 1920–33.

Sharp, Thomas, *A Dissertation on the Pageants or Dramatic Mysteries Anciently Performed at Coventry*, Wakefield, [1825] 1973.

Shoemaker, Robert, and Mary Vincent (eds), *Gender and History in Western Europe*, London, 1998.

Siraisi, Nancy G., *Medieval and Early Renaissance Medicine: An Introduction to Knowledge and Practice*, Chicago, 1990.

Smith, Lesley, 'Scriba, femina', in Lesley Smith and Jane H. M. Taylor (eds), *Women and the Book: Assessing the Visual Evidence*, London, 1997.

Smith, Richard M., 'The people of Tuscany and their families in the fifteenth century: medieval or Mediterranean?', *Journal of Family History*, 6 (1981), 107–28.

Smith, Richard M., 'Families and their land in an area of partible inheritance: Redgrave, Suffolk 1260–1320', in Richard M. Smith (ed.), *Land, Kinship and Life-Cycle*, Cambridge, 1984.

Smith, Richard M., 'Some issues concerning families and their property in rural England 1250–1800', in Richard M. Smith (ed.), *Land, Kinship and Life Cycle*, Cambridge, 1984.

Smith, Richard M., 'Women's property rights under customary law: some developments in the thirteenth and fourteenth centuries', *Transactions of the Royal Historical Society*, ser. 2, 36 (1986), 165–94.

Smith, Richard M., 'Coping with uncertainty: women's tenure of customary land in England *c.* 1370–1430', in Jennifer Kermode (ed.), *Enterprise and Individuals in Fifteenth-Century England*, Stroud, 1991.

Smith, Richard M., 'Geographical diversity in the resort to marriage in late medieval Europe: work, reputation, and unmarried females in the household formation systems of northern and southern Europe', in P. J. P. Goldberg (ed.), *Women in Medieval English Society*, Stroud, 1997.

Somerset, Anne, *Ladies in Waiting: From the Tudor Period to the Present Day*, London, 1984.

Spencer, H. Leith, *English Preaching in the Late Middle Ages*, Oxford, 1993.

Stock, Brian, *The Implications of Literacy: Written Language and Models of Interpretation in the Eleventh and Twelfth Centuries*, Princeton, 1983.

Strohm, Paul, *Social Chaucer*, Cambridge, MA, 1989.

Strohm, Paul, 'Queens as intercessors', in *Hochon's Arrow: The Social Imagination of Fourteenth-Century Texts*, Princeton, 1992.

Swabey, ffiona, *Medieval Gentlewoman: Life in a Widow's Household in the Later Middle Ages*, Stroud, 1999.

Swanson, Heather, *Medieval Artisans: An Urban Class in Late Medieval England*, Oxford, 1989.

Swanson, R. N., *Religion and Devotion in Europe, c. 1215–c. 1515*, Cambridge, 1995.

Tasioulas, J. A., 'Between doctrine and domesticity: the portrayal of Mary in the N-Town plays', in Diane Watt (ed.), *Medieval Women in their Communities*, Cardiff, 1997.

Tasioulas, J. A., 'Seeds of perfection: the childlike soul and the resurrection of the body, in P. J. P. Goldberg and Felicity Riddy (eds), *Youth in the Middle Ages*, York, forthcoming.

Taylor, Andrew 'Chivalric conversation and the denial of male fear', in Jacqueline Murray (ed.), *Conflicted Identities and Multiple Masculinities: Men in the Medieval West*, New York, 1999.

Taylor, J., 'The Plumpton Letters, 1416–1552', *Northern History*, 10 (1975), 72–87.

Tentler, Thomas N., *Sin and Confession on the Eve of the Reformation*, Princeton, 1977.

Thompson, Henry Yates, *Illustrations from One Hundred Manuscripts in the Library of Henry Yates Thompson*, 7 vols, London, 1907–18.

Thrupp, Sylvia L., *The Merchant Class of Medieval London [1300–1500]*, Ann Arbor, 1962.

Vitz, Evelyn Birge, 'Rereading rape in medieval literature: literary, historical, and theoretical reflections', *Romanic Review*, 88 (1997), 1–26.

Wack, Mary Frances, *Lovesickness in the Middle Ages: The Viaticum and Its Commentaries*, Phildelphia, 1990.

Walker, Sue Sheridan, 'Widow and ward: the feudal law of child custody in medieval England', in Susan Mosher Stuard (ed.), *Women in Medieval Society*, Philadelphia, 1976.

Walker, Sue Sheridan (ed.), *Wife and Widow in Medieval England*, Ann Arbor, 1993.

Ward, Jennifer C., *English Noblewomen in the Later Middle Ages*, Harlow, 1992.

Warner, Marina, *Alone of All Her Sex: The Myth and Cult of the Virgin Mary*, London, 1976.

Warner, Marina, *Monuments and Maidens: The Allegory of the Female Form*, London, 1985.

Watt, Diane, 'Behaving like a man? Incest, lesbian desire, and gender play in "Yde et Olive", *Comparative Literature*, 50 (1998), 265–85.

Weeks, Jeffrey, *Making Sexual History*, Malden, MA, 2000.

Weinstein, Donald, and Rudolph M. Bell, *Saints and Society: The Two Worlds of Western Christendom, 1000–1700*, Chicago, 1982.

Weir, Alison, *Britain's Royal Families: The Complete Genealogy*, rev. edn, London, 1996.

Willard, Charity Canon, 'The manuscript tradition of the *Livre des trois vertus* and Christine de Pizan's audience', *Journal of the History of Ideas*, 27 (1966), 433–44.

Wilson, Adrian, 'The infancy of the history of childhood: an appraisal of Philippe Ariès', *History and Theory*, 19 (1980), 132–52.

Winstead, Karen A., *Virgin Martyrs: Legends of Sainthood in Late Medieval England*, Ithaca, 1997.

Wogan-Browne, Jocelyn, 'Saints' lives and the female reader', *Forum for Modern Language Studies*, 27 (1991), 314–32.

Wogan-Browne, Jocelyn, 'The virgin's tale', in Ruth Evans and Lesley Johnson (eds), *Feminist Readings in Middle English Literature: The Wife of Bath and All Her Sect*, London, 1994.

Woolgar, C. M., *The Great Household in Late Medieval England*, New Haven, 1999.

Wright, Rosemary Muir, 'The virgin in the sun and in the tree', in Louise Olga Fradenburg (ed.), *Women and Sovereignty*, Edinburgh, 1992.

Wright, Susan M., *Derbyshire Gentry in the Fifteenth Century*, Derbyshire Record Society 8, Chesterfield, 1983.

Wrigley, E. A., 'Fertility strategy for the individual and the group', in Charles Tilly (ed.), *Historical Studies of Changing Fertility*, Princeton, 1978.

Wunderli, Richard M., *London Church Courts and Society on the Eve of the Reformation*, Cambridge, MA, 1981.

Wylie, James Hamilton, *History of England under Henry the Fourth*, 4 vols, London, 1884–98.

INDEX

Note: page numbers given in *italic* refer to illustrations

abduction 29, 33, 148, 155
adolescence *see* age; youth
adulthood, female 36–43
Agatha, St 47
age
 of consent 27–31, 36, 130, 159
 of criminal and civil
  responsibility 32, 34–5
 of discretion 27, 31, 130
 of entry to religious life 27–8,
  30–1, 38
 of giving legal testimony 29
 of leaving home 130, 133–4
 of maidenhood 4, 6–8, 23–43, 51
 of majority 32–5
 middle 43, 46
 perfect 3, 6, 24, 43–51, 115, 116,
  146, 193, 203
 see also marriage, age at;
  puberty; sacraments (first
  reception)
ages of man 6, 43, 47, 51
Agnes, St 45, 47
Albertus Magnus 26
Alice de Bryene 111, 112
Alice de Rouclif 29–30, 37
Allhallows' Day 190
Ancrene Riwle 145
Anne, St *69* 70, 77
Anne of Bohemia 155
anthropology 4
Apollonia, St 47

apprenticeship 37, 82–3, 132–4
 female 6, 23, 36, 37, 62, 76, 82–3,
  90–2, 109, 132–4, 150–1
 male 5, 83
Aquinas, Thomas 28
Aristotle 26, 147
Augustine 43
autonomy 7–8, 13, 36, 120–31, 203–4

Bailey, Mark 37
Bailey, Peter 163
Barbara, St 47, *69*
Bardsley, Sandy 129
Barron, Caroline M. 66, 121
Bartholomaeus Anglicus 6–7, 11–12
Basset, Anne
 education 2, 66, 68, 76, 83–4,
  179–80, 181
 letters 2, 179–82
 marriage 179
 in service 114–15, 116, 119, 202
Basset, Katherine
 marriage 179
 in service 114–15, 116, 179, 180
Basset, Mary
 clandestine marriage 181
 education 65, 66, 76, 83–4, 181
Basset, Philippa 66, 181
Beaufort, Lady Margaret 25, 38–9,
  40, 71
beauty (feminine) 3, 6–7, 44, 45, 47,
  50, 88, 180, 181

Bennett, Judith M. 3, 7–8, 34, 95, 121–3

Berkeley, Elizabeth 74, 115, 116

betrothal 27, 39–40, 41, 79, 159–60

Betson, Thomas 41–2, 68, 159

Bevis of Hampton 87, 89, 165

Biller, Peter 26

Black Death 121–8

Blanchardyn and Eglantine 73, 90

Boccaccio, *Olympia* 44–5

bodies
    female 6–7, 11–12, 23–30, 39, 41, 39, 41
        and conduct 85, 92, 97
        and female service 113–14, 116, 118–19
        and perfect age 43–51
    male 6, 11–12, 28, 43

Bodmin (Cornw.) 188

Bokenham, Osbern 23, 47

Book of the Knight of the Tower 68–70, 73, 78, 80, 82, 84–7, 90, 92–5, 144, 152–3, 164, 182

books of hours 47–9, 63, 65, 71, 77, 79–80, 89–91

Bracton 32–3, 147

brewing 128, 129, 130, 131

Brews, Margery 41, 68, 182–5, 202

Bridget of Sweden, St 14, 68

Brigstock (Northants.) 8, 121, 122, 123

Bristol 1, 149, 188, 192–3

Butler, Judith 21n.37, 177, 178

Bynum, Caroline Walker 117

Cadden, Joan 26

Carpenter, Christine 41

Caxton, William 73, 84, 90, 152

Cecilia, St 47, 49, 78

Cely family
    courtship and marriage 40, 152

female service 112
    sexuality 152, 153

chastity *see* virginity

Chaucer, Geoffrey 112, 164
    Clerk's Tale 46, 165
    Franklin's Tale 167
    Legend of Good Women 167
    Merchant's Tale 45, 159
    Miller's Tale 45, 165
    Physician's Tale 45, 75, 80–1
    Prioress's Tale 165
    Reeve's Tale 166
    Shipman's Tale 166
    Squire 6
    Summoner's Tale 166
    Troilus and Criseyde 89
    Wife of Bath 196
    Wife of Bath's Tale 167

Chaucer, Philippa (née de Roet) 112–13

childbirth 13, 25–6, 28, 36, 39–40, 116–18

childhood 2, 3, 7, 9–10, 24, 27, 44, 51

Chojnacki, Stanley 42

Christina, St 23, 47, 94

Christine de Pisan, *Cité des dames* 13, 80

Clanchy, Michael 63

Clifford, Elizabeth 36, 37

clothing *see* dress

conduct 3, 70, 75–6, 77–97, 114–15, 153
    books 62, 73, 76, 78, 83–7, 90, 92–5, 114–15, 152–3, 196
    see also education; femininity; *see also under individual book titles*

consent *see* age, of consent

Cosyn, Agnes 148–9, 194–5, 196, 203

courtesy books 83, 118
    see also conduct, books

courts
  borough 122
  Church 27, 28–30, 62, 150, 157–8, 159, 161–2, 178, 185
  common law 32, 33, 34, 35, 122, 178
  manorial 2, 67, 121, 122, 127
  see also law
courtship 40–2, 63–4, 85–6, 152, 163, 168, 182–5
Coventry 191
Croscombe (Som.) 189, 190, 192, 193
crowns 3, 46, 47, 49, 50
Cuxham (Oxon.) 126, 127

Dale, Marion K. 109
damsels *see* service, female
dancing 81–2, 84, 95–6, 163–4, 189, 192–3
daughter (as legal descriptor) 122–3, 128
Daune, Cicely 183, 185
death, and perfect age 43–51
de Beauvoir, Simone 61, 97, 204
Deerhurst (Glos.) 70
defamation 62, 151, 159
devotional texts 62, 64–5, 66, 71, 77–8, 79–80, 84
Dinah 81, 82, 167
Dorothy, St 47, *48*
Dove, Mary 43
dowry 124, 125, 126, 139n.76, 149, 183, 184
drama 62, 72, 78–9, 160–1
  morality plays 72
  mystery or cycle plays 72, 79, 92
  parochial 72, 78–9, 190
dress 70, 111, 113, 115–16, 119, 164
  fashionable 2, 44, 82, 85, 92, 93, 180–1

white 46, 47, 116
duBois, Page 10, 11, 195
Dudley, Katherine 168, 203
Dutton, Anne M. 66
Dux Moraud 160–1
Dyer, Christopher 127

education 9, 61–2
  boys' 5, 9, 24, 38, 73, 76
  girls' 6, 9, 61–97, 110–11, 130, 181
  see also conduct; literacy
Edward I 158
  daughters 39, 40, 64, 67, 74
  niece 74
Edward II 74, 113
Edward III 154, 156
  daughters 39
Edward IV 109, 154
  daughters 64, 109
Eleanor de Montfort 64
Eleanor of Castile 64, 74, 114, 119
Elizabeth de Burgh 115, 116
Elizabeth of Hungary, St 14, 78
Elizabeth of York 64, 109, 118, 119
Englefield (Berks.) 126–7
Exeter 131, 133

fabliaux 95, 166
Faith, Rosamund 126–7
family
  gender roles 12–13, 61
  work within 108, 119, 120, 128–9
femininity 1–2, 6–7, 9–15, 181, 203
  authority 79, 88–9
  ideal 3–4, 6–7, 23–4, 43–51, 77–96, 182–5
  intercession 1, 13, 51, 79, 188
  maidens' response to 14–15, 77, 177–97
  rebellion 2, 13–14, 80–1, 182, 194–7, 203

self-control 94–6
subordination 11–15, 61, 89–90, 168, 203
training in 13, 61–97
feminist scholarship 8, 10, 11, 14–15, 122, 177
Fitzherbert, John 85
Floris and Blancheflour 9, 87, 167
food, and female service 111, 112, 117–18, 129, 130
French, Katherine L. 188, 190, 193
Froide, Amy M. 7–8, 121
Froissart, Jean 1, 75, 154, 156, 163

garlands 3, 46, 47, 49, 189, 190
gender roles 9–15, 61–2, 116–18, 129
    and status 12, 13, 14, 61, 83–96
    see also femininity; masculinity
Generydes 87, 166
Geoffrey de la Tour Landry 84, *84*, 182
    see also Book of the Knight of the Tower
Geoffrey of Vinsauf 45, 47
Gesta romanorum 160
Giles of Rome, *De regimine principum* 26, 147
Glanvill 32
Godiva, Lady 46
Goldberg, P. J. P. 3, 8, 37, 79, 109, 121–2, 130–1
Good Wife Taught Her Daughter 62, 76, 92–5
Good Wyfe Wold a Pylgremage 46, 62, 92–5
Goody, Jack 123–4
governesses 63, 74–5, 113
Gower, John, *Confessio amantis* 145, 167
Gratian, *Decretum* 27–8, 30
Grey, Lady Jane 66

Greystoke, Beatrix Lady 38
Griffiths, Morwenna 14–15, 178
Griselda *see* Chaucer, Geoffrey, *Clerk's Tale*
guilds
    craft 79, 109, 134
    religious 72, 78–9, 185–94
        maidens' 6, 77, 79, 186–94
        young mens' 5, 187, 188, 190
Guy of Warwick 45, 87, 88–9, 165

hair 3, 44, 45–6, 47, 49, 50
Halesowen (Worcs.) 2, 3, 33–4, 150, 195–6, 203
Hali Meiðhad 3, 46
Hanawalt, Barbara A. 3, 5, 6, 9–10, 132, 149
Harley Lyrics 45
Haute, Eleanor (née Roos) 64, 67, 109–10
Havelock the Dane 23, 45
Havering (Essex) 123, 125–6
Henry IV 25
    daughters 40, 64, 72
Henry VI 117, 188
Henry VII 25, 38–9
Henryson, Robert, *Testament of Cresseid* 89
Hildegard of Bingen 26
hocking 190–1, 193
homiletic texts 81–2, 84, 143–4, 160
    see also devotional texts; sermons
Horrox, Rosemary 108
Howden (E. R. Yorks.) 128–9
Hull, Dame Eleanor 65, 70
humoural theory 6–7, 11–12, 24–6, 28, 29, 30
    see also bodies
Hyrd, Richard (trans.), *Instruction of a Christen Woman* 66, 73, 87, 97, 112, 164

illegitimacy 95, 146, 149–50, 151–2, 153, 155–6, 159
incest 143–4, 160–1
Incestuous Daughter, The 96, 143–4, 159
inheritance 32–4, 122–8, 146–7, 170–1n.17
  underage 34
Ipomedon 88, 165
Isabella of France (queen of Edward II) 73, 74, 113, 114, 115
Isabella of France (second queen of Richard II) 75
Isidore of Seville 6–7, 28

Jacob's Well 82
Jacobus de Voragine, *Legenda aurea* 46, 47, 49
John de Burgh 31
John of Gaunt 113, 154, 155–6
  daughters 9, 83, 154–5, 160
Justice, Steven 67

Karras, Ruth Mazo 132
Katherine, St 3, 47, *69*, 94
Kibworth Harcourt (Leics.) 23, 126, 127
King Horn 89
King of Tars 166
Knighton, Henry 155, 164
Krueger, Roberta L. 8
Kümin, Beat 187

ladies-in-waiting *see* service, female
Lancaster, Elizabeth 83, 154–5
Lancaster, Philippa 160
Lancecron, Agnes 155–6
laundresses 113, 130, 158
law
  borough 30, 34
  canon 27–32, 36, 161–2

common 30, 32–3, 34–5, 147–8
customary (manorial) 30, 33–4, 35
and maidenhood 4, 8, 23, 27–36, 43, 120–1, 122
and women 12, 36
  see also courts
Leicester 188
leyrwite 150, 195–6
Liber albus (London) 46
Liber extra 27–8, 30–1
Lisle family 2–3, 75, 170–82
  female service 114–15
  see also under Basset; Plantagenet
literacy 63, 70–1
  female 25, 61–71
    reading 63–7, 69–71, 87, 112
    writing 63, 64, 65, 67–70, 87, 177, 181, 182
  male 63, 67, 72
Lollards 145
Lombard, Peter 27, 28, 43
London 5, 6, 46, 83, 121, 132–4, 149, 150, 151, 158, 188, 189, 190, 191, 193
love 41, 182–4
Lucy, St 47, 78
lyrics 44, 45, 72–3, 95–6, 166

McIntosh, Marjorie Keniston 125–6, 151
magistrissae see governesses
Malory, Thomas 166
manners *see* conduct
Mannyng, Robert 82, 148, 161
Margaret, St 3, 46, 47, *69*, 94, 188
Margaret of Anjou 64
Margaret of York 71, 72
Marie de France, *Lay le Freine* 9, 23, 45
Marrays, John 29–30

marriage 4, 13, 14, 15, 27, 33, 36, 108, 120, 121, 131, 150, 182–5, 194–5
  age at 27–31, 33, 36–42
  ceremonies 29, 36, 46, 159–60, 163–4
  impediments to 27, 158, 161–2
  underage 27, 28–30, 37, 40, 163–4
Mary, Virgin see Virgin Mary
Mary de Bohun 25
Mary Magdalene, St 45, 160
masculinity 5–6, 9–10, 11–12, 71, 146–7
Mate, Mavis E. 3, 37, 126
Matthew of Vendôme 45, 47
May festivities 46, 189–90
Meale, Carol M. 66
medical texts 23–6, 30, 43
menstruation 12, 24–5
  first 24–6
  see also puberty
merchet 121, 139n.76
Mertes, Kate 110
migration 121, 128, 129
Mirror of Justices 33
misogyny 12, 13, 21n.46, 81
Moi, Toril 10
More, Thomas, daughter 66
Morebath (Devon) 185–6, 187–8, 191–2
mothers as teachers 73–4
Mustanoja, Tauno F. 92
Myrc, John 31–2, 161

Neville, Cecily 71
nunneries and education 9, 23, 63, 65, 74, 75–6
nuns 4, 14, 27–8, 38, 39, 46
  consecration 46
  see also age, of entry to religious life

orality 62, 63, 67, 71–3
Oxford 131

parishes 63, 71, 76, 185–94
  maidens' role within 1–2, 6, 95–6, 185–94, 202–3
  young men's role within 5, 186, 188, 189
Parsons, John Carmi 39, 40
Paston, Anne 111, 115, 119, 156
Paston, Elizabeth 119, 185, 196
Paston, Margery 112, 119, 156–7
Paston family 33
  courtship and marriage 40–1, 63–4, 112, 156–7, 168, 182–5
  female literacy 68
  female service 111–12, 114, 115, 119
  see also Brews, Margery
pastourelles 95, 164–5
Payling, S. J. 124
Pearl 43–6, 47, 49, 51
pearls 44, 46, 180, 181
Perrers, Alice 154, 156
Philippa of Hainault 1, 112, 155–6
piety 64–5, 71, 77–8, 79–80, 93–4, 185–94 passim
Plantagenet, Bridget 65, 74, 75–6
Plantagenet, Elizabeth 75–6
Plumpton, Dorothy 119
Plumpton, Elizabeth 37
Plumpton, Margaret 37
Plumpton family 36, 37, 151–2
  courtship and marriage 36, 37
  female literacy 64–5
  female service 111, 119
Poos, L. R. 125, 151
post-structuralism 10, 15
Power, Eileen 9, 41, 75
Prose Merlin 46, 67, 87
prostitution 46, 131, 132, 136n.29, 143–4, 154, 159, 160, 161

puberty 9, 23–30, 36–7, 41, 42, 61
  see also menstruation, first

Ramsey Abbey 8, 121
rape 81–2, 89, 95, 132, 147–9, 160,
  161, 166–7
Razi, Zvi 37, 195
Reading 190
Redgrave (Suff.) 125, 126, 150
resurrection 43, 44, 47
Reynes, Robert 67
Richard Coer de Lion 165
Richard II 163
Richard III 109
Riddy, Felicity 8, 71, 76, 92, 93, 122
Robert de Vere 155–6
Robin Hood 72, 96, 190
romances 8, 9, 14, 44, 62, 64, 66, 71,
  77, 87–90, 113, 119
  see also under individual titles
Roucliffe, Margaret 64–5
royal family
  female education 64, 67, 74–5
  marriage 39–40
  see also under individual names
Ryche, Katherine 41–2, 68, 159

sacraments (first reception) 30, 31–2
Saenger, Paul 63
saints 14, 16, 51, 62, 71–2, 77
  virgin martyrs 3, 6, 14, 43, 46–9,
  50–1, 77, 80–1, 82, 94
  see also under individual names;
  Virgin Mary
Salisbury 189, 190
schools 5, 38, 63, 66, 67, 75
  see also education; literacy;
  nunneries and education
Schultz, James A. 144–5
sermons 12, 62, 71–2, 78, 79, 81, 82,
  92, 143

service 37, 108
  female 6, 8, 23, 36, 76, 92, 108–
  20, 121–2, 128–31, 151
  noble households 71, 74, 110–
  20, 163
  royal households 64, 71, 74,
  109–10, 112–20, 155–6,
  163–4, 179–82
  village and urban society 110,
  120, 128–31
  see also governesses
  male 5, 110–11, 116–18, 163
sexuality 6–7, 11, 26, 28, 29, 30, 36,
  39–40, 42, 46, 61, 80–3,
  85–6, 143–68, 188
  at court 84–6, 154–6, 163–4
  and children 159–60, 161, 167
  clerical 158–9, 160, 166
  control of 82–3, 132, 134, 150–3,
  168, 167–8
  double standard 152–3, 154
  historiography 144–5
  lechery 26, 82, 93, 94–6, 147, 161
  lesbianism 145, 161, 162, 168
  in literature 89–90, 164–7
  'parasexuality' 163–4
  and race/religion 158, 160, 165–6
  and social status 146–58, 162,
  164–5
  theological views 161–2
  underage 26, 159–60, 167
  see also courtship; illegitimacy;
  incest; prostitution;
  puberty; rape; virginity
Sharp, Elizabeth 1, 3, 13, 188, 193
Shoemaker, Robert 9
silkwomen 90, 109, 130, 131, 132–4,
  184
singing 81–2, 84, 95–6
singlewomen 8, 14, 36, 46, 76, 121,
  123, 125, 130

Sir Dégare 167
Sir Degrevant 67–8, 87
Smith, Richard M. 8, 37, 121–2, 125, 126, 130
space
    domestic 9, 116–18, 163
    church 193
    rural 129
    urban 93, 94–5
Spectacle of Luf 12
speech (feminine) 86–7, 92–3
Squire of Low Degree 88, 165
Stonor family
    courtship and marriage 27, 40, 41–2
    female literacy 68
    female service 111, 115
Swynford, Katherine 154, 155, 156

Tale of an Incestuous Daughter see Incestuous Daughter, The
Taymouth Hours 89–91
textile work 76, 90, 109, 111, 112, 129, 130, 132, 133
textual communities *see* orality
Thewis off Gudwomen 92–5
tithings 5, 6, 35
tournaments 163–4
Trevisa, John 6–7, 26
Trotula 25, 26
Tuscany
    female service 121
    marriage 37, 44–5

Venice 110
    marriage 42

Vincent, Mary 9
virginity 3, 6–7, 42, 43–51, 77, 80–3, 145–54, 160, 188
virgin martyrs *see* saints, virgin martyrs; *see also under individual names*
Virgin Mary 3, 6, 14, 16, 43, 47, 49, *50*, 51, *69*, 70, 72, 82, 187–8
    as exemplar 77–80
Vives, Juan Luis *see* Hyrd, Richard

wages 119–20, 129, 131
Wakefield (W. R. Yorks.) 122
Walsingham, Thomas 155
Walter de Bibbesworth 73
Ward, Jennifer C. 37
wardship 32, 33, 37, 38, 134
Westminster Chronicler 154–5
Whitsuntide 188–9
widows 12, 13–14, 122, 125–6, 130
William of Pagula 31
Woodville, Elizabeth 64, 109, 117
work
    maidens' 8, 9–10, 62, 93, 108–35
    womens' 13, 108–9, 121, 129, 130

York 29–30, 70, 76, 79, 83, 130–1, 132, 133, 148, 149, 157
Yorkshire 37, 128–9, 150, 194
youth 4–8, 9–10, 203
    female 2, 3, 4, 6–10, 51
    historiography 4–5, 18nn.9 and 10, 19n.11
    male 4–6, 51
    see also age